WITHDRAWN

BERTOLT BRECHT

WORLD DRAMATISTS

BERTOLT BRECHT

KARL H. SCHOEPS

WITH HALFTONE ILLUSTRATIONS

FREDERICK UNGAR PUBLISHING CO.

NEW YORK

Copyright © 1977 by Frederick Ungar Publishing
Co., Inc.
Printed in the United States of America
Designed by Edith Fowler
Library of Congress Cataloging in Publication Data
Schoeps, Karl-Heinz, 1935–
   Bertolt Brecht.
   (World dramatists)
   Bibliography: p.
   Includes index.
   1. Brecht, Bertolt, 1898–1956—Criticism and
interpretation.
PT2603.R397Z8677   832'.9'12   76-15658
ISBN 0-8044-2807-7

CONTENTS

CHRONOLOGY

1898	10 February—Eugen Berthold Brecht is born in Augsburg, Bavaria.
1900	29 June—His only brother, Walter, is born.
1904–08	Attends primary school in Augsburg.
1908–17	Attends high school in Augsburg; writes contributions to the school newspaper *Die Ernte*.
1914–18	World War I.
1917	October Revolution in the Soviet Union (October in Julian calendar; November in Gregorian calendar).
1917–21	Enrolls in the University of Munich to study medicine.
1918	Is drafted as medical orderly; works in the venereal disease ward in the Augsburg military hospital.
1918–19	*Baal* (first version).
1919	Communist uprisings in Munich and Augsburg.

Titles used in chronology and throughout text are literal translations of German titles. Unless otherwise indicated, all quotations from German writers have been translated by me. Dates offered in chronology and in chapter titles are the years in which Brecht wrote the first version of the play to which the dates are appended.—K.H.S.

1919	30 July—Paula Banholzer ("Bi") gives birth to Brecht's son Frank.
1919–21	Serves as theater critic for the *Augsburger Volkswillen*.
1919	*Drums in the Night*.
1920	May 1—Brecht's mother dies.
1920	Moves to Munich.
1922	Receives the coveted Kleist prize for literature.
1922	3 November—Marries actress Marianne Josephine Zoff
1923	12 March—His daughter Hanne is born to his wife, Marianne.
1923	Meets the actress Helene Weigel (later to become his second wife).
1923	8–9 November—Hitler attempts revolt in Munich.
1923	Height of the inflation in Germany. (Revaluation on 15 November: 1,000,000,000,000 old marks = 1 new mark.)
1924	Moves to Berlin. Becomes *Dramaturg* (dramatic consultant on the staff of a repertory theater) at Max Reinhardt's Deutsches Theater.
1924	3 November—His son Stefan is born to Helene Weigel.
1926	Reads Karl Marx's *Kapital*. Meets the Marxist philosopher Karl Korsch.
1927	2 November—Brecht and Marianne Zoff are divorced.
1927	*The Little Mahagonny*. First collaboration with the composer Kurt Weill.
1927	Close working relationship with producer/director Erwin Piscator.
1927	Acquaintance with sociologist Fritz Sternberg leads Brecht to more intensive studies in Marxism.
1928	*The Threepenny Opera*.
1929	10 April—Brecht marries Helene Weigel.

1929	Wall Street crash in the United States and beginning of a worldwide economic crisis.
1929–30	*The Measures Taken* (Brecht's first collaboration with composer Hanns Eisler).
1930	18 October—His wife, Helene Weigel, gives birth to his daughter Barbara.
1932–33	Attends lectures on Marxism by Karl Korsch.
1933	30 January—Hitler and the Nazis come to power.
1933	27 February—Reichstag building in flames. On 28 February, Brecht and his family (Helene Weigel and their two children) leave Germany.
1933–39	Exile in Denmark.
1935	Nazis revoke Brecht's German citizenship.
1936–39	Civil War in Spain.
1938	*Galileo* (first version).
1939–45	World War II.
1939–40	Exile in Sweden.
1939	*Mother Courage and Her Children.*
1940–41	Exile in Finland.
1941–47	Exile in the United States (Santa Monica, California).
1943	31 January—The German army suffers a decisive defeat at Stalingrad.
1944–45	*The Caucasian Chalk Circle.*
1944–47	Second version of *Galileo;* collaboration with Charles Laughton.
1947	30 October—Brecht before the House Committee on Un-American Activities.
1947	31 October—Leaves the United States and takes up residence near Zurich, Switzerland.
1948–56	Takes up permanent residence in East Berlin.
1948	*Short Organum for the Theater.*
1949	West Germany (Federal Republic of Germany) and East Germany (German Democratic Republic) are founded.

1949	Brecht's theater, the Berliner Ensemble, is established in East Berlin.
1950	Becomes an Austrian citizen.
1950	Receives membership in the Academy of Arts in East Berlin.
1951	Is awarded Nationalpreis erster Klasse, a high East German recognition.
1953	Stalin's death.
1953	Becomes chairman of the International PEN Center (*P*oets, *E*ssayists, *N*ovelists; an international writers' organization, founded in 1921).
1953	17 June—Workers' uprisings take place in East Germany; crushed by the Russians.
1954	Receives International Stalin Peace Prize.
1956	14 August—Brecht dies in East Berlin.

INTRODUCTION:
LIFE, TIMES, AND WORK

Today, some twenty years after his death, Bertolt Brecht remains what he always was and intended to be: controversial. Some of his critics have idolized him and made him into a classic. Others still regard him as something of a charlatan or ignore him altogether. Some critics are attracted by his art but repelled by his politics; others emphasize his politics at the expense of his art. Some producers implement the so-called estrangement effect at all costs, while others stage his plays in total ignorance of his intentions. In addition, an ever-increasing number of books and articles on Brecht and his theater are published each year. One can, therefore, easily understand why there are those who feel that the "real" Brecht (the man and his work) has been effectively buried under a deluge of secondary literature. Even after the publication of several of his diaries and numerous efforts to depict Brecht, the man, much of him still remains shrouded in a cloak of ambiguity. That, however, is precisely what Brecht wanted; he always felt that his work was of much greater importance than he was.

Brecht came from the Bavarian town of Augsburg, where he was born Eugen Berthold Friedrich Brecht on 10 February 1898. His father, an employee and later an executive in an Augsburg paper company, was a Roman Catholic, his mother, a Protestant. Brecht himself was raised in his mother's faith, although not very successfully: "The church is a circus for the masses."[1] (He did, however, get to know the Bible extremely well, as is evident throughout his work.) Both parents came from the Swabian region of the Black Forest in southern Germany, a point mentioned occasionally in his writing. ("I, Bertolt Brecht, came from the black forests," he wrote in 1920 in the poem "Of Poor B.B.") He was a gifted and precocious child, but nothing in his background foreshadowed the socialist writer he was to become. As late as 12 September 1920, in fact, having listened to a certain Herr Goldschmidt talking about the Soviet Union in a Munich beer hall, he wrote in his diary: "I am horrified by the kind of order they want to establish, not by the current disorder there. Right now I am very much against bolshevism."[2] Instead of the drab uniformity of life the bolshevists proposed, he preferred to own a car.

Brecht himself considered his time in elementary and high school wasted because "I did not succeed in being of any appreciable help to my teachers."[3] But as Brecht later said about himself in his *Dialogues in Exile:* "This student has learned one thing in school: how to think."[4] What was equally important—"knowledge of the teacher"—was learned. "The pupil must recognize the weaknesses of the teacher and learn how to exploit them."[5]

His early love of dialectics (in the Hegelian sense) is evident from one of his experiences at school, which he describes in *Dialogues in Exile.* Some pupils erased red marks on their graded papers and then challenged the teacher, who easily saw through their trickery by simply holding the papers to the light, thus revealing the scratch marks. Brecht, however, resorted to a different method. Instead of erasing red marks, he added some to perfectly correct passages. Then, with a grieved and innocent demeanor, he asked the teacher about these marks. Thereupon the embarrassed teacher admitted to what he thought was an error on his part and raised the grade.[6]

Some of Brecht's lifelong friendships also date back to his school years at the Augsburger *Realgymnasium* (a high school that emphasizes the physical sciences). One of these was his classmate Rudolf Caspar Neher, who was later to become an important theater designer and to work on many of Brecht's productions.

Brecht's literary career, too, began in his *Realgymnasium* period. In 1913, at the age of fifteen, he published some poems and articles in the school newspaper, *Die Ernte*, under the pseudonym of Bertolt Eugen. In 1914, some of his writing was printed in *Der Erzähler*, the literary supplement to the local newspaper, *Augsburger Neueste Nachrichten*. Many of Brecht's first writings were quite chauvinistic in nature. Like most Germans, the sixteen-year-old Brecht was not dismayed by the outbreak of World War I in 1914. He called the war "unavoidable" and had high praise for Kaiser Wilhelm II. Yet, by 1916, his attitude had noticeably changed. His critical essay on the topic "Dulce et decorum est pro patria mori" (sweet and honorable it is to die for your country) almost resulted in his expulsion from school and marked the beginning of his lifelong pacifism.

Brecht's preference for parables, and his detached and analytical method of presentation in order to stimulate the audience's intellect, were apparent as early as 1913, when he wrote the short story "The Balkan War," which describes the two Balkan Wars of 1912 and 1913. In the same year, he also wrote his first dramatic work, which was published in *Die*

Ernte in January 1914. The main theme of this brief one-act play, *The Bible,* was derived from the nineteenth-century German playwright Friedrich Hebbel's five-act tragedy *Judith.* Brecht's play is an early example of his criticism of narrow-minded religion.

In 1917, Brecht matriculated at the University of Munich as a medical student. For a time it seemed that he would enter upon a conventional bourgeois career, as did his only brother, Walter (born in 1907), who was to become a professor at the Technical University of Darmstadt. But Brecht neglected his studies in medicine in favor of reading literature, going to the theater, and playing the guitar. Although he had rented a room in Munich, he still spent much of his time in nearby Augsburg. He wrote theater reviews of local performances in Augsburg's municipal theater— in which he generally found few redeeming features: "The repertory lacks every sense of direction."[7] He lived in a separate attic room in his parents' house, where he could come and go at his pleasure without seeing his parents if he did not want to. (This arrangement is not uncommon in Germany even today.) There he wrote poems and composed songs that he tried out on various girlfriends and in nightly revels with a group of friends in and around the town of Augsburg. He preferred the local fairs, where he admired the clowns and puppeteers, to the contemporary theater.

Two women in particular occupied much of Brecht's time and thoughts in the early 1920s: Paula Banholzer ("Bi"), a local Augsburg girl, and Marianne Zoff, daughter of the writer Otto Zoff and an actress at the Augsburg theater. His diaries of the time show his concurrent and deep involvement with both women. In 1919, Bi gave birth to Brecht's son, Frank. Although this caused quite a stir in his family, Brecht never married Bi. Frictions had developed between them. Brecht had no money and felt that he was not ready for marriage. (Immediately after his birth Frank was placed in a foster home. Later he lived in Vienna with a sister of his father's second wife, Helene Weigel. After 1935, Frank lived with his mother, who had married a doctor in 1924. In 1943 Frank was killed in Russia while serving in the German armed forces.) Nevertheless, several entries in his diary reveal that Brecht continued to feel a deep emotional attachment to Bi: "She is worth more to me than everything else. . . . I am never sure of her, she has more power over me than all others, I love her."[8] This passage is one of the very few that allows us a glimpse into the emotional side of Brecht. He usually made every effort to give a cool, detached, unemotional, and sometimes even cynical impression—especially the young Brecht. In later years, Brecht mellowed somewhat. His mature works show great compassion for mankind. But even then he revealed very little about himself.

The best analysis of Brecht, the man, is probably summed up in a note he jotted down on 20 May 1921. In it he quotes from a book by the art critic Julius Meier-Graefe about the painter Delacroix: "Meier-Graefe says about Delacroix: in him a hot heart beat in a cold man. And this, essentially, is a possibility for greatness."[9] This passage was of such importance to Brecht that he confessed on 10 February 1922: "Few dicta about art have affected me more than Meier-Graefe's sentence about Delacroix: 'in him a burning heart beat in a cold man.' "[10]

On 21 May 1921 Brecht wrote another self-analytic entry: "The businessman is an idealist when talking but a cynic when acting; it is the reverse with a writer."[11] Again the phrasing is of a general and impersonal nature, but it is obvious from the context that Brecht refers to himself and a wealthy businessman by the name of Recht. Brecht and Recht were the two poles between which Marianne Zoff oscillated for years. Finally Brecht married Marianne on 3 November 1922. (They had one daughter, Hanne Marianne, born 12 March 1923, who is now an actress in Hamburg, under the name of Hanne Hiob.)

A large portion of Brecht's early diaries records the agonizing and somewhat melodramatic relationships between Brecht and Marianne and Brecht and Bi. Marianne Zoff was torn between the rich Recht, who plied her with expensive gifts, and the poor Brecht, whom she apparently loved. Brecht's feelings for her were ambivalent: "At times I feel nothing for this woman, Bi is always close to me."[12] Then again, he and Marianne spent countless nights together in his attic room; he wrote: "It is good to live with her and never boring."[13] During this period he tried frantically to make money by writing film scenarios, but he had little success. At times his personal problems seemed too much for him: "I am tired of it. I am consumed by these affairs. The film projects take too much of my time and my strength and my enemies bury me."[14]

Periods of extreme self-confidence were followed by pangs of doubt: "Today when I was eating cherries in front of the mirror, I saw my idiotic face. In contrast with the solid black balls disappearing into my mouth, it looked even more unrestrained, lascivious, and contradictory. There are many elements in it—brutality, calm, slackness, boldness, and cowardice—but only as elements. It shows more variety and less character than a landscape under drifting clouds. Therefore many people cannot remember my face ('there are too many' says Hedda [another girlfriend])."[15] He kept these "many faces" throughout his life, a fact that makes him difficult to categorize, but renders him all the more fascinating.

These self-reflections also illustrate Brecht's remarkable ability to look at himself coolly, from the outside, from a distance. This capability is nowhere clearer than when he realized that he was not ready for marriage: "I am still only experimenting, I need room to move, I am still growing."[16] And he knew also that some of his problems arose from wanting everything at once: "I want Timbuktu and a child and a house without a door; and I want to be alone in bed, and with a woman in bed; apples from a tree, and the wood from the tree, and not using an axe, and the tree with blossoms, apples, foliage, in a close-up shot right in front of my window! And a servant to fertilize it."[17]

His father's wishes and expectations, on the other hand, were much more definite but quite different from those of his son. He wanted his son to concentrate on his studies rather than waste his time on "dubious" literary activities. They had several confrontations in which his father objected bitterly to the actions of his son, who defended radical elements and dragged the family's good name into the mud by becoming a public nuisance (as Brecht had done in a legal feud with a member of the Augsburg theater). Brecht on his part complained that his father did not understand him ("He always leaves me in the lurch when times are difficult"),[18] and he feared that he would be asked to leave his parental home. He never was, however. Later their relationship apparently achieved some kind of equilibrium. Brecht's relationship with his mother was a much closer one. When she died on 1 May 1920, he was deeply moved ("My mother died on 1 May. Spring came. Heaven grinned shamelessly").[19]

Brecht's marriage to Marianne did not last very long —they were divorced in 1927. While still married to her, he had developed a close relationship with another woman, the Austrian actress Helene Weigel, whom he had met in 1923 while on a visit to Berlin.

They were married in 1929 and remained married until Brecht's death in 1956. (Their son, Stefan, now a free-lance writer, artist, and actor living in New York City, was born in 1924. Their daughter, Barbara, born in 1930, is now an actress in the Berliner Ensemble.) "Die Weigel," as Brecht called her, was to become one of the most important interpreters of his dramatic works, as actress as well as the director of the Berliner Ensemble. And Brecht conceived some of his characters—such as Mother Courage and Pelageya Vlassova (*The Mother*)—with her in mind. (Helene Weigel died in 1971, fifteen years after Brecht's death.)

Brecht's early literary models were the playwright Georg Büchner (1813–37), and Frank Wedekind (1864–1918), the playwright, performer of popular ballads, and actor. Around 1918, Brecht started to work on his first full-length play, *Baal*. Brecht wrote this play in opposition to expressionism, the dominant trend in the German theater from around 1910 to 1925. The expressionists stood counter to the bourgeois Wilhelminian society and desired a regeneration of mankind—a "new man." Their drama was the protest of a generation of "sons" against the hierarchic structure of a generation of "fathers." This attitude is illustrated by plays with titles that are to be translated as *The Son*, by Walter Hasenclever, or *Patricide*, by Arnolt Bronnen.

With the search for new content went the search for a new form and a new language. Although expressionism was by no means a uniform movement, the expressionist writers had one thing in common: they were far too idealistic and also too far removed from the political and economic realities of their day; they were more concerned with abstract ideas than practical realities. Brecht studied the methods of expressionism very carefully and adopted what he found of value, but he was nevertheless highly critical of this movement. He rejected their kind of idealism and the pathos of expressionistic writings. But he agreed that change was indeed necessary in the drama, in both content and form, as well as in the structure of society.

In 1918, Brecht's studies in Munich were briefly interrupted by military service as a medical orderly in the Augsburg military hospital, in which he worked in the venereal disease ward. His own experiences during this time, as well as those of his friends, increased his opposition to war. In this year he wrote the radically pacifist poem "Legend of the Dead Soldier." In 1935 this poem was to be explicitly cited by the Nazis when they deprived him of his German citizenship.

At the end of World War I (in 1918), several leftist revolts broke out in various parts of Germany, including Munich and Augsburg. On 7 November 1918 the Bavarian king, Ludwig III, was deposed, and a leftist republic of Bavaria, governed by soldiers' and workers' councils, was instituted. It was, however, soon crushed by armed forces of the central government of the Weimar Republic. Though well aware of the political events of the time, Brecht remained for the most part uninvolved.

His next major play after *Baal*, *Drums in the Night* (1919), did capture the mood of disillusion prevailing at the time. The play was originally named *Spartakus*, after the Spartakusbund, a German communist organization formed during these years. (They in turn took their name from the leader of an uprising of Roman slaves in 73–71 B.C.; at the end of 1918 the Communist party of Germany evolved out of the Spartakusbund.) But far from being a glorification of this communist group, Brecht's play ended with the main character, Kragler, turning his back on revolution in favor of going to bed with his girlfriend. This ending was later to be an embarrassment to the Marxist Brecht.

In Munich, as in Augsburg, Brecht was surrounded by a circle of friends. The most important of them were the writer Lion Feuchtwanger and the producer Erich Engel. He also met Johannes R. Becher, the expressionist poet, who was three decades later to become Minister for Cultural Affairs in East Germany. It was Feuchtwanger who suggested the title by which the "Spartakus" play is known today. Brecht also enjoyed the cabaret of Karl Valentin, and performed with him several times. (Cabarets are a mixture of studio theater and nightclub in which entertainers, in satirical sketches, focus mainly on social and political topics.) Valentin's inclination to think in contradictions—his "confounded dialectics"—particularly attracted Brecht.

From October 1919 until January 1921, he was also a theater critic in Augsburg for the *Volkswillen,* the daily paper of the Independent Socialist Party. During this brief period he managed to antagonize the ensemble of the Augsburg theater with his biting comments on their plays and performances.

By midyear of 1921, Brecht's involvement in the world of theater and cabaret and with the writers and bohemians of Munich had become so great that he abandoned his medical studies at the university. He was now firmly committed to a career as poet, playwright, and director. He continued to revise *Baal,* read extensively, went to plays, movies (especially the Charlie Chaplin films), cafés, bars, cabarets, fairs, worked on numerous projects, and tried to get his two plays performed. One of his new projects was a play called *In the Jungle,* which was later to become *In the Jungle of Cities.*

In November 1922, a Brecht play was performed

for the first time before the public. The successful performance of *Drums in the Night* in the Münchener Kammerspiele established Brecht's reputation as a new force in the theater of the Weimar Republic. The critic Herbert Ihering stated: "The twenty-four-year-old Brecht has changed the literary scene in Germany overnight."[20] He awarded him the coveted Kleist prize for this play as well as for *Baal* and *In the Jungle of Cities*, which he had read. (The latter two had not been staged at that time.)

In October 1922, Brecht was hired as a *Dramaturg* (dramatic consultant) by Otto Falckenberg at the Kammerspiele in Munich. While there, he staged *Edward the Second*, which he and Feuchtwanger had adapted from Christopher Marlowe's *Edward II*.

The political situation during this period was unstable. According to Bernhard Reich, the director of the Kammerspiele in Munich at that time, Munich had become one of the most conservative and reactionary cities in Germany.[21] The activities of groups farthest to the right increased, culminating in Hitler's abortive revolt in November 1923, in which Hitler and his followers attempted to take over the government of Bavaria. After a brief exchange of gunfire, in which several Nazis (who were to become celebrated as martyrs to the Nazi cause) and policemen were killed, Hitler was arrested by the police and jailed for high treason in Landsberg prison (where he wrote his infamous book *Mein Kampf*). Inflation was rampant, food scarce. Brecht, who was constitutionally frail-looking, appeared even thinner with his large cap and cheap nickel-rimmed glasses. His unkempt appearance, together with his Swabian accent, made him seem a rather unlikely candidate to change the course of modern drama. He possessed a sharp intelligence and an insatiable drive to experiment and to try out his ideas. His rather unpretentious outward appearance actually helped him to apply his keen powers of observation to a Western society that was beginning to disintegrate and to show its true and ugly face in the wake of the "decline of the West," which Oswald Spengler had predicted in his famous book of 1918. Paradoxically, the theaters were almost always sold out, whatever the play, because people wanted to spend their money before its value plummeted even further. This gave directors a chance to try out new plays on the audience.

While in Munich, Brecht made several trips to Berlin, hoping to gain a foothold there. In the 1920s, Berlin was not only the political but also the cultural center of Germany. If artists and playwrights were successful in Berlin, they achieved national—if not international—reputations. Berlin's theaters (which were repertory theaters, like virtually all German theaters to this day) were the best in Germany and among the best in the world. Never again has the city seen such an assembly of theatrical talent. To name only a few: the directors Erich Engel, Leopold Jessner, Piscator, and Max Reinhardt; actors such as Albert Bassermann, Elisabeth Bergner, Heinrich George, Emil Jannings, Fritz Kortner, Werner Krauss, Lotte Lenya, Peter Lorre, Carola Neher, and Max Pallenberg; playwrights such as Georg Kaiser and Carl Zuckmayer; a host of prominent critics such as Herbert Ihering and Alfred Kerr.

On one of his visits to Berlin, Brecht met the expressionist playwright Arnolt Bronnen. Despite Brecht's disapproval of expressionism, he and Bronnen became good friends. They roamed through the Berlin theaters and collaborated on several projects, such as a film play in five acts called *Robinson Crusoe on the Island of Asuncion,* and a historical play, *Hannibal,* which remained a fragment. In fact, in 1922 Brecht made his debut as a director in Berlin with Bronnen's play *Patricide* in the repertory theater Junge Bühne. But because of serious differences and disputes with the actors, particularly Heinrich George, Brecht had to resign. Thus Brecht gained the reputation as "the terror of the average producer and the horror of every theater director."[22] He maintained this distinction until his death: Not only was he the writer of a play, but he also had in mind as he wrote it an exact concept of staging, scenery, directing, casting, and even music.

In September 1924, Brecht finally took up permanent residence in Berlin. The city impressed him at first as a "cold" city, a thicket, and a jungle. His play *In the Jungle of Cities* contains many of his personal experiences, which, mixed with poetic elements, he transposed to Chicago—in the United States.

In Berlin, Brecht started out as a *Dramaturg* at the Deutsches Theater under Max Reinhardt. This was, however, a brief and relatively unproductive period. Its shortcomings can be charged to the fact that Brecht did not particularly care for the famous director. He generally went to the theater only to collect his pay and to watch rehearsals, but was especially attentive at the rehearsals of Bernard Shaw's *Saint Joan* (which was later to become one of the models for his own *Saint Joan* play).

Again Brecht was surrounded by a circle of friends, among them John Heartfield, a specialist in photomontage; John's brother, Wieland Herzfelde, who was later to start publishing an edition of Brecht's works in his Malik Verlag in Prague and London; George Grosz, the creator of satirical drawings; the author Klabund (pen name of Alfred Henschke) and his actress wife Carola Neher; the boxer Samson-Körner, whose biography Brecht began to write; the writers Georg Kaiser and Alfred Döblin, whom Brecht used to call his "illegitimate fathers"; and Elisabeth Hauptmann, Brecht's most important collaborator in the Berlin period.

In December 1925, Brecht began to work on a play called *Dan Drew.* This project, which deals with the construction of the Erie railroad in the United States, was never finished. Another play, *A Man Is a Man,* which Brecht had been working on since around 1920, now reached the finished stage. This play, like most of Brecht's plays, was written in close collaboration with others (in this case, Elisabeth Hauptmann, Caspar Neher, Bernhard Reich, Emil Burri, Slatan Dudow), although Brecht unquestionably dominated the group. Brecht preferred to work with teams of people in developing his ideas. He, in turn, also collaborated with other writers on their ideas. In return for Feuchtwanger's help with *Edward the Second,* which appeared under Brecht's name, he worked with Feuchtwanger on *Calcutta, May 4th,* which appeared under Feuchtwanger's name.

By the end of his first year in Berlin, Brecht had achieved a firm foothold in that city. He was invited to contribute to many literary and theatrical discussions and opinion polls conducted by a variety of journals. In 1927, as a judge in a competition among four hundred young lyric poets, he shocked his contemporaries by rejecting all of the poems and recommending instead a poem about a racing cyclist by the virtually unknown poet Hannes Küpper, who was not even a participant in the competition. In this same year, Brecht himself published one of his most famous volumes of poems under the title *Manual of Piety.* (The main themes of this volume of poems, which is conceived in the manner of a Lutheran breviary, are the sufferings of an oppressed mankind, and carefree life and love, later expressed in the character of Baal.)

One of Brecht's most important relationships in Berlin was his association with Erwin Piscator, who was one of the leading German stage directors in the 1920s and the father of the German documentary theater that developed in the 1960s. Breaking radically with the conventional theater, Piscator used placards, film strips, projections, photomontage, and various mechanical devices for his productions in order to set his plays in a wider sociological and political context. Brecht was involved in several of these productions, the most notable being the 1927–28 stage version of Jaroslav Hašek's novel *The Adventures of the Good Soldier Schweik*. It was from Piscator, and before him Feuchtwanger, that Brecht received some of his most important ideas for the development of his epic theater.

By 1926, some important changes in Brecht's philosophy began to develop. First, he came into contact with the theory of behaviorism, which examined the question of the influence of environment on human behavior. According to John B. Watson, the leading representative of the behaviorist school, behaviorism "is concerned with the prediction and control of human action and not with an analysis of consciousness."[23] Watson believed that the only way to change a personality was by changing the environment so that new habits were formed.

More important, however, was Brecht's study of Karl Marx. In connection with his work on his play *Wheat,* which Piscator had announced for the 1926–27 season, Brecht needed information about the sale and distribution of wheat. He read extensively and talked to grain brokers, but failed to obtain the desired understanding. Brecht later wrote about this period: "From every point of view . . . the grain market remained one impenetrable jungle. The planned drama was not completed. But instead, I began to read Marx. It was only at this point that my own scattered practical experiences and impressions came

clearly into focus."[24] He also began to attend evening
classes in economics and Marxism-Leninism. His
Marxist teachers were Fritz Sternberg and Karl
Korsch, who were considered heretics by the orthodox
communists; Korsch was expelled from the party in
1926. Brecht, however, kept in touch with Korsch
throughout his lifetime. This intense study of Marx led
to Brecht's most doctrinal phase. His *Lehrstücke* (the
didactic plays—among them the one-acters *The Measures Taken* and *The Exception and the Rule,* and the
full-length play *The Mother*) were written around
1930.

Yet parallel to this doctrinal and austere period ran
Brecht's excursion into the world of opera: In Kurt
Weill, Brecht found a congenial composer who set
several of his works to music; their greatest success
was *The Threepenny Opera,* in 1928. During this
period Brecht and Weill also collaborated on *Happy
End* (1929), a sequel to *The Threepenny Opera; The
Rise and Fall of the City of Mahagonny* (1928–29);
and *The Seven Deadly Sins* (1933).

On finding some of François Villon's verses in the
text of *The Threepenny Opera,* the famous critic Alfred Kerr accused Brecht of plagiarism. Brecht freely
admitted having taken the verses from Villon's work,
although he had made some slight but significant
changes. More important, however, was Brecht's attitude toward literature and literary tradition, which
Kerr did not share. Brecht did not believe in the concept of the writer as *alter deus,* another god, one who
withdraws from the world to create a completely
original work of art in the seclusion of his study. Like
many other writers, he picked up a good thing where
he could find it. When he was accused of doing so,
he answered: "Well, Shakespeare was a thief, too."[25]
He insisted that it was necessary to lessen the importance of the concept of "originality" since, as he

Bertolt Brecht in his Charlottenburg apartment (Berlin), in the late 1920s.

wrote, "copying is not easier—it is an art in itself."[26] He went on to say that "the pitiful fear of members of our society that one could question their originality is closely connected with their shabby concept of property."[27] *The Threepenny Opera* caused further controversy in 1930 when the Nero Motion Picture Company in Berlin, which had bought the film rights to the opera, was sued by Brecht because he wanted more control over the filming. Although Brecht lost the suit, he was not overly concerned since he regarded the trial as a "sociological experiment" that exposed the bourgeois legal system.

In 1933, Brecht completed *Saint Joan of the Stockyards,* but the play did not reach the stage at that time. The play reflects the chaos the Wall Street crash of 1929 caused in Germany. Millions of workers were out of work, and the polarization between the political right and the political left increased. Poverty was widespread and inflation rampant. In January of 1933, Hitler came to power. After the Reichstag—the seat of the parliament of the Weimar Republic in Berlin— had burned down on 27 February 1933, Hitler immediately blamed the communists, his most vociferous and most powerful opponents. Under the pretense of keeping law and order, he ordered mass arrests of leftists. Thousands of them were arrested during the night of the fire. Among them were prominent writers such as Egon Erwin Kisch, Erich Mühsam, and Carl von Ossietzky. In order to incarcerate them, the first concentration camps were constructed. Soon after the fire, Marinus van der Lubbe, an unemployed Dutchman, was arrested, tried, and executed for arson. It is alleged, however, that the Nazis themselves deliberately started the fire in order to gain absolute power.

Brecht, who had been on the Nazis' blacklist for some time, left Germany the day after the fire, on 28 February 1933. His fifteen years in exile began, a period during which he "changed countries more often than shoes," as he later wrote.[28] In Germany, the Nazis, branding him a communist and cultural bolshevist, burned his works, together with those of many other writers such as Heinrich Heine and Heinrich Mann. In 1935 they also revoked his German citizenship (other exiles—for example, Thomas Mann—were likewise deprived of their German citizenship.)

From Berlin, Brecht went to Denmark via Prague, Vienna, Zurich, and Paris. From August 1933 until April 1939, he and his family (his wife Helene Weigel and their two children) lived in a house near Svendborg in Denmark. There Brecht led a rather secluded life, surrounded only by his family and a few friends, among whom were the German actress and writer Margarete Steffin, the Danish actress Ruth Berlau, and the Danish writer Martin Andersen Nexö. He also entertained fellow exiles on occasion. Among them were the essayist and literary critic Walter Benjamin, the composer Hanns Eisler, and the Marxist philosopher Karl Korsch (who actually lived in Brecht's house from the end of 1933 until 1936). Various trips took Brecht to London (1934 and 1936), Moscow (1935), Paris (1935 and 1937), and New York City (1935). These trips were mainly undertaken in connection with performances of his plays or for the purpose of attending meetings of German exiles. In Paris, for example, he attended the International Writers' Congress (June 1935). In New York, he went to the rehearsals of his play *The Mother* at the Theater Union.

While in Moscow, Brecht saw performances by the Chinese actor Mei Lan-fang, who made a lasting impression on him. In the style of Mei Lan-fang's performances, Brecht saw many features of the acting style for the epic theater he himself envisioned. He wrote about this encounter with the Chinese theater in an article entitled "Estrangement Effects in the Chinese

Art of Acting." This article, written in 1937, became part of *The Purchase of Brass* (begun in 1939), in which Brecht explained his theory of theater in the form of dialogues. Brecht's interest in Chinese philosophy, especially the school of Mê Ti, dates back to the late 1920s. And in 1934, Brecht began collecting texts for his *Mê Ti: Book of Changes* (which remained unfinished).

While in Denmark, Brecht finished *The Threepenny Novel*, which was published in 1934 in Amsterdam. It was translated into English in 1937 by Desmond Vesey and Christopher Isherwood, under the title *A Penny for the Poor*. This novel is based on the material of *The Threepenny Opera*, but the social and political aspects that, in the opera, tend to get somewhat glossed over by Weill's fascinating music were brought out more clearly. With *The Horatians and the Curiatians*, Brecht completed the last of his didactic plays.

The next two plays, *The Round Heads and the Pointed Heads* (1931–35) and *Fear and Misery of the Third Reich* (1934–38), are direct attacks upon the hated Nazi regime. When the Spanish civil war broke out in 1936, Brecht wrote a play with which he indicated his support for the struggle of the Spanish people against fascism, *Señora Carrar's Rifles*. In 1938, Brecht began an attempt at a more detached analysis of the nature of dictatorships in the form of a novel about Caesar, *The Affairs of Mr. Julius Caesar*. Although he never finished the novel, the fragment is itself an excellent example of Brecht's fine narrative prose.

In November 1938, Brecht wrote his first version of his play *Galileo*. Through the English translation of this play by Desmond Vesey, Brecht hoped to secure for himself a source of income in the event that he had to emigrate to the United States (for which he was already preparing). At the same time, he was also working on the last major play of his Scandinavian exile, *The Good Woman of Setzuan* (1938–41).

When it became evident that Hitler was preparing for war, Brecht moved to Sweden on 23 April 1939. (Brecht often referred to Hitler only as *Der Anstreicher*—"the [house] painter"—alluding sarcastically to Hitler's futile attempts in his youth to become a fine arts painter.) The sculptor Ninan Sanesson offered him her house on the island of Lidingö just off the mainland from Stockholm. Brecht had obtained his visa for Sweden in order to deliver a lecture on Experimental Theater to a Stockholm student theater on 4 May 1939. In this important speech, Brecht outlined the basic principles of his theory of theater.

Brecht finished two one-act plays in June of 1939, *Dansen* and *What Is the Price of Iron?* The latter was translated into Swedish and performed by a workers' theater group under the direction of Ruth Berlau. In the summer of 1939, the Swedish actress Naima Wifstrand brought to Brecht's attention Johan Ludvig Runeberg's story about the itinerant vendor Lotta Svärd. This work inspired Brecht to write one of his best-known plays, *Mother Courage and Her Children,* which he completed in November 1939.

Like other refugees from Nazi Germany, Brecht was not allowed to be politically active. The Swedish government feared reprisals from the Nazis too much to allow the refugees this kind of freedom. With the radio play *The Trial of Lucullus,* written with Margarete Steffin in November 1939, Brecht felt that he "had about reached the limit of what could be said."[29] Thus when he did write something concerning the immediate political situation, he used the pseudonym John Kent (for *What Is the Price of Iron?*) or Sherwood Paw (for a satirical article on Russia's war against Finland in the winter of 1939–40).

To assist his wife Helene Weigel in teaching his style of epic acting to students of Naima Wifstrand's acting school in Stockholm, Brecht wrote several "Practice Pieces for Actors," such as *Murder in the Porter's Lodge* (which recalls the porter scene in Shakespeare's *Macbeth*, II, 2), and *The Quarrel of the Fishwives* (in which he transplants to a fish market the meeting of Elizabeth I and Mary Stuart that occurred in the third act of Schiller's play *Mary Stuart*).

But once again the immediate political situation required Brecht's full attention. When German forces invaded Denmark and Norway in April of 1940, and the Swedish government showed signs of nervousness (some German émigrés were returned to Germany), Brecht and his family moved on to Finland on 17 April 1940. In Finland, they lived with the Finnish writer Hella Wuolijoki, who supplied the plot for Brecht's play *Herr Puntila and His Servant Matti*. While in Finland, Brecht also wrote his witty *Dialogues in Exile*, in which two characters, Kalle and Ziffel, reveal Brecht's dialectical way of thinking, as well as his attitude toward current events. The last of his works that dealt directly with the Nazi rule in Germany was the satirical play *The Resistible Rise of Arturo Ui*, which he wrote in Finland in collaboration with Margarete Steffin.

In spite of the dismal political events around him, Brecht continued to work on themes not directly related to these events. He found this a paradoxical situation. On 16 September 1940, he wrote in his *Work Journal:*

> It would be incredibly difficult to describe the frame of mind in which I follow the news on the radio and in the bad Finnish–Swedish newspapers about the Battle of England—and then go to work on *Puntila*. This phenomenon shows that literary production can go on in the face of such wars.

Puntila does not affect me at all, but the war affects me greatly. Yet about *Puntila,* I can write everything, about the war, nothing. And I mean not only "may" but really "can." It is interesting to see how far the practice of writing literature is removed from the most crucial events.[30]

The state of the war had by this time left German refugees little hope of an early return to the fatherland. After the defeat of Poland in September 1939, Hitler quickly occupied Denmark and Norway early in the spring of 1940, and in June 1940 France asked for an armistice. In the spring of 1941 Hitler's troops moved against Yugoslavia and Greece, and in June 1941 they attacked the Soviet Union. Shortly before the German army invaded Russia, Brecht left Finland and went to Moscow via Leningrad. On 13 July 1941, he noted in his *Work Journal:*

The situation in Finland quickly became threatening. We received our American immigration visas on 2 May 1941, and our Finnish friends urged us to leave. The German motorized divisions in the country increased; Helsinki was full of German "travelers" [soldiers in disguise]; the tensions between Germany and the USSR increased.[31]

But Brecht stayed only a few days in Moscow. He and his family took the trans-Siberia express to Vladivostok, and from there they sailed on the Swedish freighter *Annie Johnson* to the United States. They arrived in San Pedro, California, on 21 July 1941, almost exactly one month after Hitler had attacked Russia (on 22 June 1941). While on the train to Vladivostok, Brecht received the news that Margarete Steffin, whom they had had to leave behind in a Moscow hospital, had died of lung disease. She had been one of Brecht's closest friends in his period of Scandinavian exile, and her death was a severe blow to him. At the beginning of August 1941, shortly after his arrival in California, he also learned that the writer Walter Benjamin, whom he held in high esteem, had committed suicide while fleeing from the Nazis.

The reasons Brecht, an avowed Marxist, did not choose to remain in the Soviet Union are complex. To begin with, there was a very practical reason: with Hitler's early victories against the Soviet army, Moscow did not seem to be a safe place. Indeed, late in 1941, German troops came dangerously close to the Soviet capital before being repulsed by the Red Army. But perhaps more important was that Brecht's views of Marxism and art were contrary to many of the Stalinist concepts of Marxism and art dominating the Soviet Union at that time. Many of Brecht's friends in the Soviet Union—Soviet citizens such as the writer Sergei Tretiakov and German exiles such as the actress Carola Neher—died in Stalin's concentration camps for their alleged deviationism. Exile in the Soviet Union would therefore have been dangerous for Brecht.[32]

In California, Brecht and his family settled down in Santa Monica. Around them were many other exiles from Germany: Lion Feuchtwanger, Hanns Eisler, Peter Lorre, Fritz Lang, Fritz Kortner, Max Horkheimer, Friedrich Pollock, and Heinrich Mann. There also was Heinrich's brother, Thomas, whom Brecht disliked intensely. For Brecht, Thomas Mann epitomized the ivory-tower intellectual whose disdain for politics and everyday life was partially to blame for the "resistible rise" of the Nazis. The dislike was a mutual affair. (It should be added, however, that Brecht's view of Thomas Mann was somewhat clouded by personal animosity: By the time they both lived in California, Thomas Mann had long reversed his earlier apolitical attitude and openly opposed the Nazi regime in Germany.)

Yet Brecht's circle of friends was not limited to exiles alone. He met Charlie Chaplin, whose films he so admired; the actor Charles Laughton, with whom he wrote the English version of *Galileo;* W. H. Auden, with whom he adapted Webster's *Duchess of Malfi;* and Eric Bentley, scholar, writer, critic, who was to become Brecht's foremost champion in the United States. Brecht's reunion with Feuchtwanger led to the conception of a new play, *The Visions of Simone Machard,* in which he used the familiar topic of Joan of Arc for the second time.

From Los Angeles, Brecht made several trips to New York City, where he saw Erwin Piscator, Paul Dessau, and Kurt Weill, his old friends. Weill had in the meantime berome quite a celebrity on Broadway with his musicals (such as *Knickerbocker Holiday,* 1938, and *Lady in the Dark,* 1940). Piscator hoped to collaborate with Brecht on a new *Schweyk* production, but to his great disappointment and annoyance, Brecht wrote *Schweyk in the Second World War* without him. (The name "Schweyk" was of course that of Hašek's "Svejk," from the novel with the World War I background.)

While close to Hollywood—and mainly to earn money—Brecht also made several attempts to write film scripts, a task he found very difficult. In a poem entitled "Hollywood," he wrote:

> Every morning, to earn my bread
> I go to the marketplace, where lies are bought.
> Full of hope
> I join the other salesmen.[33]

Only one project was realized, although not at all in the form Brecht had envisioned. This movie, *Hang-*

men Also Die, directed by Fritz Lang, deals with the assassination of the SS officer Heydrich, in Prague.[34] Brecht wanted more and stronger scenes showing the resistance of the people and even managed to convince the American screenplay writer John Wexley to begin a second film script and to talk Lang into adopting more of his ideas. But, with the box office in mind, Lang dared not depart too far from Hollywood tastes, which generally preferred entertainment to enlightenment.

Unlike Feuchtwanger and Thomas Mann, Brecht never gained access to a large audience in the United States. His works were not published, and, with the exception of seventeen of the twenty-four scenes from *Fear and Misery of the Third Reich,* none of his plays was performed in the United States while he lived there. But he began and completed writing one of the most successful examples of his epic theater while in Los Angeles: *The Caucasian Chalk Circle.*

Although he found the people friendly, Brecht never liked living in California. What he wrote in his *Work Journal* shortly after his arrival in 1941 remained true for the whole six years that he lived there:

> Nowhere has life been more difficult for me than here, in this showplace of the "easy going." I feel as if I had been removed from this age ... 15,000 kilometers away there is a bloody massacre in Europe, day and night, deciding our fate. It generates only a faint echo here in the busy market of artificiality.[35]

The defeat of the German Sixth Army at Stalingrad in January 1943 marked the turning point of World War II. In May 1943 the German force in Africa capitulated. With the landing of British and American forces on the beaches of France's Normandy coast in June 1944 the last phase of the war began, which ended with a total victory for the allied forces in May 1945.

In 1947, the House Committee on Un-American Activities began to take a look at possible subversive activities in Hollywood's film industry. On 30 October 1947, Brecht was summoned before the committee. The committee was unable to produce any incriminating evidence against him. Brecht had already decided to leave the country, which he did the day after the hearings.

On 1 November 1947, Brecht arrived in Paris and traveled from there to Zurich, where he was reunited with old friends such as the designer Caspar Neher and the publisher Peter Suhrkamp. He moved into a house near Zurich and immediately set to work once more. In 1948, he finished *Short Organum for the Theater,* one of the most important treatises demonstrating his theory of theater.[36] He adapted Sophocles' *Antigone,* which was first performed in 1948 in the Stadttheater Chur, Switzerland, under the direction of Brecht and Caspar Neher. The first of the "Model" books (illustrated books that discuss every detail of every step in the preparation for the production), the *Antigone Model of 1948,* published in Berlin in 1949, is derived from this performance. Before Brecht left Zurich for Berlin, he had the opportunity to see another first performance of one of his plays: on 5 June 1948, the Schauspielhaus Zurich, the only prominent German-speaking theater that had remained outside the control of the Nazis during the war, staged his play *Herr Puntila and his Servant Matti.* Brecht and Kurt Hirschfeld directed, but, because of immigration regulations, only Hirschfeld's name appeared on the program. While in Switzerland, Brecht also met the aspiring Swiss playwrights Max Frisch and Friedrich Dürrenmatt, in whose works Brechtian influence is clearly distinguishable.

Before he finally decided to go to Berlin, Brecht

had also entertained the idea of settling in Salzburg, Austria, to work with the famous Salzburg Festival. He thought it desirable to have a residence outside Germany and to have an Austrian passport, since he wanted to be active in both parts of the now-divided Germany. Yet, as a man without a country, Brecht had difficulties obtaining travel papers and, consequently, he was unable to go to Salzburg.

In 1948, Brecht managed to get papers to travel to East Berlin, where he was invited to stage *Mother Courage and Her Children*. At that time Germany was divided into four occupation zones (American, British, French, Soviet), and free travel was impossible. Since Brecht was denied a visa for the American zone (for political reasons), he traveled from Switzerland to Berlin via Czechoslovakia—ironically, the reverse of the route by which he had left Berlin as a refugee fifteen years earlier. Walking through Berlin, or what was left of it, Brecht was deeply moved. He wrote in his *Work Journal* on 23 October 1948:

> Last night when we arrived, I only saw the ruins of the Friedrichstrasse in the dark. This morning at 6:30 A.M., I walked down the Wilhelmstrasse [location of Nazi government offices] to the Reichskanzlei [Hitler's former office]. To smoke my cigar there, so to speak. I saw a few men and women clearing debris. The ruins impressed me less than the thought of what the people must have suffered when the city was destroyed. A worker showed me the way. I asked him: "How long will you have to work before this looks like something again?" He answered: "I guess by then we will all have a few more gray hairs. If we had people with money, it would go faster, but we have run out of people with money." To me, the ruins seemed at least to point to the former presence of people with money.[37]

This passage contains a good deal of irony—both tragic and sarcastic. It recalls one of Brecht's most famous, most autobiographical poems, "Of Poor B.B.," written in 1920 when he was only twenty-one. In this poem, he predicted that, of the cities thought indestructible, nothing would remain but the wind that swept through them. But it was his hope that in the coming periods of upheaval he foresaw, he would not have his "cigar extinguished by bitterness." Now this prophecy had been tragically fulfilled. But he had survived to "smoke his cigar" on the ruins of the former seat of the Nazi government. The ruins, however, also reminded him of the tragedies caused by capitalists—the "people with money." (In Brecht's Marxist view, Hitler was merely a tool of German capitalists, fighting an imperialistic war to gain new markets.)

Although Brecht took up permanent residence in East Berlin in 1949, he never became a citizen of East Germany. Because his wife was an Austrian citizen, he was able to obtain an Austrian passport in 1950, and he remained an Austrian citizen until his death. Brecht felt that with an Austrian passport he would have access to all German-speaking theaters, rather than only to those behind the iron curtain.

Immediately after his arrival in Berlin in 1948, Brecht began rehearsals for *Mother Courage,* and started discussions with friends and officials about other theater plans. But soon he sensed "the stale breath of the province," as he noted in his *Work Journal*[38] after discussions about his proposed theater projects with SED party officials and East Berlin's Mayor Ebert. (The Socialist Unity Party—SED—is the ruling Communist party of East Germany.) Although Brecht was a supporter of the regime in East Germany, and was, in turn, highly respected by it, he had his share of troubles with small-minded functionaries. He was frustrated by the concept of socialist realism in the early 1950s, when much of his work was regarded by the party as too "formalistic." (By "formalistic," the party meant that the emphasis was on form rather than on socialist content. Because of Brecht's use of parables and other devices of his estrangement technique, his work, according to the party, was guilty of formalism.) Thus, in 1951, for instance, the opera *The Trial of Lucullus* (a parable) by Brecht and the composer Paul Dessau, ran into difficulties with party critics. After some changes, it reappeared under the title *The Condemnation of Lucullus*. This controversy was eagerly condemned by Western critics as an example of communist censorship. Brecht, however, dryly replied that it would probably be difficult to find a Western statesman willing and able to meet with a playwright and discuss his play for more than eight hours, as the East German officials had done with him.

The concept of socialist realism was first outlined by Andrei A. Zhdanov at the First Congress of Soviet Writers in 1934. "Socialist realism as the fundamental method of socialist literature demands from the artist a correct, historically concrete representation of reality in its revolutionary development."[39] Essential requirements were faithfulness to life (realism), representation of the social struggle as a struggle for progress, adherence to social optimism and hope for a better future, and a positive hero figure (such as a model worker). The style had to be simple and straightforward, all experimenting was to be avoided. Thus most modern expressions of art and literature were branded as decadent and formalistic (for example, expressionism, futurism, James Joyce, and jazz).

Brecht agreed that the content should be socialistic, but argued that the writer should be free to chose his own style without limitations. He felt one could learn from such modern writers as James Joyce and Franz Kafka. Brecht had already formulated his views on realism in his contributions to the so-called debate on "realism" in the late 1930s. There were several contributors to this debate, but the two most prominent antagonists were Brecht (at that time in exile) and the Hungarian Marxist critic Georg Lukács. The debate was for the most part carried out in *Das Wort,* a journal published between 1936 and 1939 in Moscow by German exiles; its editors were Brecht, Feuchtwanger, and the writer Willi Bredel.[40] It should be added, however, that many of Brecht's replies to Lukács were never printed in *Das Wort.* One reason was that Brecht did not want to cause a division in the socialist camp at a time when unity in the fight against fascism was needed.

In 1950, socialist realism in the narrow concept defined in 1934 became the official and obligatory standard for art in East Germany. (The concept has since been modified somewhat to allow for greater freedom in the choice of styles.)

In June 1953 East Germany faced a serious crisis. There was an uprising against the communist government that began with a group of discontented workers and spread rapidly to the general populace. This uprising was swiftly and brutally squelched by Russian troops. On this occasion, Brecht expressed his support for the government. At the same time, however, he composed a poem in answer to the official party poet Kuba (pen name of Kurt Barthel), who had admonished the workers to hide their faces in shame. In his poem, Brecht satirically suggested that since, according to Kuba, the people had lost the trust of the government and could only regain it by doubling their efforts at work, "wouldn't it be simpler in this case if the government just dissolved the people and selected another?"[41] Brecht also criticized some aspects of the cultural policies of the SED, but he strongly rejected applause from the West for his criticizing the SED:

> Even the smallest minds,
> If their intent is peace,
> Are more welcome in the arts
> Than those patrons of art
> Who are also the friends of the art of war.[42]

And, when asked about the political situation in East Germany, Brecht maintained that an imposed socialism was still better than none at all.

In the days of the cold war, Brecht's support of the SED during and after the workers' uprising on 17 June 1953 was severely criticized in the west. Many performances of his plays were canceled and his Western supporters faced many difficulties. (In 1966, Brecht and his part in the events of 17 June 1953 even became the subject of a play, *The Plebeians Rehearse the Uprising*, by Günter Grass, author of *The Tin Drum*.) Yet Brecht remained undeterred. He continued to work for the socialist cause through his theater and letters to newspapers and fellow artists. In July 1956 he even wrote to the West German legislature (Bundestag) in order to protest against the rearmament of West Germany. He also became interested in Mao Tse-tung. In February 1955, when asked which book had made the strongest impression on him in 1954, he named Mao's work *On Contradiction*.

During his post-exile period in Berlin, Brecht devoted most of his time to the practical aspects of theater. After more than fifteen years of exile, he could once again produce his plays. The actors he had gathered together for the performance of *Mother Courage* in January 1949 formed the nucleus of the Berliner Ensemble. The first director of the Ensemble was Brecht's wife, Helene Weigel. It included not only

many actors and actresses who had returned to Berlin
after the war, but, thanks to Brecht's personal efforts,
young talent as well. At the beginning, the Ensemble
had to share the stage with the Deutsches Theater.
Finally in 1954 it was granted separate quarters in the
Theater am Schiffbauerdamm, a building with a beautiful baroque interior. Brecht saw to it that this was
carefully restored. The Ensemble's activities were
generously subsidized by the East German state.
Thus, it could afford a staff of some two hundred and
fifty people and allow plenty of time for experiments
and rehearsals.

With actors such as Helene Weigel, Ernst Busch,
Erwin Geschonnek, Angelika Hurwicz, and Ekkehard
Schall, the Ensemble achieved worldwide fame, particularly after the highly successful performance at
the International Theater Festival in Paris in 1954.
It attracted and trained young talent such as Benno
Besson, Hans-Joachim Bunge, Claus Hubalek, Egon
Monk, Peter Palitsch, Käthe Rülicke, Manfred Weck-
werth—a list that almost reads like a Who's Who on
the East and West German theater scene. (Since the
deaths of Brecht and Helene Weigel, the Ensemble,
under the directorship of Ruth Berghaus, underwent
some very difficult periods, and many talented
directors and actors have left. But it nevertheless remains one of the leading theater groups in Europe. Its
current director is Manfred Wekwerth.)

For the Ensemble, besides preparing some of his
own plays for production, Brecht adapted plays from
other writers, among them *The Tutor,* by the *Sturm
und Drang* playwright Jakob Michael Reinhold Lenz;
Anna Seghers's radio play *The Trial of Joan of Arc at
Rouen 1431;* Shakespeare's *Coriolanus;* Molière's *Don
Juan;* and George Farquhar's *The Recruiting Officer.*
He also finished some of his earlier projects, such as
The Days of the Commune and *Turandot, or the Con-*

Bertolt Brecht in later years.
GERMAN INFORMATION CENTER

gress of Whitewashers. Brecht also helped the East German novelist and playwright Erwin Strittmatter with his play *Katzgraben.* He set out to collect material for a play of his own about a contemporary East German "model" worker (Hans Garbe) who had set new production records. The play, however, was never completed.

During these years in East Berlin, Brecht received

many official honors. In 1950, he became a member of the Akademie der Künste in East Berlin. In 1951, he was awarded the Nationalpreis erster Klasse, one of the highest distinctions the East German government can bestow. In 1953, he was elected chairman of the International PEN Center. In 1954, he won the International Stalin Peace Prize, and traveled to Moscow to receive it personally. But the strain of all this activity began to show. Brecht returned from Moscow exhausted. He continued his work, although his deteriorating health often confined him to his country house in Buckow, near Berlin. In the spring of 1956, a severe attack of influenza forced him to leave the direction of the rehearsals for *Galileo* to his old friend Erich Engel, and to undergo treatment in a hospital. After his release he participated in the preparation for the Ensemble's tour to London. On 10 August 1956, he attended his last rehearsal for *Galileo*. Four days later, on 14 August at the age of 58, he died of a heart attack.

Brecht left behind not only several finished yet unrevised plays but also numerous fragmentary plays. Among them are *Hannibal, Gösta Berling, Nothing Will Come of Nothing, The True Life of Jacob Geherda, Life of Confucius, Salzburg Dance of Death, The Breadstore,* and, of particular importance to Brecht (he returned to it time and again), *The Decline and Fall of the Egoist Fatzer.*

Two of these fragmentary plays have since been adapted for production. In 1967 two of Brecht's students, Manfred Karge and Matthias Langhoff, staged *The Breadstore* with the Berliner Ensemble. And in 1976, Frank Steckel produced *The Decline and Fall of the Egoist Fatzer* in West Berlin's Schaubühne am Halleschen Ufer, one of the leading German theaters today.

Before he left for his trip to Moscow, Brecht had

specified in his will that, upon his death, he did not want any public ceremonies. He also left instructions that he be buried in the Dorotheen cemetery, which is next to his last residence in East Berlin (Chausseestrasse 125). His wishes were fulfilled—his simple grave is next to those of Heinrich Mann and the philosophers Fichte and Hegel.

BRECHT'S
THEORY OF THEATER

Brecht called his theater epic or dialectic theater.[1] Here the term epic does not mean heroic or on a grand scale. For Brecht it simply meant that the theater tells a story on stage using dramatic means. Many of his plays actually have a narrator, or they use devices in place of a narrator, such as projected titles and summaries of the content before individual scenes.

Later the term epic seemed insufficient to Brecht ("too formalistic"). He preferred the term dialectic theater, reminiscent of Karl Marx's dialectical materialism; it also evokes Hegel's theory of thesis-antithesis-synthesis. Brecht's plays contain many contradictions and paradoxes. His hope was that the reader would see them and supply the synthesis himself.

Brecht never felt that either term was adequate to describe his kind of theater. Nevertheless the term epic theater, more than dialectic theater, has become more or less a synonym for Brechtian theater today. Bertolt Brecht developed his epic theater in direct opposition to the Aristotelian theater tradition. It is therefore necessary to take a brief look at some aspects of Aristotle's theory.

According to Aristotle, the plot is the basis and the

"soul" of the drama, and the main stimuli for the creation of a drama are the pleasures of imitation and learning. The learning process in the Aristotelian theater is initiated through the emotional involvement of the audience, in other words, through empathy. Empathy in the traditional Aristotelian sense means—for the actor and the audience—identification with the roles and events portrayed on stage. The purpose of Aristotelian theater is to purge the audience through pity and fear (the so-called catharsis effect).

The emphasis on the emotional involvement of the audience also requires a certain structure of the play. The plot must be presented in a linear progression building to a climax and descending to a denouement. In this type of structure all parts have their specific place; together they form one organic whole. If one part is rearranged or removed the play disintegrates.

Aristotle's observations, which he built up empirically from ancient Greek tragedy, were modified in later centuries, but some of his pronouncements were codified and became almost iron-clad rules. One of the essential characteristics of Aristotelian drama still is the emotional involvement between actors and audience.

Brecht agreed with Aristotle in his assessment of the importance of the plot and the pleasures of learning through a theatrical performance. But he vigorously objected to the Aristotelian concept of catharsis because it prevents the spectators from thinking about the events presented on stage: "A completely free and critical attitude of the viewer, bent on solutions of problems here on earth, is no basis for a catharsis."[2] Brecht maintains that the theater must be a place of fun and pleasure. But the pleasure the spectator derives from a theatrical performance must come from the involvement of the intellect, not the emotions. The purpose of Brechtian theater is to make the audience think. Brecht's plays are concerned with social issues. The spectator is asked to observe the play, think about the issues presented, and then contribute his share to the development of a better society.

Because Brecht specifically does not wish total emotional involvement of the spectator, he does not want a play in which the individual parts have a specific place and are smoothly integrated into an organic whole. The audience is not allowed to become entranced. Brecht purposefully incorporates ragged corners and contrasting elements into his plays to prevent such a trance.

Aristotelian theater enwraps the spectator, leads him up to an emotional climax, then releases his tensions and leaves him exhausted at the end. Accordingly, the structure of an Aristotelian drama could be compared to a landscape with one high peak.

Brechtian theater also starts out to build an illusion. It is not entirely without emotion. But it never reaches the point where the spectator is totally immersed in it, forgetting the reality around him. Before it takes hold in the spectator, it breaks off. This process is repeated many times throughout a Brechtian play. The structure of a Brechtian play could therefore be compared to a landscape with many small peaks.

In order to break the theater illusion and to allow, and indeed to encourage, the playgoer's reasoning to operate during and after a theatrical performance, Brecht obviously needed devices other than the Aristotelian catharsis. He found them in what he called the "estrangement effects"—*Verfremdungseffekte* or *V-Effekte*. As Brecht wrote in 1939 in an essay entitled "Experimental Theater," estrangement means "to strip actions or characters of what seems to be self-evident and familiar and to thus create astonishment, curiosity."[3]

Estrangement creates a distance between the events and characters on stage and the audience, so that the viewer can think about what he sees, and understand why a character in the play acts the way he does. This enables the viewer to see other possibilities and solutions to the problems presented on the stage. "To estrange means to portray events and characters as historical and as transient."[4] Thus the audience

> sees the characters on stage not as unchangeable, unsusceptible, helplessly relinquished to fate. He sees: this man is the way he is because the circumstances are the way they are. And the circumstances are the way they are because man is the way he is. But we also can imagine man and circumstances to be different from what they are ... the theater no longer attempts to make him [the spectator] drunk ... it presents the world as improvable.[5]

The estrangement effect can be created in several different ways. Brecht employed the technique of estrangement in the text, in the structure, in the production (the direction, the sets, the costumes), and in the style of acting.[6] Music also is assigned an important part in this technique.

The estrangement effect can extend to the whole structure of the play, such as parables set in unusual, "exotic" places (China, Chicago), montage (no linear progression), prologues, epilogues, interludes, and other means of preventing illusion (songs, introduction of dramatist's name into the play). But we find it also in smaller structural units such as sentences ("Shame on you for going after women without indecent thoughts,"[7] or "Terrible is the temptation to do good").[8] It can be seen even in single words: "hired heads"—as opposed to "hired hands"; or descriptive names such as "Lakeitel" for Hitler's chief of staff, General Keitel. (In German, *Lakai* means lackey, which suggests his role as Hitler's lackey, and *eitel* means vain).

Brecht's favorite source for estrangement effects was the inversion of patterns to which the viewers were accustomed. Proverbs, well-known literary quotations, the Bible, even plays of other playwrights, provided him with an abundance of materials.

In *The Purchase of Brass*,[9] Brecht presents us with "the street scene as a basic model for epic theater." A traffic accident has happened, and "an eyewitness demonstrates to a group of people how the accident occurred."[10] The witness demonstrates but does not create an illusion. The same is true of an actor in Brecht's theater. He must remain an actor and only demonstrate the character he is portraying. Brecht wrote in *The Short Organum*:[11]

> In order to produce an E-effect, the actor must refrain from everything he has learned about how to bring about audience identification with the character he portrays. In order not to entrance the audience, he must not be in a trance himself. ... A critique like "He did not play Lear, he was Lear" would be devastating for him. ... He must be on stage in two versions, as Laughton and as Galileo [here Brecht refers to the actor Charles Laughton playing Galileo].[12]

Brecht's anti-illusion theater, and its underlying assumption that the world is capable of being changed for the better, are also underscored by the sets and the technical aspects of his stage. The sets must not mirror a certain place as realistically as possible. A few particularly characteristic items for the place to be represented are sufficient, but they themselves must be of a highly aesthetic and artistic quality. Brecht wanted a mentally active spectator, and his stage "opposes the paralysis and atrophy of the imagination."[13] The stage must also allow for rapid changes.

And the source of the lighting must be visible: "It can be one of the means of preventing unwanted illusion."[14] The light itself should be steady and bright: "Thus the audience never forgets that it views theater, not life."[15] Moreover, "comedy is more effective in bright light,"[16] and bright light forces actors to be better actors.

One of the best-known trademarks of the Brechtian stage is the half-high curtain at the front of the stage, rather than the traditional heavy curtain that conceals the stage. It lends a certain levity to the performance, does not totally separate the audience from the stage, and allows the audience to see the mechanical workings of the stage.

Other anti-illusion devices of a Brechtian production are placards, projections, titles, copious program notes, and a certain usage of music. Rather than enhancing an emotional effect, the music serves instead to interrupt the flow of events. For example, in the 1928 production of *The Threepenny Opera,* every time a song was presented, there was a change in the lighting, a musical symbol was lowered from the loft, and the actors changed their positions on stage. Brecht demanded singing actors, not acting singers with polished voices. The music often goes "against" the lyrics—that is to say, the effect of the text and the effect of the music are often at odds (for example, a crude lyric may be sung to sentimental music).

Brecht strongly disliked the star system and prima donna behavior. His theater, the Berliner Ensemble, was a theater of stars indeed, but no one actor dominated a performance. An actor or an actress who played the lead in one play might appear in a very minor role in the next production. The same democratic spirit governed the rehearsals. Brecht wrote about his own directing: "Brecht's direction was much less obtrusive than that of famous directors.... The actors were not his 'instruments.' On the contrary, together with them he tried to bring out the story the play narrated, and he helped each one to find his strong points."[17] Brecht eagerly accepted suggestions and incorporated them in the production. And when long theoretical discussions threatened to erupt, he would say: "Don't talk about it, do it."[18]

Brecht also called for the development of "the art of viewing," because he felt that the spectator could not fully enjoy the art of theater "without any knowledge, without the capability for comparison, and the knowledge of the rules."[19]

Although we can trace a development in Brecht's view of theater, some of the main ingredients of his epic theater go all the way back to his early years. After several early attempts at writing in the contemporary (for the most part expressionist) style, Brecht grew more and more dissatisfied with the society around him and its literature. His *Baal* was already a protest against expressionism, and in his *Diary* he noted: "*Galgei* and *Summer Symphony* [two plays he never finished] must be completed. Then expressionism will be finished, and the term will be discarded. This movement was a (small German) revolution, but when some freedom was allowed, it became apparent that there were no free men."[20]

His Augsburg theater reviews were the earliest manifestation of Brecht's dissatisfaction with the state of the theater. Although the vitriolic attacks of the angry young man were sometimes overdone, his basic criticism of the Augsburg theater, that it lacked any kind of concept and progressive ideas, was valid; this criticism extended to the situation of German theater in general.

The viciousness of Brecht's criticism was partially a

compensation for his own insecurity. He knew what he did not want, yet he had not found what he wanted. His *Diary* clearly reveals these self-doubts:

> At times it occurs to me that my work is perhaps too primitive and old-fashioned, or too clumsy and not bold enough. I am in search of new forms and I experiment with my feelings like a young child does. But then I always return to the view that the essence of art is simplicity, greatness, and sensitivity, and that the essence of its form is coolness.[21]

In a paragraph he wrote a few days later, he gave more detail:

> I have many ideas. . . . When an action is presented in a certain style, it results in a certain mood that achieves a balance in the emotional reaction of an audience. In addition, the material presented not only seems to have been seen and arranged from one single point of view, it also seems to have happened at, and to have been experienced from, this viewpoint. . . . But where is the stylistic possibility to put these theoretical insights into practice?[22]

One major problem with which Brecht saw himself confronted (as indeed did many modern writers) was the fact that most topics had already been treated. Brecht saw one possibility of writing by inverting, even "putting to death," established literary traditions.[23]

Simplicity, coolness, and attack on established traditions—these were indeed important ingredients of his theory of theater, which became known as epic theater. An entry in his *Diary,* dated 10 February 1922, clearly defines his plays *Baal* and *In the Jungle of Cities* as early examples of his epic theater, although he did not use the term at that time:

In *Baal* and *Jungle* I hope I have avoided one big mistake of traditional art: its efforts to emotionally involve the audience. Instinctively I allow for distance in my plays, and I take care that my effects (both poetic and philosophical) remain confined to the stage. The spectator's splendid isolation will not be broken; it is not his story that is being acted out. He will not be mollified by being invited to feel with the stage heroes, to identify with them ... there is a higher kind of interest, that of parable, that of what is different, difficult to comprehend and astonishing.[24]

In 1930, Brecht formulated his theory of the epic theater in a way so antipodal to the conventional, Aristotelian, emotional theater that it has never been completely realized in his plays—nor did he ever actually intend that it should be. At no time, even in its most austere form, was Brecht's theater totally devoid of feelings and emotions.

In his notes to the opera *The Rise and Fall of the City of Mahagonny,* in which he complained about the traditional "culinary" opera, he wrote: "The modern theater is the epic theater."[25] (Brecht used the term "culinary" to designate a work providing pure aesthetic pleasure unburdened with heavy didacticism.) Then he pointed out some differences between the dramatic (the Aristotelian) and the epic theater, stressing however that these did not represent total opposites but merely a shift in emphasis. Here are some of Brecht's examples:[26]

DRAMATIC (ARISTOTELIAN) THEATER	EPIC THEATER
action	narrative
involves the spectator in the action	makes the spectator an observer
depletes his energy	awakens his energy
provides room for emotions	forces him to make decisions

DRAMATIC (ARISTOTELIAN) THEATER	EPIC THEATER
man portrayed as unchangeable	man changeable and effecting change
attention directed toward the end	attention directed toward the progress of the action
one scene preparing the other	each scene for itself
growth	montage
linear progress	progress in curves
human thought determines social conditions	social conditions determine human thought
feeling	reasoning

Brecht also argued against the Wagnerian-style "total work of art," in which all elements contributed to create and enhance a uniform effect: "Such magic, of course, is to be opposed."[27] He demanded "a radical separation of the elements" (music, text, acting).[28]

Whereas *Mahagonny* was itself fairly "culinary," as Brecht himself admitted—despite its criticism of the culinary opera and the society that needed it—the play *The Mother* (written in 1931 and 1932) was conceived as a model of epic theater: "The play *The Mother*, written in the style of the didactic plays but requiring professional actors, is an antimetaphysical, materialistic, non-Aristotelian play. It does not appeal to the spectators' empathy as unrestrainedly as the Aristotelian theater, and it has a totally different relationship to certain psychic effects, such as the catharsis-effect."[29]

It is important to bear in mind that Brecht does not totally rule out empathy and emotion. When watching a performance of *The Mother* or *The Good Woman of Setzuan*, one certainly experiences an emotional impact. But this effect is controlled, tempered by reason and directed against social injustice. As Brecht stated in 1949 in a discussion he had about *Mother Courage* with the playwright Friedrich Wolf: "Epic theater by no means dispenses with emotions. Least of all with love of justice, desire for liberty, and justified anger. . . . It even strives to increase or create these emotions. The 'critical attitude' that epic theater wants to instill in its audience cannot be passionate enough."[30]

Brecht was also quick to admit that his technique of estrangement was not entirely new: "The theater of past ages has already achieved artistic effects by means of the estrangement effect—the Chinese theater, the classical Spanish theater, the popular theater of Bruegel's time, and the Elizabethan theater"[31] (Shakespeare was always one of Brecht's great models). And Brecht freely tapped all these sources for his own theater. But Brecht made perhaps the most consistent and—owing to his considerable gifts as an artist—most successful use of this technique.

What is more, he employed this artistic device for an end beyond just theater: With its help he intended to portray society as open to improvement. This, again, was not entirely new; the Jesuit plays of the fifteenth and sixteenth centuries made the same attempt. But by virtue of this estrangement effect, many of Brecht's plays are a highly successful blend of art and propaganda unrivaled in the history of playwriting.

In 1939, when his youthful exuberance had somewhat abated, Brecht was also ready to admit that his technique was not a panacea for modern theater: "It is only *one* way; the way *we* took. . . . The solution we sought is only *one* of the perhaps possible solutions to the problem: How can the theater be entertaining and instructive at the same time?"[32]

It may appear that Brecht's theory of theater overrates the capabilities of the average theatergoer, who is accustomed to, and partially ruined by, a long tradition of fairly undemanding stage fare. Yet Brecht also stressed again and again that theory—although helpful—is secondary: "If the critics would view my theater as spectators do, without first emphasizing my theories, then what they would see would be simply theater, I hope, of imagination, fun, and intelligence."[33] And he reassured the audience: "Theater remains theater, even if it is a theater for learning; and provided it is good theater, it is entertaining."[34] He did not want anyone to feel intimidated by his theory.

Wolfgang Roth, who worked with Brecht on several productions between 1929 and 1933, summarized his impressions of Brecht:

> He was an intuitive man whose work came first, his theories later. There is no Brechtian method— the attempt by people less talented than Brecht to recreate a Brechtian theater by applying Brechtian theory can only lead to failure. This general assumption that "Brecht-Theater" is only possible with the use of placards, exposed lighting equipment, half-high front curtains, and similar devices, leads to a great misunderstanding and is not necessarily epic theater. He himself often debunked the epic label.[35]

In his later years, Brecht took great pains to mitigate the rigidity of his earlier theoretical pronouncements. He was aware that they could become either serious obstacles to good theater or a sterile gospel for uncritical believers, and he took every opportunity to point out that his theater—not his theories—was of primary importance.

His attitude toward his theory is nicely illustrated by an encounter with a group of young Italian admirers on the occasion of his visit to Milan, Italy, in

February of 1956 to attend rehearsals and the first performance of his *Threepenny Opera*, directed by the famous Italian theater director Giorgio Strehler. With copies of his *Short Organum* tightly clasped in their hands, the young people approached Brecht, addressing him as "Maestro." Brecht replied through an interpreter: "Tell them that I am not a maestro." The young people asked him questions: "Here in the *Organum* you write that epic theater...." Brecht replied: "What I wrote in the *Organum* is true only up to a certain point; ... Don't take it too literally. Theater takes place on the stage."[36]

And since Brecht never regarded his works as complete and final products, there is no reason why producers in different times and circumstances should not experiment with Brecht's work. It is necessary only that they understand Brecht's basic intentions: to generate a socially aware and critical audience, and to offer good theater, since, in Brecht's view, the learning process occurs in direct proportion to the artistic quality of the production.

AUGSBURG, MUNICH, BERLIN
(1918–26)

Baal (1918–19)

    Baal, Brecht's first full-length play, was a shocking play in its day, and even today many theatergoers find it quite unpalatable. The play shows the decline and death of a poet named Baal through a life of debauchery. It is permeated with a fascination for vivid colors, sensuality and decay, obscenity and perversion, morbidity, and even brutality—everything to revolt the bourgeois mind.

Brecht does not present Baal's life in the linear progression of a developing plot, but rather in a series of situations and images often stressing only mood and atmosphere. The fragmented form of the play mirrors Baal's fragmented and profligate life. The numerous scenes of various length loosely follow the chronology of Baal's life, but one scene does not necessarily build upon another scene, and the scenes do not build up to a climax in the Aristotelian sense.

The play opens with the "Hymn of the Great Baal" as prologue. The first scene is set in the dining room of a wealthy industrialist and publisher named Mech, who plans to publish Baal's poetry. Mech is treating his guests—including Piller, a literary critic—to a lavish meal. Baal is the center of attention. The guests liken him to Homer, Paul Verlaine, and Walt Whitman. Everyone is very "cultured"; a young lady reads aloud expressionistic poetry. Baal, however, is only interested in eating, drinking, and seducing Mech's wife Emilie, and pays no attention to the conversation. Finally, in disgust, Mech orders him out of his house. Baal has refused to be incorporated into the establishment, thus forfeiting a promising literary career. He retreats to his garret ("Klauckestrasse 64"), where he and his friend Johannes sit near the window and spend the starry night talking about Johannes's seventeen-year-old girlfriend Johanna—in beautifully poetic language with sexual undertones, underscored by chords from Baal's guitar.

Next we see Baal sitting with some truck drivers in a tavern. Emilie (Mech's wife) is madly in love with Baal and follows him everywhere. When she comes to the tavern, Baal embarrasses her with his coarse talk, his drinking, and by flirting with the waitress and with Johanna when she appears with Johannes. Baal is repulsive and fascinating at the same time, "and with his awful but wonderful talk, he drags the girls to his trough" (Emilie).[1] And it is not only his talk. There are also his guitar and his earthy songs, such as the song about Orge: "Orge told me that his favorite place/ On earth has always been the toilet./ This is the place, where one is sure/ That the stars are above and the dung is below."[2] (Orge was the name of Georg Pfanzelt, one of Brecht's schoolmates and friends in Augsburg; the play *Baal* is dedicated to him.)

Ekart, Baal's closest friend, tries to lure Baal away from the tavern to accompany him in his carefree and unfettered life. But Baal refuses—this time. First, he has other plans.

At dawn in his garret, Baal seduces Johanna. Then he sends her back to Johannes. Hours later, at noon, he is visited by two sisters who want to go to bed with him. Baal, however, is too lazy. They mention casually that Johanna has drowned herself in the river Laach (recalling Lech, the river through Brecht's native Augsburg). Baal cynically inquires whether she is still floating. Baal's landlady ("a bitch with a good heart")[3] puts a quick end to this scene. She leads the girls out of the room and evicts Baal ("My garret is not a brothel").[4]

In the evening, Baal sits at his table, writing and drinking. Someone is playing Wagner's "Tristan" on a harmonium. Before he moves out, he wants to seduce one more woman. In the street he picks up Sophie Barger. When he returns to his garret with Sophie, he finds Johannes there, but he literally throws him out because now Johannes is only an annoying reminder of Johanna. Sophie puts up a half-hearted resistance, but succumbs to Baal. He says: "You are a woman like all others. Only the head is different. Their knees are all weak."[5]

Now Baal is ready to join Ekart to roam freely through the green fields and blue plum trees, to lie by the river and under the trees in the rain, to talk to tramps and to make love to Sophie ("The sky is black and we ride in a swing, with love in our bodies, and the sky is black").[6]

In order to obtain more schnapps, Baal works as an entertainer in a small, dingy night spot called Night Cloud. When the proprietor refuses to give him the schnapps, Baal sings an obscene song and disappears through a window in the toilet.

In a village inn, Baal and Ekart cheat some peasants out of schnapps. Upon being repoached by the local priest for leading a godless life, Baal reveals his religion: "My heaven is full of trees and bodies."[7]

When Baal steals schnapps from the belongings of a woodcutter who had just been killed in an accident, the dead man's colleagues lament: "Nothing is sacred to this fellow.—God have mercy on his drunken soul. —He is the most hardened sinner that ever ran around between God's hands."[8] Yet Baal has only contempt for their moralizing: "Sit down, I don't like your preaching. There will always be those who are brighter and those who are weaker in the head. The weaker ones make up for it by being better workers. As you noticed I work with my brains."[9]

Seeking shelter from the rain in a hut, Baal vows to go on although his body is being consumed by his violent passions: "I want to live even without my skin; I withdraw all the way into my toes."[10] When Sophie, now pregnant by Baal, comes to the hut, Baal is cruel to her. His only concern is that she might come between him and Ekart, with whom he is now carrying on a homosexual relationship.

Out in the open fields, Baal now sees the world only in terms of decay: "It is the dear Lord's excrement."[11] Sitting under a maple tree in the wind, Baal anticipates his own end in the song entitled "Death in the Woods": "Died like an animal desperately digging for roots."[12]

After eight years of wandering, Baal and Ekart return to the tavern whence they started. Johannes, now totally dissolute, is still thinking of Johanna in the river ("She is still floating. No one has found her. . . . Now she has rats and water weeds in her green hair, suits her well . . . a little bloated and whitish, filled with stinking mud of the river, rather black. She was always so clean. That's why she went into the river and began to rot.")[13] Baal takes a guitar, smashes the light with it, and sings. When the light is turned on again, he sees the waitress on Ekart's lap. Furious and full of jealousy, Baal throws himself on Ekart and stabs him with a knife.

Baal, with his guitar, escapes into the woods ("I

must put that little affair behind me").[14] On a country road, two policemen fight their way against the wind and rain in search of Baal, the "murderer who started out as a performer in a cabaret and a poet, then owner of a merry-go-round, lumberjack, lover of a million-airess, jailbird, and pimp."[15] Baal, who has overheard the policemen, now knows that Ekart died: "Poor little beast! Getting in my way! Now it gets interesting!"[16]

Baal spends the night playing cards with wood-cutters in a hut in the forest. They have little sympathy for him, although it is apparent that he is dying ("Just think: a rat is dying").[17] When the rain stops, the men leave. Baal asks them to stay; he does not want to die alone. But they only spit in his face. Yet there is no sentimentality—Baal regrets nothing ("Everything was beautiful").[18] Since he does not want to die like a rat in a hole, he crawls out into the starlit night. He dies early in the morning in the forest, "still listening to the rain."[19]

The foregoing synopsis of *Baal* gives us a basis for discussion. To begin with, the play has an interesting history that reveals a great deal about Brecht's method of playwriting and about Brecht as a playwright.

The first version of *Baal* was written in the spring and summer of 1918 (not in four days, as some critics would have it). Brecht, then twenty years old and a student in Munich, took in everything a big city like Munich had to offer, particularly its theaters and cabarets. He was an angry young man full of vitality and eager to smash the fetters of bourgeois convention. When he discovered the works of the tempestuous French poet François Villon (1431 to *circa* 1463), he took an immediate and great interest in this man. In February 1918, Brecht wrote a song about Villon, and in March 1918 he mentioned him in a letter to his friend Caspar Neher: "I plan to write a play about

François Villon who, in the fifteenth century, was a murderer and a highwayman, as well as a writer and singer of ballads, in Brittany, France."[20] It was the beginning of his *Baal* project. The origins of the name Baal are not certain; Brecht could have borrowed it from a pagan god mentioned in the Old Testament or from contemporary literary works in which he is alluded to.

At the end of March 1918, Brecht saw the play *The Loner* by Hanns Johst in the Münchener Kammerspiele. This play, written in the expressionist fashion, dealt with the life and death of the German poet Christian Dietrich Grabbe (1801–36). Grabbe's way of life in many ways resembled that of Villon; he defied all bourgeois categories (although he did work at his profession as a lawyer for a time). But Brecht thought that Johst had done an injustice to his subject ("too idealistic," "hollow pathos").[21]

He conceived *Baal* as a counterversion to *The Loner*. Although Brecht used expressionistic elements in *Baal*, they serve in part as a parody on expressionism. The general tone of Brecht's *Baal*, furthermore, is vastly different from the visionary, mystic, and ecstatic character of most expressionist plays. Brecht's Baal is the epitome of vitality and anticonventionality. Brecht wanted to express this in the first title he chose for the play: "Baal eats! Baal dances!! Baal is transfigured!!!"[22]

According to Hans Otto Münsterer, a friend of Brecht's during this early period, Brecht also incorporated into Baal many characteristics of the German writer Frank Wedekind (1864–1918), and the French poet Paul Verlaine (1844–96), both of whom led lives of dissipation and debauchery.[23] When Baal kills his best friend, Ekart, in Brecht's play, the scene recalls Verlaine shooting and wounding his best friend, the poet Arthur Rimbaud (1854–91).

Undoubtedly Baal is also—to some extent at least—
a self-projection of Brecht. Baal gives as his address
an attic room, "Klauckestrasse 64," which was in the
immediate vicinity of the Brecht family's house in
Augsburg. Like Baal, Brecht had many associations
with women. Again like Baal, he was a poet who expressed his feelings in poems and songs, which he
sang to his friends, accompanying them with his guitar.

Brecht asserted in 1926 (in connection with a *Baal*
production in Berlin) that there was a real model for
the character Baal—a welder named Josef K. This
claim, however, is discounted by Hans Otto Münsterer, since Brecht had never before mentioned the
name during all the months and years he worked on
Baal.

In 1918, Brecht wrote in a prologue to *Baal:*

> This play tells the story of a man who, in a
> tavern, sings a hymn to summer without having
> selected his audience—and includes the conse-
> quences of summer, of brandy and of song. This
> man is not an especially modern poet. Baal is
> not ill-favored by nature. He belongs to the times
> in which the play is performed. . . . Baal is neither
> a comic nor a tragic figure. He possesses the
> seriousness of all animals. As to the play itself,
> after long deliberation its author has discovered
> a message: the play wants to show that it is pos-
> sible to make your art if you are prepared to pay
> for it. And if you are not prepared for it. As long
> as you pay. . . . The play is not the story of one
> or many episodes but the story of a life.[24]

In the prologue to the 1926 version, Brecht added:

> In this biography dramatized by Bertolt Brecht
> you will see Baal's life as it took place at the
> beginning of this century. You see Baal, the
> abnormal man, as he tries to get along in the
> world of the twentieth century. Baal the relative
> man; Baal the passive genius; Baal the unusual

phenomenon, from his first appearance among civilized men to his terrible end; Baal with his insatiable consumption of ladies from the best social circles; Baal in his dealings with other men. This man's life was of sensational amorality, which, however, was toned down somewhat in its adaptation for the stage. The play opens with the poet Baal's first appearance among civilized men in 1904. As an introduction, you will see Baal from all sides, and you will hear how he used to perform his well-known "Hymn of the Great Baal," accompanied by the tin-stringed banjo he himself invented.[25]

Like many of Brecht's plays, *Baal* went through several stages of development. There were five versions, differing in length and in the arrangement of the scenes—in some versions new scenes were added, others were left out or changed.[26] The first version was written in 1918; its relation to Johst's *The Loner* is quite obvious. In 1919 Brecht completely reworked *Baal;* this second version is generally considered by Brecht scholars to be his best, though it was never published by Brecht. A third version, somewhat milder and shorter, was prepared in 1919 and 1920 with publishers and theater producers in mind. In 1920, the publisher Georg Müller, in Munich, printed the third version of *Baal,* but it never reached the market for fear of censorship. The first publisher to print and deliver *Baal* (the third version) was Kiepenheuer in 1922. In 1926 Brecht prepared a fourth version for a production in Berlin. (Around 1930, Brecht worked on yet another version of *Baal* in light of his recent conversion to Marxism. This version, *The Evil and Antisocial Baal,* was printed by Malik Verlag in Prague, in 1938, but was lost in the turmoil following the German invasion of Czechoslovakia in 1939 and never reached the market.) Suhrkamp printed the play for the first time in 1953, based on the Kiepenheuer version of 1922, and Brecht revised *Baal* again in 1954, thus creating the fifth and last version.

It is the language and the imagery, not the unorthodox plot, that make *Baal* a memorable play. There are vile images of decay and decomposition: "Oh, Johanna, one more night in your aquarium and I would have rotted among the fish."[27] There is also powerful nature imagery described with vivid colors reminiscent of expressionist paintings: "Where life is decent: if one shoots down a rapid stream lying on one's back, naked under an orange-colored sky, and one sees nothing but the sky turning violet, then dark as a pit...."[28] Ekart wants to return to the woods, where "the light is lemon-colored between the trunks."[29] The trees are "like rotten stumps of teeth in the sky's black mouth."[30] Throughout the play Brecht also uses olfactory images: "Come, brother Baal! Like two white doves we fly blissfully into the blue! Rivers in morning light! Graveyards in the wind and the smell of the endless fields before they are cut down."[31]

These images express Baal's sensuality, which permeates the play. One of the most powerful passages in the play is the passage in which Ekart attempts to persuade Baal to go with him:

> Come with me brother! To the roads of hard dust. In the evenings the air will be violet. To the taverns filled with drunken men; the women you have had will fall into black rivers.... Come with me brother! Dancing and music and drinking! Rain and sun drenching the skin! Darkness and light! Women and dogs![32]

In 1954, Brecht wrote an article intended for the 1955 edition of his plays, entitled "On Rereading My Early Plays." He tried to reinterpret *Baal* in the light of his Marxist views:

The play *Baal* may pose many problems to those who have not learned to think dialectically. In it they will probably see no more than the glorification of pure egotism. But in the play an individual is confronted with the impositions and discouragement of a world that recognizes only an exploitable productivity, not one that can be useful. The play is not intended to show how Baal would react to a utilization of his talents: he fights the degradation of them. Baal's art of living shares the fate of all arts in a capitalistic society: it is opposed by this society. Baal is antisocial but in an antisocial society.[33]

Yet for the fifth version he changed only the first and last scenes: "Otherwise I leave the play as it is since I lack the strength to change it." And he added: "I admit (and give warning): the play lacks wisdom."[34] But he did not withdraw the play. In fact, twenty years after writing *Baal* he wanted to write an opera centered around the Chinese god of happiness. The topic was similar to that of *Baal:* man's indestructible desire for happiness and pleasure.

Because of its unconventional nature (producers felt it was too daring), it was several years before *Baal* reached the stage. It was first performed on 8 December 1923 in the Altes Theater Leipzig (director: Alwin Kronacher; sets: Friedrich Thiersch; Baal: Lothar Körner; Ekart: Hans Zeise-Gött). It was hailed as one of the outstanding theatrical events of the year. Even the two leading Berlin critics, Herbert Ihering of the *Berliner Börsen-Courier* and Alfred Kerr of the *Berliner Tageblatt,* ventured into the "province" to see it. The performance caused quite a scandal, and the Leipzig city council intervened, canceling further performances.

The reaction of the critics was mixed. Ihering, a Brecht supporter from the beginning, found the play "an ingenious ballad in scenes," but thought the per-

Baal, Deutsches Theater Berlin, 1926. Baal: Oskar Homolka; Ekart: Paul Bildt; sets: Caspar Neher; directors: Brecht and Homolka.
THEATER-MUSEUM MÜNCHEN

formance "inadequate," particularly Lothar Körner's Baal. Egbert Delpy of the *Leipziger Neueste Nachrichten,* on the other hand, found his high expectations (after the earlier success of Brecht's *Drums in the Night*) deeply disappointed. He called the play a failure, a "mud-bath," an "ecstasy of puberty" deficient of any poetic power. He found Kronacher's direction uneven, but Körner's Baal "outstanding."

Kerr preferred *Baal* to *Drums in the Night.* He found lyrical parts in this "Baalad," (Kerr's pun on

Baal and ballad) but in his opinion it should not be called a play: "Who will give us a drama instead of mood, coincidence, and delirious language? Who will give us a house instead of a quarry?"

Nevertheless, the applause for the play drowned the protests.

When Brecht himself directed a revised version of *Baal (Baal's Biography)* in Berlin on 14 February 1926 (sets: Caspar Neher; Baal: Oskar Homolka; Ekart: Paul Bildt), the reaction of the audience and the critics was about the same as it had been in Leipzig. Parts of the audience accompanied the performance with yelling, whistling, and shouting—indicating either their approval or disapproval. At one point in the production, a soprano voice from the second balcony could be heard: "Why don't you throw that guy [meaning Baal] out?" To this a bass voice from the stalls answered: "You are not really indignant, you just pretend to be." During the ensuing turmoil in the audience, one of the actresses on stage jumped on the piano, jangled the keyboard with her feet, and sang the first words of the Marseillaise: "Allons, enfants de la patrie!" The playwright Hans Henny Jahn, who had come from Hamburg to see the play, thought that pandemonium would break out any minute—it did not, he was just not accustomed to a Berlin audience.[35]

On 2 February 1963, William Gaskill directed Peter Tegel's translation of *Baal* in London's Phoenix Theater (sets: Jocelyn Herbert; Baal: Peter O'Toole; Ekart: Harry Andrews). Gaskill did not spare his audience—he did not attempt to tone down the obscenity, the pornography, or the brutality of the text. Now, almost forty years after *Baal's* premiere, critics were reminded of Brendan Behan, Jean Genet, Samuel Beckett, and Jack Kerouac, as well as Jean-Luc Godard's film *Vivre Sa Vie*. They had some doubts about the play itself, but they generally agreed that the production was outstanding. Especially admired was O'Toole's portrayal of Baal. According to Milton Shulman of the *Evening Standard,* O'Toole saved the play: "Without Peter O'Toole's dedicated, relentless, overpowering performance, this play would crumble into an old-fashioned relic of Teutonic expressionism."[36] Every performance was sold out, but the play failed to become a favorite with audiences. The critic Kenneth Tynan blamed this on the audience itself: "It is hard for a work like *Baal* to thrive in the mink-and-mohair atmosphere of a West End premiere; thus circumstanced, it resembles a pot of vitriol flung in the public's face."[37]

On 6 May 1965, *Baal* opened in New York City's off-Broadway Martinique Theater, adapted by Eric Bentley and Martin Esslin (director: Gladys Vaughn; Baal: Mitchell Ryan; Ekart: James Earl Jones). The play was presented by The Circle in the Square company. Howard Taubman of *The New York Times* was repelled and attracted at the same time: "There is strong stuff, both horrible and fascinating, in *Baal* ... this bitter Brechtian attack on respectability and sanctimoniousness." In all the degradation, he saw "a fundamental life force" at work. He found Gladys Vaughn's direction "taut, stark," the cast "competent and drilled intensively for this crisp production." And Taubman concluded: "*Baal* is raw, occasionally rancid meat, obviously not for all tastes. But it is well worth investigating by those who care about the directions the theater has taken. For in this play, which antedates his Marxian orientation, Brecht presages innovations to be made not only by himself but also by several schools of playwrights."[38]

Herbert Kupferberg of the *New York Herald Tribune* left the theater "not convinced by the validity of the savage Brechtian vision of life as outlined in

Baal," nor even sure whether he "found a way through all the symbolism and significances with which Brecht loaded this early work." Yet he felt that *Baal,* while "pretty strong meat for its time," still managed to "generate a degree of electricity" and that the play qualified as a "vivid theatrical experience, which despite occasional crudities and confusion is stamped with dramatic vigor and vision."[39]

Baal is not a didactic play; it is not the work of a politically engaged playwright. On the contrary, it revels in socially destructive behavior. But it abounds with poetic power of language and imagery, and it presents on stage what must remain a dream for most people: a life completely free of convention and obligation.

Drums in the Night (1919)

Following the defeat that ended World War I in 1918, Germany went through a period of severe political upheavals that could well have resulted in a communist form of government for the whole of Germany. During the war, the left wing of the Social Democrats (SPD), claiming that the SPD had become too conservative, had already broken away to found an Independent Social Democratic Party (USPD). The radical core of this party formed the so-called Spartacus group under the leadership of Rosa Luxemburg and Karl Liebknecht (both of whom were killed by right-wing forces on 15 January 1919). The group

German title: *Trommeln in der Nacht.*

called itself Spartacus after the leader of an uprising of rebellious slaves in the Roman Empire that was brutally suppressed by Crassus and Pompeius in the year 73 B.C. In December 1918, Spartacus group members formed the Communist Party of Germany (KPD).

Augsburg, Brecht's home town, and Munich, where he attended the university, were not immune from unrest. In fact, in 1919 a communist Republic of Bavaria, with Munich as headquarters, had existed briefly until it was brutally crushed by government troops of the Weimar Republic. In Berlin, the setting for *Drums in the Night*, there was also fighting between government troops and leftists.

Brecht, although not yet committed to the Marxist cause, took great interest in the events around him. But his leftist leanings at that time stemmed "less from political insight than from youthful exuberance," as Hans Otto Münsterer, one of Brecht's friends of that time, reported.[40] Artistic interests far outweighed political engagement. Most of Brecht's energies were directed toward surveying and attacking the bourgeois concept of art. Yet in 1919, he did write a play—his second—that dealt with the contemporary events. Its original title was *Spartacus*. But it was a far cry from a revolutionary play (in a political sense). On the contrary, Brecht called the play a comedy. At the end, the main character, Andreas Kragler, does not join the revolutionary forces, but chooses instead to go to bed with his girlfriend—to make love, not revolution, so to speak.

Brecht told his friend, the playwright Lion Feuchtwanger, that he had written the play only to make money. Feuchtwanger, however, who was Brecht's senior by fourteen years, was so enthusiastic about this play and its author that he not only did what he could to further the career of the young dramatist, but set out immediately to write a play of his own, which he called *Thomas Brecht* (it eventually appeared as *Thomas Wendt*). In 1930, he made Brecht a character in his novel *Success,* and it was also Feuchtwanger who suggested the final title for the Spartacus play: *Drums in the Night.*

Feuchtwanger later recalled their first meeting at the end of 1918 when Brecht came to his Munich apartment soon after the outbreak of the leftist revolution in Germany in November of 1918:

> He was slight, badly shaved, shabbily dressed. He stayed close to the walls, spoke with a Swabian accent, had written a play, was called Bertolt Brecht. The play was entitled *Spartacus.*
> Most young authors presenting a manuscript point out that they have torn this work from their bleeding hearts: but this young man emphasized that he had written *Spartacus* purely in order to make money.

And, as Feuchtwanger also noted, the play contained none of the "long and echoing dramatic declamations" that came forth from young expressionist playwrights who "tore open their breasts" to preach "that social institutions were bad, but that man, on the other hand, was good."[41] Quite the contrary, Brecht's play presented a rather unsavory assortment of characters.

The play is set in Berlin in 1919.

ACT I: The living room of the Balicke family. The daughter, Anna, is still waiting for her fiancé, Andreas Kragler, who has been missing in action for four years. Karl Balicke, her father, chides her for her "damned sentimentality," tells her that Andreas is "dead and decomposed," and strongly recommends that Anna marry Friedrich Murk (*murk* means murky), a repulsive profiteer who has been courting her. This arrangement would also be of advantage to Balicke, since Murk's shrewdness and his theory for getting ahead in the world ("you must have elbows")[42] are quite compatible with Balicke's own shady business methods.

Karl Balicke had made a good profit during the war with the production of ammunition boxes. He is still profiting from the raging revolution, but he already has a plan in mind for peacetime: the manufacture of baby carriages. When Murk appears, it turns out that Anna's grief for Kragler is actually very superficial. She is already expecting Murk's child and fears that Kragler might return some day. To the great pleasure of her scheming parents, Anna decides to get engaged to Murk.

During the engagement dinner at the Balickes' home, the conversation centers around the current political situation ("the number of troublemakers is increasing ... the government is soft on the vultures of revolution ... the stirred-up masses are without ideals").[43]

During the dinner, Babusch, a family friend and journalist, comes to inform them that the Spartacists are planning an attack. All agree that the German family and home ("my home is my castle") have to be protected and that Spartacists are "sinister riffraff" that "ought to be shot."[44] Despite the threatening disorder, they decide to move the celebration to the Piccadilly Bar, "now called Café Fatherland." As they are about to leave, Kragler suddenly returns from having spent the last four years in an African prisoner-of-war camp. Balicke informs him that Anna has just become engaged, "barely thirty minutes ago." After she has overcome her initial shock, Mrs. Balicke recommends that he look for another girl and that he "learn to suffer without complaining"[45] (as Kaiser Wilhelm II often said before he fled the country at the end of World War I).

ACT II: The Piccadilly Bar. There is a large window at the rear, with a red paper moon hanging in the window. The engagement party is not going well—an uneasy atmosphere pervades the room: "Everything is topsy-turvy. It is the end of the world."[46] In order to squelch these feelings, they drink. The Balickes are anxious to get Anna married, not so much because of her pregnancy but because they sense that having Murk in the family would be advantageous to their business. They also fear that she may be persuaded by Andreas to return to him.

But just as they are drinking a toast to the date of the wedding, Kragler appears in the door like a ghost, and the wind extinguishes the candles. Murk wants him thrown out. Balicke shouts at him: "Anarchist! Front-line soldier! Pirate!"[47] But Kragler moves inexorably toward Anna, while, in the background, a phonograph plays Gounod's "Ave Maria." Kragler tries to reestablish his relationship with Anna. But Anna feels that her affair with Murk has created a gulf between them: "I should have waited . . . but I am bad."[48] From outside comes the sound of machine-gun fire. Balicke now tries to appease Kragler: "You fought for the Kaiser and the Reich? . . . That was brave. . . . Our army has achieved great things."[49] Kragler, however, ignores everyone but Anna; he wants her to come with him. He has a confrontation with Murk. But before they come to blows, the waiter opens the window so that everyone can hear the "Internationale," the communist song of international brotherhood, being sung in the streets. A revolt has broken out, there is shooting in the newspaper districts. Balicke rages: "Spartacus! Your friends, Mr. Andreas Kragler! . . . Beasts! Beasts! Beasts! You must all be exterminated."[50]

Inside, the fight over Anna reaches a climax when Anna moves closer to Kragler and Murk calls her a whore. At that Kragler attacks Murk. Then Murk tries to get Anna to tell Kragler that she is expecting his

(Murk's) child. Anna, however, cannot bring herself to do this, and comes close to breaking down. At this emotional moment, Brecht shifts the point of view to one of detachment: he has the waiter comment on the action. Kragler gives up and leaves the bar accompanied by the waiter and Marie, a prostitute.

ACT III: Kragler is running toward the newspaper district, followed by Marie. It is night, the stars are shining dimly, the wind is blowing. Kragler wants to forget, either by committing suicide or by drowning his sorrows in schnapps.

Anna appears in search of Kragler, followed by Manke, the waiter, and Babusch, who is dragging the drunken Murk along. Anna says that though everything has been arranged for her wedding and a comfortable married life thereafter, she now wants to give it all up for Kragler: "My linen is purchased, I put it in a closet, piece by piece, but now I don't need it. The apartment has been rented, the curtains and the wallpaper are up. But he has arrived who has no shoes and only one coat with moths in it."[51] Not even the thought of the child she is carrying deters her.

ACT IV: A small schnapps bar. Glubb, the proprietor, sings Brecht's famous "Ballad of the Dead Soldier," accompanying himself on his guitar. (It was this ballad, which is about a dead and decayed soldier who is sent back to the front as combat-ready with the blessings of the doctors and priests, which later so incensed the Nazis.) Through an open window, the guests can hear the cannon of the government troops rumble by. Suddenly Kragler appears in the door, again a ghostlike figure. When Marie, who is still following him, tells the guests that his name is Andreas, Kragler vaguely remembers: "Andreas, yes, Andreas, that was my name."[52] And he keeps feeling his pulse as if to convince himself of his physical presence. When a newspaper seller enters and announces that the Spartacists have taken the newspaper district ("Red Rosa [Luxemburg] is giving an open-air speech")[53] Glubb closes his bar. Upon Kragler's suggestion, they all go to the newspaper district.

Act V: Anna and Babusch, still looking for Kragler, encounter the group from Glubb's bar. All are in various stages of intoxication. Anna now has the courage to admit to Kragler that she is pregnant. His reaction is bitter: "Is your body big with air or did you become a whore? I was gone, I could not keep an eye on you. I was lying in the mud. Where were you lying when I was in the mud?"[54] All these years he fought to survive only to see Anna. Now he learns she has deceived him: "And I wanted to see you! Otherwise I'd be where I belong, with wind blowing through my skull, dust in my mouth, and would know nothing."[55] In desperation, he picks up lumps of dirt and throws them wildly in all directions.

Events in the newspaper district go badly for the Spartacists. But when Kragler has recovered from his rage, he has lost interest in joining the revolution: "I am no longer a lamb. I don't want to die."[56] He does not want to hear any more about Anna's guilt, his sole aim now is to go with Anna into "the large, white, broad bed."[57] Anna agrees. The play ends as they leave together.

Private desires win over revolutionary engagement; the emphasis is on the right to individual happiness. When he wrote *Drums in the Night,* Brecht was not interested in revolution: "The revolution which served as background milieu did not interest me any more than the volcanic mountain Vesuvius is of interest to a man who only wants to heat his pot of soup on it. And my pot of soup seemed to me very big in comparison to Mount Vesuvius."[58]

The play has several weaknesses. There is a break in tone and tempo after the second act; the first two acts use more naturalistic elements, the rest is more expressionistic. As we know from his diary, Brecht himself had great difficulties with the fourth act. But as Martin Esslin attests, the play has turned out to be one of the best plays ever written about returning soldiers after World War I.[59]

The play already contains many features of Brecht's epic theater. Sentimentality and stage illusion are avoided. Kragler refuses to be a hero. Signs in the theater instruct the audience: "Don't gape so romantically!"[60] At the end of the play, which could have been an excellent occasion for an outpouring of feelings to touch the audience's lachrymal glands, Kragler proceeds to tear down the stage properties, exclaiming: "This is just theater—a few boards and a paper moon."[61] The stage directions have him throw a drum at the paper moon, and both the drum and the paper moon fall into a waterless imitation river. The often crude language and several repulsive characters add to the antiromantic effect.

Later, in 1954, the Marxist Brecht sharply condemned this early play: "Of all my early plays, the comedy *Drums in the Night* is the most problematic. The protest against an outworn literary convention almost led to the condemnation of a great social revolution."[62] In 1920, Brecht had felt that Kragler's action at the end of the play was the only possible one, and he stated that the whole play was written because of it. Now, thirty-four years later, the ending seemed to Brecht to be "the worst of all possible variants, particularly since one can sense the playwright's approval."[63] To have at least a shadow of a counterpart to Kragler, in 1954 Brecht added another character—Glubb's nephew, a young worker who dies in the revolution (he never actually appears on stage, but is mentioned in the conversation). But

Brecht did not retract the play: "Only the considera-
tion that literature is part of history, as well as the
feeling that my present views and capabilities are
worth less without knowledge of my early ones, kept
me from erecting a small pyre."[64]

Drums in the Night does, however, portray a certain slice of reality. In Kragler, Brecht depicted the
type of person who joins a revolution—until he finds
something better to do. This "diversity of interests"
amongst the people was also, according to Brecht,
the main reason that the revolution of 1918–19 did
not succeed. Looking back, he thought that the failure
of socialist politics at that time resulted from a failure
to make clear to the Kraglers of society where their
own interests lay. Many of Brecht's literary contemporaries had attempted to do this, but they had worked
in terms too abstract and too ideological to be of any
value. Their talk of "universal mankind" and "ideal
interest" and dying for an abstract "idea" so infuriated
Brecht that he, as he later said, lost sight of those
forces fighting for the real and concrete interests of
the common man.

The red paper moon which appears throughout the
play until it is destroyed by Kragler at the end also
took on a new meaning after Brecht's conversion to
Marxism. Brecht then pointed out that it was more
than just an antiillusionary device: for Kragler, "this
fake-proletarian, who sabotaged the revolution,"[65] a
revolution would be unthinkable without a romantic
moon. For Kragler, as for many pseudo-revolutionists
of the American or European leftist movements of the
1960s, there was something thrillingly romantic about
"the revolution." But as soon as they found something
more interesting to do, the revolution was tossed
aside; the revolutionists returned to their bourgeois
existence.

The first performance of *Drums in the Night* took
place on 29 September 1922 in the Kammerspiele
München (director: Otto Falckenberg; sets: Casper
Neher; Kragler: Ernst Faber). "Behind pasteboard
screens, about two yards high and representing the
walls of a room, the large city was painted in a childlike manner. A few seconds before each of Kragler's
entrances, the red moon lit up."[66]

It was the first performance of a play by Brecht—
and his first success. Hermann Sinsheimer noted in
the *Münchner Neueste Nachrichten:* "A dramatist

Drums in the Night, Kammerspiele München, world pre-
miere, 29 September 1922. Director: Otto Falckenberg.
Scene in the Piccadilly Bar.
THEATER-MUSEUM MÜNCHEN

showed his claws, a director his art, and a dozen actors their talent. We are full of hope."[67] Brecht was awarded the coveted Kleist prize for this play.

Three months later, on 20 December 1922, the prestigious Deutsches Theater in Berlin opened its doors to Brecht's play, again directed by Falckenberg, with Alexander Granach as Kragler, Blandine Ebinger as Anna, Werner Hollmann as Murk, and Heinrich George as Glubb. The success in Munich and the Kleist prize obviously had convinced Felix Hollander, the director of the Deutsches Theater, who had formerly refused to stage the play.

Although not so overwhelmingly as in Munich, the play repeated its success. Nevertheless, Alfred Kerr found it "half disappointing." He found the second act best, and from then on it was all downhill. For Kerr, Brecht was only a minor talent who gained attention because no one else was around. According to Kerr, Brecht simply mixed ingredients from plays by other playwrights (like a "ragout cook") and made entirely too much noise doing it.[68] Brecht never forgave Kerr for this—"at least not for the next ten years"—according to Arnolt Bronnen, who was one of Brecht's friends at that time.[69]

Herbert Ihering took an entirely different view. For him, the Munich performance of this play was "*the* artistic event of the year." He did not deny that the play had its weak moments, but he attributed them to Brecht's lack of experience and, most of all, to deficiencies in acting and staging, not to lack of talent on the part of the playwright, as Kerr would have it. The greater portion of Ihering's review is actually an attack upon Kerr's critical and rather condescending view of contemporary dramas and dramatists (particularly Brecht), which marked the beginning of a lifelong feud between these two great critics.[70]

On 17 May 1967, *Drums in the Night* opened in

New York City's Circle in the Square theater in an English adaptation by Frank Jones (director: Theodore Mann; sets: John Annus; Kragler: Ralph Waite; Anna: Joanna Miles). The performance and the play both received good notices from Dan Sullivan of *The New York Times.* The "exquisite sense of balance" made "Theodore Mann's distinguished production ... a fine play to argue about on the way home." The argument: whether Kragler has a right to his own happiness after years of war or whether he should have joined the revolution. Sullivan thought the cast "remarkably strong," though "the palm goes to Ralph Waite." He also thought that "besides its other virtues," the play could be taken as a good introduction to Brecht's other works; "Hopefully it will be so taken by the crowds it ought to draw to the Circle in the Square."[71]

Despite its crudities, *Drums in the Night* also has its genuinely moving scenes, such as the encounter between Anna and Kragler in the Piccadilly Bar. In general, the language and the plot are much more straightforward than in *Baal.* Being set against the background of the Spartacus uprising, the play is also more dramatic than *Baal.*

Yet like *Baal,* it is an attack on bourgeois conventions. Traditionally, an unwed but pregnant girl was supposed to hide her head in shame because to have a child out of wedlock was a great sin against the strict but superficial bourgeois conventions. Many dramas wallow in the tragic fate of the unwed mother, Goethe's *Faust* being among the best known of them. Not so Brecht's *Drums in the Night.* Anna, the pregnant "heroine," is more concerned about her waistline than her shame.

Drums in the Night is also one of the best plays ever written about a soldier returning from war. The returnee, Kragler, is alienated from a bourgeois society that he has outgrown through his experiences.

Early One-Act Plays (1919)

Today, Brecht's first one-act play, *The Bible* (*Die Bibel*), which was also his first dramatic production in general, is only of interest to literary historians and Brecht scholars. This play, which he wrote when he was fifteen years old, was published in January 1914 in his high school newspaper, *Die Ernte,* under the pseudonym Berthold Eugen. The historical setting is The Netherlands, where a Protestant city is under siege by Catholic forces. The Catholics promise to spare the city if its inhabitants become Catholics and if one of the maidens of the town spends the night with their leader. The play is written in the expressionistic fashion and shows little originality. But the emphasis on rational behavior and the distrust of rigid religion pave the way for later developments.

In 1919, while a student in Munich, Brecht performed occasionally with Karl Valentin (1882–1948), a comedian from Munich. In cabaret-style sketches— many of them in the local Munich dialect—Valentin used word play and seemingly absurd logic to ridicule habitual modes of speech, thought, or behavior. Brecht admired Valentin, and the five one-act plays he wrote in 1919 owe a great deal to Valentin. And Hans Otto Münsterer recalls that Brecht himself also mentioned Cervantes's "Autos intermedios" or "Entremeses" (one-act farces presented between the acts of a play), as a source for his one-act plays.[72]

In *The Wedding* (*Die Hochzeit*), the guests have assembled at the dinner table for the wedding meal. Everything is very proper and stiff. The bride proudly announces that her bridegroom has made all the furniture himself. But as the meal progresses, the furniture begins to disintegrate—and so do the manners of the guests. At the end, after everyone has left, the groom takes the bride to bed—which also breaks apart with a loud crash.

The play gives a satiric glimpse of petit bourgeois family life. The bride's father is appalled at modern literature—such as "that play *Baal*," which he thinks is "unadulterated filth": "Modern writers drag family life into the dirt. Yet it is the most precious thing we Germans have."[73] Brecht destroys this illusion by showing the reality behind the appearances—the guests quarrel, the father keeps telling stories no one wants to hear, the bride is pregnant.

The Wedding was first performed in Frankfurt on the Main on 11 December 1926. According to Martin Esslin, it was a complete failure.

In November 1970, the German-language troupe Die Brücke presented a very successful production of *The Wedding* in German at the Barbizon Plaza Theater in New York City. The program contained ample notes in English so that even those spectators who knew little or no German could enjoy the comedy, which was, according to Howard Thompson of *The New York Times*, "as funny as it could be."[74]

The Beggar, or The Dead Dog (*Der Bettler oder Der tote Hund*), a dialogue between a blind beggar and an emperor, outside the emperor's palace, is a stab at the conventional method of regarding history merely as a gallery of gallant heroes. The emperor has just defeated his greatest enemy, and being in a gracious mood, he decides to stoop down and talk to the beggar, the "nonentity." But in his conversation with the beggar, the tables are turned: the beggar, far from being humble, is the dominant figure. He shows his disdain for "conventional" history and the ways of the mighty:

> EMPEROR: And Alexander the Great? And Caesar? And Napoleon?
> BEGGAR: Only stories! What Napoleon do you mean?[75]

The only Napoleon the beggar knows about is a galley slave. The recent death of his dog, his only friend, is closer and more important to him than the heroes of history.

The play anticipates much of the Marxist Brecht's view of history, but some critics also regard it as a precursor to the theater of the absurd.[76] So far as I could ascertain, this play has never been performed.

He Drives Out a Devil (*Er treibt einen Teufel aus*) is set on a farm on an evening in August. It is a conventional story of love made difficult by stuffy lower-middle-class morality. Boy meets girl, girl says no, but acts yes. The parents try to separate them out of moral scruples and fear of what the neighbors would say, but they do not succeed. When the father frightens them out of the girl's room (the boy had used a ladder to enter), they climb on the roof to embrace each other. Soon the whole village, including the minister, assembles to look at the "new weathercock" and "the stork's nest" on top of the house. The parents become the laughingstock of the village and the object of the minister's scorn.

The play, written in terse dialogue, is a humorous attack on narrow-minded middle-class morality. It has not been performed.

Light in the Darkness (*Lux in Tenebris*) consists of nine short scenes set in a street in a red light district. To the right and in the background are brothels with open red glass doors and red lights. To the left is a large canvas tent, with an opening at the front which is covered by a flap. There is a sign on the tent saying "Let there be light! Sex instruction for the people!"[77] From the top of the tent a bright white light illuminates the scene.

Paduk, the organizer of this mass-education campaign, is sitting in front of the door selling tickets to his exhibition of the gruesome effects of various venereal diseases: soft chancre, gonorrhea and, the most expensive exhibit—syphilis. Paduk explains to a reporter that he does it for the love of humanity and as a warning against prostitution, which he diagnoses as the source of all evil. For a Catholic chaplain and the members of his young Catholic Workers' Association, he agrees to give a special performance.

Paduk gleefully observes that he has almost ruined business in the red light district. But Madame Hogge, the proprietor of the red light establishments, discloses Paduk's real motives: he is seeking revenge for having been thrown out of her brothel. Paduk believes that Madame Hogge is angry only because the young Catholics this time came to him instead of going to her. Egged on by his success, he delivers a flaming speech against the vices of prostitution and the exploitation of prostitutes, directing his attention mainly toward Madame Hogge's establishment. The very next scene, however, shows him exploiting his own assistant: Paduk demands all the tips his assistant had received.

His business, too, seems to be at a turning point. With alarm, Paduk notices some visitors in the red light district—the first in weeks. A mollified Madame Hogge returns to suggest a business deal. Since he, Paduk, actually lives on prostitution, his business would disappear if prostitution were wiped out.

Therefore she suggests that—having mutual business interests—they go into business together rather than fight each other, an idea that makes perfect sense to Paduk.

This play, the best of Brecht's early one-act plays, presents many of Brecht's later themes, particularly the combination of prostitution and exploitation. In this early play, prostitution has already taken on a more general meaning. Paduk prostitutes his rhetorical abilities in the service of hatred, revenge, and greed. A direct line can be drawn from this play to *Turandot, or the Congress of Whitewashers,* one of Brecht's last plays (written in 1953 and 1954). In this late play, Brecht calls those people who prostitute their intellectual abilities "Tuis" (he coined this term from syllables of the word "intellectual"), and Paduk is undoubtedly one of Brecht's first Tuis. *Light in the Darkness* is also the first statement of Brecht's opinion that prostitution is the result of a rotten society, not its cause.[78]

With the encounter between the chaplain and Paduk, Brecht also wanted to point out the unholy alliance between religion and capitalism, a theme that was to dominate many of his later works (*Saint Joan of the Stockyards, The Threepenny Opera*).

The light that shineth in the darkness (*lux in tenebris*) is Paduk's light shining into Madame Hogge's establishments and onto her shady business with prostitution. But its ironic function becomes translucent when Brecht sheds light on Paduk's own shady motives.

Technically, the play also contains many elements that are known as Brecht's "estrangement technique."

The play was apparently performed in 1968, but no details are available.

The Catch (*Der Fischzug*) is set in a fisherman's

cottage. The fisherman comes home drunk, supported by two of his drinking companions. He has been drinking all day instead of catching fish. In his drunkenness, he orders his wife around. But he is not too drunk to plan a big catch. He builds a trap in his bed with a fishing net. His wife and one of his drinking companions are caught in the trap while the fisherman is asleep on the couch. Awakened by the noise of his trap snapping shut, he discovers his wife and his companion in bed together. With his shouts of "Fish! Fish!" he attracts the whole neighborhood into the house. They carry off the big catch in triumph and dump the couple into the water.

But the play comes to a conciliatory end. The wife returns and takes control of the situation. She throws all the other people out and takes care of her husband. In her resoluteness, she is undoubtedly a precursor of the self-reliant woman of Brecht's later plays (Leocadia Begbick, Mother Courage, Señora Carrar, Pelageya Vlassova).

The Catch is a parody both of Simon Peter's catch (Luke 5:1–11) and an episode in the eighth book of Homer's *Odyssey*.[79] Ares and Aphrodite had a love affair, but were caught in bed in a net of chains that Hephaestus, Aphrodite's husband, had prepared for them. But, instead of in the realm of the gods, Brecht's play is set in a small fishing village. This early play is already a good illustration of the Brechtian technique of inversion of traditional concepts. Again, so far as I know, this play has not been performed.

These early one-act plays are of interest since they foreshadow many of the techniques (irony, satire, humor, alienation effects) Brecht was to use in his later and more famous plays. Some of the one-act plays, *The Wedding*, *The Catch*, or *Light in the Darkness*, would be exciting items for an evening of one-act plays at colleges or high schools.

In the Jungle of Cities: The Fight Between Two Men in the Giant City of Chicago (1921–24)

You are in the city of Chicago in 1912. You observe an inexplicable wrestling match between two men and the ruin of a family that has come from the prairies into the jungle of the big city. Do not rack your brains over the motives of this fight, but make yourself share in the human stakes. Judge impartially the fighting form of the contenders, and direct your attention to the finish.[80]

Thus Brecht introduced his third full-length play, which he wrote between 1921 and 1924. For the first time, he chose the city of Chicago as background for a play. The action takes place in an "unreal, cold Chicago." From then on, "the cold Chicago" became a frequent image in his work.

Readers (and viewers) should be forewarned that this play is perhaps the most difficult one of all of Brecht's plays.

The play opens on the morning of 8 August 1912 in C. Maynes's Lending Library in Chicago. Shlink, a Malaysian lumber dealer, and Skinny, his Chinese clerk, enter and try to start a fight with Garga, a white library employee—for no apparent reason. To provoke him, they offer to buy his opinions—despite his protests that he will not prostitute himself by selling his opinions ("I will sell you the opinions of Mr. J. V. Jensen and those of Mr. Arthur Rimbaud, but not mine").[81] They try every means to make Garga change

German title: *Im Dickicht der Städte: Der Kampf zweier Männer in der Riesenstadt Chicago.*

his mind, but even when they start destroying books, he refuses. It is only when Maynes fires him that he is ready to fight back. Somehow he feels relieved: "This is freedom."[82] He runs out of the library, symbolically leaving his coat behind for others to bargain over.

Several days later, on the evening of 22 August, shortly before seven o'clock, Garga enters Shlink's office. The recent events are still incomprehensible to him. He does not know what they want of him; he feels pulled in by invisible ropes. But he does not ask for reasons. Shlink at this point hands over his lumberyard to Garga, and says that from now on his fate is in Garga's hands. Garga then proceeds to ruin Shlink's business by making several crooked business deals and then closing down the lumberyard.

Later that night, Garga returns to his home. Since he no longer has a job, his parents face starvation in the "cold city," where insecurity is everywhere. Although they urge him to stay, Garga hands them some money and leaves to find work in the south. When Shlink (his lumberyard now ruined) appears and asks Garga's father for a place to stay, he is offered Garga's place in their home. From then on, Shlink supports the Garga family by hard menial work. He spends his spare time looking for Garga among the people who board the ships for Tahiti.

But Garga has not left town. A month later, he surfaces at a seamy Chinese hotel. Shlink's spell is still upon him; he cannot escape from Shlink. Garga and Shlink meet in the hotel. Shlink appears submissive, but this is deceiving; he is actually the one who is in control. (Brecht noted: "By feigning passivity, Shlink cuts the lines that connect Garga with the world around him. He forces him into a desperate struggle against the jungle of Shlink's intrigues, a jungle that becomes thicker and thicker.")[83]

In the course of the fight, both sides make considerable sacrifices. Shlink's lumberyard and Garga's library job have been lost; Garga's sister, Marie, as well as his girlfriend, Jane, are driven to prostitution by Shlink.

On 29 September 1912, it looks as if Garga has won. In his parents' now well-furnished living room, Garga celebrates his wedding to Jane. When Shlink appears, Garga tells him that there is no room for him and that their acquaintance is over, although it had been very profitable (Shlink had supplied the funds for the furniture and the wedding). As for himself, Garga has decided to regain his job at Maynes's Lending Library. But Shlink has another weapon ready. He sees to it that Garga gets a three-year jail term for the fraudulent deals he made with the lumber company. Before he goes to prison, however, Garga prepares for revenge by writing a letter accusing Shlink of sexual assault on both his wife, Jane, and his sister, Marie. He plans to release this letter shortly before his release from prison.

About a month later, Shlink looks like the winner. He has rebuilt his business and vows to have nothing more to do with the Garga family. But on 20 October 1915, a man enters Shlink's private offices to warn him that Garga has made public the incriminating letter. Shlink disappears immediately—and none too soon. A lynch mob is after him, his lumberyards are on fire, and the "yellow men" are hanging on the Milwaukee bridge like laundry. But when Garga thinks he has finally rid himself of his enemy, Shlink reappears. Garga again falls under his spell and leaves with him.

On 19 November 1915, around two o'clock in the morning, Shlink and Garga have their last and decisive confrontation in a deserted railroad workers' tent in the gravel pits near Lake Michigan. This key scene of the play gives us some insight into the nature of the seemingly inexplicable fight between the two men. Garga recognizes that Shlink has been lonely all his life, and that Shlink's reason for the fight was to establish contact with another human being through enmity. Shlink agrees: "Now you understand that we are comrades, comrades in a metaphysical conflict."[84] Shlink is attracted to Garga, but even human contact through enmity seems impossible: "Man's infinite isolation makes enmity an unattainable goal."[85] What separates people from each other is speech. Shlink agrees; for him the only means of establishing a relationship is through bodily contact. But that does not bridge the gap created by speech. The isolation of the individual is so great that there cannot even be a fight. With nostalgia, he looks back to the beginnings of mankind: "The woods! From here mankind originated. Hairy, with teeth like the apes, good animals who knew how to live. Everything was so easy."[86]

But Garga has enough of Shlink's "blabbering." He wants to put an end to the fight. It is Thursday night, and, like Judas, Garga plans to betray Shlink to the lynchers. There will never be a resolution or an understanding in this fight. Garga has decided to go to New York City to begin a new life; he feels that he has sacrificed enough. Shlink is disappointed: "You did not comprehend what it was. You wanted my downfall, but I wanted the fight. It was not the physical aspect I sought, but the spiritual."[87] But for Garga, the tangible world is more important: "The spiritual, as you see, is nothing. Being the one who survives, not being the stronger, is what is important."[88] Shlink commits suicide just before the lynch mob arrives.

Eight days later we see the private office of the late Shlink. The burned-out lumberyard is for sale. Marie has returned to her father. Garga sells the lumberyard to Manky, a sailor, and leaves for New York City. He looks forward to a new beginning, but regrets nothing: "It is good to be alone. The chaos is spent. It was the best time."[89] The play ends with these words.

For Brecht, a new period began in 1927, around the time he prepared the third version of this play; anarchic nihilism gave way to disciplined Marxism. Perhaps he expressed his own feelings at that time in the last words of this play. (Though the first version of 1922 also contained the passage in question, it was neither in this form nor at the very end of the play, where it receives more emphasis.) Much later, in 1954, Brecht wrote:

> It was the fierceness that interested me about this fight. And since in those years (after 1920) I enjoyed sports, especially boxing—one of the "great mythical amusements of the giant cities beyond the big pond" [referring to America and the Atlantic]—my new play should present "a fight for fighting's sake," a fight without any cause other than the joy of fighting. It had no goal except to find "the better man."[90]

And Brecht, the Marxist playwright, added that even at the time he wrote *In the Jungle of Cities,* he had the—then still rather vague—notion that the fight between Shlink and Garga symbolized the fight for survival in a capitalist society.

In the Jungle of Cities went through several stages of development (carefully traced in Gisela Bahr's volume of study materials to the play).[91] Here it may suffice to point out that there seem to be three different versions: *In the Jungle* (1923), *Jungle* (1924), and *In the Jungle of Cities* (1927). There is little difference between the first two versions, whereas the 1927 version (reprinted in the 1950s in Brecht's collected plays with only minor changes) was substantially revised. Brecht changed some of the names and characters and added precise times and dates. This last version is less anarchic and atmospheric and more urban and technological than the other two. In addition, there are also some changes in the plot itself. It is this last version on which the plot summary is based.

Brecht combined several literary influences in this play, some of which he himself mentioned: Schiller's *The Robbers* ("With *Jungle,* I wanted to improve *The Robbers*");[92] Shakespeare's *Othello* (particularly the lighting effects of the Jessner production he had seen in Berlin); Verlaine; Rimbaud (especially his prose poem "Une Saison en Enfer"); a collection of letters (probably Charlotte Westermann's novel *Knabenbriefe* of 1908); and, perhaps most important, the novel *The Wheel* (1905) by the Danish novelist Johannes Vilhelm Jensen (1873–1950). *The Wheel,* set in Chicago, also describes a strange fight between two human beings that ended with the destruction of one of them.

According to Brecht, the atmosphere, as well as the crude and sensational plays of the fairs of his native Augsburg, also played an important role. He wrote most of the play on thin typing paper, folded to fit into a little notebook, and, while writing, he used to walk around in the suburbs of Augsburg, along the crumbling old city walls and past the algae-covered moats. While working on plot and character, he developed whole scenes of words of a certain texture and color to affect the senses. As strange as it may sound today, Brecht also regarded *In the Jungle* as an historical play at the time he wrote it.

> The history of mankind is a pile of unsifted material. It is difficult to see who the people with the responsibility were for each period. One

should make a survey of the appearance of great individuals, the creation of important ideas, and the clash between individuals and ideas, a clash which does not always take place in battles and revolutions. The individual who, in 1923, fought the first fight for the sake of fighting, that first fight devoid of all ulterior motives, C. Shlink, is an historical person.[93]

Later, in 1954, after he had been an adherent to the Marxist view of history for some twenty-five years, he himself called this early concept of his "strange."

There have been several attempts at interpreting this strange, but fascinating, play. Some interpreters have stressed the homosexual relationship between Shlink and Garga. This seems to be supported by Brecht when he noted that Garga "resembles A. Rimbaud in appearance. Essentially he [Garga] is a German translation from French into American."[94] His relationship to Shlink, then, would in some ways reflect Rimbaud's homosexual relationships to Verlaine. (A similar parallel occurs in *Baal* between Baal and Ekart.)

One critic saw this play as the dramatization of the inner psychic conflict of a young man (Garga) thrown into modern urban life; all other characters only externalize conflicting aspects of his personality. Other interpreters see the play as a forerunner of contemporary existentialist plays, most of which depict the overwhelming isolation of modern man, such as Beckett's *Waiting for Godot* or Ionesco's *Rhinoceros*.

Brecht soon found that audiences were seriously puzzled by *In the Jungle of Cities*—something he had actually expected. Therefore he felt himself compelled to give another explanation of this "fight without enmity" when the play was performed in Heidelberg in 1928. The rather extensive program notes offered the following:

The actions of people of our times, which are occasionally, though not always completely, reported in our newspapers, can no longer be explained by familiar motives. . . . Increasingly, police reports list "motive unknown." Thus you must not be surprised that certain characters in modern dramas act differently from what you expect or that your assumptions about the motives of a certain action prove to be wrong. *In this world and in these plays a philosopher is more at home than a psychologist* [Brecht's own italics].[95]

On 9 May 1923, the first performance of *In the Jungle of Cities* took place in Munich's Residenztheater (director: Erich Engel; sets: Caspar Neher; Garga: Erwin Faber; Shlink: Otto Wernicke; Marie: Maria Koppenhöfer). Few understood the play; most remained confused. Herbert Ihering, the critic who "discovered" Brecht, was enthusiastic: "*In the Jungle* is Bertolt Brecht's third and richest play. . . . You can either say yes or no to it. One immediately feels the suggestive power of Brecht's language—or one remains cool and unreceptive toward the play."

Most other critics, however, remained unreceptive: Georg Jacob Wolf, in the *Münchener Zeitung,* asked: "What's the point?" Horst Wolfram Geissler, in the *München-Augsburger Abendzeitung,* wrote: "I must confess that I am not at all sure that my attempt at an interpretation is correct. Perhaps the play describes nothing more than the best method of pickling cucumbers. Such is the play's confusion, such its writer's failure to present clear ideas or create characters. A greater fiasco has seldom been presented on stage."

And there was outright hostility on the part of the far right. Josef Stolzing, of the Nazi paper *Völkischer Beobachter,* wrote: "My worst expectations were far surpassed. . . . My time is too valuable to argue with the scrawls of today's literature." In his view, how-

In the Jungle of Cities, Residenztheater München, world premiere, 9 May 1923. Director: Erich Engel; sets and costumes: Casper Neher.

In the Jungle of Cities, Berliner Ensemble, 1971. Director: Ruth Berghaus; sets: Andreas Reinhardt. Shlink: Ekkehard Schall (left).

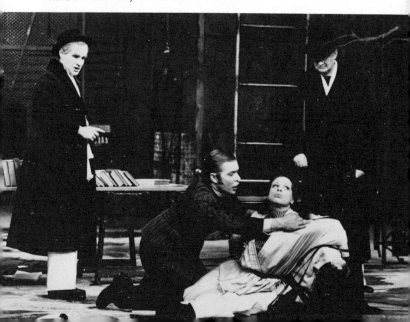

ever, Brecht's worst offense was that his characters spoke Yiddish. (They did not; the charge reveals Stolzing's anti-Semitism).

On 29 October 1924, the play was performed in the Deutsches Theater in Berlin, again directed by Erich Engel (sets: Caspar Neher; Garga: Walter Franck; Marie: Gerda Müller; Shlink: Fritz Kortner, who even refused a role in Max Reinhardt's staging of Bernard Shaw's *Saint Joan* in order to play this role). The reaction to the play was more or less the same as in Munich.

Monty Jacobs, of the *Vossische Zeitung,* did not understand it, but was fascinated by Brecht's wild and chaotic play, Engel's production, and the actors' performance, particularly that of Kortner. Alfred Kerr, of the *Berliner Tageblatt,* on the other hand, was disgusted: "End of politeness: this is completely worthless stuff. Completely worthless stuff." But he conceded that it was well directed and well played.[96]

On 20 December 1960, The Living Theater presented *In the Jungle of Cities* in New York City; translated by Gerhard Nellhaus (director: Judith Malina; sets: Julian Beck; Garga: Jamil Zakkai; Shlink: Khigh Dhiegh; Marie: Ethel Manuelian). It was in repertory with other plays and closed after forty-four performances on 15 April 1962.

The reaction of the New York critics was not unlike that of their colleagues in Berlin and Munich some thirty-five years earlier. Howard Taubman of *The New York Times* tried to make some gracious remarks about this "bewildering play," but wondered whether the play was worth the efforts that the producers and theatergoers put into it: "It takes a long time to discover what the author is trying to say, and when he has reached his destination, you wonder whether the twisting, confusing journey was worth it." He thought the play might be stimulating to those who were willing to accept Brecht on his own terms: "Other-wise, you will find it arty, even a bore." To him, the staging, too, left something to be desired: "It leans heavily on ferocity of movement, but it fails to achieve subtlety." Yet Taubman did not write off the play completely. Although "hardly Brecht at his best," he conceded that the play had "numerous examples of pungent observation and harsh poetry.... You may have difficulty finding the straight path to the play-wright's thought, but you will encounter bright and shrewd theatrical moments."[97]

Walter Kerr of the *New York Herald Tribune,* too, was slightly puzzled: "You have, then, an event that is intended for specialists, that is impenetrable as any sort of rational experience, but that is nevertheless possessed of an odd and eerie authority. Its authority, I'd say, is wholly theatrical; but that is nothing to be lightly dismissed."[98]

In February 1970, *The New York Times* critic Clive Barnes, surfeited on Broadway trivia, traveled to Bos-ton to see *In the Jungle of Cities,* in Anselm Hollo's adaptation, staged by Louis Criss at the Charles Play-house (Garga: Michael Moriarty; Shlink: Nicholas Kepros). Apparently the time was ripe for this early Brechtian play. Barnes found it "absolutely marvel-ous," and most appropriate for those times of unrest in the country (the Vietnam war, unrest on college campuses and in the cities):

> It is a strange and wonderful play, perhaps—
> and this will be sacrilege to true Brechtians—
> more interesting to us today than the epic
> thought and beauty of *Galileo.* Because *Jungle
> of Cities* not only has tremendous dramatic im-
> pact, it also is a psycho-intellectual power
> struggle between two men, and in its inconse-
> quential natural motivation it anticipates Samuel
> Beckett and Harold Pinter. It is modern.[99]

In the Jungle of Cities, Studio des Champs Élysées, Paris, 1962. Translator: Gilbert Badia; director: Antoine Bourseiller; sets and costumes: Jacques Schmidt; music: Jean Podromidès. *Above,* Sami Frey and Claire Duhamel. *Right,* Sami Frey (in foreground).

As to the production itself, Barnes thought the Bostonians "superb."

Brecht's own theater, the Berliner Ensemble, tackled the play relatively late. It was first performed in 1971, after long deliberations concerning the problems of producing Brecht's early and nihilistic works in a socialist society (director: Ruth Berghaus; sets: Andreas Reinhardt; Shlink: Ekkehard Schall; Garga: Hans Peter Reinecke). According to Hans-Jochen Irmer, a spokesman for the Ensemble, *In the Jungle of Cities* fit well into the company's repertory because there was a line of development from *In the Jungle of Cities* (1921–22) to *Arturo Ui,* (1941) and then to

Turandot (1953–54); all three plays "portray the increasing manipulation of men and the increasing brutality of the world."[100] It was the Ensemble's intention to present the play critically, as " 'illustrative material' from the years 1921–22."

Ernst Wendt, the reviewer for the West German theater journal *Theater heute,* felt that the production left something to be desired. The program announced that the producers took a critical approach to the play, yet Wendt was unable to detect it in the production itself, and the producers' real intentions remained unclear to him. His most serious criticism, however, concerned the careful avoidance of any allusion to the homosexual relationship between Shlink and Garga— despite strong hints in the text itself. In his view, this relationship, born out of desperation since all other means of communication fail, is central to the play. By avoiding this aspect, the play, in his opinion, was not accessible to the theatergoer.

Wendt approved of the sets, which attempted to suggest a city jungle by wire fences, bizarre iron doors, and scrap metal. The acting, especially that of Schall, seemed too stylized for him.[101]

As is evident from the plot summary, the reviews, and the reaction of audiences, *In the Jungle of Cities* is indeed a very difficult play. What makes this play so particularly hard to understand is the apparent absence of a tangible motive for the fight between Shlink and Garga and the seeming lack of a rational and logical cohesion of the scenes. But some explanation can be gained from a look at the play's history. It was written in times of turmoil and unrest following World War I by a young, nihilistic playwright in search of stability. Central to the play are irrational fear, isolation, loneliness, and chaos as well as pleasure in disorder and destruction. This was precisely the background for the superficial glitter of the so-called roaring twenties that Brecht has captured for us in this play.

A Man Is a Man (1924–26)

In this play Brecht takes us to the bustling barracks of the British Imperial Army in Kilkoa, India. The year is 1925. The main character of the play is the poor docker Galy Gay. He is a man who has two great faults: he cannot say no, and he loves to make a deal. It is his transformation from a poor and simple but peaceful packer into a pugnacious platoon member of a British machine-gun unit that Brecht wants to show us in his play.

SCENE 1. Kilkoa. Galy Gay tells his wife that he has decided to go out briefly to buy a fish. She warns him of dangerous women and soldiers, but he thinks they will not bother a simple packer.

SCENE 2. Street near a pagoda. The town of Kilkoa is full of British soldiers preparing for action at the northern borders. Four soldiers of a machine-gun unit —Uria Shelley, Jesse Mahoney, Polly Baker, and Jeraiah Jip—break into the pagoda in order to obtain some money to buy more beer. But before they proceed, one of them collects their military passes to keep them safe: "Military passes must not be damaged. A man, however, can be replaced at any time."[102] Thus, if someone is injured, killed, or caught in this venture, it will be difficult to identify the man. Moreover, the others have his pass to furnish a substitute with necessary papers. On his way out of the

German title: *Mann ist Mann.*

pagoda, Jeraiah Jip's red hair gets caught in the door. To free him, his friends cut it off. But now the bald spot on his head will betray him and his friends as being the ones who broke into the pagoda. They keep his pass and leave him behind.

SCENE 3. Road between Kilkoa and the camp. Sergeant Fairchild, known as Bloody Five (because he once shot five helpless Hindus), is posting a warrant for the arrest of those persons who broke into the pagoda; the most important evidence is a tuft of red hair. The three soldiers read the warrant with horror, and Sergeant Fairchild warns them of dire consequences if they show up at roll call without a fourth man. While they are debating what to do, Galy Gay arrives on the scene carrying a basket of cucumbers for widow Leocadia Begbick, a canteen proprietress. (This is a character of whom Brecht was particularly fond; he used her again in *The Rise and Fall of the City of Mahagonny*.) Begbick tries to seduce Galy Gay, but he is too stupid to realize this—he is only concerned about getting his fish. Since he cannot say no to anything, he is quickly talked into buying a cucumber he did not want. The three soldiers realize they have found their fourth man. They have no difficulty in persuading him to come with them and share a cigar in Begbick's canteen.

SCENE 4. In Widow Begbick's canteen (a railroad car that is pulled across India along with the military trains—a more modern version of Mother Courage's wagon). The soldiers sing "The Song of Widow Begbick's Bar." The three men of the machine-gun unit ask Galy Gay to substitute for Jeraiah Jip, their missing fourth man. In return for three cases of cigars and five bottles of beer, Galy Gay agrees and dons the uniform they have bought for him.

Widow Begbick sees trouble ahead and decides to divert Sergeant Fairchild's attention to her own charms.

Particularly on rainy days, Fairchild is subject to "terrible attacks of unrestrained sensuality."[103] She manages to delay him while the roll is called, at which Galy Gay, without being noticed, substitutes for Jeraiah Jip.

Galy Gay's service has now ended, but he decides not to leave. He might be needed again and hopes for another deal. The process of his transformation has begun; upon Begbick's question, he denies that he is Galy Gay.

SCENE 5. Interior of the pagoda. The bonze (a Buddist priest), Wang, finds the genuine Jip drunk in a chest. The priest has no real use for him but decides to pass him off as a new god so that he can attract the money of pious pilgrims. The three soldiers return for Jip and threaten the bonze, but he convinces them that if the four of them are seen together with extra money, the theft will be traced to them. They quickly realize that he is right. Although they can hear Jip moaning in the chest, they leave again.

SCENE 6. Late at night in Begbick's canteen. The three soldiers find Galy Gay asleep in a chair. Once again, they have a use for him.

SCENE 7. The pagoda, early the next morning. Jip wakes up in the chest, without knowing exactly where he is or what has happened to him. The bonze talks to him and pretends to the pilgrims that he is talking to a god. When Jip bangs on the lid of the chest to get out, the bonze counts the number of knocks and tells the pilgrims that the god is telling them how much money he wants them to offer. Finally, after all the pilgrims are gone, Wang lets Jip out, but a beefsteak dinner convinces Jip to remain safely in the pagoda.

SCENE 8. Begbick's canteen, early the same morning. Since Jip has not returned, his three colleagues know that they have to persuade Galy Gay to stay with them permanently. They paint the life of a soldier in glow-ing colors: "The soldier's life is especially pleasant in wartime. It is only in the battle that a man achieves true greatness."[104] Galy Gay is unimpressed—until Uria suggests a business deal. He will sell Galy Gay an elephant at a bargain price if he will agree to be their fourth man. Galy Gay cannot resist: "For almost any kind of deal, I am your man."[105] He even disavows his wife, who has come looking for him. Uria is confident that his plan will work. There is no problem in transforming one man into another man because "one man is like any other man. A man is a man."[106]

Interlude. The action is interrupted by Leocadia Begbick, who comments on the play and addresses the audience: "Mr. Bertolt Brecht claims: a man is a man. And that is something anybody can claim. But then Mr. Bertolt Brecht proves that you can do anything you want with a man. Tonight, right here, a man will be reassembled like a car."[107]

SCENE 9. Begbick's canteen. The soldiers prepare to move north to the war, commenting: "When they need cotton, it's Tibet, if they need wool, it's Pamir."[108] Begbick sings the "Song of the Flow of Things," and verses of this song recur throughout this rather long scene. In it Galy Gay's transformation is portrayed. The refrain of the song points out that hope lies in constant change:

> "Don't hold to the wave
> That breaks over your foot, as long as it
> Is in the water,
> Other new waves will break over it."[109]

The news that war has broken out is good news to Uria: "Comrades, war has broken out. The times of disorder are over."[110] The three men of the machine-gun unit now desperately need Galy Gay. Uria has a plan for transforming him irrevocably into Jeraiah Jip. They intend to have Galy Gay sell a fake army elephant and then arrest him for selling army property. Polly and Jesse take a tarpaulin and a stuffed elephant's head from the wall and disguise themselves as an elephant. Uria assures them that Galy Gay will pass off anything as an elephant, even a beer bottle, as long as he can make a deal. Begbick agrees to pose as a prospective buyer.

The spectacle following Scene 9 is divided into five sections, announced by Uria:

Number one: The elephant business. Galy Gay receives Billy Humph, the elephant.

Number two: Galy Gay sells the elephant to Begbick and is arrested when he accepts the check.

Number three: The trial of Galy Gay—who is no longer sure that he really is Galy Gay. Begbick comments: "Of all certainties, the most certain is doubt."[111] Galy Gay is convicted and sentenced to death.

Number four: Galy Gay's execution. Galy Gay is frightened and now insists that he is not Galy Gay. Before he is "shot" (with fake bullets), he faints. To Galy Gay, this period of unconsciousness means the "death" of Galy Gay.

Number four (a): An interlude, during which Sergeant Fairchild is transformed into a civilian. He appears on stage in civilian clothes to seek Begbick's favors. But out of uniform, he is an easy target for the soldiers' hatred. His change is the reverse of that of Galy Gay. Galy Gay has now become a man (that is to say, a soldier), whereas Fairchild has degenerated into a civilian and is mocked by his soldiers.

Number five: Galy Gay's funeral and his funeral oration. The military trains are leaving. Galy Gay, now fully identifying with Jeraiah Jip, is sitting on "the former Galy Gay's" casket, preparing a eulogy, and fighting the temptation to look inside the casket. Luckily for him, he does not. Uria was standing by, ready to shoot him if he did. Begbick makes sure that

Galy Gay has his dog tag "so that one knows to whom he belonged when he is found and he can receive a place in a mass grave."[112] Galy Gay's dog tag now reads Jeraiah Jip. The transformation is complete. Before he enters the railroad carriage, he delivers the funeral speech for "Galy Gay . . . who went out in the morning to buy a little fish, owned a big elephant in the evening, and was shot on the same night."[113]

SCENE 10. In a moving train, Galy Gay wakes up but does not quite remember where he is and who he is. Sergeant Fairchild, in dirty civilian clothes, finds himself in a similar situation. Galy Gay consoles him: "A name is a very uncertain thing: you cannot count on it."[114] Fairchild realizes that it is his sensuous desire that cost him his reputation. He takes his revolver and castrates himself. Galy Gay finds a pass in his pocket that reads "Jeraiah Jip." He now knows who he is. He is ready for action.

SCENE 11. In Tibet, near the fortress Sir El Dchowr. To the surprise of the machine-gun unit, the real Jeraiah Jip shows up again. But they ignore him since he cannot prove that he is Jeraiah Jip. Only Galy Gay (now Jeraiah Jip) takes pity on him and gives him the papers of "a certain Galy Gay." Galy Gay has now changed completely from a simple, peaceful citizen into a "human fighting machine," who single-handedly destroys the fortress Sir El Dchowr with seven thousand refugees inside. He has "smelled blood," and is now ready to "bury his teeth in his enemy's throat."

In addition to the play, Brecht also wrote the interlude "The Elephant's Baby," which is to be played in the theater lobby by the characters of the regular play. This farcical whodunit examines whether the elephant baby (played by Galy Gay) has murdered his mother. As it turns out, the mother is still alive, and the baby is not her child; but, in a parody of the judicial system, the case against the baby is proven with the help of a chalk circle. In its crudeness, this farce is reminiscent of the play of the craftsmen in Shakespeare's *Midsummer Night's Dream*. The action is often interrupted by comments from the "audience" (also played by characters of the regular play), and the text contains many ironic allusions to conventional theater tradition.

The comedy *A Man Is a Man* was essentially completed in 1925, although some changes were made afterward. Scenes 10 and 11, for example, which formed the conclusion of the 1925 version, were cut in 1931 because Brecht felt that Scene 9 makes Galy Gay's transformation sufficiently clear. In 1953, however, Brecht reintroduced portions of the last two scenes.

The first plans for this play go back to 1920, when the twenty-one-year-old Brecht began to make outlines for a play, with the working titles of *Klamauk* or *Galgei*, which was supposed to portray the transformation of a carpenter into a butter salesman. In 1924 Brecht transposed this concept of transformation into the realm of the military, portraying the transformation of the peaceful Irish packer Galy Gay into the "human fighting machine" Jeraiah Jip. The scene is, of course, an imaginary India, reminiscent of Rudyard Kipling's India in "Barrack-Room Ballads."

Galy Gay has a soft heart, coupled with a weak mind, and "cannot say no." Yet he is defined not in psychological terms but rather in sociological terms. This focus points up the fact that at that time Brecht was strongly influenced by the school of behaviorism, the exponents of which focused on observable human behavior.

For the first time in Brecht's plays, economic motives gain decisive importance. In Galy Gay's transformation, his greed for material possessions plays an important role, particularly in the scene in which he acquires Billy Humph, the fake elephant.

In his initial interpretation of the character of Galy Gay, Brecht stated that Galy Gay is someone who just "apathetically and helplessly trots along like a sheep," that he is a liar and an opportunist who has no opinions of his own and can adapt himself easily to whatever situation seems to further his own interests. On the other hand, Brecht also saw Galy Gay as a precursor of "a new type of man." With the parable of Galy Gay's transformation he wanted to expose "the shallow individualism of our time." Brecht felt that in order to adapt to a changing world, the individual human being must also change. The "new man" Brecht envisioned was a man who could relinquish his individuality in favor of collective society. Brecht was aware that such flexibility could take a dangerous turn. In a technical world, it could lead to more suppression, or to greater freedom, depending on the nature of the collective society. Yet he was optimistic: "He [the new man] will not allow himself to be changed by machines; but he will change the machines."[115]

This view clearly reflected the influence of Brecht's studies in Marxism, which he began around the time he completed *A Man Is a Man*. In 1927, in the introduction to a radio broadcast of the play (on 18 March 1927, by Radio Berlin), he even went so far as to claim: "Galy Gay is not a weakling. On the contrary, he is the strongest, but this does not happen until he has ceased to be an individual. He becomes strong only in a mass of people."[116] Brecht argued that it is not a tragic affair when someone is forced to give up his individuality: "It is a comedy. Instead of losing something [individual spirit] Galy Gay gains something [collective spirit]."[117] But Brecht's optimistic

Marxist interpretation is not consistent with the underlying tragic nature of the play itself. The transformation of Galy Gay does not come across as positive in
any way. Brecht himself must have felt this at the
time, for he concluded his introductory remarks by
saying that he did not mind at all if the listener
reached a different conclusion.[118]

As a matter of fact, most people have taken another
view. And apparently even Brecht himself had abandoned his earlier interpretation when he suggested a
possibility for an updated version of the play in 1936,
a time when he was in exile and the Nazis were in
the process of "reassembling" the German people.
Brecht suggested that the events in Kilkoa could be
transferred to the Nazi party convention in Nürnberg,
and that the break-in into the pagoda could now be
the break-in into a Jewish business.[119] And in the introduction to a 1955 edition of his plays Brecht wrote
that *A Man Is a Man* shows "the false, bad collective
(the 'gang')" as opposed to the "historically timely,
genuine social collective of workers."[120]

A Man Is a Man was first performed on 9 September
1926, concurrently, in Darmstadt and in Düsseldorf.
In Darmstadt, Brecht's friend Jakob Geis directed, and
Caspar Neher was responsible for the sets (Galy Gay:
Ernst Legal; Widow Begbick: Bessie Hoffart). The
premiere was deemed important enough for such
prominent critics as Herbert Ihering and Alfred Kerr
to travel from Berlin to Darmstadt.

For the first time, the Brecht curtain (a plain white
curtain at the stage front, only half-high and screen-
ing only the set, resembling in appearance a shower
curtain) and projections of titles introducing each
scene were used. Jazz music accompanied the events
on stage.

With the exception of Kerr and Ihering, most of the
critics were puzzled by the play. Alfred Kerr, knowl-

edgeable and urbane, but bound by tradition, and always Brecht's most severe critic, thought the acting and staging were good. But the play? "It was not worth it. . . . A comedy of errors that failed"—despite the traces of Pirandello he discovered in it. Herbert Ihering, on the other hand, thought it excellent and could only wonder why Berlin had not seized at the opportunity to produce such a good comedy.

Two years later, the play did reach Berlin. On 4 January 1928, it opened in the Volksbühne under Erich Engel, with Heinrich George as Galy Gay (Ihering: "wonderful") and Helene Weigel as Begbick. Despite some negative criticism, the production was Brecht's first widely acclaimed success.[121]

C. Hooper Trask, Berlin correspondent for *The New York Times*, who saw the 1928 performance in Berlin, felt that, of the young German dramatists, Brecht showed the most promise:

> Brecht is in many ways the most talented of the present generation. He has humor, power, and poetic grasp. Some day, I feel sure, he will shake off the last husk of technical immaturity, and the personality which shall then be revealed will be of exceptional force and beauty.

In Trask's opinion, *A Man Is a Man* revealed both Brecht's faults and his virtues. Two-thirds of the play went along "in lively fashion," but the end was "elusively flung buncombe."[122]

Three years later, after he had established a worldwide reputation with his *Threepenny Opera*, Brecht himself directed *A Man Is a Man* in one of Berlin's most prominent theaters, the Staatliche Schauspielhaus. On 6 February 1931, this production opened, with Peter Lorre as Galy Gay and Helene Weigel as Begbick. This time, Brecht experimented by using partial masks, a commentator, and two projected photographs of Galy Gay. The soldiers had huge hands and ears. Moving about on stilts, they looked down at little Galy Gay. With his progressive transformation from scene to scene, Galy Gay's natural face turned slowly into a mask. Instead of a comedy, Brecht now called the play a parable, and he emphasized its didactic character. Widow Begbick's interlude was spoken as a prologue in front of the curtain.

Ihering found this production too sterile and schematic, and thought Peter Lorre unsuitable as Galy Gay. (On 8 March 1931, Brecht answered the criticism of Lorre's acting with the essay "Concerning the Question of Standards in Judging the Art of Acting," in which he took the position that a new kind of theater required a new style of acting.)

As Alfred Kerr saw it, his first negative opinion of Brecht was corroborated. He called the production a waste of artistic talent and Brecht "an incoherent small talent." That was the end of Brecht for him: "the next one, please."[123]

During the 1962–63 theater season, New York theatergoers were offered two versions of the play, produced concurrently. On 18 September, The Living Theater premiered its production of A Man Is a Man under the title Man Is Man (translation: Gerhard Nellhaus; director: Julian Beck, also responsible for the sets; Galy Gay: Joseph Chaikin; Leocadia Begbick: Judith Malina; music: Walter Caldon).

One day later, on 19 September in the Masque Theater, The New Repertory Theater Company opened its production of A Man Is a Man (translation: Eric Bentley; director: John Hancock; Galy Gay: John Heffernan; Widow Begbick: Olympia Dukakis; sets: David Reppa; music: Joseph Raporo). Bentley used the 1925 version as a model for his adaptation (eleven scenes). Nellhaus based his translation on Brecht's 1954 revision (two acts, ten scenes).

The message of the play was felt, at this time, to be

painfully modern. As Walter Kerr of the *New York Herald Tribune* noted after seeing both versions of the play, Brecht had described, in this play written thirty-five years earlier, "a curious foreshadowing of the art of brainwashing."[124]

Howard Taubman of *The New York Times* observed: "Brecht's style might begin by putting off a sophisticated theatergoer," since it often "has the didacticism of a primer." But he cautioned those who too easily condemn: "Stay with him. Being an artist as well as a sardonic moralist, Brecht knew how to modulate from bare opening motifs to large, shattering statements, like a symphonist who can transform a four-note theme into a powerful emotional experience." And this is exactly what happens in *A Man Is a Man*. Taubman continues: "It shades from a kind of a-b-c of character and structure into a slashing, pitying exposition of what can be done to man by his neighbors and environment."[125]

The critics found a marked difference in the quality of the two performances. Both Taubman and Kerr agreed that the Masque Theater's version was superior as far as text and production were concerned. To quote Taubman: "The earlier version is more effective because it is leaner and sharper" and "the Masque Theater production . . . is staged and performed with greater consistency of style."[126] Walter Kerr recommended the Masque Theater production without any hesitation. The director, John Hancock, "has got the tinsel look and the saxophone sound of Brecht's cabaret-style sermon right off." The style of this production recalled the music halls—tiny Christmas-tree lights surrounded the whole proscenium. Widow Begbick's three daughters, omitted in later versions of the play, served at the bar, and also contributed live entertainment as a three-piece jazz band. Titles, as the old silent films, appeared before each scene, and the front curtain was adorned with two pictures of Galy Gay—one "before" and one "after." Begbick, her daughters, and the soldiers, wore masklike makeup. As in Brecht's Berlin production, Galy Gay's face was at first natural, then became a mask as he was transformed.

But Kerr also had some reservations about the play: "overblown . . . repetitious . . . the bitter humor is not always funny enough."[127]

The Living Theater production, on the other hand, was, according to Kerr, "a failing work, possessed neither of a design of its own nor, it is to be hoped, of Brecht's."[128] Taubman was somewhat kinder, but equally negative: "*Man Is Man* is anything but an easy play to encompass, and the Living Theater's production is not yet the tightly knit affair it should become."[129]

The Berliner Ensemble staged *A Man Is a Man* in 1967; the premiere was on 10 February (director: Uta Birnbaum; music: Paul Dessau; sets: Hans Brosch; Galy Gay: Hilmar Thate; Widow Begbick: Felicitas Ritsch). The production was based on Brecht's 1931 version, but incorporated episodes from the 1925 version; it concluded with the storming of the fortress Sir El Dchowr. In order to fully concentrate on Galy Gay's metamorphosis, other transformation episodes were weakened or omitted (such as Fairchild's castration and the scenes in the pagoda where Jip is transformed into a god). The four soldiers had natural faces, not masks. Hilmar Thate, "one of the most reliable pillars of the Berliner Ensemble," gave a most impressive portrayal of Galy Gay.[130]

The performance was a great success, although there was some criticism. The East German journal *Theater der Zeit,* for example, thought that the sale of the elephant should have been cut somewhat because the play was too long. The critic of the West

A Man Is a Man, Minnesota Theater Company, 1970.
Above, Galy Gay/Jeraiah Jip: Biff McGuire; Mrs. Galy
Gay: Fern Sloan. *Below,* "Machine Gun Squad," Uria
Shelley: Charles Keating; Jesse Mahoney: Ron Glass;
Polly Baker: Peter Michael Goetz; Charles Fairchild
(Bloody Five): Robert Benson.

THE GUTHRIE THEATER

German journal *Theater heute* noticed most of all the highly artistic effects in the performance ("a silvery gray color tone"; "l'art pour l'art in the Berliner Ensemble"). He also noted the danger of presenting Brecht as a classic rather than bringing out the contradictions inherent in the play.[131]

In February 1971, the Workshop of the Players Art (WPA) staged a production of *A Man Is a Man* in a storefront theater on New York City's Bowery (translation: Eric Bentley; director: R. Mack Miller; Galy Gay: Dennis Dugan; Begbick: Ann Boothby Ross; Fairchild: James Hilbrandt).

The Vietnam war was still being fought, and Mel Gussow, the reviewer for *The New York Times,* thought the play, "which deals with the dehumanization of man by the war machine," extremely relevant. But, although the production used some of the devices of the Masque Theater production (1962), the performance was, in Gussow's terms, "more dutiful than inspired."[132]

A month later, in March 1971, "a thoroughly Anglicized" *Man Is Man,* a new and slangy translation by Steve Gooch, with "some jaunty new music by John Cameron," was staged by William Gaskill at the Royal Court Theater in London. According to Irving Wardle, the reviewer for *The New York Times,* Galy Gay was "shown simply as a piece of human engineering, neither good nor bad. Rather than forecasting the nightmares of lobotomy and psychological torture, [the play] emerges as a statement that human beings need attention like food and will undergo any change to get it." Kipling's India and the British barracks atmosphere came across strong. Henry Woolf's Galy Gay was, in Wardle's opinion, "a rare and fascinating piece of acting."[133]

A Man Is a Man clearly marks a change in Brecht's work. The language is less lyrical and more analytical than in his earlier plays, and the tendency toward a parabolic form is clearly discernible. Consequently, not too much importance should be attributed to historic inaccuracies (such as the fact that Brecht alludes to the soldiers of Her Majesty, the Queen, while at the time of the action, 1925, King George V occupied the British throne). Nor should the setting, India, be taken literally. "India simply means a foreign country," as Brecht himself said.[134]

In some ways, Galy Gay and Jeraiah Jip, his alter ego, foreshadow the split characters of Brecht's later plays, like Shen Te/ Shui Ta in the *Good Woman of Setzuan* or the drunk Puntila/ sober Puntila in *Puntila and His Servant Matti*. And the trial of the chalk circle in "The Elephant's Baby" plays a significant role in Brecht's play *The Caucasian Chalk Circle* (1944–45).

Although the play contains hilariously comic scenes, its underlying message is essentially tragic. The play shows how easy it is to transform a peaceful average citizen (with average human weaknesses) into a "fighting machine." After the cruel experiences of World War II and more recent wars, this interpretation seems even more relevant today than in the 1920s when Brecht wrote it.

BERLIN (1926–33)

The Threepenny Opera
(and *Happy End*) (1928)

The Threepenny Opera is perhaps Brecht's best-known and most widely played work. In John Gay's *The Beggar's Opera* Brecht found an ideal source and in Kurt Weill an engaging composer whose songs from *The Threepenny Opera* became extremely popular. One of them—"The Ballad of Mack the Knife"— became a top song on the American hit parade in the 1950s and is still well known today.

The setting for the opera is Victorian London. The opera opens with a prelude at a market in Soho. A ballad singer introduces the main character, Macheath, called Mack the Knife, in "The Ballad of Mack the Knife": "The shark he has his teeth/ In his face for all to see./ Macheath he has a knife/ But his knife cannot be seen."[1] (Brecht called this ballad a "Moritat"—*Mord* means murder; *Tat* means deed. *Moritaten* were songs usually sung by street singers at fairs; the subject was usually a bloody and hideous crime.)

ACT I, SCENE 1. In the wardrobe of his establishment for beggars, Mr. Peachum intones his morning

---

German title: *Die Dreigroschenoper.*

anthem (the only melody Weill retained from *The
Beggar's Opera*): "Wake up you rotten Christian!" He
then proceeds to complain to the audience that his
business is sagging since people are rapidly becoming
accustomed to cripples and pious phrases. His business is a beggars' racket: he has London divided into
fourteen districts, and, for a large fee, he sells each
beggar a license to beg in a certain district. Peachum
also provides the beggars with properties, such as
tattered clothes and crutches, designed to arouse the
pity of their fellow men. His beggars are required to
be artists because nowadays only a true artist can still
move the human heart. Independent beggars are "encouraged" (forcefully) to join Peachum's establishment. One of these independents, Filch, has just come
to join, after having been beaten up by Peachum's
men—who left behind Peachum's business card.
Peachum shows Filch the five basic models of human
misery, assigns him "type D" and a district.

While Filch is changing his clothing, Peachum hears
from his wife that their daughter Polly has been seeing a "fine gentleman"—Macheath. When Peachum
discovers that Polly did not come home the night
before, he and Mrs. Peachum step before the curtain
and sing a song in which they complain that, instead
of staying at home and doing their duty, young people
only want to have fun.

SCENE 2. Mack's and Polly's wedding in a horse
stable. Mack's friends bring in various items of stolen
furniture. Since some of the pieces do not match,
Mack scolds them because they have no taste. When
Father Kimball appears to perform the wedding, Mack
asks for a song. Three of his gang sing the "Wedding
Song for Poor People." Since it does not go over too
well, Polly decides to sing the song of "Pirate Jenny."

Suddenly the party is thrown into disarray by the
shout, "Police!" And, indeed, the police chief himself,

Tiger Brown, arrives. But, as it turns out, Mack and Brown are old friends who still help each other out occasionally. In memory of their days together in the army in India, they sing "The Cannon Song."

Before Mack's men take their leave, they reveal their last present—a bed: "And now there must be room for sentiment. Otherwise man becomes a mere slave to his work."[2] Polly and Mack sing a mock-sentimental duet.

SCENE 3. Polly returns to her parents and, with a song, she explains to them her marriage to Mack. The Peachums are shocked: "How can you be so immoral as to marry!"[3] They fear that Polly may tell her husband about their shady business. They insist on a divorce. Polly assures them that Mack will be a good provider: "He is an excellent burglar and a sharp-eyed street thief."[4] But the Peachums remain adamant. They believe only in business—which is threatened by their business rival, Mack—and are indifferent to the claims of love. Therefore Mack will have to be taken care of, preferably by the gallows. And they know where they can catch him: in a whorehouse in Turnbridge. The charge is bigamy. At the end of the scene, the three Peachums step forward and sing the "First Threepenny Finale: On the Uncertainty of Human Circumstances," containing the famous lines, "To be a good man—who would not like to be one? But the circumstances just don't allow it."[5]

ACT II, SCENE 4. The horse stable. Polly warns Mack that her father is plotting against him. Mack sees that he must disappear for a time, and asks Polly to run his business. He promises her that he will soon be in a legitimate business—banking. Polly agrees to take charge of the gang and immediately wins the men over by finding the right tone of addressing them. When one of the men expresses doubt about a woman running the gang, she shouts at him, "You son of a bitch! You're off to a good start!"[6] Then Polly and Macheath part in a mock-sentimental scene.

Interlude. Mrs. Peachum and Jenny, a whore from Macheath's favorite brothel in Turnbridge, step in front of the curtain. Mrs. Peachum promises to pay Jenny if she will betray Mack when he shows up at the brothel. She sings "The Ballad of Sexual Submissiveness."

SCENE 5. Thursday night in the whorehouse in Turnbridge. Jacob, one of Mack's men, is reading a newspaper; the girls are washing, ironing, mending—they present an image of domesticity, "a middle-class idyll." Mack, a man of habit, appears as usual on that day despite the dangers. His favorite companion, Jenny, slips out and informs a police constable while Mack is singing "The Ballad of the Pimp." Jenny reappears and joins in the second verse, just before the constable comes in to make the arrest. Mack manages to jump out a window. But he is confronted by more police and Mrs. Peachum, who "consoles" him: "The greatest heroes in history have always tripped up over this little obstacle."[7] She announces to the girls that Mack will henceforth lodge in the Old Bailey, London's infamous prison.

SCENE 6. In the Old Bailey. Tiger Brown is hoping that his men will not catch Mack. But he is disappointed—Mack is brought in. Mack gives his old friend one deep, rebuking look. He is then locked up. A bribe of fifty guineas gets Mack free of the handcuffs. He then sings "The Ballad of Gracious Living" ("only the well-to-do can afford comfort"). Then Lucy, Tiger Brown's daughter and Mack's old lover, comes to visit him, and reproaches him about his affair with Polly. When Polly also comes in, a jealousy scene develops. The women trade insults until Mrs. Peachum drags Polly away. Mack persuades Lucy to open the cell and he escapes. Now Peachum threatens that he will cause a disruption of the impending coronation procession by sending out his beggars in force if Brown does not recapture Mack. Curtain.

Mack and Jenny step in front of the curtain. They sing the "Second Threepenny Finale: What Does a Man Live On?" which contains an often-quoted Brechtian line: "First comes the meal, then comes the moral."[8]

ACT III, SCENE 7. Wardrobe in Peachum's establishment. Peachum is preparing to disrupt the coronation by a procession of thousands of crippled and filthy beggars ("The rich of the earth create misery, but they cannot bear to see it").[9] To prevent this from happening, Tiger Brown appears to jail the beggars and their leader. Peachum protests: "I am not a criminal. ... We all obey the law. The law is solely made for the exploitation of those who do not understand it or those who, for naked need, cannot obey it. And whoever wants a share of this exploitation must strictly obey the law."[10] He then tells Brown that though his plan sounds good, it will not work—there are more beggars, thousands of them, than he could possibly throw in jail. Before giving the morning orders to his beggars to go out and disrupt the coronation, he sings "The Song of the Futility of All Human Endeavor": "Go make yourself a plan/ And be a shining light/ Then go and make a second plan/ For neither one will work./ Since for this earthly life/ Man is not bad enough./ Yet his aspirations/ Are a nice try."[11] The curtain closes and Jenny steps in front of it to end the scene with "The Song of Solomon," about great people in history and their downfall.

SCENE 8. A room in Old Bailey. (Brecht indicated in a note in the text that this scene was inserted for those actresses playing Polly who have a gift for comedy.)

Polly comes to see Lucy to find out where Mack is

hiding. The hostile relationship between the two women has not changed since their first encounter. But the first time, their tone was the tone of the gutter; now it is that of supposedly refined society. The battle between the two women for their possession (Mack) is a marvelous piece of satire on polite society.

SCENE 9. Death cell in Old Bailey, Friday morning, five o'clock. Mack has been recaptured, again betrayed by the girls of the brothel, and is to be hanged before six o'clock—so that all the people who have flocked to the Old Bailey to view the hanging can also go to see the coronation. For one thousand pounds, police constable Smith says he could find a way to let Mack escape. But neither Mack's men nor Polly are able to gather the amount in time. When Tiger Brown appears, Mack treats him coolly and settles some business with him. Then he sees his last visitors, including Peachum, who now encounters his son-in-law for the first time. As he is being led to the gallows, Macheath recognizes that the times have changed; there is no place for small criminals like him any more: "Ladies and gentlemen, you see here the vanishing representative of a vanishing class. We common bourgeois craftsmen, who work with simple jimmies on the cash boxes of small shopkeepers, are being swallowed up by large concerns backed by banks."[12] And in a mellow and forgiving mood, he sings the "Ballad in Which Mack Begs Pardon of All"—even from "the cops—the sons of bitches."

But as Mack is about to be hanged, Peachum turns to the audience and announces that the opera will end happily. In the "Third Threepenny Finale: Appearance of a Mounted Messenger," Tiger Brown appears on horseback, bringing the announcement that, because it is her coronation day, the queen has ordered that Mack be released immediately. But the opera ends with a reminder to the audience that in real life, the fate of the small man is far different.

When Gay's *Beggar's Opera* had its premiere in London's Lincoln Inn Theater on 29 January 1728, it was an immediate and overwhelming success. It ran for ninety consecutive performances and, according to a contemporary source, "it made Gay rich and Rich [the producer] gay."[13] The opera was conceived as a protest against the elaborate productions of the Italian courtly operas and those of George Frederick Handel —and against the corrupt aristocrats (including the Prime Minister, Sir Robert Walpole) who relished these operas.

For his score, the composer Johann Christoph Pepusch, a German from Hamburg, utilized popular English songs and the tradition of the comic opera. He also borrowed from Handel, thus giving the work a quality of parody.

Gay's text used popular language and everyday scenes from life in London. The main character, Macheath, was modeled after two famous London criminals: John Sheppard and Jonathan Wild. Macheath's underworld enemy, Peachum, was given traits of Walpole himself. According to Gay, the message was: "High life equals low life." "Through the whole piece you may observe such a similitude of manners in high and low life, that it is difficult to determine whether (in the fashionable vices) the fine Gentleman imitates the Gentleman of the Road, or the Gentleman of the Road the fine Gentleman."[14]

The success of the Gay/Pepusch opera severely curbed that of bombastic Italian-style baroque opera. It also encouraged further antiestablishment satires, such as Henry Fielding's *Pasquin, a Dramatic Satire on the Times* (1736) and his *Historical Register for the Year 1736*. To this, Walpole's government retaliated by introducing theater censorship. From that time on, every play had to be licensed by the Lord Chamberlain.

In 1920, Sir Nigel Playfair revived Gay's *Beggar's Opera*, and for two and a half years it delighted audiences in London's Lyric Theater.

In the early months of 1928, Elisabeth Hauptmann, one of Brecht's closest friends and collaborators in the 1920s, heard about the great success the revival of John Gay's *Beggar's Opera* had had in London. She promptly obtained a copy and translated it into German. When Brecht read her translation, he was so interested that he immediately began to adapt it, putting aside all of his other projects.

Curiously enough, there was a Handel renaissance taking place in Germany, culminating between 1925 and 1930. Several opera houses were staging Handel operas, and there were Handel festivals in various German cities. Some leftist critics linked this Handel revival to an increasingly conservative—even reactionary—political trend. It is not surprising then that Brecht set himself the task of reviving and adapting Gay's opera.

Brecht transferred the action from the 1720s to Victorian London and added a few ballads by the French highwayman-poet François Villon. Otherwise, he followed Gay's plot very closely. But his satiric attack was directed against a bourgeois society, not against the artistocracy which had been Gay's target.

The happy end serves not only as a parody of the *deus ex machina* of Greek tragedy (the gods who intervened to solve all problems), but also of the "unreal" and sentimental bourgeois plays that always ended happily. The character of Macheath is also a parody of the petit bourgeois: he has his regular habits (every Thursday night, without fail, he visits the brothel); he insists on all the trappings of a bourgeois wedding (he does not care how they are acquired); he has a bourgeois concept of art and bourgeois manners (he is appalled when Jacob eats fish with a knife); and, for him, marriage is mainly a means of protecting and increasing his business.

Brecht noted in 1935 that he wanted a distinct break between the musical numbers and the spoken parts. To achieve this, the orchestra is placed visibly on the stage. For each song, the actors change their positions on stage, the light turns to a golden color, a musical symbol is lowered from the loft, and the title of the song is projected onto a screen. To prevent the audience from becoming too involved in the progress of the action, and to direct its attention instead to the way in which the content is presented and the lessons contained, a summary of each scene is projected onto a screen before the scene begins.

In Gay's version, the capture of Macheath was a high dramatic point of the opera. Brecht, however, avoided this type of dramatic structure, which builds up to a climax, by having Macheath arrested twice.

The first performance of *The Threepenny Opera* took place on 31 August 1928 in the Theater am Schiffbauerdamm in Berlin, today the permanent home of the Berliner Ensemble in East Berlin (director: Erich Engel; sets: Caspar Neher; Macheath: Harald Paulsen; Peachum: Erich Ponto; Polly: Roma Bahn; Jenny: Lotte Lenya, Weill's wife).

As Lotte Lenya, now living in the United States, recollects, the preliminaries to the opening performance were far from pleasant.[15] Brecht and Weill moved from busy Berlin to a small, quiet town on the French Riviera and frantically worked on the opera in order to meet the deadline. Two important actresses, Carola Neher (Polly) and Helene Weigel (Mrs. Peachum), had to drop out at the last minute, and the final dress rehearsal was an absolute disaster.

The Threepenny Opera, the famous 1928 production in Berlin. Macheath: Harald Paulsen.

The critics expected a dreadful flop. But by the time the premiere reached the second scene, it was quite clear that the opera was going to be a tremendous success. Apparently not even the Marxist social message (the rich get richer by exploiting the poor; the bourgeoisie is a class of robbers and thieves) stood in the way. To C. Hooper Trask of *The New York Times,* the spectre of Marx loomed "somewhere on the horizon" but remained sufficiently nebulous to allow him "three hours of joy undiluted."[16]

In 1930, the German Nero film company made a film version of *The Threepenny Opera,* with G. W. Pabst directing and Rudolf Forster (German version) and A. Prejan (French version) as Macheath. This film version is still frequently shown today. Originally, Brecht and Weill collaborated with the company on the film. But soon serious differences arose between them and the film company. Brecht insisted on more emphasis on the social criticism.

The result was the famous "Threepenny Trial." Suing the film company, Brecht lost the suit; he called the film "a miserable piece of patchwork" and "a shameless disfiguration of *The Threepenny Opera*."[17] There are many people, however, who question Brecht's judgment here. Now considered a film classic, it continues to be played. Its social message, too, is at least as pungent as that of Brecht's play.

The Threepenny Opera first reached the United States on 13 April 1933. It opened in New York City's Empire Theater as "a musical show," adapted into English by Gifford Cochran and Jerrold Krimsky (director: Francesco von Mendelssohn; Peachum: Rex Weber; Polly: Steffi Duna; Jenny: Marjorie Dille; Macheath: Robert Chisholm; music: Kurt Weill).

Although the reviewer for *The New York Times* found *The Threepenny Opera* "on the whole worth seeing,"[18] Percy Hammond of the *New York Herald Tribune* wrote that the opera was "geared only for the pleasure of those who are fond of senility in its most abandoned form."[19] Since at that time Brecht was unknown in America, both critics saw the show mainly as a dubious attempt to revive John Gay's *Beggar's Opera*—"the *Of Thee I Sing* of 1728," as *The New York Times* critic noted. And even with Weill's "stylish" and "splendid" music, the work seemed quite old-fashioned in juxtaposition to the musicals by George Gershwin and Richard Rodgers, which had begun to dominate Broadway in the late 1920s. (*Of Thee I Sing*, with book by George S. Kaufman and Morrie Ryskind, lyrics by Ira Gershwin, and music by

The Threepenny Opera, 1933. Set: designs by Gaston Baty.
FRENCH CULTURAL SERVICES

George Gershwin, had won the Pulitzer prize in 1932.)

For the next twenty years, the play was performed only on college campuses here and there, mostly in the English version by Desmond Vesey and Eric Bentley. But, in March 1954, *The Threepenny Opera* once again returned to a commercial theater in New York City in an English adaptation by Marc Blitzstein, with Kurt Weill's music. It opened on 10 March 1954 in the off-Broadway Theatre de Lys in Greenwich Village (director: Carmen Capalbo; sets: William Pitkin; Macheath: Scott Merrill; Peachum: Leon Lishner; Polly: Jo Sullivan; Jenny: Lotte Lenya, the same part she had played in Berlin twenty-six years earlier).

The first reactions were mixed. Jay S. Harrison of the *New York Herald Tribune* praised Weill's music and Lenya's performance, but he was critical of Blitzstein's adaptation, which, in his opinion, "failed to maintain, for a host of reasons, the bittersweet flavors and alternating comic and dramatic stances assured by the work." He also felt that Blitzstein should have pared away its "dull and interfering political asides."[20]

The reviewer for *The New York Times* saw it differently: "To Mr. Blitzstein this morning this department extends heartfelt thanks." He felt that the text retained "the bite, the savage satire, the overwhelming bitterness underlying this work." In his opinion, Lotte Lenya's performance was beyond criticism, and, in general, the young company did rather well despite some minor flaws ("there is evidence of inexperience").[21]

Yet despite this initial mixed reaction, *The Threepenny Opera* became one of the most successful productions ever staged in New York City; it ran for six years, from 1954 to 1961, and reached a total of 2,611 performances. (In comparison, the number of performances of some other long runs in New York City are: *My Fair Lady,* 2,715; *Oklahoma,* 2,248; and *South Pacific,* 1,830.)

When *The Threepenny Opera* opened at the Theatre de Lys for its second season on 21 September 1955, Lewis B. Funke of *The New York Times* was even more enthusiastic, calling Marc Blitzstein's adaptation "a splendid working book and a clear and meaningful set of lyrics that convey the bite, the irony and the sadness that pervade the story." Again he expressed his "vote of thanks" and called the opera "one of the modern gems in the musical theater." In the cast there now was "even greater cohesion and edge in the current rendition than there was in the first production."[22] Brooks Atkinson, also of *The New York Times,* agreed: the opera was a "brilliant work" and the production "superb."

Walter Kerr of the *New York Herald Tribune* thought Weill's music "the most wonderfully insulting music I have ever come across," and Marc Blitzstein's adaptation "altogether adequate." Kerr found "enough able action," particularly by Lotte Lenya, who "[made] a visit worth while on her own." But he wished that the dialogue passages had been equally successful: "There is a tendency to bear down hard, expose the joke until it is too naked for quick laughter." But overall *The Threepenny Opera,* for him, remained "a fascinating musical experiment."[23]

In 1956, one of the most significant productions of *The Threepenny Opera* was presented by Giorgio Strehler, one of Italy's leading directors, in his Piccolo Teatro in Milan, with Tino Buazzelli as Macheath. It was Strehler's first Brecht production, and his extensive preparations included a visit to East Berlin to discuss the production with Brecht himself.

Strehler was particularly concerned with presenting *The Threepenny Opera* as epic theater. He wanted the play to retain its shock effect and not deteriorate into a nice, but harmless, production. Upon Strehler's question about how best to train actors in the epic style of acting, Brecht advised him to have the actors practice their lines as though they were being reported —in third person singular, frequently inserting "he said." He also suggested that the actors emphasize the play's comic aspects. When Strehler asked Brecht about possibilities for a different setting for the opera, Brecht suggested the Italian quarter of New York City around 1900. Apparently Strehler took Brecht's suggestion. The setting for his *Threepenny Opera* was the United States of the time of the Keystone Cops (the insanely incompetent police force in Mack Sennett's silent film comedies from 1914 to the early 1920s).

In March 1965, in a dramatic change from the Theatre de Lys production, the New York City Opera, usually known for its productions of classic operas and ballets, presented *The Threepenny Opera* at the City Center in the original German version (director: Adolf Rott; sets: Wolfgang Roth; Macheath: Kurt Kasznar; Polly: Anita Hoefer; Jenny: Martha Schlamme; Peachum: Stefan Schnabel, son of the famous pianist Arthur Schnabel). The New York City Opera wisely decided to have "singing actors," and the acting was given priority over singing (as Brecht had intended).

According to Harold C. Schonberg of *The New York Times,* the German-speaking actors who came "from Broadway and points East" were "superb," and made the event "exciting and stimulating."[24] Most of the audience could not understand German, but apparently that posed no problem. By that time, most people were familiar with *The Threepenny Opera.*

In October 1972, the Workshop of the Players Art (WPA) in New York City staged *The Threepenny Opera* with a mixed cast—more than half of the actors, including David Downing as Macheath, were black (director: Roger Furman; Peachum: Milton Grier; Polly: June Berman; Jenny: Geraldine Fitzgerald).

According to Mel Gussow of *The New York Times*, this added a new dimension to the opera: "Macheath . . . becomes the black man forced by a corrupt, hypocritical society into an alternate lifestyle—finding economic and social opportunity in the underworld." But as Gussow noted, the performances were unfortunately not good enough (with the exception of Geraldine Fitzgerald's excellent Jenny) to underscore this provocative idea.[25]

In May 1976 Joseph Papp's New York Shakespeare Festival concluded its season with *The Threepenny Opera* (new translation: Ralph Manheim and John Willett; director: Richard Foreman; sets: Douglas W. Schmidt; Macheath: Raul Julia; Jenny: Ellen Greene; Peachum: C. K. Alexander; Polly: Caroline Kava). According to the critics, the production was a resounding success. Brendan Gill of *The New Yorker* called it "sensationally attractive."[26] Douglas Watts of the *New York Daily News* found it "fantastic and sensationally theatrical."[27]

A good deal of the credit went to the translators Manheim and Willett. They created a version more Brechtian in tone than Blitzstein's smooth lyrics. Thus Brecht's message came through more clearly. This was acknowledged by T. E. Kalem, the reviewer for *Time* magazine: "This *Threepenny Opera* honors the Brecht who wrote with a hammer and swung a sickle."[28]

In 1960, *The Threepenny Opera* returned to the Theater am Schiffbauerdamm in East Berlin—where it had had its world premiere in 1928. The production was debated at great length by the Berliner Ensemble for more than three years. The pros and cons of the project were discussed; rehearsals were scheduled and canceled. Finally, in April 1960, the opera opened, directed by Erich Engel, the director of the original

The Threepenny Opera, Berliner Ensemble, 1960. Director: Erich Engel; sets: Karl von Appen. Scene shown: "The Arrival of the Mounted Messenger."

PERCY PAUKSCHTA; BERLINER ENSEMBLE

1928 production (sets: Karl von Appen; Macheath: Wolf Kaiser; Polly: Regine Lutz; Peachum: Martin Flörchinger). As the eminent West Berlin critic Friedrich Luft observed, it was a technically perfect replica of the 1928 version—too perfect, in fact, so that "artificiality slowly came through." The production was marred by "the curse of perfection." Melancholic nostalgia replaced cynic vitality. *"The Threepenny Opera,"* said Luft, "is a beautiful work but a thing of the past." The attempts at relating the work to modern times (such as to the alleged neofascism in West Germany) were more embarrassing than effective, according to Luft.[29]

In 1965, the Berliner Ensemble presented the German original of *The Threepenny Opera* in London's

Old Vic Theater (director: Erich Engel; Macheath: Wolf Kaiser; Peachum: Peter Kalisch; Polly: Christine Gloger). In the opinion of *The Times'* drama critic, the opera's social message came through rather clearly; it knocked "some of the gloss off the legend and [re-established] the work's priorities." Yet at the same time, the reviewer found the acting of the Ensemble "the disappointment of the production—unexpected from this company."[30]

But then *The Threepenny Opera* had always had a more difficult time in London than in New York, Berlin, or Paris. In London, the memory of Nigel Playfair's brilliant revival of Gay's *Beggar's Opera* was still alive, and Brecht and Weill's work was constantly measured against Gay. When Sam Wanamaker presented *The Threepenny Opera* (in Marc Blitzstein's translation, with Weill's music) in London's Royal Court Theater in February 1956, the critics' reaction was decidedly mixed. Cecil Wilson, critic for *The Daily Mail,* for example, called it a "crude and crazy satire on the *Beggar's Opera.*" He did, however, admit: "I spent the evening veering between irritation and fascination, but the impudence, the absurdity, and the sheer vitality of it all won me over in the end."[31] Despite the critics' contradictory reactions, the production was a popular success.

G. Tana, of the East German theater journal *Theater der Zeit,* however, criticized Blitzstein's translation as "more Blitzstein than Brecht." In his opinion, it pulled the teeth from Brecht's biting satire and reduced Wanamaker's—admittedly lively—production to a burlesque.[32]

Despite the feeling of many critics and Brecht scholars that the work has lost its original bite and meaning, *The Threepenny Opera* continues to be an audience favorite. It was one of the greatest hits of the 1973–74 season on German stages, where it was seen by more than 200,000 spectators (in 1972–73, there were 155,000; in 1971–72, 104,000, according to Henning Rischbieter of *Theater heute*, May 1975).

Many theater directors seem to agree that the work cannot be performed as it was in 1928. In the 1974–75 season, for example, theaters in Cologne and Düsseldorf, West Germany, experimented with two different approaches. In Cologne, *The Threepenny Opera* was staged as a parody of the music revues of days gone by; the acting was greatly exaggerated. According to Rischbieter, this experiment failed, not because of the idea, but because of the quality of the acting. In Düsseldorf, however, another experiment was a great success. The opera was set in contemporary times, with Macheath in a pin-striped suit and Peachum as an elegant businessman. Instead of a brothel, Macheath visited a massage parlor. To increase social criticism, passages from Brecht's *Threepenny Novel* were incorporated and the ending was changed. Just as Macheath is about to go to the gallows, Tiger Brown informs Peachum that Macheath has some highly valuable stocks, whereupon Peachum immediately demands Macheath's release. He welcomes him as his son-in-law, and they form the Peachum-Brown-Macheath Company. Instead of being saved by a "mounted messenger," Macheath is saved by a business deal.

Back in 1729, the great success of *The Beggar's Opera* inspired Gay and Pepusch to write a sequel entitled *Polly*. Although the critics felt that this sequel was not as good as *The Beggar's Opera*, it turned out to be a popular book because Walpole's government forbade the production of the play.

In 1929, Brecht and Weill, too, wanted to capitalize on the success they had had with *The Threepenny Opera*, and they wrote a sequel—the *Singspiel* entitled *Happy End*. (The German *Singspiel* developed

The Threepenny Opera, The Cleveland Playhouse, 1970.
Director: John Going. Paula Duesing, David Frazier
(Mack), Noreen Abookire, Susan Burkhalter.
REBMAN; THE CLEVELAND PLAYHOUSE

in the eighteenth century as an offshoot of English
ballad opera. In contrast to serious opera, it consists
mainly of spoken dialogue, instead of lengthy recita-
tives, and lighter melodies.) Set in Chicago, the play
is a melodrama. To it a moral lesson was tacked on.
Brecht claimed that he had adapted the play from a
short story, "Under the Mistletoe," by Dorothy Lane,
which had appeared in an obscure magazine published
in the American Midwest. Brecht's claim, however, was
only a gimmick; "Dorothy Lane" was a pen name for
Brecht's collaborator Elisabeth Hauptmann.

Brecht's *Happy End* is not nearly so good as the
original work. Brecht later ascribed most of the play,

Happy End, The Cleveland Playhouse, 1974. Director: Dennis Rosa. *Above,* Charlotte Hare, C. C. Carter, David Williams. *Below,* Dan Desmond, Norm Berman, John Buck, Jr., Richard Halverson, Robert Snook.

J. R. BURROUGHS, THE CLEVELAND PLAYHOUSE

with the exception of the songs, to Elisabeth Hauptmann.

When *Happy End* was first performed on 31 August 1929 in the Theater am Schiffbauerdamm in Berlin, the Berlin critics condemned the play as a failure. But C. Hooper Trask, Berlin critic for *The New York Times,* found it "a very pleasing way to spend an evening . . . it would make an interesting production on Broadway."[33]

Happy End has not yet come to Broadway, but the Yale Repertory Theater in New Haven, Connecticut, included it in its 1971–72 season. Walter Kerr (now of *The New York Times*) wrote: "We are much in Yale's debt for rescuing and attractively mounting this curiously neglected work." Admitting that *Happy End's* mockery was less pungent than that in *The Threepenny Opera,* he enjoyed it anyway—especially the "mesmerizing rhythms" of such songs as "The Bilbao Song" or "Surabaya Johnny"—"What is so delightful about *Happy End* is its youthful, brittle, doubting, tuneful effortlessness."[34]

Productions of *Happy End* in the United States are not such a rarity as might be assumed. In 1974, for example, it was also produced by The Cleveland Playhouse (director: Dennis Rosa).

When Brecht wrote his *Threepenny Opera,* he wanted to hold a mirror up to bourgeois/capitalist society to convince the successful that they are all thieves—that bankers and shareholders, for example, are nothing but old-fashioned thieves in modern disguise: "What is a skeleton key to a bank share? What is the robbery of a bank to the founding of a bank?"[35] The famous ballad of Macheath and the shark actually draws upon a passage from Karl Marx's *Das Kapital;* it is indeed ironic that this song was to become a favorite in the capitalist United States!

The success of *The Threepenny Opera* in the capi-

talist world was not exactly in line with Brecht's intentions, as he had already stated in connection with
his play *Drums in the Night:* "I had the vague feeling that those people who wished most to congratulate
me were exactly those whom I wanted to hit on the
head, perhaps not with this play but in general."[36]

Today *The Threepenny Opera* has become a classic.
It has lost much of the sting with which it shocked
the Berlin of 1928. Because of Weill's catchy music
and the romantic Robin Hood flavor of the theme,
Brecht's original social message is largely lost on contemporary audiences. In order to become effective
again, the opera has to undergo another adaptation.

The Rise and Fall
of the City of Mahagonny (1928–29)

The year: 1927. The place: Chamber Music
Festival in Baden-Baden, Germany. A serious-minded,
cultured audience listened to austerely formal, for the
most part atonal, chamber music. Then before their
disbelieving eyes, stage hands erected a boxing ring
from which a group of actors and singers (including
Lotte Lenya) bombarded them with a series of brazen
songs. This *Songspiel Mahagonny*—now better known
as *The Little Mahagonny*—evoked a tumultuous response, but it was successful. The texts for the songs
were mostly from the *Manual of Piety,* the most famous collection of Brecht poems, published in 1927.
The Little Mahagonny premiered along with Paul
Hindemith's *Back and Forth,* Ernst Toch's *Princess*

German title: *Aufstieg und Fall der Stadt Mahagonny.*

upon the Pea, and Darius Milhaud's opera *The Ab-
duction of Europa. The Little Mahagonny* is the
product of the first cooperation between the composer
Kurt Weill and Brecht.

The Little Mahagonny formed the basis for Brecht
and Weill's full-length opera *The Rise and Fall of the
City of Mahagonny,* which they set out to write immediately after their return from Baden-Baden to Berlin. They interrupted this effort only to finish work on
The Threepenny Opera. Unlike *The Threepenny
Opera,* which was a ballad opera, *Mahagonny* was
written in the vein of a traditional full-length opera
intended for performance in opera houses, although
Weill's music required an orchestra of only about
thirty musicians.

The setting is America—albeit a mythical America
—as in many other Brecht plays. Mahagonny, "the
city of nets,"[37] is a city governed by money. It reflects
a European's view of America during the time of the
gold rush. But Mahagonny really stands for the Berlin
of the roaring twenties, "the seething cauldron of lust,
greed, and corruption that for him [Brecht] summed
up the twentieth-century world: dreadful, doomed—
and magnificent."[38]

The opera begins with the founding of the city of
Mahagonny. A battered old truck breaks down in a
desert area somewhere on the west coast. Three shady
characters—Leocadia Begbick (known to us already
from *A Man Is a Man*), Trinity Moses, and Willy the
Bookkeeper, all of them sought by the police—emerge
from the truck and decide to stay there and found a
city. Originally they had planned to go further north
along the coast in search of gold. Now they think of
an easier way: "You'll get the gold much easier from
men than from rivers."[39] They plan to attract the men
with gin, whiskey, and women.

The city springs up in only a few weeks' time and

the first "sharks" (swindlers) settle down. Jenny (who shares some traits with Jenny in *The Threepenny Opera*) and six other prostitutes appear, sit down on their suitcases and sing the "Alabama Song" ("Oh, show us the way to the next whiskey-bar").

Word about the new city of Mahagonny spreads to the big cities and lures away the men: "In your cities there is too much noise and nothing but unrest and discord. . . . Come to Mahagonny."[40]

Among the people who flock to Mahagonny are four lumberjacks from Alaska: Paul Ackermann (called Jim Mahoney or Jim Mallory in some versions), the central character ("it is his story we want to tell you")[41]; and his companions Jacob Schmidt, Heinrich Merg, and Joseph Lettner ("Alaskawolf-Joe"). The four men are met by Leocadia Begbick who asks what they would like. First she provides them with girls—when Jacob finds Jenny too expensive, Paul takes her.

But trouble looms over Mahagonny—"all great enterprises have their crises."[42] The crime rate rises and the prices increase; people begin to leave again. Paul, too, wants to leave, but his friends manage to keep him there.

In front of the Hotel of the Rich Men, the men of Mahagonny are drinking and daydreaming. They are surrounded by signs reading: "No singing of obscene songs!" "Don't make any noise!" "Take care of the chairs!"[43] Paul does not like this state of affairs; he feels he deserves something better after seven years of hard work in Alaska. He protests the sterile atmosphere of Mahagonny: "There's nothing going on here."[44]

But change is on the way—a hurricane is moving toward Mahagonny: "A terrible event. The city of pleasures will be destroyed."[45] Everyone fears the impending doom, except Paul. He welcomes the violent

change that is coming. Begbick warns: "Bad is the
hurricane/ Worse is the typhoon/ But worst of all is
man."[46]

But Paul calls upon the people of Mahagonny "to
do everything tonight that is forbidden."[47] And he
gives out the new rule: "For as you make your bed
so you will lie./ Nobody is there to cover you,/ And
if someone is doing the kicking it will be me,/ And if
someone is being kicked it will be you."[48]

The whole scene is accentuated by the recurring
chorus of the men of Mahagonny: "Keep yourselves
upright: Be not afraid."[49]

Tension in the city rises: a map projected in the
background shows an arrow slowly approaching Mahagonny—the path of the hurricane. Loudspeakers
describe its course and the devastation it is causing.
Suddenly the arrow stops moving just outside Mahagonny, then moves around the city: "O miraculous
rescue!"[50] Mahagonny is spared, unlike its biblical
counterparts Sodom and Gomorrah. "From then on
the motto of the people of Mahagonny was 'you may
do it,' as they learned on the night of horror."[51]

Business begins to flourish again. A chorus of men
from Mahagonny announces the new pleasures of
Mahagonny:

> First—and don't forget—comes greedy eating,
> Second is a love affair,
> Thirdly, don't forget the boxing,
> And fourthly heavy drinking as prescribed.
> But most of all do observe,
> That here you may do anything.[52]

These pleasures are illustrated in this and the following scenes. First is "Gluttony." Jacob is sitting before an enlarged picture of himself. He gorges himself
until he drops dead.

Next is "Love." The men of Mahagonny line up in

front of a simple room. Begbick directs the pleasure traffic, admonishing each man not to take too much time. Paul and Jenny meet for a fleeting moment. And it is here, with Paul and Jenny in this debased and commercialized love business, that one of the tenderest love scenes in Brecht's work develops. They express their feelings through the image of flying cranes in one of the most beautiful love poems of modern literature: "Behold those cranes sweeping wide...."[53]

Then comes "Fighting." A boxing ring is erected on the stage, and a brass band provides the music. Alaskawolf-Joe will take on Trinity Moses—although Willy the Bookkeeper says this is "pure murder." The fight ends literally as Willy predicted: Joe is killed.

Next is "Drinking." Paul offers to stand everyone for a drink. But when Begbick demands the money, he confesses to Jenny that he has none left. He wants to return to Alaska because he no longer likes Mahagonny. In a very effective scene, a billiard table is converted into a "ship." Paul, Heinrich, and Jenny climb on it and pretend they are on the high seas sailing for Alaska. But Paul is torn out of his daydreams when Begbick emphatically demands the money. When Paul cannot pay, his friends all desert him. He is arrested. While he is being tied up, Jenny sings a song in which she says that she will be nobody's sucker, for "if someone is doing the kicking, it will be me, and if someone is being kicked, it will be you."[54] Paul tries to prepare himself for what is ahead, but he dreads the coming day, the day of his trial.

At the trial, the "audience" is reading newspapers, chewing, and smoking. Begbick is the judge; Willy the Bookkeeper, the defense counsel; and Trinity Moses, the prosecutor (who also sells tickets for five dollars to those who want to watch two "excellent trials"). In the first trial, a man is accused of premeditated murder—but since no "injured party" steps forward, and the man's bribe is high enough, he is acquitted.

The second trial is that of Paul Ackermann. He has no money for a bribe, and his "friend" Heinrich is unwilling to lend him any. ("Paul, I feel close to you as a person, but money is a different matter.")[55] Paul is found guilty and sentenced on five counts: two days in jail for second-degree murder, because he did not prevent his friend Joe from being killed in the boxing ring; the suspension of civil rights for two years, for "disturbing peace and harmony"; four years for seducing the prostitute Jenny, who bears witness against him; ten years in a maximum-security prison for singing forbidden songs during a hurricane; and the death penalty "because of the lack of money, which is the greatest crime on earth."[56]

Then follows "Paul Ackermann's execution and death." A total view of Mahagonny is projected against the background. People are standing around in groups; the electric chair is being readied. Paul reminds everyone that there is a God to whom they are responsible for their deeds. Thereupon Begbick orders him to sit down (on the electric chair) in order to watch a play about God in Mahagonny. When God condemns the men of Mahagonny to Hell, they reply that it makes no difference—they have always lived in Hell. Through this play-within-a-play Paul recognizes his error. When he arrived in Mahagonny, his fate was already sealed. The pound of flesh he wanted to carve out for himself was rotten. He came to Mahagonny to make his fortune. Now he finds that the pleasures and the freedom he bought with money were no real pleasures and no real freedom.

But the city of Mahagonny, too, is being destroyed: There is "increasing confusion, inflation, and hostility of everyone against everyone."[57] Demonstrations move across the stage before enlarged photographs of the burning Mahagonny. The demonstrators carry placards with inscriptions such as "For the chaotic conditions of our cities," "For the continuation of the golden age," "For private property," "For law and order."[58] While marching, the demonstrators repeat key verses of the opera that stress that the law of the jungle prevails in Mahagonny. This now is the real Mahagonny, whose law courts are no worse than other law courts, as Brecht said. It is a Brechtian vision of a capitalist society. The hurricane—besides serving as an excellent dramatic device—reveals the true nature of Mahagonny. It is a city dominated by greed and exploitation. The demonstrators represent the advocates of capitalism.

In *Mahagonny*, Brecht and Weill included elements from cabaret, vaudeville, and the sports arena. The opera, a combination of irony, parody, popularity and genuine sentiment, is enjoyable in a traditional sense.

For Brecht, however, *Mahagonny* also had a revolutionary function. He wanted to attack the society that has a need for that kind of opera. In *Mahagonny*, "the text must not be sentimental or moral, but must demonstrate sentimentality and morality."[59] Brecht claimed that the average operagoer checked his brains, along with his coat, in the cloakroom before he took his seat. It was Brecht's intent to shock the operagoer out of his complacency and to demand that he think while viewing the opera.

Weill maintained that the new opera coming into existence in the 1920s had epic character. And it was in conjunction with the opera *Mahagonny* that Brecht laid down the first principles of epic theater and epic opera versus dramatic theater and dramatic opera. In regard to opera, Brecht's main thrust was against a Wagnerian type of *Gesamtkunstwerk*, a total work of art in which all elements of scenery, text, and music are integrated and support each other. Brecht insisted on strict separation of these elements.

As the German music critic H. H. Stuckenschmidt points out in his comments accompanying the Columbia recording of *Mahagonny*:

> Weill's orchestra . . . has the at once strident and nostalgic sound of the jazz bands of 1918. Solos by the wind instruments are given preference; cantilenas by the strings are relatively rare; banjo, bass guitar, piano harmonica and accordion, zither, saxophone, and many types of percussion instruments color and flavor the tutti passages, but also are singled out for solos. In this, too, pervades the sophistication of conscious primitivism.

Parody and quotation are also part of the musical score. For example, the refrain "beautiful green moon of Alabama" in the song "Let's Go to Mahagonny" (in the fourth scene) uses chords from the bridesmaids' refrain in Carl Maria von Weber's romantic opera *Der Freischütz*. The ninth scene, which takes place in the Hotel of the Rich Men, begins with a piano solo from "The Maiden's Prayer," which was a very popular song around 1900.

On 9 March 1930, *The Rise and Fall of the City of Mahagonny* premiered in the Neues Theater Leipzig. The evening ended in one of the biggest theater scandals the German theater had ever seen. Fist fights broke out and demonstrators stormed the stage. It ended with the police clearing the theater. Here is an excerpt from the critic Alfred Polgar's personal experience on the opening night:

> And soon the epic form of the theater spread from the stage to the auditorium. . . . The woman on my left thought she was having a heart seizure and wanted to leave. But when it was pointed out

to her that this was a historic moment, she stayed.... A man behind me on the right was talking to himself: "I'll only wait until that fellow Brecht shows up!" He licked his lips to keep them prepared—readiness is all. War cries echoed through the auditorium. In places, hand-to-hand fighting broke out. Hissing, applause, which sounded grimly like faces being slapped.... And in the end: *the levée en masse* of the malcontents, accompanied by thunderous applause from the rest of the audience. There were impressive episodes: a worthy gentleman with the face of a boiled lobster had taken out his bunch of keys and waged a heroic struggle against the epic theater ... he had pressed one of the keys against his lower lip and caused streams of air of an extremely high rate of vibration to pass over the hole at its end. The noise this instrument produced had an implacable quality. It cut right through one's stomach. Nor did his spouse desert him in his hour of trial; a large, round woman, she was the ride of the Valkyries all over, with a bun and a blue dress with yellow flounces. This lady had put two fat fingers into her mouth; she closed her eyes, blew up her cheeks, and produced a whistle louder than the key.[60]

Rather than close down the performance altogether, the city council of Leipzig ordered that a large police contingent line the walls of the theater each night and that the house lights be kept on. No further incident occurred.

The unconventional nature of the Brecht-Weill opera brought unconventional reactions, and people gave unbridled expression to their feelings and opinions. The emotions ran from extreme delight with this kind of opera—its form, its message, or both—to absolute disgust with every aspect of it. But in spite of the varying emotions it aroused, the work was a success. People felt repelled and attracted at the same time. Like no other work, *Mahagonny* reflected the spirit of the times, the dichotomy between order and anarchy.

The tumultuous reception was also partly due to the worsening political situation at that time (1930). The faltering Weimar Republic was besieged by an economic crisis of major proportions and was under attack from both the right (the Nazis) and the left (the communists). The Nazis used every opportunity to cause trouble for anyone who did not fall into line behind them, and both Brecht and Weill had been on their blacklist for some time. Performances of their works were frequently disturbed by Nazi sympathizers. This was also the case in Leipzig.

On 21 December 1931, Ernst Josef Aufricht, who had produced *The Threepenny Opera* three years earlier, staged *Mahagonny* in the Berlin Kurfürstendamm Theater (Paul: Harald Paulsen; Begbick: Trude Hesterberg; Jenny: Lotte Lenya). It was a superb production; its reception could easily have surpassed that of *The Threepenny Opera,* had the political climate been different. As in Leipzig, the opera was received with "a mixture of deepest horror and unbound admiration"[61]—but without incident.

It was not until January 1963—after the Third Reich had risen and fallen—that *The Rise and Fall of the City of Mahagonny* was made available to an English-speaking audience. It was presented by the Sadler's Wells Opera in London (translation: David Drew and Michael Geliot; director: Michael Geliot; sets: Ralph Koltai; Jenny: April Cantelo; Begbick: Patricia Bartlett; Jimmy Mahoney: Ronald Dowd; conductor: Colin Davis).

The sets consisted of a wide cinema screen for projections, and a three-ton truck in which Begbick arrived on the stage. The truck was dismantled and rather ingeniously transformed to suggest all the diverse scenes of the opera. The reviewer of *The Times* thought it "the most ingenious production that Sadler's Wells have given us for many years." But he also found some flaws in the staging of this "most impressive and most provocative" work, resulting from the fact that the performers were "acting singers" rather than "singing actors": "The characterization lacks ... hard emotionless quality ... Miss April Cantelo, in particular, turned Jenny into a nice English miss."[62]

It was not until forty years after its world premiere that *Mahagonny* finally reached the United States. The American premiere opened on 28 April 1970 in the Anderson Theater, an off-Broadway theater in New York City (adaptation: Arnold Weinstein; director: Carmen Capalbo; sets: Robin Wagner; Begbick: Estelle Parsons; Jenny: Barbara Harris; Jimmy Mallory: Frank Poretta).

The producers had chosen a huge theater, mobilized vast personnel resources, and invested $400,000. But the opera closed on 3 May, after only eight performances and sixty-nine previews—despite Clive Barnes's good review in *The New York Times*. It was advertised as "a musical in three acts and twenty-two scenes."

Barnes was overwhelmed by "the altogether marvelous" production and the work: "It is a great and lovely work, one of the masterpieces of the 20th-century lyric theater, with ironically sentimental music that with all its sweetness and bitterness will stay with you as long as you live." What impressed him most was the music: "The music is fantastic. Erotic, melodic, childlike and yet sinister, it has a musical innocence, and charms as potent and as poignant as poisoned chocolates. In style it stretches back to Mahler, and forward to the Beatles, the Kinks and the Who. It is beautiful, and lingers, lingers, lingers."

Clive Barnes doubted (correctly) whether *Mahagonny* could be called a musical at all. He continued: "But if it is a musical, it leaves every other musical in town looking sick, green, and trivial." But he also had some criticism. He found "the satiric irony of Brecht's play at times too stark." He felt that "the production could with advantage have had more stylistic imprint—I never felt the Germany of the twenties."[63]

Barnes's colleague at *The New York Times,* the music critic Albert Goldman, was sharply critical about the production. In fact, he was shocked to see "a revered masterpiece being butchered by a bad production." He found the production "stripped of its rich and allusive orchestral texture and reduced to amateur vocalizing," and wondered, "what possessed Mr. Capalbo to cast this demanding work as one would an Off Broadway musical?"[64]

In his assessment of this performance, the critic and scholar Lee Baxandall also called the production a failure, which he chiefly attributed to a lack of a native American idiom.[65]

In December 1972 the Opera Society of Washington presented Brecht/Weill's opera *The Rise and Fall of the City of Mahagonny* at the Kennedy Center in Washington, D.C. (conductor: Günther Schuller; staging: Ian Strasfogel; Jim Mahoney: William Neill). After viewing this production, Clive Barnes wrote: "There can be no dispute that their [Brecht/Weill's] major collaboration, and indeed Weill's masterpiece, is *The Rise and Fall of the City of Mahagonny.*" The Washington production was, in Barnes' opinion, "far from perfect . . . [it] lacked something in vitality . . . but because of its orchestral resources it is a marked improvement on the Off Broadway version we had in New York a couple of seasons ago."

One problem, according to Barnes, was the translation by Arnold Weinstein and Lys Symonette, revised in 1960 by David Drew. As Barnes noted: "Something more is needed if this Brecht/Weill parable of human greed and indifference is to make its way on the English-speaking stage."[66]

In February 1974, the Yale Repertory Theater "rescued *Mahagonny* for the theater" after the New York premiere "provoked critical distemper and seemed, finally, to confine the work to the category of obdurate masterpieces."[67] *The Rise and Fall of the City of Mahagonny* was presented in a translation by Michael Feingold (director: Alvin Epstein; sets: Tony Straiges; Jim: Gilbert Price; Jenny: Stephanie Cotsirilos; Begbick: Grace Keagy). The cast consisted of a shrewd combination of singers who could act and actors who could sing.[68] The orchestra of Yale's School of Music was splendidly conducted by Otto-Werner Mueller; according to Mel Gussow, it was the key to the successful production: "There is such an ease and professionalism about this *Mahagonny* that one can imagine its being transferred, intact, to Broadway."[69]

Although Novick found the action in *Mahagonny* "less lively and fast moving than in *Threepenny*," and the satire "sometimes overobvious and banal," its message haunted him: "*Mahagonny* has a kind of heavy-footed, cumulative power; what moves us is not the action or the characters, but the anger and despair in the work as a whole." He was glad to have seen Shakespeare's *The Tempest* the night before "as a sort of charm against the nihilism of Brecht and Weill, a reminder that the human imagination could at least conceive a beneficent universe."[70]

The Little Mahagonny, too, finally found its way to the Anglo-American stage. In April 1967 *The Little Mahagonny*, or the *Mahagonny Songspiel*, as the English version is called, had its English premiere (producers: Geliot-Drew) at the Brighton Festival, where it was a success.[71] In July 1968, it provided "a pungent half-hour or so of entertainment" at the City of London Festival, produced by John Cox and David Drew.[72]

In 1973 the Center Theater Group of Los Angeles presented a Brecht evening in the Los Angeles Music Center. Under the title "Brecht: Sacred and Profane," they performed *The Little Mahagonny* together with *The Measures Taken*. To the tune of a ten-piece jazz band, Begbick and her clan rolled onto the stage in a flashy Detroit jalopy of the 1950s; the whole atmosphere was reminiscent of the Las Vegas of the fifties. The effect of director Edward Payson Call's production was similar to what Brecht had envisioned in 1927.[73]

The Rise and Fall of the City of Mahagonny is a peculiar mixture of Brecht's newly found philosophy of Marxism and his old carefree anarchic beliefs. The city of Mahagonny symbolizes rampant capitalism with its worship of money. As Brecht sees it, money can buy everything and the greatest sin is to be without it. But one can also sense Brecht's appreciative recognition of the unrestrained "pleasures" it has to offer. It is perhaps this ambiguous quality, together with Weill's music, that is responsible for the special fascination of this work.

Saint Joan of the Stockyards
(1929–31)

Brecht was so fascinated by the Joan of Arc theme that he employed it in three of his plays: *Saint Joan of the Stockyards, The Visions of Simone*

German title: *Die heilige Johanna der Schlachthöfe.*

Machard, and *The Trial of Saint Joan in Rouen 1431.*

Saint Joan of the Stockyards is a much more ambitious play than the other two. It was written between 1929 and 1931, that is to say, during Brecht's most doctrinal Marxist phase. (This was also the period in which Brecht composed his austere didactic plays.) In 1931, also, the Catholic world celebrated the five-hundredth anniversary of the death of Jeanne d'Arc—a fact Brecht was surely aware of.

In *Saint Joan,* Brecht takes the historic Saint Joan and transplants her to the Chicago of around 1900. Like George Bernard Shaw's Major Barbara (the protagonist of Shaw's play *Major Barbara,* 1905, and one of Brecht's models for his Saint Joan), Joan is an officer of the Salvation Army, trying to do good works among the poor in Chicago's stockyards district. She attempts to save the soul of one of the biggest exploiters in the meat business, Pierpont Mauler, but she unwittingly becomes a tool of the capitalists she opposes.

In the first scene, Pierpont Mauler receives a letter from his friends in New York warning him to get out of the meat business before the market drops. But Mauler pretends to his partner, Cridle, that he wants to quit because he can no longer stand to see the blood. Cridle agrees to buy the business if Mauler first ruins their archrival, Lennox.

The next scene opens with 70,000 workers waiting for the gates of the Lennox packing plant to open. They grumble about the low wages and the twelve-hour working day although they realize that they have no alternative. But the gates do not open. Newspaper boys cry out that Lennox has been forced out of business by Mauler: "70,000 workers out of work!"[74]

In contrast to this ruthless business move, the following scene shows Mauler, the philanthropist. Newspaper boys shout: "Meat king and philanthropist

Mauler on his way to visit his hospitals!"[75] Mauler passes by, flanked by two bodyguards. (The "philanthropist" has to be protected from the people.)

In the house of the Black Strawhats (as Brecht calls the Salvation Army), Joan Dark announces her intention of reintroducing God into the world, "which resembles a slaughterhouse."[76] With soup and sermons, the Black Strawhats try to convert workers outside the Lennox plants—but with little success; the workers leave as soon as the soup runs out.

At the livestock exchange, Joan and her companion, Martha, are waiting to talk to Mauler. On the upper level, the meatpackers Lennox, Graham, and Cridle are also waiting for Mauler. Mauler comes and demands his money from Cridle, who is balking because prices have dropped. Mauler agrees to see Joan, but pretends to be Slift (a broker and Mauler's confidant). Joan, however, recognizes him immediately. (This is an echo of the incident in which the historic Saint Joan recognized the king when she was first brought to the court.) Mauler is impressed by Joan and the Strawhats' altruistic work because they do it "for nothing." He tries to justify his own actions, offers Joan money to keep up her good work, and tells her not to take things too seriously: "The poor are bad and like animals . . . it's their own fault."[77] He orders Slift to take Joan to the stockyards and show her "the scum of the world."[78]

Slift takes Joan through Mauler's plant and tries to demonstrate to her the baseness of the poor by pointing out two cases. Four days ago, a man named Luckerniddle fell into an unprotected meat boiler and could not be saved. Now Slift makes a bargain with the widow—for twenty meals, she is willing to remain silent about the accident. In the other case, a worker named Gloomb lost his hand at his tin-cutting machine and now complains bitterly about his miserable job. Slift promises him a better job if he can find someone to take over his old job. Joan poses as a job seeker, and Gloomb immediately recommends his present job to her. Slift now hopes to have converted Joan to his opinion of the poor. But to the contrary, Joan says, "You have shown me the poverty of the poor, not their wickedness."[79]

At the livestock exchange, meanwhile, the meat-packers offer canned meat, but there are no buyers. And since the packers cannot sell meat, they will not buy cattle. In turn, therefore, the cattle breeders cannot sell. To make matters worse, Mauler pulls out of the meat market and sells all his shares, which drives the market down. In the eyes of the meatpackers, no one is to blame and there is no remedy: "No one can help these crises. We are all bound by the inexplicable laws of economics. These catastrophes of nature return in terrible cycles."[80] At this moment of crisis, Joan appears with a group of poor people who have lost their jobs, and she courageously argues for the right of each to hold a job. Mauler cannot stand the sight of the poor and agrees to buy all the meat himself for two months. The market seems to be saved, and Joan feels a sense of triumph.

Mauler goes to Slift's house in the city. He is full of fear—not of what is above (God), but of what is below (the poor people who may one day rise up and do away with him and his like). But Slift offers Mauler a rare steak in the hopes of bringing him back to his senses—his business senses, that is. Again Joan appears. Now she pleads for the "cattle breeders of Illinois." Again Mauler softens and buys meat "to save Illinois and avert the ruin of farmers and cattle breeders."[81] Yet it is not his "good heart" that moves Mauler to buy the meat and the cattle. He is being prompted by his powerful "friends in New York" (meaning Wall Street) who apparently know what the market is going to do.

In the house of the Black Strawhats, meanwhile, Major Paulus Snyder announces a change of strategy. Since the poor show an "inexplicable resistance," the Strawhats will now turn to the rich to help them fight "materialism and infidelity in the city of Chicago."[82] The meatpackers appear and agree to pay the rent for the Strawhats' house for forty months if the Black Strawhats will, in turn, keep the poor quiet by trying to convince them that their reward for living a life of poverty and suffering on earth will be eternity in Heaven. But Joan disrupts the negotiations. The meatpacking plants still have not opened; the jobless wait outside in the snow. She now doubts that help will ever come from those in control, and she chases the meatpackers out of the house in an action analogous to Jesus's driving the money changers from the temple. Paulus, however, is indignant and immediately dismisses Joan from the Black Strawhats. Joan vows to continue to fight for the poor on her own by converting Mauler and enlisting his help.

While Mauler and Slift are making plans to corner the meat market and ruin their competitors, Joan—hungry and freezing—comes to Mauler's office to try to convert him. Mauler seems deeply concerned about Joan. He wants to save the Strawhats from eviction and have Joan reinstated in the organization. He delivers an eloquent speech praising the almighty power of money and stressing the importance of the Strawhats in maintaining the capitalist system. But Joan decides that she herself would rather share the jobless workers' fate in the snow-covered stockyards.

Then follows a rapid succession of scenes in different locations, a technique that lends a sense of urgency to the events portrayed. Joan joins the wait-

ing workers in the snow-covered stockyards and tells
Mrs. Luckerniddle and Gloomb about a dream she has
had. She saw herself at the head of many demonstrations, "changing everything which my foot touched."[83]
Gloomb and Mrs. Luckerniddle are unable to understand; all they know is that because of Joan's scruples,
they no longer get warm soup.

At the livestock exchange, Mauler hears from his
friends in New York that customs barriers in the south
have fallen, which means that meat can be sold again.
Mauler has contracted for the meat from the meatpackers at a low price; now he can sell it at a high
price. He also bought up livestock at a low price,
which the meatpackers now have to buy from him at
a high price in order to meet their delivery contracts
to him. The small investors are ruined. Mauler's mer-
ciful gestures now appear to have been deliberate
business moves.

A group of Black Strawhats enters a small tavern
near the stockyards to spread the good word and
collect donations. Joan now realizes the fruitlessness
of this kind of charity. She wonders: "Are there no
people around here who really do something that
helps?" A worker answers her: "Yes, the communists."
Joan then says, "Aren't those the people who advocate
committing crimes?" The worker answers, "No."[84]

Back at the livestock exchange, the meatpackers
express their desperate need for livestock. They now
realize that Mauler is in total control of the market.

In another part of the stockyards, Joan talks to the
leaders of the workers' union. They plan a general
strike, which the city employees have agreed to join.
But information about the strike has to be taken
secretly to various groups by absolutely trustworthy
people because "the net with one mesh torn is of no
use."[85] Joan agrees to take a letter to the workers at
the Cridle factory.

At the livestock exchange, names of collapsed firms are called out. Slift, certain that the meatpackers will have to buy, keeps driving up the price of livestock. Mauler warns him not to overdo it, since they, too, will be wiped out if the meatpackers cannot buy at all.

Mauler's detectives return from the stockyards. They report growing unrest among the workers and some shooting by the police. They find no trace of Joan, whom Mauler wants to locate.

In the stockyards, news reporters discover Joan among the waiting workers and try to use her for a big story. Her fame as an advocate for the jobless has spread: "All of Chicago is with you."[86] But Joan refuses to be made into a "heroine." She now realizes: "This whole system is like a seesaw, and those who are on top are there only because others are at the bottom.... And there must be more at the bottom than there are on top—otherwise the seesaw wouldn't hold."[87]

But conditions in the yard are rough. Joan is hungry and cold, and someone steals her shawl. Machine-gun fire can be heard in the distance—army troops are firing on the resisting workers. Some workers warn Joan that only solidarity and force will help. But Joan is appalled at the thought of violence: "That which is brought about by violence cannot be good."[88] She leaves without having delivered the letter.

On a street corner in Chicago, Mauler, who is on his way to the stockyards to find Joan, learns from the papers that Slift has ruined the meatpackers—and him—by holding out too long.

In the stockyards, Mrs. Luckerniddle and Joan accidentally meet in the dense snowfall. Mrs. Luckerniddle demands the letter. Joan, afraid that it contains incitement to violence, refuses to give it to her, and slips away in the snowfall.

In another part of the stockyards, Joan overhears two workers saying that some of the workers have not received the message calling for the general strike. Joan is now haunted by voices—pangs of her own bad conscience. (In the historic story she heard the voice of God.)

At the headquarters of the Black Strawhats, Paulus Snyder and his Strawhats are being evicted. They are desperately waiting for Mauler to come with the promised rent. Mauler appears—but with no money. Accusing himself of being an exploiter, he says he only wants to hear the word of God. Snyder is bitterly disappointed. Livestock breeders and meatpackers come to seek out Mauler. Meatpacker Graham gives a vivid description, in the style of the *Iliad,* of the seven-hour-long battle at the exchange, which led to the meat industry's ruin.

The livestock breeders angrily demand their money from Mauler. Mauler is rescued by a letter from his friends in New York that tells him what to do. Since he was rejected by the Black Strawhats when he came as a mere poor sinner without money, he now returns to his business. Only harsh measures can save the capitalist system. He plans to consolidate the meatpacking industry, and advises the livestock breeders to burn a third of their livestock to raise the prices. When Snyder lamely interjects that the livestock could better be given to the poor, Mauler sets him right: "Dear Mr. Snyder, you have not grasped the situation; those poor people are the buyers."[89] Mauler's other plans include a lockout of a third of the work force and the lowering of wages for the rest. In these turbulent times, he also needs the Black Strawhats. He proposes to finance their operations if in return they help to keep law and order by singing, preaching about rewards in heaven, and distributing hot soup. When the news arrives that the strike has collapsed, and that its leaders are in jail, the capitalist system seems saved.

Driven by her conscience, Joan has returned to the stockyards finally to deliver the letter. But it is too late—the general strike did not materialize. Joan realizes the extent of her responsibility for the failure of the strike. She collapses.

For the final scene, all groups—the Black Strawhats, the meatpackers, the livestock breeders, and the wholesale buyers—are assembled in the house of the Black Strawhats (now lavishly furnished). Two policemen enter with Joan, who is close to death. She is guilt-ridden by her failure to deliver the letter. Slift and Mauler begin to make plans to establish Joan as a saint and the angel of the stockyards "as proof that we hold humanitarianism in high esteem."[90]

Joan now clearly sees that her "doing good but getting no results" has only been exploited by the oppressors and that "those who are below are kept below so that those who are above can stay above."[91] She now says that nothing can help but a complete change of the world—"it needs it." But no one is listening to her; her agonized words are drowned out by ecstatic praise of the system (expressed in the highly poetic language of German classical poetry) and a chorale in which everyone joins. Joan dies, and her body is ceremoniously covered by the lowered flags of the Black Strawhats. The final moments of the scene are flooded with a rosy light (a parody of the ending of Schiller's romantic drama *The Maid of Orleans*, 1801). While the capitalist system is praised in poetic declamations, loudspeakers announce the news: "Eight million unemployed in the United States." "Six million unemployed in Germany." "In front of Henry Ford's factory in Detroit, a battle rages between police and the unemployed."[92]

Brecht's *Saint Joan* is basically a play about economics, written at the time of the great worldwide depression. To prepare for this play, Brecht consulted many books on economics and talked to specialists. He studied the mechanisms of the Chicago wheat exchange and—most important—he read Karl Marx's *Das Kapital*. He also conducted intensive research into the activities of the Salvation Army.

In its structure, the play follows the pattern of Shakespearean history plays. It was influenced by several other literary works, such as Upton Sinclair's novel *The Jungle* (which describes the tragic fate of a young immigrant who worked in Chicago's stockyards); the Danish writer Johannes Vilhelm Jensen's novel about Chicago, *The Wheel;* and Bernard Shaw's *Saint Joan* and *Major Barbara.* As in many of his other works, Brecht uses numerous biblical references. (For example, to express the bankruptcy of the meat buyers who could no longer bid in the stock exchange, Brecht used the tone of the Old Testament: "And there was silence across the waters.") Particularly obvious in this play also are Brecht's allusions—mostly parodistic in nature—to the writings of Goethe, Schiller, and Hölderin.

With Joan Dark and Mauler, Brecht created two especially interesting characters. Joan is a good-hearted and well-meaning nonviolent idealist who is brought to the realization that the good, charitable, and well-intended deeds of an individual are not enough to change the world. Although for Joan this realization comes too late, the audience is supposed to learn while there is still time.

Mauler is one of Brecht's most intricate characters. Is he really affected by Joan Dark's goodness? Or is he so ruthless that he only pretends human feelings to gain economic advantage? Is there a good core in him that, because of his circumstances, has no chance to develop? Is Mauler an early version of Brecht's split characters? Interpretations vary, often depending upon the critic's own political convictions. Peter Wagner's version seems the most convincing: there are indeed residual feelings of humanity in Mauler but, as Wagner sees it, Mauler too is a victim of capitalism —by the time of the play he is too corrupted to be influenced by the voice of humanity.[93]

Brecht had often been accused of attacking Christianity in *Saint Joan*. But, as he points out in his annotations to the play, he wanted only to expose one characteristic commonly displayed by so-called Christians and Christian organizations: the readiness to talk about God and goodness but a reluctance to remedy the injustices of the daily life around them.

Saint Joan is allied with Brecht's didactic plays in its total lack of humor—its didactic austerity. Its parodies, rather than providing comedy, add to the tone of angry bitterness that pervades the play. For example, when Mauler, who has just ruined hundreds of workers and small investors, praises Joan's humanity in Goethean style, the parody is no longer humorous. It is precisely this discrepancy between words and actions that Brecht wants to uncover. Some of the stage effects, however, can elicit laughter—as indicated below in the discussion of the Berliner Ensemble production.

When *Saint Joan of the Stockyards* was completed in 1931, the political influence of the Nazis was already so strong that no stage dared to produce the play, although several attempts were made. In the increasing polarization between right and left toward the end of the Weimar Republic, the Nazis managed to exploit the fears of communism of a great many people. Thus even before the Nazis came to power in 1933, they encouraged the people to resist anything coming from the left.

One of those attempts at producing *Saint Joan* was

made at the Landestheater in Darmstadt, which had already produced several of Brecht's plays. But as soon as it became known that the Landestheater planned to stage Brecht's *Saint Joan,* a violent press campaign was begun against it, and the city council held a session to discuss the matter. Based on reading the play, the *Kölnische Zeitung* of 1 February 1933 expressed the prevailing sentiment when it wrote: "The play is not without poetic value. As a matter of fact, it is probably Brecht's best achievement. But . . . at its core it is unequivocally bolshevist and blasphemous propaganda . . . directed against the foundations of western culture." The production was terminated.[94]

Although *Saint Joan* did not reach the stage until after World War II, it was broadcast over Berlin radio in an abridged version on 11 April 1932. Fritz Walter, of the *Berliner Börsen-Courier* said it was a memorable but sad moment in the cultural history of our age that the theater had to leave the transmission of one of the greatest and most important dramas of our time to the radio." The studio had assembled some of the best actors Berlin had to offer to speak the parts: Joan: Carola Neher (Brecht had actually written the part with her in mind); Mauler: Fritz Kortner; Slift: Peter Lorre; Mrs. Luckerniddle: Helene Weigel.[95]

It was not until 30 April 1959 that *Saint Joan of the Stockyards* had its world premiere—in the Deutsches Schauspielhaus in Hamburg (director: the famous German actor/director Gustav Gründgens; sets: Caspar Neher; Joan Dark: Hanne Hiob, Brecht's daughter from his first marriage to Marianne Zoff; Mauler: Hermann Schomburg). This evening was one of the very few times in postwar German theatrical history that artists from East and West Germany came together in anticipation of a historic event in the theater. They were not disappointed. The audience received the play with a standing ovation that lasted more than half an hour. Helene Weigel, who had come from East Berlin to see the play, summarized her impressions: "Superbly done by Gründgens."[96]

Gründgens retained the revolutionary message of the play; he pointed up the paradoxes and bitter ironies, but also emphasized the play's poetic side. For the West German critic Johannes Jacobi (*Die Zeit*), Brecht's 1930 political message seemed almost meaningless to the world of 1959. But he complimented Gründgens for having brought out the dramatic and artistic qualities beyond the propaganda.[97]

André Müller, the East German critic of *Theater der Zeit*, joined in the chorus of praise for Gründgens's great artistic and dramatic achievement. But, unlike Jacobi, he did not think that the content was outdated. He found it courageous of Gründgens to present the play with so few changes. There was one exception: he noted that Gründgens had carefully omitted any direct reference to communists.

Since the music Kurt Weill had originally composed for the play had been lost, Paul Dessau composed a new score. Gründgens, however, decided to use music by the virtually unknown Siegfried Franz—which Müller found "decidedly weak."[98]

All critics were in agreement, however, when it came to Neher's sets and the ensemble of actors: "Extraordinary, without exception."[99]

In 1964, Tony Richardson directed a production of *Saint Joan of the Stockyards* at London's Queen's Theater (Joan: Siobhan McKenna; Mauler: Lionel Stander). According to B. A. Young, who reviewed the play for *The New York Times*, the production was "a highly effective theatrical spectacle," mainly because it was completely "un-Brechtian." Mauler and his associates were played as comic figures so that it was difficult for the reviewer to hate them—as he felt he should. And the songs gave a romantic quality to the play: "The songs that can be so tiresomely intrusive in Brecht have been set to music by John Addison with an emotional quality reminiscent of nineteenth-century oratorio and are dovetailed into the play so that they actually help it on its way." (From this review, it would seem that this production was indeed most un-Brechtian!)[100]

On 12 June 1968, *Saint Joan of the Stockyards* was performed by the Berliner Ensemble (directors: Manfred Wekwerth and Joachim Tenschert; Joan: Hanne Hiob; Mauler: Martin Flörchinger; Slift: Ekkehard Schall; sets: Karl von Appen; music: Hans-Dieter Hosalla).

Whereas, in 1930, Brecht's intention had been to provide insights into the dominating forces in society, Wekwerth's intention in 1968 was to warn against allowing capitalism to cover up social injustice by modern means of mass communication and by talk of the alienated man. By overemphasizing capitalist methods of whitewashing, Wekwerth hoped to teach his audience to recognize the whitewash for what it was. According to Wekwerth, Mauler does indeed have moral scruples, but he exemplifies the double moral standard prevalent in individuals in capitalist societies. Many a captialist tycoon is ruthless and inhumane in his business methods, but at the same time he can also be philanthropic. And in the last scene, Wekwerth revealed who carries the burden in such a society: the platform on which Joan's "canonization" takes place rests on the backs of workers.[101]

The production by the Berliner Ensemble underlined the austerity and didactic elements of the text, as well as its poetic qualities. One moment of humor was allowed: Mauler's entrance into the house of the

Black Strawhats was accompanied by the tune "O When the Saints Go Marching In," played by the Salvation Army band.

The critic of *Theater der Zeit,* Ingrid Seyfarth, felt that the production was less than a complete success because Wekwerth/Tenschert did not always accomplish what they set out to do. According to Seyfarth, the production often displayed a kind of artificial perfection bordering on sterility and oscillated between naturalism and a strange mystification (the "voices" that haunt Joan). She was also unhappy with the way the two leading actors, Hanne Hiob and Martin Flörchinger, conceived their roles. For Ekkehard Schall's Slift, however, she had nothing but praise.[102]

In November 1970, the famous Italian producer/director Giorgio Strehler created his version of Brecht's *Saint Joan of the Stockyards,* in Franco Fortini's translation, for his Piccolo Teatro in Milan (sets: Ezio Frigerio; music: Fiorenzo Carpi; Joan: Valentina Cortese; Mauler: Glauco Mauri).

Arturo Lazzari, who reviewed the play for the East German *Theater der Zeit,* found it a very impressive production of high aesthetic quality, one that abounded with ingenious and imaginative staging devices. In his view the production ably demonstrated Brecht's "originality and vitality" to the Italian audiences. But the production also raised some questions in his mind; he feared that the artistic beauty might detract from the social message. Also, in spite of the fact that the play does end with a victory for the capitalists, Lazzari would have liked to see the play conclude on a note of optimism, not in a mood of bitterness as had Strehler's production.[103]

Brecht's *Saint Joan* can be as provocative today as it was when he wrote it. In 1974, the city council of Tokyo, Japan, prohibited a performance of *Saint Joan of the Stockyards,* ostensibly because the dialogue would "hurt the feelings of the stockyard workers."[104]

What makes Brecht's *Saint Joan* so extraordinary a drama is the combination of down-to-earth economic conditions and highly poetic language (often a parody on specific lines from famous classical works). The experiment is highly successful: Graham's account of the events at the livestock exchange, for example, is superb writing. From a purely literary point of view, *Saint Joan* is undoubtedly one of Brecht's best plays.

Yet it is precisely this combination of economics and poetry—especially the reverberations of classical German works—that may prevent the play from being effective on the American stage, particularly in a commercial theater. (Gisela Bahr's volume containing study materials for *Saint Joan*[105] lists only one performance in America: a Barnard-Columbia Summer Theater production in the Minor Latham Playhouse, New York, in June 1963.) Such poems as Schiller's "The Bell," Goethe's "The Magician's Apprentice," or Hölderlin's "Hyperion's Song of Fate" are (or should be) as familiar to German high school students as poems by Frost or Longfellow are to American high-school students. But most Americans, cannot respond to Brecht's effective use of parodies of these works because the works are not part of their culture.

The American setting could also lose its effectiveness as a metaphor because the audience—taking the Chicago setting literally—might claim that Chicago is not like that, at least not any more. But when seeing this play the theatergoer must accept the premise that Brecht created a model to illustrate a theory, to teach, and to entertain. To Brecht, and the German audience for which he wrote, the setting—whether Chicago, America in general, India or China—simply meant an exotic environment. He used it as a metaphor in the hope that people would gain insights they could not gain from looking at their all too familiar immediate surroundings. Had he written for Chicagoans, he would most likely have transplanted the action to Berlin or some other "strange, exotic place." The setting is only a means to an end; the play is supposed to alert the audience to the intolerable conditions of a capitalist society in general.

Lehrstücke

Most of the *Lehrstücke* (didactic plays; plays for learning) were written between 1928 and 1930 although in 1934 Brecht used this form once more for his play *The Horatians and the Curiatians*. The *Lehrstücke* (singular: *Lehrstück*) mark a special phase in Brecht's development as a playwright. Since in their intent and design they stand apart from virtually all other Brecht plays, they can be grouped together as the characteristic product of Brecht's most doctrinal Marxist period. They were primarily written for the political instruction of students and workers who would learn by acting out the plays themselves.

What troubled Brecht most in the traditional theater was the passive and receptive attitude of the audience. Particularly in view of his newly found Marxist creed, he wanted to combine reception and action:

The bourgeois philosophers see a big difference between those who act and those who observe. A person who thinks does not make this differentiation. If one makes this differentiation, one leaves politics to those who act and philosophy to those who merely observe. In reality, however, politicians must be philosophers and philosophers must be politicians. There is no difference between genuine philosophy and genuine politics. Having recognized this, the thinker proposes to educate young people by performing plays that make them actors and observers at the same time.[106]

One of the most important ideological sources for Brecht's *Lehrstücke* was a speech Lenin had given on 2 October 1920 to the third all-Russian congress of the Russian communist youth organization. In it Lenin stressed that the single most important task for the young generation was to *learn*. But Lenin had also pointed out: "There is not yet an answer to the most important, most essential question: How and what shall one learn? One thing, however, is clear: during the reorganization of the old capitalistic society, the training and education of these new generations who will form the communist society cannot be carried out with the old methods."[107]

The *Lehrstücke* constitute Brecht's contribution to Lenin's postulations. One requirement for the *Lehrstücke* therefore was, in Brecht's words: "These plays must be invented and executed in such a way that they serve a useful purpose for the state. It is not the artistic beauty of a sentence, a gesture, or an action, that determines its value but its usefulness for the state."[108] His *Lehrstücke* were "educational experiments" for which he did not need a theater, although he employed theatrical means. The traditional theaters were too commercialized for his goal, which was "to develop a type of theatrical event that would influence the thinking of those participating in it." He wanted "art for the producer rather than art for the consumer."[109] Thus the *Lehrstück* in its purest form is not intended for an audience: "The *Lehrstück* teaches people by having them act out the play, not by having them watch it. In principle, no spectators are required for a *Lehrstück.*"[110]

The *Lehrstück,* as conceived by Brecht, has a strict form. But, as Brecht stressed, this makes it easier "to introduce one's own ideas or contemporary references . . . the *Lehrstück* provides room for a vast variety of possibilities."[111] One thing, however, Brecht thought essential: "The presentation must follow the rules for *epic theater.* The study of the estrangement effect is indispensable."[112]

Brecht himself was not satisfied with the German term *Lehrstück,* although he never changed it. For the English version of the term, Brecht suggested "learning-play." Today, this term, as well as "play for learning" and "didactic play," are used—though none seems totally suitable to designate this particular group of plays, since all of Brecht's plays were written to instruct.

The didactic plays were indeed used in schools and workers' organizations more or less without audience, as Brecht intended. But they also have often been performed as normal plays in theaters.

The first of the didactic plays, *The Flight Across the Ocean* (*Der Ozeanflug*), was written in 1928 and 1929 in collaboration with Elisabeth Hauptmann and Kurt Weill. Its original title, *The Flight of the Lindberghs* (also *Lindbergh's Flight*), was changed by Brecht because Lindbergh allegedly expressed admiration for the Nazi air force.

Although Brecht eliminated all references to Lindbergh in the play, it is still obvious that the plot is based on Lindbergh's historic flight, which is described in fifteen short scenes or acts. The play is dedicated to "that which has not yet been achieved."[113] This flight symbolizes every great achievement in man's progress: "It represents the battle against everything that is primitive, and an effort toward improvement of our planet, just as does the dialectic [Marxist] economy that will radically change the world."[114] This fight against "anything that is primitive" includes the fight against organized religion that, in Brecht's view, had been standing in the way of progress for centuries.

With this "didactic radio play for boys and girls," Brecht developed a method of using the radio for didactic purposes, thereby attempting to change it from a "mere distribution system to a communication system."[115] He wanted to activate and involve the listener. In *The Flight Across the Ocean*, Brecht intended the part of the flier to be spoken and sung by the listener or listeners (in a classroom, for example— presumably with copies of the script in hand). The radio was to supply the chorus and all sound effects, such as the noise of waves, engines, and masses of people. There were two musical scores: one by Paul Hindemith and one by Kurt Weill.

This play (performed on a conventional stage before an audience) was the first Brecht play to be performed in the United States. On 4 April 1931, the Philadelphia Orchestra Association presented it at the Academy of Music in Philadelphia under the title *Lindbergh's Flight*. Weill's music was conducted by Leopold Stokowski; the musical aspect was far more important than Brecht's text, which had been translated by the American composer George Antheil.

The production was not well received. Linton Martin of the *Philadelphia Inquirer* called the piece "preposterous" and "merely an addition to the illustrious line of more or less grotesque portraiture of American subjects approached from outside." And he continued: "Of course the composer can't be called to account for the ritualistic and ridiculous libretto provided by Bert Brecht, filled with vagaries so vulnerable that chance quotation shows its incredible crudity and naive inaccuracies . . . but the composer contents himself with trivial tunes."[116]

The Baden Didactic Play: On Consent (*Das Badener Lehrstück vom Einverständnis*) consists of eleven scenes and is in many ways a continuation of *The Flight Across the Ocean*. It was written in 1929 in collaboration with Slatan Dudow and Elisabeth Hauptmann. (The Baden of the title refers to the city of Baden-Baden in the Black Forest; the play was commissioned for a music festival there.) Again the airplane, the fliers, and mechanics represent man's domination over nature. But the play is not a report of a successful flight. On the contrary, in their desire to reach new heights of technical achievement, the fliers crash: "Our thoughts were on machines and the struggle for greater speed." Technological progress has outdistanced social progress as the fliers say: "We forgot our names and our faces in those struggles. . . . Poverty has increased in our cities."[117]

A "learned chorus" of Marxists teaches the mechanics that everything and everyone must be changed: "You must agree that everything must be changed, the world and humanity, and most of all the disorder of the class system, because there are two types of men: exploiters and those who are ignorant."[118] Humility, discipline, and self-denial are required of those who want to accomplish the change.

This play also contains one of the most shocking and grotesque scenes in any of Brecht's plays: the "investigation as to whether man helps his fellow man."[119] In this scene, three clowns, in the pretense of being of service to a giant named Mr. Smith, remove his arms and legs, leaving him disabled and helpless at the end. The message: Under the existing system, man obviously does not help his fellow man. Or, in the interpretation of the scholar and critic Lee Baxandall:

"Smith is the proletariat, vast in potential power but victimized again and again until it is helpless."[120]

The play's concept remains somewhat puzzling, and its ideology has been criticized by Marxist critics because there is too much emphasis on the concept of abnegation rather than on the optimistic foreshadowing of a glorious future. Yet, according to Baxandall, it is also a fascinating statement of Brecht's personal conflicts, such as the struggle for self-discipline, during his transition from bourgeois to Marxist writer.

When the play was presented at the music festival of Baden-Baden on 28 July 1929, with Paul Hindemith's music, it shocked the audience. The famous German playwright Gerhart Hauptmann is said to have left the theater in disgust.

In May 1969, both plays, *The Flight of Lindbergh* and *A Lesson in Consent* (as the titles were translated), were presented in what must have been a rather strange production by the New York City Theater Workshop in the Grace Rainey Rogers Auditorium of the Metropolitan Museum of Art. The director was Gordon Duffey, and his troupe consisted mostly of black and Puerto Rican actors, largely drawn from ghetto neighborhoods. Here is an account of the events on stage by Donald Henahan of *The New York Times:*

> The two short dramatic works, linked and presented as one, were interwoven with original material (words by Mr. Duffey, music by Richard Peaslee), improvisations, and sometimes simple horseplay. Allusions and references to flying flew —to Icarus, the Wright Brothers, Leonardo, and Daedalus. At the close there was "A Ceremonial Dance to Which There Is No End," in which the actors mimed mechanical, meaningless acts while a speaker screamed quotations from a Charles A. Lindbergh speech made in 1954, to the effect that modern man is becoming the "slave of science."[121]

Before the performance, the actors, dressed in leo-
tards and tights, ran through the audience distributing
paper and instructions for the members of the audience to make their own paper planes and shouting, "I'm
not allowed to fly!" Jumping on stage, they added, "We
are allowed to take our clothes off." According to
Henahan this was intended as a parody of The Living
Theater's *Paradise Now*. (*Paradise Now*, a collective
creation of the unorthodox group of actors working
under Julian Beck and Judith Malina, was first performed by The Living Theater at the 22nd Festival
d'Avignon, France, on 24 July 1968. The play is a
loosely structured series of episodes about "The Beautiful Nonviolent Anarchist Revolution.")[122]

He Who Says Yes (*Der Jasager*), and its counterpart, *He Who Says No* (*Der Neinsager*), written in
1929 and 1930 (collaborators: Elisabeth Hauptmann
and Kurt Weill; music: Kurt Weill), are what Brecht
called "school operas," intended to be used in schools.

He Who Says Yes is an adaptation of an English
version (by Arthur Waley) of the Japanese No play
Taniko. In his adaptation, Brecht followed the Japanese play very closely. The relation to *The Baden
Didactic Play* is stated in the first line of the play: "It
is particularly important to learn to agree."[123]

In Brecht's play, a teacher and three students plan
a trip across the mountains to obtain medicine for a
disease that is ravaging their village. A boy whose
mother has contracted this disease begs the teacher to
take him along on this dangerous trip so that he can
get medicine for his mother. The trip, however, proves
too strenuous for the boy. There is an old custom that
says that during such a trip, those who cannot go on
must be left behind. Rather than endanger the whole
mission, the boy agrees to accept the dictate of the
custom. But in order not to die a slow and lonely
death, he asks to be thrown into the valley and thus

killed instantly. The play ends with his companions reluctantly throwing him into the valley and proceeding on their mission.

A discussion with students caused Brecht to write a counter-version to the first play. According to Brecht, both plays form a unit and should be played together.

The plot of *He Who Says No* is basically the same as that of *He Who Says Yes,* but there are some significant changes. The disease that the mother has is not serious, and the expedition to the other side of the mountain now takes place mainly for the purpose of research. The old custom as described in the second play is much more rigid: it demands that anyone who cannot go on must be thrown into the valley. This time the boy does not agree to abide by the custom: "As to the old and venerable custom, I see no reason in it. I propose to introduce a new custom immediately —namely the custom to think anew in each new situation."[124] That which is reasonable, not that which is heroic, is important. Thus they all return to the village, and the boy's life is spared.

In both plays a chorus accompanies the actions with comments, descriptions, and plot summaries.

The emphasis in the first play is on the sacrifice of one person for the common good. Although it is a hard decision, one can understand the actions of the boy's companions under the circumstances described.

With the changes Brecht introduced in the second play, he also changed the central issue. There is now much less reason to adhere to the old custom. The emphasis is on the necessity of changing old customs that have become obsolete.

The two playlets focus on the questions of discipline, sacrifice, and change of outdated customs, which were very much on Brecht's mind in those years. Recognizing that these qualities were necessary for the advancement of society as he envisioned it, he tried to come to grips with them himself. He also presented them as problems to be acted out and to be discussed by others.

The plays were first produced on 23 June 1930 by the Central Institute for Education and Instruction in Berlin under the directorship of Brecht and Weill, with Otto Hopf as the teacher and with local schoolboys playing the other parts and an amateur orchestra playing the music.

In May 1946 the Hebbel Theater in Berlin produced *He Who Says Yes.* According to Friedrich Luft, the reaction of the audience was mixed; some liked it, some did not know how to react to it, others left the theater. Luft belonged to those who liked it. He found Brecht's austere style and Kurt Weill's clear and tart music a welcome change from the traditional, elaborate theater style. For Luft, "the evening was one of the most interesting of the last theater season."[125]

He Who Says Yes was also among the first of Brecht's plays to be performed in the United States. On 25 April 1933 in New York's Grand Street Playhouse, the music school of the Henry Street Settlement House gave four performances of *He Who Says Yes.* The reviewer of *The New York Times* called the work, which reminded him of "the abstract quality of early Greek drama," "an unusual and curiously moving experience." He thought this school opera had "more authentic emotional blood than the majority of modern works offered uptown under much more pretentious circumstances."[126] The critic of the *New York Herald Tribune* thought the music "not too exacting," but ascribed to the opera "undoubted educational value."[127]

But neither *The Times* nor the *Tribune* mentioned Brecht at all. His name may not even have appeared on the program. *The Tribune* reviewer said only, "The rather dour libretto [was] adapted, it was announced, from the Japanese and presented last night in Alice Matterlath's English translation."

How unknowledgeable the reviewers were about Brecht is to be seen in the comments of the reviewer of *The Times*, who saw the play as a defense of Nazism: "Recent events in the Reich perhaps explain somewhat why a piece whose ideology combines devotion to an abstract virtue with personal callousness has achieved such popularity there." With "recent events," he presumably referred to Hitler's rise to power on 30 January 1933, a time when Brecht was decidedly not popular in Germany!

The Measures Taken (*Die Massnahme*), written in 1929 and 1930 in collaboration with Slatan Dudow and Hanns Eisler (who also composed the music), is perhaps the most interesting and most controversial of Brecht's didactic plays. The play was severely criticized by communist critics ("abstract and undialectic"). It was also used by the House Committee on Un-American Activities in their hearings against Eisler and Brecht in 1947 (HUAC had it translated and gave the play its first American "production").

As in *The Baden Didactic Play* and *He Who Says Yes*, the topic is agreement, self-effacement, and the sacrifice of the individual for a higher goal. But *The Measures Taken* by far surpasses the previous didactic plays in its austerity and ideological severity. Brecht's most doctrinal play, it expresses his first frank and unreserved profession of communism, and his only attempt to present the extreme sacrifice required by the class struggle. Its purpose is "to teach politically correct behavior by showing politically incorrect behavior."[128]

The action of the play takes place in Moscow and Mukden, Manchuria, an industrial area in northeast China. The time is the early 1920s. (At that time the communists, aided by the Soviet Union, struggled for control of the *Kuomintang*, the Chinese national party. They were defeated by General Chiang Kai-shek in 1927. But after long and arduous battles the communists, under the leadership of Mao Tse-tung, came to power in 1949.)

As the play opens we see four communist agitators who have just returned from a successful mission in China. They report back to the communist party, here represented by a "control chorus," which praises them for their work: "Your work was good, the revolution is now well on its way in this country."[129] But they had to kill one of their comrades because he endangered the success of the movement: "He wanted to do what was right, but he did what was wrong."[130] Now they have to justify their actions before the control chorus.

The eight scenes that follow the prologue are a dramatized report of the events that took place in China, played by the agitators before the control chorus. The agitators play themselves as well as all other characters involved; the chorus interrupts with judgments, comments, or songs.

The four agitators go from Moscow to the city of Mukden to spread the teachings of Marx and Lenin, guided by the young comrade. To accomplish their mission, they relinquish their individuality and become "empty sheets upon which revolution can write its instructions." (To indicate this loss of individuality on stage, the actors put on masks.)[131] The chorus comments: "He who fights for communism must be able to fight or not fight, to tell the truth and not tell the truth . . . keep promises or not keep promises. . . . He who fights for communism has only one virtue: he fights for communism."[132] The chorus then presents the song "Praise of Illegal Activities."

But the young comrade, although his intentions are good, makes four mistakes, each one more serious than the preceding one, mainly through misguided compassion and a false sense of honor.

He is sent to agitate among the coolies, whose work consists of pulling boats filled with rice through canals. His mission is to convince them to act to improve their lot. When the coolies slip and fall in the mud, he first recommends that they demand better shoes. The coolies seem convinced. But when they slip again and the supervisor continues to whip them, the young comrade takes pity on them and helps them get up rather than encouraging them to protest and demand shoes. The coolies and the supervisor, however, think he is a fool and chase him away, thereby obstructing the agitators' work.

Next the comrade is sent to a factory to distribute leaflets urging workers to support a strike by workers in another part of the factory. But he sees a policeman make an unjust arrest, and he knocks the policeman down. Now he must flee and the leaflets cannot be distributed—the strike fails.

In his next mission, the comrade is to contact a Chinese merchant to persuade him to form an alliance with the coolies against the common enemy, the English. But the merchant is one of the exploiters of the coolies, and the young comrade refuses to sit down to dinner with him. The chorus admonishes that one must work to change the world, even if it means sitting down with one's enemies.

The fourth mistake is the most serious. Unrest increases in and around the city of Mukden. The new leader of the unemployed convinces the young comrade that the time for the uprising has come. The agitators disagree. They warn the comrade that this man is an agent of the merchants and a traitor to the communist cause. They recommend that the young comrade expose him and try to convince the soldiers

the government has brought in to quell any disturbances to join their common cause with the workers.
They speak for the communist party and the party
knows best. The chorus comments with the "Praise
of the Party" song: "The individual has two eyes, the
party has a thousand eyes . . . it is the vanguard of the
masses and leads the fight using the methods of the
classics [Marx, Engels, Lenin], methods taken from
their knowledge of reality."[133]

The young comrade does not listen, however. He
cannot wait any longer: "I have seen too much. I can
no longer be silent."[134] He imprudently tears off his
mask and reveals his identity as an agent from Moscow to the oppressed people of Mukden, telling them
that he has come to help. Prematurely exposed, he becomes too great a risk for his comrades and the cause
for which they are fighting, for if he is exposed, their
plan will be known too soon, and their work will be
unsuccessful. With their enemies on their heels, they
have no choice but to shoot the young comrade and
to throw his body into a lime pit, thus leaving no
trace of him. The young comrade himself sees that he
has failed and agrees to the measures to be taken. The
four agitators comment, "It is terrible to kill." But it
must be done "in the interest of communism."[135]

At the end, the control chorus approves of the agitators' actions: "Your report shows us what is necessary
in order to change the world: anger and hardness,
knowledge and indignation . . . cold patience and endless perseverance."[136]

There are several versions of the play. The last one,
which Brecht prepared in 1938 for the Malik Verlag
(on which the above plot summary is based) differs in
several respects from the first version of 1930, particularly as far as the action and motivation of the young
comrade is concerned. Communist critics, notably
Alfred Kurella (who is still today an important critic

in the German Democratic Republic), maintained, in a discussion of the first version in 1931, that as Brecht presented it, it was not the comrade who acted against the party line. He claimed that the comrade, rather than the agitators, represented the true view of a radical revolutionist and a bolshevik. Thereupon Brecht made several changes, mainly in the scenes that demonstrate the young comrade's mistakes, in order to make it clear that he was endangering the cause of the revolution and that the measures taken by the agitators were necessary. The play still does not sit well with communist critics. In their view, Brecht's play presents a distorted view of communism.

Martin Esslin calls *The Measures Taken* "without doubt one of Brecht's best works."[137] But one suspects that his judgment is based less on artistic reasons (although the play undoubtedly has its artistic merits) than on his own aversion to communism, for he continues: "Years before the great Soviet purge trials it expressed the essential nature of Stalinist Communism." However well this interpretation may seem to fit, it is a far cry from Brecht's intentions. His play was intended to assist in the educational process of a communist, and Brecht's attitude toward Stalin was never unfavorable, despite some misgivings. Esslin's interpretation points up one of the reasons Brecht refused to release the play for production between the years 1933 and 1956; he did not want praise for the wrong reasons.[138]

The Measures Taken was first performed on 13 December 1930 in the Philharmonie Berlin by three combined workers' choirs from Berlin, with Hanns Eisler, the composer, among the singers (musical direction: Karl Rankl; director of the play: Slatan Dudow; actors: Ernst Busch, Alexander Granach, Anton Maria Topitz, and Helene Weigel).

The first-nighters formed an unusual group: a mixture of workers and prominent intellectuals. The reaction to the performance was rather complex, although mostly along political lines. It evoked praise from the left ("a performance of monumental importance"), despite ideological reservations ("not Marxist"), and elicited utter rejection from the right (text "primitive," music "astonishingly regressive," the whole work "a dangerous contamination of our cultural values"). Between right and left, a number of critics attempted an objective evaluation on purely artistic merits. Hans Heinz Stuckenschmidt (*Berliner Zeitung*) wrote: "It is not up to me to judge the political implications of the play. But one thing is certain: the attempt at instructing the people through artistic means has never found a more appropriate and more inspired but less demagogic form, . . . we register: a work of prophetic nature, a tremendous success."[139]

Perhaps never before nor after has a play by Brecht caused so much discussion, particularly in leftist circles. The discussions have not ended; even today the play remains what it was from the beginning—uncomfortable for both the left and the right.

In June 1966, a Dutch company, the Nieuwe Komedie Den Haag, presented the play in Pittsburgh—with little success; ten to twenty people left the theater in disgust each night. (Or perhaps this was a sign of success, depending on one's point of view.) In June 1970, however, the play was well received on the campus of the University of Wisconsin in Milwaukee, where it was presented by a mixed group of students and workers.

In 1973, the Center Theater Group of Los Angeles presented *The Measures Taken*. There were no sets; the four agitators—played as political fanatics rather than cool political agents—acted in front of a large red flag. Although the production was apparently a somewhat melodramatic distortion, it was effective and provocative. As in Pittsburgh, a number of people left in protest.[140]

In October 1974, Joseph Papp brought *The Measures Taken* to New York City's Public Theater, staged by Leonardo Shapiro and the Shaliko Company. According to Jack Kroll of *Newsweek*, it was "one of the most fascinating products he [Papp] has ever brought into Public Theater." Kroll heralded the play as "perhaps the most powerful and disturbing political play ever written." He gave high marks to the players, including their singing of Hanns Eisler's songs. In his opinion, the singing made "Pete Seeger sound like Teresa Brewer."[141]

Among the spectators were Clive Barnes and Walter Kerr of *The New York Times*. "For 28½ reasons," Barnes thought it "a valuable play. . . . Brecht's nervily antithetical thinking . . . nowadays seems disturbingly relevant." But the message Barnes received was more existential than political: "Despite politics, this is a play, at a physical dramatic level, about survival." As to the quality of the production, Barnes "felt it could have been more interesting. . . . The actors seemed as if they were caught up with a debating society on the way to the theater," and he remained in search of the "real" Brecht. ("But where was Brecht when the lights went out? This was one of the few plays that might have shown us.")[142]

Walter Kerr found the play "historically most interesting." But the play obviously had a deeper effect on him. Although, intellectually, he understood the play's harsh message, he sided with the young comrade: "It [the play] has . . . slammed shut in our faces and outraged our hearts. . . . If we can grasp the political issue in our heads, all the rest of us votes for the man who is kind."[143]

For Brecht, *The Measures Taken* was the most significant of his *Lehrstücke*. As late as 1953 he noted

that he had plans for a play about Hans Garbe, an
East German worker-hero who had set new produc-
tion norms. It was "to be written in the style of *The
Measures Taken* or *The Mother.*" And when Manfred
Wekwerth asked him to name a play for the theater
of the future, Brecht answered unhesitatingly, *"The
Measures Taken."*[144]

At the same time (1929 and 1930) that Brecht was
working on *The Measures Taken,* he also wrote another, much less doctrinal, didactic play: *The Exception and the Rule (Die Ausnahme und die Regel),* in
collaboration with Ernst Burri and Elisabeth Hauptmann, with music by Paul Dessau. The play is centered
around the ironic fact that a good deed, if it occurs,
must necessarily be misunderstood in a society where
the bad deed is the rule.

Before the play begins, the actors ask the spectators
to watch closely "the conduct of the people" in the
play and not to assume that "that which happens all
the time" is God-given and unchangeable.[145]

A merchant, accompanied by a guide and a coolie,
hastens through a desert in Mongolia in order to beat
all of his rivals to an oil deal. He drives his servants
mercilessly. When they are about to enter a deserted
stretch where there is no police protection, the merchant decides to dismiss the guide, so that he has only
one potential enemy—the coolie.

When the merchant and the coolie reach a river
swollen by torrential rains, the merchant forces the
coolie across at gun point. The merchant makes it
across safely, but the coolie almost drowns and breaks
his arm. The merchant grows increasingly nervous
about the coolie: "I have hurt him possibly for life.
It would be only right if he tried to pay me back."[146]

Events come to a head when the coolie loses the
way. The merchant beats him and orders him to

pitch the tent. Their communal water bottle is empty, but the merchant has concealed another one. He secretly drinks from it, always thinking that if the coolie catches him, he will surely kill him—"provided he has even a trace of intelligence."[147] The coolie, however, also has another water bottle. He approaches the merchant in order to share its contents with him. But the merchant, convinced that the coolie is carrying a large stone with which to murder him, shoots the coolie and kills him.

In the last scene, the dead coolie's wife brings the matter to court. But the judge decides against her, since "the accused acted in justifiable self-defense."[148] The court holds that the coolie, as a member of an underprivileged class, and after all that he had suffered at the hands of the ruthless merchant, had every reason for revenge and that the merchant could not possibly have assumed that the coolie only wanted to give him something to drink. As the guide comments: "In the system they [the ruling classes] have created, an act of human kindness is an exception." [149]

The play ends with the actors addressing the audience with an echo of the message of *He Who Says No:* "Question that which is the custom./ Recognize that as abuse which is the rule./ And where you recognize abuse, abolish it."[150]

The play was not printed until 1937, and its first performance took place in 1938 at Givath Chajim, Palestine, in Hebrew. On 20 May 1965 it opened at the Greenwich Mews Theater in New York City, presented by the Greenwich Players (director: Isaiah Sheffer; music: Stefan Wolpe; Merchant: Paul E. Richards; Coolie: Joseph Chaikin; Guide: Richard Hamilton).

Howard Taubman of *The New York Times* at first felt "patronized" by Brecht's "transparently dogmatic" manner. But toward the end his resistance "ebbed," and he was touched by the play's message of "truth and humanity."[151]

Louis Snyder of the *New York Herald Tribune* maintained that the play was, "in theatrical terms, something of a throwback to the stage of day before yesterday." Yet he felt that since Brecht was in vogue in 1965, the play was "required seeing and hearing."[152]

As a contrast to this "bleached-out" performance, Lee Baxandall recommended the performances of this play given in May 1965 by the San Francisco Mime Troupe—"the leading theatrical expression of the New Left." They transposed the action from a meta-phoric desert to the black ghetto of Oakland, California. The merchant became a white policeman; the coolie, a black boy; and the water canteen, a harmon-ica. The policeman shot the boy, thinking that the har-monica was a knife.[153]

Brecht's *Lehrstücke* have often been compared with medieval morality plays, religious plays in the service of the Protestant or Catholic cause, and oratorios. And, indeed, the didactic play was frequently used during the seventeenth century by the Counter Reformation in Germany, particularly by the Jesuit order to illus-trate and teach their doctrine. The primary purpose of the religious or morality play was to teach correct behavior and to spread the gospel. With communism being a kind of secularized gospel, it comes as no sur-prise that Brecht resorted to this dramatic form.

Diversified as they are in subject matter, Brecht's *Lehrstücke* are characterized by a certain rigidity and uniformity of purpose. They are also good examples of his progressive concept of epic and dialectic the-ater as well as of his newly found creed, Marxism-Leninism. It is an indication of Brecht's versatility, however, that during this, his most doctrinal period, he also created such works as *The Threepenny Opera* and *The Rise and Fall of the City of Mahagonny.*

> *The Mother: Life of Pelageya Vlassova, Revolutionist from the City of Tver* (1931–32)

The Mother, written in 1931, demonstrates the transformation of Pelageya Vlassova, "widow of a worker and mother of a worker," into a revolutionary fighter. We also see the effects of her political activities, particularly in the way she brings about the transformation of Nicolai, the teacher, from a cynical independent to a sympathizer with the revolutionary cause. With Pelageya Vlassova, Brecht created a model to be imitated in the revolutionary struggle: "The play *The Mother* was first performed on the anniversary of the death of Rosa Luxemburg, the great proletarian revolutionist. With its songs and choruses it is dedicated to the workers, especially to the women who fight for the proletarian cause in Germany."[154]

The plot and the characters are taken from the revolutionary novel *The Mother* by the Russian writer Maxim Gorky. Gorky himself participated in the anti-czarist revolution of 1904–5, which he describes in the novel. Because of the censorship in czarist Russia, the novel was first published in English in a New York magazine in 1906 and 1907.

Brecht's collaborators on this play were Slatan Dudow, Hanns Eisler (who also composed the mu-

---

German title: *Die Mutter: Leben der Revolutionärin Pelagea Wlassowa aus Twer.*

sic), and Günther Weisenborn. With Günther Stark, Weisenborn had already created a dramatic version of *The Mother*, which was commissioned by Gorky himself.

But Brecht's play is far more than just an adaptation of Gorky's novel. Brecht wrote in 1951: "My play *The Mother* is loosely based on motifs of Gorky's novel, but it is not an adaptation of the classic novel. Nevertheless, it was authorized by Gorky himself."[155] One of the most obvious changes Brecht made was to extend the time period covered; like Gorky's novel, his play begins in 1905, but it ends on an optimistic note with the beginning of the successful Russian revolution in October of 1917. (The revolution of 1905, on the other hand, had failed.)

When the curtain opens, we see Pelageya Vlassova's room in the city of Tver, in the year 1905. She attempts to cook a good soup for her son, but, because of her poverty, she lacks the necessary ingredients. A chorus of revolutionary workers summarizes her situation: "Your situation is bad/ It is getting worse/ It cannot go on like this/ But what is the way out?"[156] But one thing is clear: "The decision about the meat that/ You don't have in the kitchen will/ Not be made in the kitchen."[157]

Pelageya's son, Pavel, has recently joined a group of revolutionary workers. Four of them arrive early in the morning at Pelageya's and Pavel's apartment, carrying a mimeograph machine. They hope to find, here, a safe place to print leaflets to be distributed in the Suchlinow factory on this decisive day when the workers have to decide either to accept a reduction in pay or to go on strike.

Pelageya does not approve of what is going on. She is afraid these people will drag her son into something terrible: "With concern, I notice how he reads these books, and with grief I see him run to those agitators' meetings instead of staying at home and resting. In doing this, he will only lose his job."[158] Masha, one of the workers, admonishes Pelageya with "The Song of the Way Out," which says that if the weak unite, they will be strong. At this moment, the police arrive and ransack Pelageya's room—but they find nothing, for the incriminating evidence has been well hidden.

Now the leaflets must be distributed, and it is Pavel's turn. Pelageya, however, is determined that Pavel should not get involved and she forbids him to distribute the leaflets. Instead, she will go herself. In order to get into the factory, she takes the place of a friend who sells food in the plant. Her plan is to wrap the food she sells in the leaflets. She herself has no idea what the leaflets say because she cannot even read.

Pelageya manages to convince the guard to let her into the factory. The workers buy food from her and read the leaflets. Some marvel at the courage and ingenuity of those who stand behind the movement: "Courageous fellows . . . there must be something to what they want."[159]

Members from the workers' council return from their negotiations—they were unable to prevent the wage reduction. The best they could do was to get an agreement that the money the company would save in wages would be used to dry out the swamp outside the factory, and then to expand the factory, which would, in turn, create new jobs. This, however, is unacceptable to the radical members: "We need the whole factory. And the coal and the iron and the power in the state."[160]

Some of the workers are caught reading the leaflets and are arrested by the security police.

Back in Pelageya's apartment, the workers explain to Pelageya that Mr. Suchlinow can do a lot of damage with his private property, the factory; he can ruin

many people who have nothing but their labor. Yet
at the same time, Mr. Suchlinow's factory with all its
machinery would be worth nothing without the workers. Thus he also depends on the workers. And that
is precisely what they mean to show him through the
strike. Pelageya understands, but she does not see
why the police have apprehended workers who were
caught with the leaflets, since, in her eyes, it is a
matter between Suchlinow and the workers. The
workers intend to have a peaceful demonstration for
their rights on 1 May. Pelageya naively believes that
the police will not interfere.

The actual demonstration and the ensuing bloody
confrontation with the police are not shown. But some
of the participants give reports in retrospect about
what happened, punctuated by pantomime and descriptive music. The peaceful demonstrators—Pelageya Vlassova among them—were confronted by the
police and the military, who opened fire when the
demonstrators refused to stop and surrender their red
flag. When the bearer of the red flag was shot,
Pelageya was appalled and took over the flag herself.
Her conversion to communism began at that point.
But so did her misfortunes: her son Pavel was arrested
and she was evicted from her apartment.

One of Pavel's friends, Ivan, takes Pelageya to his
brother, Nicolai, because Pavel's friends have promised him that they will take care of his mother while
he is in prison. Nicolai, a teacher, disapproves heartily
of his brother's political actions ("all nonsense"), but
he agrees to give Pelageya a place to stay. While
Pelageya and some neighbors are in Nicolai's kitchen,
discussing politics, Pelageya defends communism in
her song "Praise of Communism": "It [communism]
makes sense, everyone understands it, it is easy....
It is a simple thing but difficult to bring about."[161]
When Nicolai returns, tired from long discussions

about politics at the local bar, he is annoyed to find that Pelageya is attempting to win other people to communism; he does not want politics in his home.

Pelageya now realizes that if she is to become a successful revolutionary, she must learn to read. Nicolai begins to teach her to read—using such words as "branch," "nest," "fish." But Pelageya wants him to use such words as "worker," "class struggle," and "exploitation," since they are much more useful to her. She also wonders whether the soldiers—themselves sons of peasants—would have fired on the demonstrators if they had been able to read the posters the demonstrators were carrying. But, as the workers explain in the song "Praise of Learning," learning to read and write is only a first step: "Learn how to spell. It is not enough, but learn it. . . . You must know everything! You must take the lead."[162] Nicolai, on the other hand, displays a rather cynical attitude: "Generation upon generation has piled knowledge upon knowledge; they have written books upon books. And what good did it do? The confusion is greater than ever before."[163]

Ivan comes to visit Pelageya and to bring her the membership card of the communist party. Pelageya has no news of Pavel, but she is not distressed; she is proud to have a son who is serving to further the revolution. She expresses her pride by reciting "Praise of the Revolutionist." The teacher Nicolai continues to declare: "Russians will never start a revolution. That is something for the west. The Germans, they are revolutionists; they will start a revolution."[164] But to Ivan's surprise, Nicolai has changed: he has taken down the czar's picture.

Pelageya visits her son in prison. Despite the strict supervision of the guards during her conversation with Pavel, she learns the name of several farmers who want to read the communist newspapers. At this point, the actor who plays Pavel steps out of his role and sings about the impossibility of stopping communism, despite jails, laws, priests, professors, tanks, cannons, police, and soldiers.

While on the way to deliver the papers to the farmers, Pelageya and two workers are pelted with rocks by strikers who take them for strikebreakers. The two workers run away, but Pelageya, although wounded, talks to the strikers, who tell her that strikebreakers have been brought in and that some workers have not joined the strike. Pelageya comments: "Thus worker fights worker and the exploiters are laughing at us."[165]

Pelageya goes to the kitchen, where the butcher (who has not joined the strike) is serving a meal to the strikebreakers. There she justifies the strikers' attack on strikebreakers, even though she herself suffered from it. To her surprise, the butcher is pleased. This was the push he needed. He now recognizes that "rage and discontent alone are not enough. There must be action."[166] He joins the strikers and throws the strikebreakers out of his kitchen. In a song, he praises the "Vlassovas of all countries, the unknown but indispensable soldiers of the revolution," whether they are in "Tver, Glasgow, Lyon, Chicago, Shanghai, or Calcutta."[167]

The year is now 1912. Pelageya and her friends are getting ready to print leaflets in Nicolai's house. Although Nicolai is now "theoretically in sympathy with the cause,"[168] he is, however, still unable to translate theory into action. He is against printing leaflets in his home. Pelageya simply registers his complaint and continues the printing.

When Pelageya returns from a neighbor's apartment with some material to soften the noise of the printing machine, she finds her son, Pavel, waiting for her. He has returned from spending long years in Siberian prisons. But their reunion is cut short; Pavel has received orders from the communist party to move on to a new assignment in Finland. Observing the strict party discipline and the sacrifices the party demands, Nicolai comments: "I hear you are fighting for freedom, but you have the worst slavery in your own party. A nice freedom that is! Nothing but orders and coercion."[169] But they explain to him that it is necessary if they want to be successful. Pelageya understands that Pavel must leave again. She feels united with him through the cause they are both working for, as she explains in "The Song of the Third Cause."

During his attempt to cross the Finnish border, Pavel is captured and shot. We see Pelageya in Nicolai's kitchen reading the letter which contains the sad news. But her immediate reaction is not dramatized. Instead a chorus of revolutionary workers reminds Pelageya and the audience that there are still many people who actually help their own oppressors: "Comrade Vlassova, your son was shot. But when he stepped up to the wall to be shot, he went to a wall made by people like himself. And the rifles pointed at him were made by people like himself. These people still must be liberated."[170]

Pelageya's neighbors come and try to console her with religion: "Mrs. Vlassova, man needs God. He is powerless against fate." But Pelageya prefers to trust her own reason: "We say that man's fate lies in the hands of man. . . . It is not God's inscrutable plan that has taken away my son Pavel, but the czar's scrutable plan."[171]

Nevertheless, Pelageya's revolutionary fervor has been subdued by Pavel's death and by other setbacks for the revolutionaries. She is almost broken in spirit and health. But when she hears the news that World War I has broken out and the party calls her to mobilize against the czar and his war ("Arise, the party is in danger! Arise quickly! You are sick, but we need you"[172]), she awakens from her apathy.

While spreading propaganda on a street corner, Pelageya is severely beaten by policemen for shouting "Down with the war, long live the revolution!"[173] When two nonrevolutionary workers try to tell her to forget her revolution and go home, she implores them to see that in this war, worker is fighting against worker instead of uniting against the common enemy of their class.

Pelageya continues to work for the cause. In another scene we see her among a group of women who are standing in line in front of a "patriotic collection center for copper." They are waiting to hand in copper items to be used by the war industry. She succeeds in driving several of the women away. Finally, in 1917, we see Pelageya Vlassova, "the mother," marching in the ranks of striking workers and mutineering sailors who, in that same year, overthrow the hated czarist regime.

Here again we see a good example of epic theater. Brecht uses the device of a historical report. Rather than showing the revolution on stage, he has the characters report what happened and what they did. For instance, a maid recounts: "Our flag was carried by a sixty-year-old woman. We told her: 'Isn't the flag too heavy for you? Give us the flag!' But she said [and at this point Pelageya speaks herself]: 'No, if I get tired I will give it to you.'"[174] And Pelageya then recalls her development from initial passive desperation to active participation in the revolution, that many said they would never achieve their goal. Pelageya says: "He who is still alive must never say never! That which seems certain is not. Things will not remain as they are."[175]

The primary purpose of the play was undoubtedly to further the communist cause at a time when the struggle between rightists and leftists for the control of Germany was particularly fierce (at the beginning of the 1930s). Repeatedly, the actors step out of their roles to address the audience with revolutionary messages.

Rote Fahne, the newspaper of the Communist party of Germany (KPD) at that time, now finally began to count Brecht as a true communist, although he was never to join the Communist party, even after his return to East Germany after World War II.

With this play, Brecht hoped to achieve the same purpose as did the progaganda plays of the various communist agitprop groups (agitprop means agitation and propaganda); instruction by far outweighed entertainment. Brecht stressed in 1932 that: "The performance of *The Mother* pursued the goal of teaching its audience certain forms of political struggle. . . . It demonstrates methods of illegal revolutionary struggle. . . . It was particularly directed toward women."[176]

But Brecht by no means neglected the artistic side of the play. Its apparent simplicity is the result of years of experimentation: "Highly complicated considerations and years of stage experiments have led to its inception."[177] Brecht sought a radical form for a radical content, but what he desired most was to be understood by the masses. *The Mother* became one of the models of his epic theater, although it does not reach the artistic heights of his later plays.

Sentimentality and audience empathy were avoided at all cost—which at times places undue constraints on the play. The critic Herbert Ihering, for example, found the beginning scenes "austere and limited." But, in his opinion, the reunion of mother and son and the handling of the demonstration scenes were masterful pieces of epic theater.[178]

The play's artistic qualities and its revolutionary content are enhanced by Hanns Eisler's revolutionary music. Eisler, one of Arnold Schönberg's most gifted students, used modern musical techniques for his score. *The Mother* also contains one of Eisler's most famous songs, "Praise of Learning," "a classic song of the workers' movement which has been translated into almost all languages of the world."[179] Originally, the music was written for solo voice, chorus, trumpet, trombone, piano, and percussion. Later, while in exile in New York, Eisler composed a cantata version of *The Mother* (using only two pianos as instruments). In 1951 he added more songs and instruments.

The Mother was first performed on 17 January 1932 in the Komödienhaus Berlin by Gruppe Junger Schauspieler (Young Actor's Group; directors: Brecht and Emil Burri; sets: Caspar Neher; Pelageya Vlassova: Helene Weigel; Pavel: Ernst Busch). It was the last of Brecht's plays to be staged in Germany before he was forced to flee the country. The performance also marked Helene Weigel's breakthrough as an actress. The sets were artful but simple; there was no attempt to create the illusion of reality as a room or a street. In order to stress the universality of the content, the costumes did not suggest a particular time or place. In each scene, Neher used projections of titles, plot summaries, photographs, or slogans from Marx or Lenin. At the end, he had planned to show a film strip of the Russian October revolution, but this was forbidden by the censor. In the auditorium, he placed a placard with a Lenin slogan: "There is no real mass movement without women."

Herbert Ihering, critic of the *Berliner Börsen-Courier,* placed Brecht's version of *The Mother* next to Vsevolod Illarionovich Pudovkin's memorable Russian film version of Gorky's novel *The Mother* (along with Sergei Eisenstein's *Potemkin,* one of the great Russian film classics). Ihering found some roles still too mechanical and unnatural, but he felt that Brecht was definitely on the right path and that in Helene Weigel and Ernst Busch, Brecht had found two outstanding performers of his work.

The rage with which Alfred Kerr lambasted Brecht and the play appears almost pathetic in hindsight: "It is a play by a primitive author. Epic drama is a synonym for bad drama, for an idiotic play (I am sorry to say) ... false childishness as a result of dramatic impotence.... The German worker is by far not so retarded as the author.... For how long will people tolerate such impotence?" Yet he did acknowledge the acting of both Helene Weigel ("simply magnificent") and Ernst Busch. Kerr was by no means against the idea of a play about workers; indeed, he found it "extremely important—except there is no author."

And from the far right, Ludwig Sternaux commented: "Red, super-red, party theater under the sign of hammer and sickle. Gorky's old-fashioned novel mutilated for illiterates."

Brecht rebuffed these accusations by pointing out that thousands of workers had seen the play and they did not think it was "primitive." The leftist paper *Welt am Abend* counted *The Mother* "among the most fascinating proletarian plays of the decade."[180]

In 1935, the Theater Union in New York, the most famous American socialist theater, planned a production of Brecht's *The Mother*. Paul Peters adapted the play. But—having no understanding of epic theater, and with an American audience in mind—he made several changes, reintroducing stage illusion and empathy. His most serious alteration was moving Pavel's death to the end of the play. Brecht was furious. To straighten out matters, Brecht was invited to New York. But there were constant clashes between Brecht and the Theater Union people concerning the staging. Emotions became so bitter that Brecht (and Eisler) were literally thrown out of the theater two days before the opening performance.[181] The only person at the theater who understood what Brecht intended was the designer Mordecai Gorelik—with whom Brecht entered on a lifelong friendship.

The production opened on 19 November 1935 (director: Victor Wolfson; sets: Mordecai Gorelik; Pelageya Vlassova: Helen Henry; Pavel: John Boruff). The production lasted thirty-six performances. It met with a cool, even hostile reaction from the newspapers: "Poor stuff amateurishly presented" (*Daily Mirror*); "An entertainment for children, for it is a simple kindergarten for communist tots" (*Brooklyn Daily Eagle*).[182] To Brooks Atkinson of *The New York Times,* it was "an interesting experiment in stagecraft without much emotional vitality."[183] Only the communist *Daily Worker* had good things to say ("an exciting new play"[184]).

After the production, Brecht wrote a letter to the Theater Union in which he showed understanding for their problems and explained—in poetic verse—what he wanted to achieve with the form and content of his play. He admonished his comrades in New York not to shy away from experiments: "Comrades, the form of the new plays is new. But why are you afraid of what is new?"[185]

It is of great interest to see how *The Mother* is staged in a country where communism rules. On 12 January 1951, *The Mother* premiered with the Berliner Ensemble in East Berlin (director: Bertolt Brecht; sets: Caspar Neher; Pelageya Vlassova: Helene Weigel; Pavel: Ernst Kahler; and Ernst Busch in the relatively minor role of the teacher's brother). The events of the play were presented in a historic light, "as a poetic representation of a classic period," as Brecht called the period of struggle before the communists came to power.[186] The play was also in-

The Mother, Berliner Ensemble, 1951. Helene Weigel in the title role.

tended to render homage to the Soviet Union and to be a contribution to the re-education of the people of the young German Democratic Republic (established in 1949): "We wanted to make the Soviet Union likable to our workers, our middle class, and our intellectuals."[186] Artistic considerations, too, received more emphasis, and Brecht stressed the relationship of the play's form to the so-called classical period of German literature at the end of the eighteenth century ("from Goethe's *Götz* to Büchner's *Woyzeck*")[186] and the plays of Shakespeare. This production became one of the model performances of epic theater, described in detail in *Theaterarbeit.* This volume also contains Hans Garbe's review of the performance; one of East Germany's outstanding worker heroes, Garbe was strongly reminded of the class struggle in his youth.

When the Berliner Ensemble presented a guest performance in June 1960 in Paris (in the French Théâtre des Nations), the critics of the bourgeois press reacted much the same as had those in New York and Berlin. Jean-Jacques Gautier of *Le Figaro* felt—despite the great achievements of the director and the actors—that it was like being in "a night course for mentally retarded persons."[187] The French playwright Arthur Adamov, however, came to Brecht's defense in a very informative article in *Les Lettres Françaises*, in which he showed how well motivated Pelageya's transformation is. He demonstrated why, although she is one of the few "purely positive heroes" in Brecht's work, she is not presented in the traditional heroic fashion. Some of the critics obviously would have preferred a heroic presentation, but Brecht heartily disliked this style.[188]

The Mother has been performed in many Western countries but seldom in the established commercial theaters.

In November 1974, *The Mother*, in Lee Baxandall's translation, returned to New York City when the visiting San Francisco Mime Troupe staged a production of the play at the Chelsea Theater Center's Westside Theater, with Sharon Lockwood in the title role, and music by Hanns Eisler and the Mime Troupe itself. According to Mel Gussow of *The New York Times*, the Mime Troupe reinterpreted Brecht's text, attempting to relate it to the America of the 1970s. They colloquialized the dialogue and incorporated references to the new feminism and the current political situation. In his view, *The Mother* thus became "one of Brecht's most timely and relevant plays . . . both an explosive political incitement and bold, entertaining theater."[189]

On the other hand, Jost Hermand, reviewer for the *Brecht Yearbook,* who saw a production of the Mime Troupe's version of the play at the University of Wisconsin in Madison in the winter of 1973, found the production nothing more than a "grotesque cartoon . . . a mere pop-revolution."[190]

The Mother can be considered a *Lehrstück,* even though it does specifically require actors, thus deviating from the purest form of Brecht's *Lehrstücke.* Brecht himself noted: *"The Mother,* written in the style of the *Lehrstücke,* but requiring actors, is a play of the antimetaphysical, materialistic, non-Aristotelian dramatic composition."[191] It is Brecht's most revolutionary full-length play, not only in its form but also in its political content.

EXILE (1933–47)

The Seven Deadly Sins (1933)

In 1933, while in Paris, his first station in exile, Bertolt Brecht wrote the text for the ballet *The Seven Deadly Sins*. This biting satire on the values of bourgeois society was the last major work on which he collaborated with the composer Kurt Weill.

The ballet depicts the seven-year-tour made by two sisters from Louisiana to a number of American cities (among them Memphis, Los Angeles, Boston, Philadelphia, and San Francisco) in order to earn money for their family's "little house on the Mississippi River in Louisiana." The sisters are both named Anna— Anna I and Anna II—and actually personify only two aspects of one person. Anna is one of Brecht's many split characters: "We have one past and one future, one heart and one bank account."[1] Anna I is the manager, the salesman, always practically oriented; Anna II is the beauty, the artist, the commodity for sale.

Each of the seven scenes illustrates a "sin" that one must not commit if one wants to get ahead in a capitalistically oriented society. In scene two, for example,

German title: *Die sieben Todsünden.*

which is called "Pride," the people in a nightclub want to see sex, not art; Anna II must debase herself to give the customers what they want if she wants to make money. To refuse would be to commit the sin of pride. Anna's family back home in Louisiana prays that Anna will find the right path: "May the Lord enlighten our children that they find the path leading to prosperity. May he give them strength and ambition so that they do not trespass against the laws which lead to wealth and happiness."[2]

George Balanchine, who had commissioned the ballet for the troupe he had just established ("Les Ballets"), first performed the work on 7 June 1933, under the title *Anna-Anna, ou les Sept Péchés Capitaux* in the Théâtre des Champs Élysées in Paris, with sets by Caspar Neher and with Lotte Lenya as Anna. The ballet had little success, either in Paris or in London, where it was staged the same year. When it opened at the Royal Theater of Copenhagen, the Danish king left in protest, and the ballet had to be canceled after one performance.

In 1958, George Balanchine produced *The Seven Deadly Sins* in New York City (translation: W. H. Auden and Chester Kallman; Anna I: Lotte Lenya; Anna II: the young dancer Allegra Kent). *Time* magazine called it "a smash hit." James Lyons of *World Theatre* added: "It was unquestionably a remarkable theatrical achievement and deservedly a success with the press and the public alike."[3]

The ballet has seldom been performed, but with its witty text and Weill's catchy music, it surely deserves better.

The Horatians and the
Curiatians (1934)

Four years after he had written the last of his *Lehrstücke,* or didactic plays, Brecht used the *Lehrstück* form once more for his play *The Horatians and the Curiatians.* He himself called it "a *Lehrstück* for children about dialectics" or "a school play" when he published it in 1955. It was written in 1934 when he was living in Scandinavian exile. For the most part it is in irregular free verse. According to Hans Bunge, it was "commissioned by the Red Army."[4] Brecht's collaborator was Margarete Steffin. The source for the play was Livy's history of Rome. In Livy's work, Brecht found the description of the Horatians' fight against the Curiatians. (The Horatians were triplets from an established patrician family in ancient Rome who fought victoriously against the Curiatians, triplets from Alba Longa, near Rome.)

The play teaches a lesson in tactics: how a determined but underarmed army can beat a superior enemy through willpower, persistence, and cleverness. To divert attention from internal strife (struggle for real estate and iron-ore mines), the Curiatians decide to wage war against the neighboring Horatians and capture their land and possessions. Each army is composed of three units: archers, lance-fighters, and sword-fighters. In the battle of the archers, the Curiatians win over the Horatians, although they suffer losses. The Curiatian lance-fighters also win. Although their losses are quite severe, victory seems at hand for the Curiatians when the Horatian sword-fighters re-

---

German title: *Die Horatier und die Kuriatier.*

treat before their combined army units. But their joy is premature. The Horatians' retreat was only a strategy to separate the Curiatian armies in order to divide and conquer.

Brecht, of course, does not require whole armies on the stage in the Hollywood style. The leader of each of the armies represents his whole army. After the fashion of the Chinese theater, the individual parts of an army are indicated by little flags on wooden ledges which each army leader carries on his back. For each part of the army that is defeated, one flag is removed. Brecht suggested that the scenery be stylized in the fashion of a medieval etching; a landscape with knee-high trees and hills, constructed on a slanting stage, slowly rises toward the rear so that the audience can clearly see the landscape.

There are no direct references to communism or socialism in the play, and its lesson of encouragement is generally applicable in times of trouble. At the time Brecht wrote the play, this encouragement, however, was of particular importance for the socialist cause, since the Nazis had won in Germany and fascism was gaining ground in other countries. Thus the chorus of the Horatians encourages its lance-fighters: "Well then, retreat. You have lost time. You must lose more! You are weakened. Double your efforts! ... He who has victory before him will overcome many difficulties. It is difficult to face anew the old dangers while retreating and to redouble courage after defeat. ... Yet retreat is only part of a new advance for him who keeps on fighting."[5]

The play was never staged during Brecht's lifetime. It was first produced on 26 April 1958 in Halle, in the German Democratic Republic, by the Theater der Jungen Garde. The music was composed by Kurt Schwaen in 1956. It remains one of Brecht's rarely performed works. The play has been translated into English, but there is no record of a performance in the United States.

The Round Heads and the Pointed Heads, or Rich and Rich Stick Together (1931–35)

The Round Heads and the Pointed Heads is a horror story in the form of a parable in eleven scenes, using free verse, prose, and song. Brecht's collaborators were Emil Burri, Hanns Eisler, Elisabeth Hauptmann, and Margarete Steffin; the music was composed by Hanns Eisler. With this play, Brecht set out to show that in the fierce struggle between the right (the Nazis) and the left (the communists) at the beginning of the 1930s in Germany, Hitler used his racial theories only as a coverup to divert attention from the class struggle between poor and rich, regardless of race. And in the play Brecht wanted to demonstrate that the only significant conflict in our world is the conflict between wealth and poverty, "the only difference that really matters."[6]

The setting of the play is the city of Luma in the country of Yahoo. (In earlier versions it was Lima, Peru, which accounts for the Spanish names.) The people of Yahoo are of two different races; they are either Czichs (*Tschichen*), who have pointed heads, or Czuchs (*Tschuchen*), who have round heads.

The country is facing serious political and economic difficulties. Because a surplus of grain has brought

German title: *Die Rundköpfe und die Spitzköpfe, oder Reich zu Reich gesellt sich gern.*

down the selling price, the tenant farmers cannot pay rents to the landlords. An increasing number of impoverished tenant farmers join the Sickle Movement, which promises to free them by force from their oppressive landlords. In the eyes of the government, a solution to the economic problems would be an imperialist war, which would keep the people's minds off economics and at the same time create new markets. But first the landowners must be placated (their money is needed to finance the war), and the Sickle Movement has to be suppressed (the poor people are needed to fight the war). To solve these internal problems, the rulers of Yahoo (the vice-king and his advisor, named Missena) call upon Iberin, who himself comes from the lower classes, to serve as governor.

Iberin knows perfectly well that people tend to lay the blame for their own problems on other groups of people, so he "replaces the fight of rich against poor with the fight of Czichs against Czuchs."[7] Iberin blames everything on the Czichs, whom he describes as being "a foreign element ... without a home of their own ... shrewd and cunning." He claims the Czichs take advantage of the Czuchs, who are, though somewhat simple, "honest and faithful" and "from the beginning deeply rooted in the native soil."[8]

He promises the peasants that he will help them by curbing the power of the rich landowners. The rich landowners support him because he promises to destroy the feared Sickle Movement.

At this point, attention is focused on Callas, a Czuch tenant farmer. His poverty has forced his daughter Nanna to work in Mrs. Cornamontis's establishment as waitress and prostitute. Callas himself, suffering under his landlord Guzman, had joined the Sickle Movement. But when Iberin claims that it is the Czichs, not the rich, who are responsible for all of Yahoo's difficulties, Callas leaves the Sickle Movement. He deems it only just when he helps himself to the horses that belong to Guzman, a wealthy Czich. Still threatened by the Sickle Movement, the government does not dare to make Callas return the horses. In this period of instability, they cannot afford to affront the peasants.

At first, Callas is celebrated as a folk hero for this deed. Soon after, the government troops defeat the depleted Sickle Movement in a bloody battle. The race war has thus served its purpose of diverting attention from the class struggle. The old order, with its division between poor and rich, is firmly reestablished. Callas is then forced to give the horses back to Guzman.

In their place, he receives as a "gift" from the state a steel helmet and a military overcoat, so that he may go and fight in the imperialist war the government is preparing. And Guzman, the Czich, who, in the time of the racist turmoil, had been sentenced to death for "seducing" the Czuch prostitute Nanna Callas, is now absolved of all guilt and set free. The internal rebellion has been suppressed. The rulers of Yahoo can go to war and conquer new markets for their surplus goods. And for this endeavor they need the combined services of the rich landowners (such as Guzman) to finance it, the poor people (such as Callas) to fight it, and Iberin, the manipulator, to lead it.

In the last scene, after the remnants of the Sickle Movement—which consisted of both poor Czuchs and poor Czichs—have been executed, a festive banquet is held for Iberin, now Yahoo's vice-king, and the rich landowners, both Czuchs and Czichs. They celebrate peace, but a big gun barrel, lowered from the loft, exposes the nature of their "peace."

The play ends with a note of hope for the oppressed, however. A large red sickle appears on the wall of the dining hall (recalling the biblical hand-writing on the wall) and sends a shudder through the diners. The curtain closes as the tenant farmers sing the "Song of the Sickle Movement" that opens with the words "Peasant arise!"

The play presents an allegory of the political developments in Germany as Brecht saw them in 1934. The communists (the Sickle Movement) were gaining ground when Chancellor Hindenburg, the landowners, and the industrialists called Hitler (Iberin) to destroy the communists. Hitler accomplished this—according to Brecht—by promising to help the impoverished classes, and by appealing to their racist feelings in order to divert attention from the real social problems: class differences and exploitation by the rich. To open new markets, war was inevitable, and the capitalists needed Hitler and the common man to fight the war for them. In 1934, Brecht truly believed that Hitler, the newly elected chancellor of the German Reich, was only a tool in the capitalists' hands.

Originally this play was intended to be an adaptation of a Shakespearean play. In November 1931, Brecht was asked to adapt Shakespeare's *Measure for Measure* for a group of young actors in Berlin. He interrupted his work on this project, however, to write the play *The Mother,* which he considered more important. When he took up the project again, during his exile in Denmark, his plans for the adaptation had changed. *The Round Heads and the Pointed Heads* emerged in 1934, after passing through several versions, as a very different play from what Brecht had originally intended. Only a few details are reminiscent of Shakespeare's *Measure for Measure,* such as the meeting of Guzman and his sister Isabella (Brecht's scene eight), which is based on the conversation between Claudio and his sister Isabella in Shakespeare's play (III, 1). In *Measure for Measure,* the discussion in this scene centers around Claudio's impending execution. Claudio will be pardoned if his sister Isabella gives herself to the lustful Angelo, the Duke's deputy. Fearing death, Claudio attempts to persuade his sister to sacrifice her honor in order to save him, but his sister is appalled. Brecht closely followed the pattern of this scene. Guzman's life, too, is to be spared if Isabella fulfills the desires of Zazarante, Iberin's right-hand man. She, too, is horrified at the thought that Guzman would ask this of her.

Other important sources for the play, apart from Shakespeare's *Measure for Measure,* are the story *Michael Kohlhaas* by Heinrich von Kleist, and Jonathan Swift's *Gulliver's Travels. Michael Kohlhaas* (published 1808) is the story of a horse dealer who was robbed of two of his horses by a corrupt nobleman. When the courts, which were under the control of the nobility, denied him justice, he took the law into his own hands. He was caught and sentenced to death. *Gulliver's Travels* (published 1726) is a biting satire on the political life of England in Swift's time— the reigns of George I and George II and their powerful prime minister, Sir Robert Walpole. Swift used the term Yahoo, and even the title of Brecht's play is modeled after the Big-Endians and the Little-Endians of Swift's novel. Brecht's play also contains references to Hitler's book *Mein Kampf* (1925–27) and Hitler's hatred of "pointy-headed intellectuals."

On 4 November 1936, the first performance of the play was given in Danish in the Riddersalen theater in Copenhagen (director: Per Knutzon; Iberin: Asbjorn Andersen; Nanna Callas: Lulu Ziegler). It was a very important occasion for Brecht, who had little opportunity to see his plays performed while in exile. Most important for him were the measures undertaken to nullify stage illusion.

Brecht himself wrote a detailed description of how this was done. According to his description, the lighting apparatus was visible to the audience. The two pianos used in the production were illuminated when played, and the changes of scenery took place behind a half-high curtain. The audience was allowed to eat and smoke during the performance.

The director made it clear that the motivation of the characters did not stem from the "externally human condition," but from a particular time and particular circumstances in history. Brecht also described each role and how it was portrayed. Callas, the overworked tenant farmer, for instance, was portrayed as being opportunistic, yet he was not without his virtues. Iberin was not made to look like Hitler, but he used some of Hitler's gestures.

Furthermore, Brecht gave intricately detailed descriptions of the sets for each scene. For scene one, for instance: "small chair for the vice-king; a billiard table covered with newspapers, a map on a wooden stand; a broken lamp with only one bulb burning, a hat stand for the vice-king's hat; a door frame with door with a small emblem (a hyena holding a scepter) on top; in front of the door, a chair for the waiting Iberin."[9]

The play has seldom been performed. Even the Berliner Ensemble has yet to produce it.

The American premiere took place on 9 November 1973 on the campus of Cornell University (translation: Leonard Lehrman and Gesa Valk; director: Leonard Lehrman). As the program notes tell us, the producers felt that "a production of this parable of war, racism, whitewashing, and corruption seems especially appropriate in 1973. The parallels are so striking that one is tempted to feel that it could have been written some time this year." (The two most important and most controversial political issues in 1973 were the Vietnam war, which was still raging, and the Watergate scandal.)

Though *The Round Heads and the Pointed Heads* is not among Brecht's greatest works, it does contain some impressive scenes. The street scenes, for example, capture precisely the mood of the common man in Germany in the early 1930s. We also gain insight into how Iberin/Hitler was able to manipulate the common man; the play is a case study of political manipulation. There are many good examples of wit, satire, and parody (particularly in the political speeches given by Iberin, which parody Hitler's speeches).

The play also contains several well-known songs, such as "The Ballad of the Water Wheel." It may, in fact, be better remembered and appreciated for Hanns Eisler's excellent score than for the content of the play itself, although the play does remain an interesting experiment in epic theater.

Fear and Misery of the Third Reich (1935–38)

Between 1935 and 1938, while in exile near Svendborg, Denmark, Brecht wrote (in collaboration with Margarete Steffin) several scenes, varying in length and quality, about life inside Nazi Germany. The original title, *Germany—A Tale of Horror* (*Deutschland—ein Greuelmärchen*), was based on the Ger-

---

German title: *Furcht und Elend des Dritten Reiches.*

man poet Heinrich Heine's epic poem *Germany—A Winter's Tale* (*Deutschland—ein Wintermärchen*), which Heine wrote in 1844 while in exile in Paris. There are two musical scores for the play, one by Paul Dessau (1938) and one by Hanns Eisler (1945).

The scenes are based on eyewitness reports and newspaper articles. In his *Work Journal,* Brecht called the play a montage of scenes of life in a country ruled by a dictatorship. He wanted to show that his epic theater could also include naturalistic elements. Brecht advised the actors to study basic models of epic theater, but he also wanted them to master the techniques of arousing empathy. Thus each individual scene comes close to traditional theater.

In writing these scenes, Brecht kept in mind Slatan Dudow's proletarian German theater in Paris as a place for a possible performance, and the restrictive conditions of German performances in exile. He therefore kept the number of characters to a minimum. He also worked in terms of a flexible structure, so that a rearrangement of scenes or even the omission of several scenes was possible. Originally, there were twenty-seven scenes. For an edition to be published by the Aurora Publishing Company, New York, in 1945 (the Aurora company was a publishing house founded by Wieland Herzfelde and other German exiles, including Brecht), Brecht omitted four scenes and added one new scene. The 1967 Suhrkamp edition is based on this version, which contains twenty-four scenes, each introduced by an explanatory verse that provides the interpretation.

For an American version that was presented simultaneously in San Francisco and New York in June 1945, under the title *The Private Life of the Master Race,* Eric Bentley selected and translated seventeen of the twenty-four scenes.

The only link between the individual scenes is the

frame of reference: aspects of Nazi Germany, scenes presenting people living under a dictatorial regime and demonstrating how it affected them and their relations to each other. The staging can give further cohesion to the scenes, as Brecht noted in connection with the American performances: an armored personnel carrier of the German army appeared four times between the individual scenes, manned by twelve to fifteen soldiers with chalk-white faces. Between the other scenes, one could hear the rumbling sound of the carrier moving overland and a voice commenting on the events.

Twelve of the major scenes are synopsized in the following sketches.

"Betrayal." Breslau, 1933: lower-middle-class apartment. A husband and his wife have betrayed to the police a neighbor who was listening to a foreign radio broadcast. Hearing the sounds of the neighbor being dragged violently down the staircase, they make excuses for their action.

"The Chalk Cross." Berlin, 1933: kitchen in a mansion. The maid's boyfriend, now a proud Nazi storm trooper, demonstrates with the cook's brother, a jobless worker, how traitors are marked during cross-examinations by the Nazis. With a slap on the back, the person being interviewed receives a chalk cross mark, so that when he leaves, he is immediately arrested. During this mock cross-examination, many of the characters' real opinions about the Nazis are revealed in a rather humorous way. But the conversation in the kitchen also has a very ominous side because of the ever-hovering possibility that the storm trooper's remarks about the Nazis are intended as a serious test of the worker's opinions and as a possible trap. At the same time, this scene also gives a portrait of the characteristic storm trooper—an average lower-middle-class man who now feels very important and powerful. Although he takes all of his girlfriend's money for his Nazi activities, he treats her with condescension. She no longer understands him, he is completely changed ("they have totally ruined him").[10] She feels that he is now capable of betraying her, too.

"Justice." Augsburg, 1934: room in the courthouse. Three storm troopers have robbed and ransacked a Jewish store. The matter is now in court, but the judge faces a dilemma. The new legal principle "justice is what is good for the German people" is of no help. If the judge indicts the law-breaking storm troopers, as the townspeople expect him to, the Nazis will put an end to his career. On the other hand, if he acquits the storm troopers, an influential landlord, who needs the Jew's money, will see to it that the judge's career comes to an end. And the Jew certainly could not have provoked the storm troopers verbally, as they allege, because of an injury received in World War I that robbed him of his speech. The scene shows how difficult it was to administer justice under the Nazi regime.

"Occupational Disease." Berlin, 1934: hospital ward. A worker who has been severely beaten is brought in from a concentration camp in Oranienburg. Diagnosis: "occupational disease."

"Physicists." Göttingen, 1935: physics building at the university. Secretly, two physicists excitedly discuss Einstein's revolutionary theories. Publicly, they denounce them as Jewish sophistry.

"The Jewish Wife." Frankfurt, 1935. This is one of the most moving scenes. The Jewish wife of a non-Jewish doctor is packing to leave because she realizes that she now stands in the way of her husband's career. Neither her husband nor their friends want to admit that her continued presence would be an impediment. But her husband makes no real attempt to stop her from leaving. The scene is mostly monologue; the wife telephones friends to say goodbye.

"The Informer." Cologne, 1935: a rainy Sunday afternoon in a teacher's home. The teacher makes a few anti-Nazi remarks to his wife. When their small son goes out to buy himself some chocolate, the parents begin to fear that he may have gone to the Hitler youth quarters to denounce his parents (as the young people were instructed to do by the Nazis). The scene shows how fear stands between father and son, man and wife.

"Winter Aid." Karlsruhe, 1937: apartment of an older woman and her daughter. Two storm troopers, volunteers for the Winter Hilfe (a charitable organization of the Nazis), bring a package of food and money "from the Führer." But when the mother inadvertently mentions that her daughter has complained about rising prices, the storm troopers take away her daughter for spreading horror stories.

"Two Bakers." Landsberg prison, 1936. One baker is jailed because he did not add bran and potatoes to his bread (as the law demanded because of serious food shortages). The other is jailed because he did— two years earlier, when adding these things was illegal.

"Old Party Members." Calw, 1938: a city square of small shops. The Nazis no longer spare their own faithful members. They have just ruined a butcher who had supported them since 1929. He no longer had meat to put in his display window, and he refused to use the cardboard imitations of meat they wanted him to display in his window. Now he has hung himself in his display window, wearing a price list around his neck. On it he has inscribed: "I voted for Hitler."

"The Sermon on the Mount." Lübeck, 1937: living room of a fisherman. This scene illustrates the precarious position of the church under Nazism. A dying fisherman accuses the Nazis of preparing for war rather than taking care of the needs of the people. In the presence of his son, who is a Nazi storm trooper, the fisherman insists the minister tell him whether Jesus was right when, in the Sermon on the Mount, he praised those who love peace, or whether it was only "the babbling of a Jew," as the Nazis claim. The minister manages to evade the issue by quoting Luke (20:25): "Render unto Caesar that which is Caesar's and unto God that which is God's."

"Work Procurement." Spandau, 1937: apartment of a worker. The parents receive a letter telling them that their son has been killed in a crash during a training flight near Stettin. In reality, however, he was shot down in the Spanish Civil War (1936–39, in which Hitler sent troops to support the fascist Franco). Ironically, the bomber he was flying was built in the factory where his father has just been given a desperately needed job. The scene illustrates how Hitler reduced the ranks of millions of unemployed by providing jobs in the war industry.

The play includes several other scenes: "Community of People" shows the reign of fear and terror. "Moor Soldiers" and "Service for the People" are two scenes from concentration camps. "The Black Shoes" illustrates the pressures put on parents by the Hitler youth. "Labor Service" exposes the fraudulence of the Nazis' alleged abolition of class differences. In "The Hour of the Worker," "happiness through National Socialism" is exposed as a sham. In "The Box," a worker is shot for criticizing bad working conditions. In "Discharged," a released concentration camp prisoner is shunned by his friends because they fear he is an informer. In "The Peasant Feeds His Sow," a farmer has difficulties feeding his animals, because the government demands all his grain. In "The Word of Admonition," Hitler youth exploits youngsters and parents. In "In the Barracks the Soldiers Learn About the Bombardment of Almeria," soldiers fear that the civil war in Spain will soon spread to Germany. In "Plebiscite," resistance workers prepare leaflets against Hitler containing only one word. NO.

Seven scenes of this play were first performed on 21 May 1938 in Paris under the title 99%, with Slatan Dudow directing and Helene Weigel and Ernst Busch as actors. The songs in this production were the first Brecht texts that Paul Dessau set to music.

The first performance of the play in the United States took place on 28 May 1942 in New York City, when Berthold Viertel produced four scenes in German. The scenes presented were "Justice," "The Chalk Cross," "The Jewish Wife," and "The Informer." They were staged by The Forum for Free German Literature and Art in America, a group composed mostly of German émigrés. The actors included Ludwig Roth, Lotte Stein, Elisabeth Neumann, and Eleanore von Mendelsohn. The proceeds were earmarked for refugees from fascism. According to a review by Hermann Kesten in *Aufbau* (5 June 1942), the production was well received.

Seventeen scenes, in Eric Bentley's translation, were performed in Los Angeles (7 June 1945: University of California) and New York (12 June 1945; presented by the Theater of All Nations at the Pauline Edwards Theater). Berthold Viertel directed the New York performance; the actors were German émigrés (among whom was the famous Albert Bassermann) and Americans (including Clarence Derwent and Dwight Marfield). Brecht was there to advise Viertel. He also got a glimpse of Broadway, which, in Brecht's words, "mirrors the intellectual life of the States—nervous, commercialized, standardized." When he read the reviews of the play, he was disappointed: "They attack the production, but spare the play; nowhere is there a discussion of its content."[11]

Otis L. Guernsey, Jr., the critic for the *New York Herald Tribune*, called Brecht's documentary play "a dull and muddled experimental production." He wrote: "The case as stated in this play is obsolete, and it is not spoken eloquently."[12]

Lewis Nichols of *The New York Times* was not quite as negative. In his opinion, the play was "an interesting experiment" and "forceful," but the individual scenes were uneven in quality and seemed "dated." The production and the acting, according to Nichols, were not what they should have been.[13]

The less than enthusiastic reception of the play was perhaps also due to bad timing of the performance. In June 1945, a few weeks after the war in Europe was over, the Americans were very tired and sad. Moreover, their attention was now focused on ending the war against Japan. Brecht's play was designed to arouse people against the Nazis. This was necessary in 1938, but in 1945 the Nazis had already been defeated and their atrocities had been exposed to the world.

On 30 January 1948, exactly fifteen years after Hitler's ascension to power, and almost three years after his downfall, the Deutsches Theater in East Berlin staged seven scenes of *Fear and Misery of the Third Reich*. Directed by Wolfgang Langhoff, it offered such famous actors as Werner Hinz and Angelika Hurwicz. Berlin critic Friedrich Luft found the scenes a precise and exemplary analysis of Germany's most shameful historical period. The play had a deep and powerful impact on him, especially the scene "The Jewish Wife."[14]

In January 1956, The Opera Stage theater group in New York City presented *The Private Life of the Master Race* ("a bitter cartoon of totalitarian life"), with Norma Frances directing. According to Brooks Atkinson of *The New York Times,* the scenes (in Eric Bentley's translation) were "crisp and incisive," the production "talented and interesting," and some of the acting "exhilarating." But Mr. Atkinson found the play dated: "Brecht's method is more interesting today than what his play has to say."[15]

One of the best scenes in *Fear and Misery of the Third Reich,* "The Jewish Wife," was also part of *Brecht on Brecht,* a selection of works by Brecht assembled by George Tabori. In a 1961 production of this work by the Greater New York Chapter of the American National Theater and Academy in New York City's Theatre de Lys, Viveca Lindfors gave "a trenchant performance in the role of the wife."[16]

Many of the scenes of *Fear and Misery of the Third Reich* still affect audiences, including the younger members, as shown by a performance in Wuppertal, West Germany, in September 1973. One reviewer wrote: "At the premiere, the audience, consisting mainly of young people, was very quiet and pensive.' What made the Wuppertal production particularly shocking was the contrast between the optimistic and cheerful superficiality of the popular songs of the Nazi era, which were presented between the scenes (for example, *"Das kann doch einen Seemann nicht erschüttern"*—"Nothing can upset a sailor") and the cruel reality of the scenes themselves.[17]

We are still being swamped with books and movies about World War II and the Third Reich. Most of them, however, are of dubious quality, emphasize the sensational, and make little or no attempt at historical accuracy. Brecht's play remains one of the few sources presenting an objective and gripping picture of life under the Nazi dictatorship.

Señora Carrar's Rifles (1937)

Brecht wrote this one-act play in 1937, first using the title "Generals over Bilbao"; his collaborator was Margarete Steffin. According to John Willett,[18] the play can be considered "a modern version of the Irish playwright John Millington Synge's *Riders to the Sea*." But Brecht shifted the action from Ireland to Spain, changed the time, and gave the play a political background.

Since 1930, Spain had had a liberal, democratic government. In 1936, when leftists gained a slight majority in the elections, the rightists under General Franco staged a coup against the democratically elected government. It was the beginning of the Spanish Civil War, which Franco's rightists finally won in 1939 after a long and bitter struggle. International brigades of volunteers from numerous countries, including the United States and the Soviet Union, supported the republican government, while Hitler and Mussolini came to the aid of Franco.

At the time Brecht completed the play, the Spanish Civil War had been in progress for a year, and Brecht intended the play to be his contribution to the loyalist cause.

The play is set in an Andalusian fishing village in April 1937. There is only one set: a room in the house of Teresa Carrar, the forty-year-old widow of a fisherman. It is night; through the window one can see the light of the fishing boat belonging to her son Juan Carrar. The roar of cannon can be heard in the distance. Juan is fishing alone, for all the other able-

German title: *Die Gewehre der Frau Carrar.*

bodied young people are at the front. But Teresa Carrar wants to keep her two sons, José, fifteen, and Juan, twenty-one, out of the war at all cost: "I do not want my children to become soldiers. They are not cattle raised for slaughtering."[19] She believes that if she remains neutral, no one will harm her.

The other people in the village, however, suspect that she is on the generals' side. (Franco and his military leaders are called generals in the play.) The children sing verses mocking Juan as a coward, and Juan's girlfriend breaks off with him. Juan wants to go to war, but Teresa Carrar remains adamant; she does not want a repetition of a great mistake she made once before and for which she had to pay dearly. Two years before, she had encouraged her husband, Carlo, to join the struggle on the side of the leftists, and he came back in a coffin. Therefore, she keeps Carlo's rifles well hidden and a close eye on her sons. The village priest is not unsympathetic to the republican cause, but he insists "thou shalt not kill." He supports Teresa in her efforts to keep her sons at home.

When a decisive battle between the republicans and the generals is shaping up, Teresa's brother Pedro appears. He wants her to give him Carlo's rifles, and he also wants her two sons. In sharp arguments, he tries to convince Teresa and the priest that by not taking sides, they "condone every bloodbath the generals are causing among the Spanish people."[20] Pedro's arguments silence the priest, but they do not convince Teresa Carrar. She threatens to hang herself if her sons go, and she refuses to give Pedro the rifles.

When she notices that the light of Juan's fishing boat has disappeared, she suspects that she has been tricked so that Juan could run away and join the republican army. But she is wrong—minutes later, two fishermen come, carrying Juan's body. While fishing peacefully, he was shot by the fascists. Now Teresa realizes that everything her brother said about the generals is true: "They are not humans. They are like leprosy, and must be burned out like leprosy."[21] Suddenly the roar of the cannon increases; the generals' troops have broken through. Now Teresa urges her brother and her son José to hurry to the front, and she herself joins them with her rifles—"for Juan."

Although Brecht was at this time working to develop his theory of epic theater, *Señora Carrar's Rifles* is the only play he wrote almost entirely in the traditional theater style: "It is Aristotelian theater using dramatic illusion." Realizing that, for him, this was a step backward, he added: "The disadvantages of this technique can be compensated—at least to some extent—by presenting the play along with a documentary film of the events in Spain."[22]

Señora Carrar's Rifles is not representative of Brechtian theater, but as Martin Esslin writes, it is "effective theater," affording "great opportunities to the actress playing Señora Carrar."[23] Brecht himself, however, thought differently; he considered the play an expression of his solidarity with his fellow leftists, written by and large as a dutiful act. In the summer of 1937, he attended the International Writers' Congress in Paris. The Spanish Civil War was discussed extensively at the Congress, and at its conclusion, many participants traveled to Spain, among them Brecht's friend and collaborator, the Danish actress Ruth Berlau. Brecht, however, thought the situation in Spain too dangerous. Returning to Denmark, he wrote his play in support of the leftist cause in Spain. He feared for the safety of his friends in Spain and blamed himself for being too cowardly to go. Neither at the time of its completion, nor later, did he have much to say about his play *Señora Carrar's Rifles*, except that it was "too opportunistic."[24]

The published drama does not use names to identify characters. By referring to them only as "the mother," "the boy," "the priest," Brecht wanted to imbue the play with universal meanings. His characters are individuals, but they also represent types and patterns of behavior.

The propagandist and emotional effect is increased by the inclusion of famous songs of the Spanish Civil War. We hear the international brigades moving past Señora Carrar's house singing "Die Heimat ist weit" (Germans), "Bandiera rossa" (Italians), "Hold the Fort" (Americans), and "Los cuatros generales" (Spaniards).

The first performance of *Señora Carrar's Rifles* took place on 16 October 1937 in Paris. Advertising posters stated: "Brecht's new play is dedicated to the Spanish people's heroic struggle for freedom." Brecht himself traveled from Denmark to Paris to participate in the rehearsals of the play, which was presented by a group of German exiles, directed by Slatan Dudow, with Helene Weigel as Teresa Carrar.[25]

On 19 December 1937, Ruth Berlau directed a Danish version of the play in Copenhagen's workers' theater; the title role was played by Dagmar Andreason. Brecht, who attended the performance, made notes comparing the ways Weigel and Andreason played the title role. These notes convey some interesting information about Brecht's theory of acting. Neither actress, in his opinion, tried to identify completely with the part she played. But Andreason's portrayal did not provoke the audience to take a position as Weigel's had done in Paris. The Danish audience took Señora Carrar's initial neutrality as "natural" without questioning it. One of the most important demands Brecht made of an actor was that the actor present the events in such a way that the audience must take a position, either for or against. Brecht, however, did not necessarily attribute the Danish production's "neutrality" to Andreason's lack of acting talent; rather, he thought it merely reflected Denmark's political neutrality.[26]

The first American production of the play, in Keene Wallis's translation, was staged by San Francisco's Theater Union under the direction of George Altman. It opened on 3 February 1939 in San Francisco's Green Street Theater.

Shortly after the end of World War II, in May 1946, the Hebbel Theater in Berlin produced *Señora Carrar's Rifles* (director: Peter Elsholz; Carrar: Lu Säuberlich). The critic Friedrich Luft liked Brecht's pungent and ingenious language and the production, particularly the scenery, which was not designed to achieve a naturalistic effect. But he found the content of the play dated.[27]

On 9 and 10 December 1968, the American National Theater and Academy (ANTA) matinee series at the Theatre de Lys, New York City, presented two performances of *The Guns of Carrar* (translated by George Tabori; director: Harris Yarlin; Teresa Carrar: Viveca Lindfors; José: Kristoffer Tabori; Pedro: Billy Macy; priest: Michael McGuire).

For Clive Barnes of *The New York Times,* it proved "among the most interesting evenings of a so-far poor Off Broadway season . . . much more rewarding [than] so much rubbish . . . put on for a run of eternity." He noted that the play was "at heart . . . nothing but a propaganda tear-jerker." Nevertheless, "Brecht's little play, as subtle as a recruiting poster and as balanced as a pistol, is still oddly moving in its simple naturalistic writing and the depth of its feeling." He thought Miss Lindfors played "beautifully," and that the acting was "of a good honest standard."[28]

In March 1972, the Chilean-North American Cultural Center in Temuco, Chile, was inaugurated with a production of *The Rifles of Mother Carrar,* performed by the theater workshop of the University of Chile, directed by Gaston Iturra. The socialist-oriented company also performed this play for peasants at agrarian-reform sites and for workers in factories. This play was chosen because at that time the Chilean socialist regime of President Salvador Allende Gossens was struggling to gain the confidence of the country. Director Iturra felt that the play was "an important work to present at this moment because it raises the issue of commitment and neutrality in a revolutionary situation."[29]

Teresa Carrar, "the mother," has many traits in common with Pelageya Vlassova in *The Mother.* Both want to keep their children out of danger, yet both finally join the struggle on the side of the oppressed. Yet, it is interesting to note, in comparing the two plays, that *The Mother* (written six years earlier, in 1931) is a model of Brecht's epic theater, while *Señora Carrar's Rifles* is written almost entirely in the Aristotelian theater tradition.

Galileo (1938, 1944–45, 1953–56)

Galileo, the astronomer and physicist (1564–1642), discovered the moons of Jupiter, which provided scientific proof of Copernicus's theory that the earth was not the center of the universe. Galileo was forced by the Roman Catholic Church to recant his discovery since the church's teachings were based on Aristotelian physics and the Ptolemaic system, which stipulated

German title: *Leben des Galilei.*

that the earth was the center of the universe. Brecht became interested in Galileo because he saw parallels between the Roman Catholic Inquisition methods and German Nazism.

There are three versions of Brecht's *Galileo:* the first version, written in 1938; the second version, written between 1944 and 1945 (with Charles Laughton; in English), and the third version, written from 1953 to 1956. The following summary is based on the third version.

The opening scene shows the forty-six-year-old Galileo in his modest study in Padua. It is morning. Andrea Sarti, his landlady's young son, brings Galileo his breakfast and reminds him that the milkman's demands for the money owed him can no longer be ignored. At this moment, however, Galileo's mind is directed more toward the movements of the stars than the price of milk. In an exuberant mood, he demonstrates Copernicus's theory that the earth moves around the sun by picking up Andrea and his chair and carrying him around the washbasin. The Ptolemaic system, with the earth as center of the universe, is the officially accepted view, however. But Galileo wants to break down these "walls and scales of immobility."[30] He feels that he is on the threshold of a new epoch in which everything will be reexamined— although he is quite aware of the fate of Giordano Bruno, who was burned at the stake in 1600 for propagating Copernicus's theories.

But first the urgent problem of money must be resolved. Fortunately, a rich nobleman by the name of Ludovico comes to Galileo to take private lessons. He also brings with him from Holland the latest discovery, a telescope.

The procurator of the University of Padua, where Galileo is a professor of mathematics, appears to bring the bad news that Galileo's request for a salary increase has been denied. He suggests that Galileo accomplish something of practical value in order to impress the dignitaries of the Republic of Venice. Galileo sees a chance to put the telescope to good use.

In a big ceremony (which covers the entire second scene), Galileo offers the leaders of Venice the telescope, claiming that it took him seventeen years to devise it. He knows that this is a lie, of course, but he needs the money to carry out more important research —and to eat well, which he also likes to do. The success of Galileo's ploy is assured when the usefulness of a telescope in the case of war is pointed out to the officials of Venice.

Galileo, however, has another application: with the telescope he can watch more closely the movements of the stars. On the cold winter night of 10 January 1610, Galileo and his friend Sagredo, clad in thick coats, are observing the heavens. Their discoveries lead them to believe that the moon and the earth are celestial bodies like millions of others reflecting light from the sun. They also discover that Jupiter has four moons circling around it. The Copernican hypothesis is thus proved to be true.

The traditional fundamental concept of "Heaven" (God in heaven, above the earth) has ceased to exist. Alarmed, Sagredo asks, "Where is God in your system?" And Galileo answers: "Within ourselves or nowhere!"[31] Despite Sagredo's warnings, Galileo decides to move to Florence, where he will receive more money and have more time for his research. In Florence he will also have a more comfortable life. Galileo trusts in the rationality of man, including the monks, and he believes they will not resist rational arguments and proof: "I believe in man and that means I believe in the power of reason."[32] He hopes that the theologians will make the necessary adjustments.

But in the next scene events prove ominous for Galileo. His Highness, the Archduke Cosimo de' Medici of Florence, and members of his court come to hear about Galileo's moons of Jupiter. While his entourage is waiting for Galileo to arrive, Archduke Cosimo (who is only nine years old) manages to slip upstairs to Galileo's room, where Cosimo and Andrea soon get into a fight over the miniature models of the Ptolemaic and Copernican systems. By accident, the Ptolemaic model breaks into pieces. (Unfortunately, this delightful scene, which allows us a satiric glimpse at the feudal system and gives a hint of the eventual fate of the Ptolemaic system, is missing in Laughton's English version).

The wrestling match is interrupted by the arrival of Galileo and the dignitaries. But before they look through the telescope, the dignitaries insist on a formal disputation. Their philosopher states that according to the teachings of Aristotle, the newly discovered moons are neither possible nor desirable because they would destroy the beautiful harmony of the spheres. In vain, Galileo begs them simply to trust their eyes and look through the telescope. They leave in order to attend a state ball, without ever having seen the moons.

The next scene shows Galileo working to find proof for his hypotheses while the plague is ravaging the city of Florence. He even refuses to take the carriage that Archduke Cosimo—who has already fled the city —has sent to rescue him. This scene (also missing in Laughton's version) shows Galileo's tremendous devotion to his work, because Galileo hopes that he will be able to convince the Collegium Romanum, the Vatican's research institute, that his theories are correct. This scene also has a symbolic function: in the eyes of the church, Galileo's discovery is like a plague. (There is no historic record of a plague in Florence at this time; Brecht simply invented it for dramatic purposes.)

The next scene opens in the hall of the Collegium Romanum; the year is 1616. At any moment Clavius, the chief astronomer, may appear to announce his findings after examining Galileo's theories. On one side of the hall, a group of high clergymen, monks, and scholars make fun of Galileo's findings: "I am getting dizzy, the earth is revolving too fast!"[33] Galileo is waiting silently by himself at the other end of the hall. In a very impressive scene, a very old cardinal, supported by a monk, steps forth to make a speech about the importance of man as the pinnacle of creation and the earth as the center of the eight crystal spheres of the universe. In the middle of his speech, he—"the pinnacle of creation"—collapses.

At this moment, Clavius appears and walks briskly through the hall. Just before leaving, he remarks almost casually, "It is true." No one speaks; all are in deep shock. Galileo feels he has won: "Reason has prevailed!"[34] But there are omens of trouble to come. The very old cardinal discovers a similarity between Giordano Bruno (who was burned for heresy) and Galileo. As Galileo leaves the hall, he meets the towering figure of the cardinal inquisitor, who has been brought to see the telescope. (The appearance of the inquisitor is missing in the Laughton version, but, although short, it is a very significant and effective scene.)

These forebodings become reality in the confrontation between Galileo and the ruling system, embodied in the Cardinals Bellarmin and Barberini. In this most impressive scene, which takes place at a masked ball in Cardinal Bellarmin's house, the two cardinals, one wearing the mask of a dove, the other the mask of a lamb, show their real faces behind the masks. They do not deny the truth of Galileo's discovery. Neither are they upset about it. They are even willing to allow Galileo to pursue his research in astronomy as mathematical hypotheses. But they do not like the implication of the discovery. In Galileo's words, the implicit message of Galileo's discovery is: "If a man can misunderstand the universe, he could also misinterpret the Bible."[35] In an effort to avoid unrest among the people, the Holy Office has banned Copernicus's teachings as heresy because they are contrary to the doctrines of the Church. The cardinals freely admit that Christianity serves as a tool in the hands of the clergy to assert its authority and to keep the people quiet and submissive: "If there were no God, we would have to invent one."[36]

Virginia, Galileo's daughter, is totally ignorant of her father's situation. She therefore becomes an easy tool by which the cardinal inquisitor can spy on her father.

What the two cardinals presented in a rather cynical manner at the masked ball is shown to be a serious concern for the common people in the next scene, which is a conversation between Galileo and the Little Monk. The monk points out the anguish that would result if people were to lose the comfort of the Bible and of the accepted order of the world; they would learn that they in fact inhabit only a minor planet spinning in a vast universe, and that all of their sufferings are for nothing, since there is no Heaven above. "We must be silent from the highest of motives, the peace of mind of those unfortunate people."[37]

But Galileo answers bluntly that truth cannot be regulated: "The sum of the angles in a triangle cannot be changed to suit the wishes of the pope."[38] On this occasion, we also hear that the cardinals have offered Galileo all the comforts of the good life they themselves enjoy if he remains silent about his discoveries. But Galileo feels he must pass along what he has learned. Once he has tasted of the tree of knowledge, he cannot stop doing further research—like the Little Monk, who in the meantime is fervently reading Galileo's manuscripts.

In the next scene, we see Galileo once again teaching the old Aristotelian physics to his students. Apparently he has heeded the cardinals' warnings after all. He has remained silent for the past eight years and ceased to do research into the movements of the earth. Even the discovery of sunspots and scientific hypotheses concerning their origin leave him outwardly unmoved, at first. But when he hears that Cardinal Barberini, himself a mathematician, is about to become pope, he resumes his inquiries into the movements of the stars, the sun, and the earth. And neither his housekeeper, Mrs. Sarti, nor his daughter Virginia, nor her rich fiancé, Ludovico, can stop him. Ludovico leaves after a serious argument with Galileo —the engagement with Virginia is broken off. But nothing can deter Galileo from closely examining the sunspots to find proof for the earth's revolution: "I must know."[39]

Since Galileo records his findings in Italian rather than in the customary scholarly Latin, his discoveries can be read by the common people. Galileo's findings gain wide popularity. To demonstrate this on the stage, the next scene takes us to a market square in an Italian city during the carnival festivities of 1632. A ballad singer entertains the people with songs about the "teachings and opinions of the court physicist Galileo Galilei" and "a taste of the future." The ballad singer seemingly makes fun of Galileo's findings. But in the mask of the fool, he dares to suggest that since the celestial order has changed, why not change the terrestrial order, too. The stars no longer move in the paths the Church has prescribed; why should the people?

In the next scene, we find Galileo and his daughter Virginia in front of the palace of the Medici in Florence; the year is 1633. Galileo has come to submit the *Discorsi* to Archduke Cosimo. But he is kept waiting and the people he sees are noticeably constrained. Only the iron founder Vanni (called Matti in Laughton's text) gives him encouragement: "I don't know much about the movement of the stars, but for me you are a man who is fighting for freedom."[40] He assures Galileo that he, Galileo, has widespread support among the Italian manufacturers, who hope that greater freedom to learn about scientific discoveries will improve their production. He advises Galileo to leave Florence. Finally the archduke emerges, but he totally ignores Galileo's book. An official of the court explains that Galileo has been ordered to go to Rome: "The carriage of the Holy Inquisition is waiting for you, Mr. Galileo."[41]

The next scene opens in a private room in the Vatican. Pope Urban VIII, formerly Cardinal Barberini, is being dressed in ceremonial robes for an audience with the scholarly world, representatives of all religious orders, and the entire clergy. They have come to be reassured by the Pope in the face of the growing unrest evoked by Galileo's teachings. The noise of the crowd outside the room gives a sense of particular urgency to the scene. With the Pope is the inquisitor, who eloquently points out the adverse effects of the work of Galileo and other scientists: "These people doubt everything. Shall we build human society upon doubt rather than upon faith? . . . What would be the result if everyone trusted only in his own reason!?"[42] (This brilliant speech is considerably shortened in the Laughton version.) The Pope tries to defend Galileo, but the pressures on him are too great: from within, the state of the Church and social unrest; from without, the Thirty Years War, a battle between Protestants and Catholics which has been raging in central Europe for the past fifteen years.

The next scene shifts to the palace of the Florentine ambassador in Rome, where Galileo's students are waiting for the news as to whether Galileo has recanted or is holding firm. The day is 22 June 1633. Andrea recalls the words Galileo once used when scolding one of his students: "He who does not know the truth is only a simpleton. But he who knows the truth and calls it a lie is a criminal."[43]

If the bell of St. Mark's rings at five o'clock, it will be a sign that Galileo has recanted. When five o'clock arrives and the bell does not ring, the students are elated: "So much is gained if only one man arises and says no!"[44] But their joy is short-lived—a moment later the bell strikes and a town crier announces Galileo's recantation. Galileo's daughter Virginia, however, is relieved. Then Galileo enters—almost unrecognizable from twenty-three days in jail and the Inquisition procedure.

Andrea loses his composure and shouts at him: "So you saved your precious skin, didn't you!?" Andrea leaves in disgust, pitying the "country without heroes." But Galileo replies: "Unfortunate is the land that needs heroes."[45]

The next scene is most significant in that it shows Brecht's view of Galileo and discusses the role of a scientist and his responsibility to society. Galileo, now an old man and half blind, is in a country house near Florence, still a prisoner of the Inquisition. His daughter Virginia, now forty years old, and a monk watch over all Galileo's actions, experiments, and writings. In addition, he has to write regular reports about his activities to the archbishop. While Virginia and Galileo are composing their weekly letter to the archbishop, Andrea Sarti enters. The meeting is at first awkward. But when Andrea learns that Galileo has secretly made a copy of his *Discorsi,* Andrea is elated and praises Galileo's cunning wisdom: "You hid the truth from the enemy. Even in the field of ethics you were ahead of us hundreds of years."[46]

Andrea believes it was all carefully planned, but Galileo ruthlessly destroys his illusions. He tells Andrea that he recanted because he feared torture and death and proceeds to explain to Andrea why he is a failure as a scientist: "I believe that the only goal science has is to ease the burden of human existence. If scientists, intimidated by powerful potentates, accumulate knowledge only for knowledge's sake, science could be crippled, and new machines could only mean further oppression and suffering.... The joy over each discovery could turn into a universal cry of horror." Galileo feels that if he had resisted—and the times were favorable then because "astronomy reached the market places"—scientists could have developed something similar to the Hippocratic oath of the medical profession, a vow that they would use their knowledge only for the betterment of mankind. He feels that he has betrayed his profession because he delivered his knowledge into the hands of the authorities instead of the people.[47]

But the scene does not end on an entirely pessimistic note. When Andrea leaves, he secretly takes the *Discorsi* with him to Holland, hoping that Galileo's pessimistic view will not be the last word in this matter.

The last scene is very brief. It shows Andrea crossing the Italian border. A new age can now begin.

Brecht's plans for a play about Galileo Galilei go back to about 1933. But it was not until 1938 while in exile in Denmark, after extensive studies on the historical Galileo, that Brecht wrote the first version of his play *Galileo.* (Initially he had planned to call it *The Earth Moves.*) It was Brecht's sixth year in exile, and Hitler's rise, since his assumption of power in 1933, seemed destined to continue. In those dark times, Brecht wanted to give some hope and encouragement to those living under fascism. In Brecht's play, Galileo's progressive *Discorsi,* which was written secretly under an oppressive system, is a symbol of hope.

Soon after Brecht had completed the manuscript, the news went around the world that the German physicists Otto Hahn and Fritz Strassmann had succeeded in splitting the atom. When Brecht heard about this marvelous discovery, he added one passage to his finished manuscript: Galileo says to his young student Andrea,

> While in some places great discoveries, which should immensely increase the happiness of men, are being made, large parts of the world are still in darkness. Darkness has even increased in those places! Take care when you travel through Germany with the truth [the *Discorsi*] under your coat.[48]

After having his scientific facts checked by an assistant to the physicist Niels Bohr in Copenhagen, Brecht completed his play in three short weeks, in November of 1938.

As Brecht pointed out in connection with the first version, the technique of the play is somewhat of a regression from the methods of strict epic and dialectic theater. At least in its first version, the play occupies a middle ground between epic theater and the more traditional Aristotelian theater. Brecht gives a very practical reason for this. In view of the ever-increasing threat from Nazi Germany, he had already made plans to leave Denmark and go to the United States. In order to secure some financial means upon his arrival there, he said that he had written *Galileo* for New York City. (It was immediately translated into English by Desmond Vesey. But it took more than five years before the play reached the New York stage, and then it was not in Vesey's translation.)

During 1944 and 1945, while living in Santa Monica, California, Brecht worked with the actor Charles Laughton to create a second version of the play in English, based on the German text Brecht had written in Denmark.

In the first version, Galileo was presented as a positive but contradictory figure. Although Galileo recognized the social significance of his discoveries, he failed to join the class struggle on the side of the oppressed. In Brecht's view, Galileo's secretly finishing the *Discorsi*, however, far outweighed this negative aspect.

But after the destruction of Hiroshima by the atom bomb in August 1945, Brecht's views of Galileo, and of a scientist's duty to society in general, changed drastically: "From one day to the next, the biography of the founder of modern physics appeared in a different light."[49] Although Brecht still acknowledged Galileo's contribution to science, he condemned his recantation as a social crime, "for which the book [the *Discorsi*] could not make amends despite its immense importance."[50]

In the second version, written with Laughton, Brecht presented Galileo as a social criminal who delivered his discoveries into the hands of the ruling classes to be misused as they chose. Galileo thereby set a precedent that eventually led to the social irresponsibility of the atomic scientist in the capitalist society.

To further illustrate and stress Galileo's social failure, Brecht introduced the character of Vanni. Vanni assured Galileo of widespread support among the common people if he remained steadfast. But Galileo recanted. Recognizing his failure, Galileo's self-criticism is much more devastating in the second version. The negative social implications of Galileo's recantation, too, became much more apparent in the second version; for example, the passage in which Galileo refers to the "universal outcry of horror" at each new scientific discovery is missing entirely in the first version.

Brecht, however, did not totally rewrite the play. There are critics who feel that the changes in Brecht's view of Galileo are not always consistent with Galileo's portrayal in the play. The point is well taken, and it rests with the producer of the play to rectify this imbalance.

In 1953, Brecht wrote a third version of *Galileo*, in German, for the Berliner Ensemble.

The question of a scientist's responsibility toward society had again gained worldwide attention with the development of the hydrogen bomb and the highly publicized judicial case against the American physicist J. Robert Oppenheimer. (The Atomic Energy Commission declared Oppenheimer a security risk in May 1954 because of his leftist views and friends in the 1930s.) Brecht studied these developments very carefully in books and newspapers and deemed a new German version of *Galileo* an absolute necessity.

This third version was a combination of the first and second versions. The third version is less ambiguous and longer than the second. Brecht reintroduced several speeches and scenes from the first version. Otherwise there is little difference between the second and the third version, and the treatment of the protagonist remains the same in both. In form, however, the third version, particularly in its production by the Berliner Ensemble, is considerably more "epic" than the first version of the play.

Brecht stressed that it would be wrong to assume that his play was directed against the Catholic Church. For Brecht, the Church simply stood for the powers that be, and "with a few changes, the old cardinal in the fourth scene can easily be turned into a Tory, or a Democrat from the state of Louisiana."[51] The dignitaries of the church in *Galileo* are the bankers and senators of today. Galileo himself says several times that he is a faithful son of the Church, and Brecht took great pains not to present officials of the Church as monsters. On the contrary, they are generally portrayed as impressive and capable figures, whose actions are not entirely without logic from their point of view. In fact, Brecht's Pope Urban VIII has much stronger scientific interests than the historical Urban VIII ever had. And in his directions to actors for the 1957 production of *Galileo* by the Berliner Ensemble, Brecht wanted the inquisitor played as a modern, flexible, and very able young Jesuit, whose pronouncements were quite reasonable. He insisted that "Galileo's opponents, clergy and courtiers" be presented in "as good a light as possible."[52]

It was not Brecht's intention to paint a historically accurate portrait of Galileo. Brecht therefore felt at liberty to alter the historical facts to suit his own purposes. The historical Galileo, for instance, did not have particularly strong feelings about being on the threshold of a new epoch. Brecht needed this change because the dramatic character Galileo represented the dawn of a new age of science, in conflict with the old and established order of the Church. Historically accurate, on the other hand, is the attitude of the learned scholars, who insisted that anything contrary to what Aristotle had said could not possibly be true, and thus refused to look through the telescope. Brecht also changed historical dates; he did this mainly to give each event its full weight. Father Clavius actually confirmed Galileo's findings in 1611, not 1616. He did not say that theologians would have to make the necessary adjustments, as he does in Brecht's play; instead he said that astronomers would now have to fit this discovery into the already accepted teachings of the Church.

Brecht also brought in the ballad singer for his own purposes. Carnivals were indeed popular at the time, and occasionally singers did concern themselves with topical themes. But there is no indication that entertainers popularized Galileo's findings, as Brecht's play would have it. As a matter of fact, historians have pointed out that people ridiculed Galileo's discovery of the moons circling Jupiter—indeed, they tell us that the Jesuits actually had to defend Galileo against the insults of the people after his discoveries became known.

The characterization of Galileo's daughter, Virginia, is Brecht's invention. The only thing Brecht adopted from the historical Virginia is the name. (He could not have adhered to facts if he had wanted to. About all that is known about Virginia is that she entered a religious community in 1616 and died in 1634.) But through Virginia, Brecht wanted to show that the ruling powers do not hesitate to invade private spheres when such invasion suits their purposes.

Brecht also omitted actual events that could have been dramatic highlights—such as the historically established encounters between Galileo and Pope Urban VIII in 1624 in Rome. Brecht was afraid that such a scene could turn into pure melodrama on the stage, thus detracting from the real issues of the play. For this same reason, Brecht did not show the inquisition and the recantation on the stage.

The main issues in the play are the scientist's responsibility to society, the reasons ruling powers resist change, and how rulers use ideology (Christianity in this play) to keep the people under their control. These issues are, of course, not confined to the seventeenth century in Italy: the lessons of the play have a much more universal application. But Brecht himself did believe that the historical Galileo could have changed the course of history.

The collaboration in 1944 and 1945, during Brecht's exile in California, between Brecht, who knew little English, and the British actor Charles Laughton, who knew no German, is probably rather unusual in the history of playwriting—particularly since at that time the armies of their respective countries were slaughtering each other in Europe. That Brecht enjoyed this collaboration tremendously is indicated by the fact that he wrote extensively about it, once in a fragmentary poem and, particularly, in "Building of a Role; Laughton's Galileo" ("*Aufbau einer Rolle*"). For Brecht, Laughton was "a realistic artist of our times," and, in Brechtian terms, that was high praise.[53] Their main aids in their work together were huge volumes of synonyms and their own gestures. Brecht would act out scenes in bad English or even German. Laughton would then imitate Brecht, and translate into English until Brecht was satisfied. Then Laughton wrote down the result sentence by sentence, often making changes on the following day. Thus discussions about the psychology of characters were almost totally avoided; everything was directed toward the performance. It was "acting as a method of translation. We were forced to do what translators, better versed in languages, should also do: translate gestures."[54] Anyone interested in performing *Galileo* should by all means read Brecht's highly interesting account of his collaboration with Laughton to learn about the creation of the play and how carefully every detail of the production was planned, from the choice of words to the choice of colors for the decor, the background, and the costumes.

It is always tempting to look for an author's traits in his characters. The German writer Gerhard Szczesny professes to see a close affinity between Brecht and

his Galileo; he attributes some of Galileo's opportunistic traits (for example, the telescope episode) to
Brecht himself.[55] Another interesting biographical element in *Galileo* was pointed out by Guy Stern, who
convincingly suggested that the play contains many
allusions to the plight of exiles, such as "the refugees'
flight from Germany, their economic straits, loss of
identity, and intellectual suppression."[56] (Laughton,
to whom these allusions meant nothing, deleted them
from the second version; Brecht restored all of them
when he created his third version.)

It was not until 1943, when Brecht was living in
California, that Leonard Steckel produced the first
version of *Galileo* in the Schauspielhaus Zürich. The
premiere was on 9 September 1943 (director: Leonard
Steckel; Galileo: Leonard Steckel; sets: Teo Otto;
music: Hanns Eisler). The audience, including many
refugees from fascism, was quick to make analogies
between the Inquisition and the Gestapo, between
Galileo's struggle to circulate the forbidden scientific
discoveries and the activities of the resistance fighters.
This aspect was also emphasized in the newspaper
reviews (*Bund, Neue Zürcher Zeitung,* and *Basler
Nachrichten*). Galileo's recantation was generally approved of as a pragmatic method of saving his life
and continuing the fight for freedom of thought. The
critic of *Weltwoche,* on the other hand, saw *Galileo*
as an expression of the philosophy of existentialism,
emphasizing the tragic existence of mankind in a
world in which people are hopelessly at cross purposes.

Steckel's Galileo and Teo Otto's stage design earned
general praise. But one prominent Swiss critic, Elizabeth Brock-Sulzer, regretted that Brecht had not pursued the idea that Galileo, the believer, paved the way
for unbelievers. (Galileo was a faithful son of the
Church. But as a father of the scientific thought that

Galileo, Schauspielhaus Zürich, world premiere, 9 September 1943. Director: Leonard Steckel; sets: Teo Otto. Andrea: Robert Bichler (left); Galileo: Leonard Steckel.
THEATER-MUSEUM MÜNCHEN

was eventually to effect rejection of Christianity, he sowed seeds that led to the weakening of religion.) She was also critical of the historical costumes and settings and would have preferred a more "timeless" setting. (In 1965, this aspect was also criticized by the East German critic Ernst Schumacher: the play was presented as a historical play.)

The first American performance of *Galileo* took place on 30 July 1947 at the Coronet Theater in Beverly Hills (Galileo: Charles Laughton; Cardinal Barberini: Hugo Haas; director: Joseph Losey; music: Hanns Eisler; sets: Robert Davison). The audience included many Hollywood celebrities, among them Charlie Chaplin. It was a very hot day—before the days of air-conditioning—and Laughton insisted that blocks of ice and fans be placed around the small theater so that the spectators "would be able to think."[57]

For Brecht, this was a very important performance —one of the very rare chances during his many years of exile to participate actively in a production of one of his plays. And for the first time, he had the chance to demonstrate his epic theater in the United States. (His first attempt, with *The Mother* in 1935 in New York City, had failed.) Mindful of the importance of this performance, Brecht and Laughton undertook most careful preparation. They had one of the best cartoonists from the Walt Disney studios prepare satirical drawings as backdrop; they searched through books of costumes and old paintings (notably Pieter Bruegel the Elder) for suitable costumes; they carefully selected the colors of setting and costumes for each scene (ranging from a deep blue for the first scene to dull gray colors at the end); and they searched in a New York museum for samples of technical drawings by Leonardo da Vinci to use as background projections.

The roles were acted by young actors whom Laughton prepared by reading Shakespeare to them. The settings were nonillusory, but the historical time of the seventeenth century was indicated by several pieces of furniture and the costumes. The actors stood in groupings to evoke the characteristics of the Bruegel paintings.

The production played to full houses for twelve days. It ended when Laughton had to return to film engagements. But the performance was not a breakthrough for Brechtian theater in the United States, although it won admiration from many members of the audience (including Charlie Chaplin). Because of the large cast involved (fifty actors) and the small seating capacity of the theater, the performances netted little profit. And the reception by the reviewers was less than exuberant.

Gladwin Hill of *The New York Times* wrote about the play, which was "one of the current theater's most-talked-of projects": "Mr. Laughton...makes the scientist an appealing human figure. The production, however, somehow lacks the impact implicit in the story. It seems barren of climaxes and even sparse in stirring moments...it seems questionable whether the episodic technique is as facile a vehicle for a theme that is less expository than emotional."[58]

Edwin Schallert's review in the *Los Angeles Times*, 31 July 1947, was guarded and cautious: "Argumentative inspiration will be found not only in the theme of *Galileo* itself and the manner in which it is treated, but also will likely extend to discussions pro and con as to the manner of its giving, which is in the sphere of the revolutionary." He was equally cautious about the message of the play: "The play might be said to draw parallels through the ages on the holding back of that knowledge which might seem to spell an overthrow of accepted systems."

Euphemia Wyatt of *The Catholic World* did not see the play as relevant in any way to the contemporary world. She thought the play overlong and saw in it little artistic merit. The critic of *Variety* was more outspoken: he condemned the whole play.

Such critical approval as the play did evoke came from a few European émigrés. John W. Winge was impressed by the striking parallels to modern times. Ludwig Marcuse called it—despite a few minor criticisms—his "most important theatrical experience of the past seven years."[59]

The next milestone for the Laughton version was a performance in New York City by the Experimental

Theater, sponsored by the American National Theater and Academy. Beginning on 7 December 1947, the play ran for six nights in Maxine Elliott's Theater (director: Joseph Losey; Galileo: Charles Laughton). Brecht was not present; he had left the United States on 31 October of that year. World War II had ended more than two years before, and America was at this point in the grip of an anticommunist fever. Brooks Atkinson wrote in *Broadway*: "*Galileo* was suspected of being communist when the Experimental Theater produced it after Nazism had been defeated."[60] It took courage to perform a play by a playwright who was an alleged communist, and to present the music of the composer Hanns Eisler, who had been expelled from the United States in 1947 as an undesirable alien after a hearing by the House Committee on Un-American Activities (HUAC). Again, the reaction of the public and the press was mixed—Brecht considered it outright "bad."

Brecht himself had been concerned that the play's speeches might present problems on an American stage. Under the impression that the American theatergoer liked action, he feared the long speeches would be considered intrusive. How right he was (although he and Laughton had cut several of the longer speeches) is pointed out by Howard Barnes's review in the *New York Herald Tribune* of 8 December 1947: "The collision of science and religion is often more loquacious than theatrical." In general, though, his review was quite favorable: "*Galileo* is a fascinating and brilliantly articulated production." Laughton gave a "commanding portrayal" of Galileo, the supporting players were "uniformly excellent." Joseph Losey's direction was "resourceful" and had "immense style and imagination." But "that it [the play] would be popular in the regular theater, with its discursive and episodic outline, is questionable."

Brooks Atkinson of *The New York Times* also took a critical view of the structure of the play: "It is a loose and episodic play that is unnecessarily enigmatic and puts form ahead of contents." (This despite the fact that Brecht himself claimed he had written the play in a more conventional vein. It appears, however, that for his own production in America he again emphasized the epic elements.) Atkinson was less enthusiastic than Barnes about Laughton's acting—although he commended Laughton for coming all the way from California to play for the Experimental Theater's standard fee of ten dollars a performance; "but like a showman, Mr. Laughton pretty effectively throws the part of Galileo away . . . his Galileo is good Laughton, it is not Galileo."[61]

Most reviewers saw the play as a play about the historic Galileo. Only a few of them saw the play as containing content relevant to the contemporary world. One of them, Irwin Shaw, writing in *The New Republic* (29 December 1947), drew a parallel to the contemporary communist witch hunt in the United States. By spreading fear and insecurity, this witch hunt infringed upon the freedom of thought and expression. Shaw was also one of the few critics who tried to explain to his readers the characteristic features of epic theater.

On 16 April 1955, the first production of Brecht's third version took place—not in Brecht's Berliner Ensemble, but in Cologne's Kammerspiele (director: Friedrich Siems; Galileo: Kaspar Brüninghaus). Apart from its artistic merits, the performance also had a political significance. It achieved a breakthrough in the boycott against Brecht in West Germany that had followed his open support of the East German regime during the workers' uprising on 17 June 1953. Generally, the West German critics were much more aware of the play's dramaturgic qualities and its rele-

vance to modern times than their American counterparts. But they carefully tried to divorce the political
Brecht from the artistic Brecht. Several of them also
saw a parallel between Brecht and his character
Galileo—that both men were forced to make com-
promises with the ruling powers—and interpreted this
as Brecht's veiled protest against the East German
regime. From then on, Brecht's plays were again
regularly performed in West German theaters.

Galileo was the last production Brecht prepared for
the Berliner Ensemble. (He did not live to see the
premiere on 15 January 1957. After his death on 14
August 1956, his old and trusted friend Erich Engel
took over the direction.) The great Brechtian actor
Ernst Busch was cast as Galileo—but only after some
hesitation on the part of both Brecht and Busch. The
actor who portrays Galileo should be portly, vivacious;
he must convince the theatergoer that Brecht's Galileo
enjoys good living. Charles Laughton was well suited
for this part, whereas Ernst Busch was more the tense,
ascetic type. Busch, in his interpretation, put more
emphasis on Galileo as a technician, a creator of
means of production.

Yet problems remained. Brecht wanted Busch to
stress Galileo's recantation as a crime—in sharp contrast to Galileo's earlier eager pursuit of the truth at
all costs. Busch understood Brecht's intention. But
he admired the historical Galileo and found it difficult
to portray him as a criminal. Apparently this problem
was not solved because several of the otherwise extremely positive reviews (such as those by Andrej
Wirth in *Kultur* and Henryk Keisch in *Neues Deutschland*) mentioned that Busch's concept of Galileo
did not implement Brecht's conception of Galileo.
Fritz Erpenbeck in *Theater der Zeit* also noted this
incongruity. But he felt that it was to be attributed not
to Busch's acting but to the fact that the revised last

scene was not consistent with the rest of the play. And that, indeed, seems to be the play's major problem.

The West Berlin critic Friedrich Luft wrote about the production of *Galileo,* which he called "probably Brecht's best play": "The performance ... came close to perfection." In this judgment he included the stage design by Caspar Neher, the direction by Erich Engel, and the actors, particularly Ernst Busch, although he did make the qualification that Busch was "not as sensuous as Charles Laughton."[62] He also found political relevance in the play because he saw behind Galileo's fate the plight of the intellectual under the communist East German regime—something Brecht probably did not intend.

One of the eminent non-German critics who saw the Berliner Ensemble's performance was the English critic Kenneth Tynan, Brecht's foremost proponent in Great Britain. Tynan found the play "an incomparable theatrical statement of the social responsibilities of the intellectual."[63] He was full of praise for this production, particularly the ballad-singer scene and the scene in which Cardinal Barberini, newly installed as Pope Urban VIII, is getting dressed in his papal garb, and at the same time also gradually changing his view of Galileo's discovery. Initially he vigorously defended Galileo's right to free research. At the end he agrees that Galileo *must* be threatened with torture in order to persuade him to stop his "free" research.

Tynan's review was equally favorable when *Galileo* opened at London's Mermaid Theater in 1960. What his American colleagues regarded as a weakness—the play's epic form—constituted for Tynan the greatness of the play. In his view, most traditional plays "follow the pattern of the sexual act; they begin evenly, work up to a climax of emotion, and then subside. . . . To break up the clinch, along comes Brecht bearing a bucket of cold water in the shape of a play about the

Italian Renaissance in which nobody rants or raves or even raises his voice. The nearest approach to a climax —Galileo's recantation before the Inquisition—takes place offstage."

To Tynan's surprise, the English actors proved themselves quite capable of handling Brecht's requirements for acting in the epic theater. Bernard Miles, the director, used Laughton's translation and—successfully—the description of the exemplary performance given by the Berliner Ensemble in 1957. He also excelled in the part of Galileo. Tynan felt intellectually bothered by the questions the play raised, and he advised his readers, "Go then, and be bothered likewise."[64]

On 14 December 1962, the San Francisco Actors' Workshop (director: Herbert Blau; Galileo: Robert Symonds) opened "an impressive production"[65] of the Laughton version of *Galileo*. And on 13 April 1967, The Repertory Theater of Lincoln Center opened its production of *Galileo* in the Vivian Beaumont Theater, at which the play ran for eighty-seven performances. The Laughton version was directed by John Hirsch; the British actor Anthony Quayle starred in the title role.

The performance was, according to Walter Kerr of *The New York Times*, "on the whole, better than average for the house," but suffered somewhat from "Hollywooditis." Presumably, it was overly dramatic. In Kerr's view, this was not only a flaw of the production but also of the play, which "occupies a curious and somewhat awkward middle ground between epic theater and historical melodrama." Kerr felt that the overly simplistic language of Laughton's adaptation "sacrifices a good bit of [the play's] natural intellectual interest." He wished that Bernard Shaw had written the play: "More words are given to attitude than to argument; and you frequently find yourself

Galileo, Théâtre National Populaire, Paris, January, 1963. Translators: Armand Jacob and Edouard Pfrimmer; sets and costumes: Alfred Manessier; music: Hanns Eisler. Galileo: Georges Wilson (second from right).

wishing that Shaw had written the play so that the intricate coiling of contending minds might have been charted in every devious, rational and irrational, precision-tooled pretzel twist." (One must keep in mind, however, that Kerr was reviewing the Laughton version of *Galileo*, in which the speeches had been considerably shortened.) Kerr also felt that the explanation of Galileo's recantation ("simple physical cowardice") had been tacked on.[66]

In contrast to the somewhat lukewarm reception *Galileo* has evoked in the United States, the play was an outstanding success, according to all reviews, when Giorgio Strehler produced it in his Piccolo Teatro in Milan in 1963, with excellent sets by Luciano Damiani and a superb performance by Tino Buazzelli as Galileo. Every performance was sold out. In order to give more than the planned number of performances of *Galileo,* the repertory theater company had to rent a second theater to present other plays in their repertory. The performance lasted five hours, but according to Ossia Trilling, reviewer for *Theater der Zeit,* it was not a minute too long. Next to the director, the designer, and the actors, Trilling also gave high marks to Gideo Baroni, Italy's greatest expert in stage lighting. Baroni had developed special low-voltage bulbs to give a uniformly mild light that created a special atmosphere for the play. With this lighting effect, the scene in which the Pope is dressed in his ceremonial robes took on the aspect of a Renaissance painting.

The test of a play is its realization on stage. And here Brecht's versions of *Galileo* provided ample material for excellent and stimulating productions. The issues are topical and of concern to all people. The characters are superbly drawn in their complexity, Galileo's adversaries no less than Galileo himself.

Mother Courage and Her Children: A Chronicle from the Thirty Years' War (1939)

In *Mother Courage and Her Children,* in twelve loosely connected scenes, Brecht presents the travels and travails of the canteen woman Anna Fierling during twelve years (1624 to 1636) of the Thirty Years' War (1618–48).

It was perhaps the most cruel and devastating of all the wars central Europe has been assaulted by. After Martin Luther's reformation at the beginning of the sixteenth century, the independent German

German title: *Mutter Courage und ihre Kinder: Eine Chronik aus dem Dreissigjährigen Krieg.*

states elected Lutheranism or remained within the Roman Catholic fold. Animosities between them grew as the efforts of the Roman Catholic counterreformation intensified.

The reasons for the war were religious and political. Each side wanted to increase its territory and its influence. Open hostility broke out in 1618, when angry Protestants threw two envoys from the Catholic German Emperor through a window and into the moat of the royal palace in Prague. With the entry of Sweden (1630) and France (1635), the war involved virtually all major central European powers.

On the battlefields, the main heroes were the generals Tilly and Wallenstein, on the Catholic side, and the Swedish King Gustav Adolf, who came to the aid of the beleaguered Protestants in 1630. The longer the war lasted, the more widespread and anarchic it became. Marauding soldiers terrorized the population. Vast stretches of land were left uncultivated; whole cities were totally destroyed. At the end of the war, the German states had lost two-thirds of their population.

In those days soldiers were not accompanied by their own supply troops; they were forced to find their own food and other necessities. This they did by plundering farms and towns or by buying from the wagons of canteen women, who followed the armies all over Europe. Brecht's Anna Fierling—better known as Mother Courage—is one of these women.

Mother Courage was written in 1939 when Brecht was in exile in Sweden, while in Germany yet another devastating war was being prepared. There is, however, nothing specific in the play that suggests Hitler and his preparation for war.

The play begins in the spring of 1624 in Sweden, far away from the war being waged in Central Europe. The stage is totally bare of scenery or properties. There are two men on stage—a sergeant and a recruiting officer who are trying to enlist men for the war in Poland. Encountering difficulties in finding men who are willing, they blame it on the peace in Sweden, because "peace means disorder, only war generates order."[67] Then Mother Courage's canteen wagon appears. It is pulled by her two sons, Eilif and Schweizerkas (Swiss Cheese, so named because his father was Swiss), and carries supplies, Mother Courage, and her mute daughter, Kattrin. The recruiters stop the wagon and demand identification. Mother Courage answers with a song about her trade that has the refrain:

> Christians, awake! The winter's gone!
> The snows depart. The dead sleep on.
> And whoever has not died yet
> Takes to his feet again.[68]

At the sight of Eilif and Schweizerkas, the recruiters see their chance to enlist two men. But Mother Courage does not want her sons to go to war. When the recruiters try to lure Eilif away, she threatens them with a knife. When the recruiters glorify the war and a soldier's life, she tears up a sheet of parchment and has the recruiters, her sons, and Kattrin draw lots to see what the war will bring them. Each of them finds a black cross on his slip of parchment. This indicates that the war will bring each of them only death. Nevertheless, the recruiters manage to enlist Eilif. One of them draws Mother Courage aside to bargain with her over a buckle, while the other leads Eilif away. Mother Courage is too deeply involved in her bargaining to notice. The sergeant comments: "If she wants to live off the war, I reckon she'll have to give it something, too."[69]

Two years later, Mother Courage and her wagon

reach Poland in the entourage of the Swedish army. We see her bargaining over a capon with a cook. In the tent next to them, Eilif's commander is honoring him because he killed some farmers and took their cattle. Eilif, in good spirits, performs a dance and sings a song. Mother Courage recognizes her son's voice, and mother and son are reunited. But when she hears of his heroism, she slaps him because he exposed himself to danger.

Three years later, Mother Courage is doing a good business in the Swedish camp in Poland. Her second son, Schweizerkas, has now also joined the Swedish army and is paymaster. We meet Mother Courage's friends at the camp: a Dutch cook, a Protestant chaplain, and Yvette, who sells her favors to the soldiers. The discussions between the cook, the chaplain, and Mother Courage serve to bring out the irony of the war: "In a way it is a war, since people burn, kill, plunder—not to mention rape—yet it is different from all other wars because it is a religious war."[70] The Swedish king (Gustav Adolf), of course, only wants to "free" the people from Catholic rule. But if someone does not want to be "freed," the king will not stand for such nonsense. And the Poles are faced with war only because "they meddled in their own affairs and attacked the king when he moved peacefully through their land."[71]

This conversation is suddenly brought to an end when the Catholic forces attack and overrun the Swedish camp. Although the mute Kattrin is not pretty, Mother Courage promptly covers Kattrin's face with ashes to make her appear even less attractive and prevent her from being raped. The cook manages to get away, but not the chaplain, who quickly changes into secular clothes and raises the Catholic flag.

Mother Courage is not particularly concerned for her own safety. Business is business—"A peddler is not asked for his creed, but his price. Besides, Protestant pants keep one just as warm as others."[72] But honest Schweizerkas is captured; the Catholic forces are after the army cashbox that he has hidden. Mother Courage can ransom him from the Catholic soldiers if she sells her business to Yvette and Yvette's rich lover, but because she bargains too long over the price, Schweizerkas is shot. And, for her own safety, Mother Courage has to deny that she knows her son when she is confronted with his body.

After a lapse of another two years, during which she has moved through Poland, Moravia, Bavaria, and Italy, Mother Courage's wagon appears in a destroyed Bavarian village. Tilly, the Catholic general, has just won the Battle of Magdeburg—a major defeat for the Protestants. For Mother Courage, this important event in 1631 means only the loss of four of her beautiful officers' shirts. The chaplain, who has accompanied Mother Courage and Kattrin through the years, took the shirts to dress the wounds of the farmers injured in the battle. Much to her chagrin, Mother Courage receives no pay for the shirts. She complains: "Your victories only bring me losses."[73]

When Tilly is killed in 1632, and the war threatens to come to an end, Mother Courage is still in Bavaria and afraid that she will be left with twenty-two pairs of socks. Her main concern now is whether or not to buy new supplies. The chaplain convinces her to purchase additional merchandise by arguing that the lull is only temporary. Even a war has to pause to catch its breath, which is what some people call peace. Mother Courage sends Kattrin to buy goods. On the way back, Kattrin is attacked by soldiers. With a large wound on her face, she returns with the supplies. As the scene ends, Mother Courage curses the war.

Yet, at the beginning of the next scene, as Mother Courage, the chaplain, and Kattrin are moving to new markets with a well-stocked wagon, she praises the war again. "I won't let you spoil my war for me. They say war destroys only the weak. But they are also destroyed in peace. The only difference is that war feeds its people better."[74] But when King Gustav Adolf is killed in the battle of Lützen, Mother Courage's livelihood is again gravely threatened by the prospect of peace: "Don't tell me that peace has broken out! I've just bought new supplies."[75] She promptly goes to town to sell her goods before the prices drop. While she is gone, her son Eilif appears. He is chained and guarded by soldiers. He has come to say goodbye before he is executed. He has again killed some farmers and stolen their cattle, but, unfortunately for Eilif, what was an act of heroism during the war has become a criminal act in these few hours of peace.

Luckily for Mother Courage, war resumes before she sells all of her goods. She moves on with the Dutch cook, who has returned during this brief period of peace. But they leave the chaplain behind, for he accompanied Eilif to comfort him on the way to his execution.

Mother Courage's business, however, does not go well. War has impoverished the country. Two years after Eilif's death, they are begging in front of a vicarage in the Fichtel mountains of northeast Bavaria. There is one solution: the cook has inherited a bar in Holland that can support him and Mother Courage—but not Kattrin. Mother Courage refuses to desert Kattrin; thus she and Kattrin move on alone.

Kattrin's great scene comes when she and Mother Courage are staying at a farmhouse near the Protestant city of Halle. Catholic soldiers come to the farmhouse and force the young farmer to show them the way to Halle. After the soldiers leave, the farmers lament that nothing can be done to save the innocent people of Halle; they can only pray. Kattrin, however, climbs to the roof of the farmhouse and beats a drum as hard as she can. She succeeds in awakening the people of Halle. She herself is shot down from the roof by the Catholic soldiers. Mother Courage, who was on a business trip to Halle at the time, returns to the farmhouse to find Kattrin dead. She pays the farmers to bury Kattrin, and harnesses herself to her battered wagon. With the words, "I must get back to business,"[76] and now all alone, Mother Courage again follows the troops. The war has exacted its price from her.

Brecht did not invent the character of Mother Courage. Hans Jacob Christoffel von Grimmelshausen's novel *The Runagate Courage* (1670) and Johan Ludvig Runeberg's story *Lotta Svärd* (1921) are both stories about canteen women. Brecht's canteen woman is called Courage because, during one battle, she drove her canteen wagon through an artillery barrage in order to sell fifty loaves of bread which were beginning to get moldy. Her courage, however, was entirely self-serving because she feared a loss had the loaves spoiled completely. But Brecht saw her also as a representative of an oppressed class. Thus her name has greater significance. As Mother Courage says: "The poor people need courage, otherwise they are lost. . . . The fact alone that they have children in this kind of world shows that they have courage. . . . And that they put up with an Emperor and a Pope proves that they have tremendous courage, because it costs them their lives."[77]

Throughout the play, Brecht stresses Mother Courage's greed for money. At one point in the play she is even called "the hyena of the battlefields." In his own production of the play in 1949, Brecht saw to it that this avarice was visible even in moments of deep anguish. At Kattrin's death, Mother Courage is shaken. But when she pays the farmers to bury her, she counts out the money very carefully. Then she puts one coin back into her purse, which she closes with a loud snap. Her grief does not distract her from her pursuit of money. She has in mind not so much the burial as its cost. It is almost like any other business deal.

Making money is necessary, of course, for Mother Courage to survive. But, as Brecht makes clear, it has become more than just a livelihood—it is an obsession. She never becomes rich, because of the losses she suffers in the war, but in peacetime, her avarice would probably have amassed for her quite a fortune. It is Brecht's intention that she appear as the prototype of a grasping businessperson in this play.

Structurally, the end of the play returns to its beginning. Mother Courage sings another verse of the song with which she introduced herself at the beginning of the play. Again the audience hears the refrain:

> Christians, awake! The winter's gone!
> The snows depart. The dead sleep on.
> And whoever has not died yet
> Takes to his feet again.[78]

Again Mother Courage makes one circle with her wagon on stage. Throughout her life she has indeed moved in a circle. She has not learned anything, despite all of her losses and her suffering.

Not all critics agree that this is the best possible ending for the play. In 1949, four years after World War II had been brought to an end, the German playwright Friedrich Wolf suggested to Brecht that the play would be more effective if Brecht allowed Mother Courage to learn from her experiences. Wolf would have liked the play to end with her curse: "The war be damned!" But Brecht found this ending too optimistic, too unrealistic. He was not sure that people learn from catastrophes. An audience would see more clearly, he believed, if it could be jolted into awareness by the example of Mother Courage's blindness. As in many of his other plays, particularly his *Lehrstücke*, Brecht preferred to teach by offering the reverse example.

Although Brecht takes great pains to point out that Mother Courage's obsession with making money was the cause of much of her suffering, he nevertheless cannot suppress his compassion for her suffering. When Helene Weigel, as Mother Courage in the memorable 1949 production by the Berliner Ensemble, hears the shots that kill her son Schweizerkas (while she is still bargaining for his freedom), she mouths an inaudible cry of agony that could not but arouse the sympathy of the audience.

Mother Courage makes her livelihood from the war —but does she have a choice? She is one of Brecht's split characters. She is torn between cursing the war because it takes away her loved ones, and praising it because it provides her with the means of survival. Although we can clearly see her faults, we also can see the external forces that made her what she is. The play causes us to wonder about the society that forces Mother Courage to be such a woman.

The audience feels both pity and disgust for Mother Courage. But the theatergoer can feel only sympathy for Kattrin. Kattrin is the representative of all the decent qualities in man: compassion, love, goodness. And she is the only major character in all of Brecht's works who is entirely positive. But—significantly—she is mute. Brecht wants to indicate that goodness and compassion have little chance to be heard in times of war. Yet, in the scene on the farmhouse roof, it is Kattrin who "speaks" through her compassionate deeds; when the people around her say that nothing can be done, she alone acts. The scene when Kattrin

saves many innocent lives by beating the drum, thus
sacrificing her life, is, according to the English theater
critic Kenneth Tynan, "the most tremendous scene to
have enriched the drama for many years."[79]

There was also a very practical reason for making
Kattrin mute. Initially Brecht had conceived this role
for his wife Helene Weigel. If the character were
mute, Weigel could then also act the part outside
German-speaking countries.

The form of the play is epic theater. *Mother Courage* does not end in an emotional climax, as Friedrich
Wolf, representing Aristotelian dramaturgy, would
have preferred; rather, it remains open-ended. In the
play itself, brief summaries of the action are provided
before each scene so that the audience knows what is
going to happen and can concentrate not on what is
happening but how it happens. The action is interrupted often by songs.

The dialogue is peppered with witty, unexpected
comments, which appeal more to the intellect than to
the emotions. Thus much of the play's social criticism
is presented in a very entertaining way—mostly
through Mother Courage's sarcasm. For example,
when one of the recruiters says, "We need discipline
in the camp," she retorts, "I thought you needed sausage."[80] Later, when the Catholic forces overrun the
Swedish camp and the chaplain mumbles, "We are
in God's hands now," Mother Courage says, "I don't
think we're that lost yet."[81]

Although there is a plot line, the play really consists of a series of fairly isolated scenes that are linked
by the physical presence of Mother Courage and her
wagon. The wagon is the source of continuity throughout the play. And the physical condition of the wagon
reflects both Mother Courage's fortune and the general state of the war, as both move across central
Europe.

The form of the play owes much to Shakespeare's history plays, as indicated by the subtitle, "A Chronicle of the Thirty Years' War," and by Brecht's notes. But instead of focusing on kings and dukes, as Shakespeare does, Brecht's main characters are the common people. The history-book heroes of the Thirty Years' War (Wallenstein, Tilly, Gustav Adolf) never once appear on stage. In this sense, *Mother Courage* is Brecht's answer to Schiller's classic Wallenstein play. In the *Wallenstein* trilogy, one of Schiller's major works and written between 1792 and 1799, Wallenstein and other high-ranking officers are the heroes. Brecht's play is an example of the reinterpretation of history he proposed in his poem, "Questions of a Reading Worker": "Young Alexander conquered India./ He alone?/ Caesar defeated the Gauls./ Did he not have even a cook with him?"[82]

In *Mother Courage and Her Children,* Brecht wanted to drive home the fact "that the big profits in wars are not made by the small people; that war is only a continuation of business by other means. War kills all human virtues and must therefore be opposed with every possible means."[83] This message is repeatedly expressed in the play itself, directly or indirectly. Thus Mother Courage explains to the chaplain: "If you listen to the big shots, you would think that they conduct wars only for fear of God and for everything that is good and beautiful. But if you look more closely, they are not that stupid—they conduct wars for profit."[84] In the play itself, however, we never see the powerful people making big profits. And in Mother Courage, Brecht created such a complex and interesting character that the playgoer is often so fascinated with her that he is distracted from Brecht's intended message.

On 19 April 1941, *Mother Courage and Her Chil-*

dren was premiered at a major Swiss theater, the
Schauspielhaus Zürich (Mother Courage: Therese
Giehse; sets: Teo Otto; director: Leopold Lindtberg;
music: Paul Burkhard). The production was highly
successful; the critic of the leading Swiss newspaper,
Neue Zürcher Zeitung, praised especially Therese
Giehse's Mother Courage, a role of "truly Shake-
spearean dimensions."[85]

Just to stage such a play in 1941 was a courageous
act—Switzerland was surrounded by Nazi troops who
could invade at the slightest provocation. This anti-
war play by a leftist author, whom the Nazis had
driven out of Germany and deprived of German citizenship, could easily have been considered a provocation. The directors of the theater, as well as Giehse,
Lindtberg, and Otto, sent cables to Brecht, who was
at that time in California, telling him about the play's
success. Upon receiving them, he wrote in his *Work
Journal:* "It is very courageous of this theater, consisting mostly of refugees, to stage one of my plays at
this particular time. No Scandinavian stage possessed
that kind of courage."[86] (Nor, one could add, did
they possess the kind of talent assembled in Zurich.
As a neutral country, Switzerland was a haven for
many German exiles. Among them were many excellent actors who could continue to work in the German-
speaking Swiss theaters, particularly in Zurich.)

Yet Brecht was not totally happy with the reception
of his play. Some critics had misunderstood Brecht's
intention in the play and talked about a "Niobe tragedy" and "the overwhelming strength of the mother
creature."[87] (In Greek mythology, Niobe, the daughter
of the Phrygian king Tantalus, boasted to Leto of her
seven sons and seven daughters, whereupon Leto had
her two children, the gods Apollo and Artemis, kill
all of them. Overwhelmed with grief, Niobe turned to

stone.) To prevent this misinterpretation from recurring, Brecht made some slight but significant changes, stressing even more strongly Mother Courage's obsession with making money. Thus at the end of the first scene, in which Mother Courage and one of the recruiters bargain over the price of a buckle, Brecht made sure it was perfectly clear that Eilif could only be enlisted because Mother Courage was too preoccupied with her business deal to notice.

The most significant performance of the play took place on 11 January 1949 in the Deutsches Theater, in East Berlin. It was the first play Brecht (together with Erich Engel) directed after his return to what was now East Berlin. Germany lay in ruins from the war. Actors and spectators alike were constantly reminded of the destruction of war on their way to the theater. Would people ever learn? Brecht sincerely hoped that the dramatization of Mother Courage's incapacity to learn would teach them.

Brecht wanted the audience to realize that Mother Courage is not just tossed about by blind fate. She acts out of her recognition that she can make a business out of the war. At the same time, her fate assumes symbolic meaning, as Brecht wrote in his *Work Journal* on 12 January 1953: "The image of Germany emerges, conducting predatory wars, destroying other countries and herself in the process, not learning anything despite all the catastrophes."[88] But he also points out that Kattrin is an exemplary character in the play, one from whom the audience can learn. Kattrin acts when others merely lament that nothing can be done.

The music for the 1949 performance was composed by Paul Dessau. In order to separate the musical parts from the action, an "emblem" (consisting of a trumpet, drum, flag, and ball-shaped lamps) was lowered from the flies and illuminated whenever a song was to be presented. The musicians were clearly visible to the audience throughout the performance. Properties were used sparingly; they were realistic and detailed. There was no attempt to create a naturalistic scene. Special care was given to small properties, such as Mother Courage's money bag, and details of Mother Courage's wagon. The whole stage was illuminated by a bright white light to prevent any sort of mysterious atmosphere. The place of the action was indicated in large black letters on a screen above the setting. The date, and a short caption summary of the scene, were projected on the half-curtain before each scene.

The 1949 performance by the Berliner Ensemble is meticulously documented in words and pictures. But this "model" performance was not necessarily intended to be binding for all performances, according to Brecht. For further productions, he suggested a compromise: neither slavish imitation of the Berlin model of 1949 nor total departure from it.

As the critics Paul Wiegler and Friedrich Luft noted, Helene Weigel made an unforgettable impression as Mother Courage in the performance of 1949. Indeed, she became so well known for this role that when she walked through the streets of Berlin, people would point her out and say: "There goes Mother Courage."

In October 1950, Brecht went to Munich to stage *Mother Courage*. The title role was again played by Therese Giehse, who had performed this part in Zurich in 1941. Again, the play was a great success.

The play was also received with great enthusiasm in other European countries. In 1954, the Berliner Ensemble, under the direction of Brecht himself, presented *Mother Courage* at the International Theater Festival in Paris. Receiving first prize, this production established the international reputation of the Ensemble as one of the leading theater companies in

the world and greatly enhanced Brecht's already outstanding stature as a playwright.

In 1954, Ruth Berlau, one of Brecht's collaborators,
staged *Mother Courage* in Amsterdam. There she ex-
perienced the tremendous power the play was to have
in countries that had been ravaged by the Nazi forces.
When the Dutch actress Aaf Bouber, in her role as
Mother Courage, started to deny that Schweizerkas
was her son when his dead body was shown to her
(the end of scene three), she was so overcome by
emotion that she could hardly go on. (Miss Bouber's
own son was taken away by the Nazis and she never
saw him again.)

The first time *Mother Courage* was presented to an
English-speaking audience was in January 1955, when
the Institute of Contemporary Arts in London arranged for a public reading. In June of the same year,
Joan Littlewood and her Theater Workshop Company
staged *Mother Courage* at the Devon Arts Festival.
In the opinion of Kenneth Tynan, this production was
not exactly a success:

> Theater Workshop, the company chosen to play
> it, was dismally unequal to the strain. Ants can
> lift objects many times their size and weight, but
> actors cannot. Mother Courage is a role calling
> for the combined talents of Anna Magnani and
> Siobhan McKenna: Joan Littlewood plays it in
> a lifeless mumble, looking both over-parted and
> under-rehearsed. Lacking a voice, she has to cut
> Mother Courage's song, which is like omitting
> the Hallelujah Chorus from the Messiah.

Tynan's criticism was directed against this production
and the performers, not against the play itself. Tynan
summarized: "The result is a production in which
discourtesy to a masterpiece borders on insult."[89]

The first American performance of *Mother Courage*
was in San Francisco at the Marines' Memorial The-

ater, staged by the Actors' Workshop of San Francisco on 17 January 1956 (director: Herbert Blau; sets: Ernest Baron; Mother Courage: Beatrice Manley). The reception of the play was somewhat mixed. The critic of the *San Francisco Chronicle* found Paul Dessau's music appropriate, and he liked the actors who played the roles of the chaplain and the cook, both of whom supplied "vitality and humor" where they were "badly needed." He found Kattrin's drum scene on the rooftop "a startling and affecting picture." But, to his regret, he could not "say much for the rest of the production," which appeared to him "rather timid." Beatrice Manley played Mother Courage with "unrelenting grimness . . . conveying neither the earthy humor nor the depredations of Father Time." He was also critical of the play itself. In his opinion the basic weakness in the play was that "it lacked suspense," and that "much of its anti-war crusading seems both repetitious and pretty old hat. . . . There have been many plays that are sharper weapons against war."[90]

On 28 March 1963, Eric Bentley's adaptation of *Mother Courage* opened in the Martin Beck Theater in New York. This was the first production of a Brecht play on Broadway (director: Jerome Robbins; music: Paul Dessau; Mother Courage: Anne Bancroft). After fifty-two performances, it closed on 11 May, a box-office failure, despite more preview performances than any other play that season.

The reviewer of *Variety* found the play "sophomorically obvious, cynical, self-consciously drab and tiresome." He asked: "Why should anyone think it might meet the popular requirements of Broadway—that is, be commercial?"

Kenneth Tynan thought the question well worth posing, but turned the tables on the *Variety* critic by writing: "The truth is that the more honestly Brecht is presented, the less likely he is to appeal to the middle-class, postprandial Broadway audience. They insist on clearly defined emotional climaxes, whether of laughter or tears; they like to be told how to feel; and the relaxed, ambiguous coolness of an authentic Brechtian production would leave them darkling in a twilight of boredom." According to Tynan, the actors destroyed the play by pandering to the audience's expectations. While Helene Weigel, as Mother Courage, had reacted to the execution of Schweizerkas with an "immobile, soundless cry . . . Miss Bancroft stumbles halfway across the stage, emitting strangled yelps. Now and then she is even willing to sob, because that is what the customers demand." Tynan was also equally unhappy with Bentley's adaptation and Mr. Robbins's direction, but he attributed the artistic failure of the play primarily to the commercialized nature of Broadway theater.[91]

Other critics were less severe. *Time* magazine of 5 April 1963 had some criticism of this Jerome Robbins production, but summarized: "Despite these shortcomings, playgoers jaded on dramatic creampuffs ought to seize the chance to swallow intellectual fire." And Howard Taubman of *The New York Times* had nothing but praise for the play itself and the production: "Since this is one of Brecht's mature, masterly works, its arrival at the Martin Beck Theater Thursday night qualifies it as an event of consequence. It comes here in Eric Bentley's vigorous adaptation, and it has been staged by Jerome Robbins in a worthy manner. . . . Anne Bancroft plays Mother Courage with surface impassivity through which gleam heartiness and cunning and, at the right rare moments, emotion." And he concluded: "*Mother Courage*, praise be, is a different theater experience. In its humor, irony, and truth, it is a work to welcome and cherish."[92]

In November 1967, the Jewish State Theater of

Poland gave a performance of *Mother Courage* in Yiddish at New York City's Billy Rose Theater, with Ida Kaminska in the title role. Although Kaminska played "brilliantly," Richard F. Shepard of *The New York Times* felt that "Brecht did not fit the Yiddish stage comfortably"; Brecht's play is on a great—and impersonal—theme, while "Yiddish theater is nothing if not personal."[93]

After extensive previews, a new and unusual production of *Mother Courage and Her Children* had its premiere in New York City on 24 February 1975. It was staged by Richard Schechner and The Performance Group in the Performing Garage, with Joan MacIntosh as Mother Courage, James Griffiths as the cook, and Stephen Borst as the chaplain. This experimental theater invited the audience to occupy the entire space of the theater, rather than confine it to one particular seating section. Schechner also dispensed with the most important property of this Brechtian masterpiece, Mother Courage's canteen wagon. Instead he crisscrossed the entire performing space with a network of ropes, like a spider web. Mother Courage, herself trapped in the web, is shown battening off other victims caught in the same web.

Jack Kroll of *Newsweek* thought this a good idea, and his review was favorable. Clive Barnes of *The New York Times*, on the other hand, although acknowledging the ingenuity of the production, was not convinced of its viability: "The fabric and fiber of Brecht's play, even Brecht's thoughts, never seemed to emerge."[94]

Nevertheless, the production was obviously a brave attempt to break out of the sterile world of poorly staged Brecht imitations, a break that was sorely needed. The Swiss playwright Max Frisch once claimed that a play that becomes a "classic" ceases to

Four productions of *Mother Courage and Her Children: Above left,* in Germany, with Therese Giehse in title role. *Above right,* at the Festival d'Avignon, 1952, with Germaine Montero. *Left,* The Guthrie Theater Company, 1975–1976. Kattrin: Marcy Mattox; Mother Courage: Barbara Bryne; Yvette: Karen Landry. *Right,* Berliner Ensemble. Mother Courage: Helene Weigel.

be effective. How close *Mother Courage* has come to suffering this fate is shown by a production offered in February 1975 by the McCarter Theater Company, in Princeton, New Jersey (director: Michael Kahn; sets: David Jenkins; music: David Raksin; Mother Courage: Eileen Heckart). According to Clive Barnes, the production was a close and well-played imitation of the classic 1949 production by the Berliner Ensemble. But he found no message in it. For him the play had "no poetic meaning, no inner truth, not even an overt political message. What you see is what it is: an epic tragedy about cowardice and avarice during the seventeenth century's Thirty Years' War."[95]

A first attempt at filming *Mother Courage* by the state-owned film company of the German Democratic Republic in 1955 was never completed. The same company made a successful film of the play in 1960, directed by Brecht's students Peter Palitzsch and Manfred Wekwerth, starring Helene Weigel and the Berliner Ensemble.

Mother Courage and Her Children shows Brecht at his best; the didactic and artistic elements are perfectly blended. There is no heavy-handed tub-thumping, although the play does convey a very serious message. The play's wit and humor appeal to the intellect, but the play also proves that there is room for controlled emotion in epic theater. *Mother Courage* undoubtedly has a strong impact on the spectator's emotions. But these emotions are not free-flowing, as in sentimental melodramas. They are never allowed to dominate; they are channeled and harnessed by the estrangement effects of epic theater.

In *Mother Courage* there is nothing of the sterile quality so often attributed to Brecht. It is permeated with wit, warmth, and a great feeling and understanding for human beings.

The Trial of Lucullus (1939)

Lucius Licinius Lucullus, the Roman consul for Asia Minor who lived from approximately 106 to 57 B.C., is remembered today for his victory over the Persian ruler Mithridates, one of ancient Rome's most dangerous enemies, and for his efficient administration of Asia Minor, his proverbial wealth, and his hedonistic life style. In 76 B.C. he brought the cherry tree from the Greek city of Kerasus in Asia Minor to Italy. (From there it spread across Europe, and the name of the tree in all European languages is derived from the Greek *kerasion*.)

Lucullus is the subject of the fourteen short scenes of a radio play Brecht wrote in 1939. Brecht's play, however, neither focuses on Lucullus's well-known epicurean tastes, nor on his military exploits, but rather on his death and subsequent reception in the netherworld, thus drawing heavily on classical mythology. It is written in unrhymed irregular verse, with the exception of one rhymed scene.

An announcer serves as commentator, giving a report of the scene. The play opens with a ceremonious burial procession. Soldiers carry the catafalque, followed by slaves carrying a huge frieze upon which Lucullus's deeds are inscribed and which is to be placed on his tomb. A children's chorus informs us that his fame has become so great that he will be immortalized in schoolbooks. The spectators watching the procession react according to their class; the merchants, who made profits under him, praise him as a

German title: *Das Verhör des Lukullus.*

great man. But the common people cannot bear to hear "this nonsense about his fame,"[96] for Lucullus drove up the prices and cost them many lives in his wars.

When the procession reaches a small building on the Appian Way, the hollow voice of the doorkeeper to the realm of the shadows (the netherworld) bids them stop and orders Lucullus to walk unaccompanied through the small gate and into the building. At this point, the solemnity is abruptly broken by the irreverence of the soldiers who are carrying Lucullus's body. Glad to be rid of him, they dump him at the building, saying, "Bye, bye, Lucullus, we are through with you, old lecher. Let's get out of this bone house and into the pub!"[97]

In the next scene, Lucullus has entered the realm of the shadows. Impatiently he waits for his trial to begin. The outcome will commit him either to the eternal bliss of the Elysian Fields or to dark Hades. Lucullus complains of being kept waiting and boasts of his great deeds on earth. But an old woman who is also waiting her turn informs him that the judgment is based on how useful a person was to his fellow men on earth.

Finally Lucullus is called before the judges. The voice that summons him mispronounces his name and Lucullus is indignant. The speaker of the court of the dead informs the audience that the inquiry is to be conducted by five jurors who, in their lives on earth, belonged to the lower classes: a peasant, a slave, a fisherwoman, a baker, and a prostitute. When they ask Lucullus to name someone who can speak in his behalf, he requests Alexander the Great, certain that Alexander was elevated to Elysium after his death. But to Lucullus's astonishment, no Alexander the Great can be found in the Elysian Fields; all his great deeds did not earn him admission to this abode of the blessed. Lucullus then demands that the frieze be brought in as testimony to his worth. This is done, and the speaker of the court describes the witnesses to Lucullus's former glory, immortalized on the frieze: a captured king; a foreign-looking queen; a man holding a small cherry tree; a fat golden god carried by two slaves; two virgins holding a plaque on which the names of fifty-three cities are inscribed; two legionaries, one standing and one dying, greeting their commander-in-chief; and a cook holding a fish.

But as each image on the frieze comes to life and tells its story, all but two of them testify against Lucullus. The two exceptions are the cook, who prepared gourmet meals for Lucullus, and the gardener with the cherry tree, who informs the court that it was Lucullus who introduced the cherry tree into Rome. But his evil deeds—the war exploits that on earth had been considered heroic—far outweigh his good deeds. Eighty thousand dead legionnaires against one cherry tree decidedly tip the scales of justice against Lucullus. The court of the dead condemns him to Hades:

> Into nothingness with him. For with all that violence only one realm grows: that of the shadows.... How much longer are they, he and his like, inhuman creatures, to rule over men by lifting their indolent hands to throw peoples against each other in bloody wars? How much longer will we and our people tolerate them?[98]

In the years between 1949 and 1951, Brecht prepared the libretto for the opera *The Trial of Lucullus,* with music composed by Paul Dessau. The text is based on the radio play of 1939. The ministry of education of the fledgling German Democratic Republic had just begun its campaign against "formalism"—in essence, any form of experimental or unusual art was banned as an unsuitable means of bridging the gulf between art and the people. The ministry also demanded that plays be set in East Germany, and that they help the Communist party cope with immediate problems. Brecht's libretto, however, is a parable. The setting is far removed from the contemporary world of East Germany. Moreover, Dessau's music is quite modern.

Although Dessau wanted to wait, Brecht pushed for a trial performance of the opera. ("One must never fear criticism; one must either oppose it or utilize it, that is all."[99]) The performance took place on 17 March 1951 in the Staatsoper in East Berlin (conductor: Hermann Scherchen; sets: Caspar Neher; Lucullus: Alfred Hülgert).

In line with the Communist party position, Brecht explained in a note to the opera that its aim was to condemn all wars of aggression. He also deemed it necessary to defend the setting of the opera (the netherworld) by explaining that this device had already been employed in the German classical period. (The period at the end of the eighteenth century, the classic period of Goethe and Schiller in Weimar still has considerable authoritative value, perhaps more in East than in West Germany.)

But the opera was severely attacked by the East German critics and the Communist party as formalistic and decadent. The official party newspaper, *Neues Deutschland,* wrote: "A highly gifted dramatist and a talented composer, whose progressive views are unquestioned, strayed into an experiment that, for ideological and artistic reasons, was bound to fail." Dessau's music was sharply criticized for following "Igor Stravinsky, a composer living in the U.S.A., a fanatical destroyer of European musical traditions."[100] (It is of interest to note that Brecht had approached Stravinsky about the possibility of his composing the music for *Lucullus*. Stravinsky refused on the basis of being too heavily committed to other projects.) There were no further performances.

Brecht argued strongly in defense of his play, though not without sympathy for the intentions of the East German government. He actually felt that it was not only the party's right but its duty to criticize the arts. Brecht defended his opinion that the opera was not "formalistic." According to Brecht, Dessau's music had "nothing to do with formalism. In an exemplary way, it serves the content; it is clear, melodic, and fresh. We are seeing ghosts if we see formalism *everywhere*."[101]

But during hours of discussion with several members of the government, including Otto Grotewohl, the prime minister of East Germany, Brecht and Dessau did agree to make some revisions, although no fundamental ones. The title was changed to *The Condemnation of Lucullus*. Several scenes were altered to eliminate certain objections of the critics. For example, the frieze was now not brought onto the stage. Instead, the people depicted on it were brought in to testify individually, thus eliminating the critics' objection that a frieze that comes to life is unrealistic. Also, lines were added to explain why the king, who was conquered by Lucullus, was himself acquitted at the trial and allowed to enter the Elysian Fields: the reasoning was that the captured king had conducted only wars of defense, whereas Lucullus was condemned because he conducted wars of aggression. And three new arias were given to Lucullus's accusers "in order to correct a certain disproportion, because musically Lucullus far outweighed the court in the first version."[102]

The revised version of the opera was first performed

on 12 October 1951, again in the Staatsoper with Scherchen conducting. The party critics tolerated it, but it never became a favorite with them. And for large parts of the audience, the work was too avant-garde, especially Dessau's music.

In recent years, however, *Lucullus* has become part of the opera repertory of East German theaters. The extent to which East Germany has modified its views in the past years is made clear by a review of two successful 1974 productions of *Lucullus,* one in Neustrelitz and one in Magdeburg (both in East Germany). Eckart Kröplin, in *Theater der Zeit,* regarded *Lucullus* as an important work "in the heritage of our young socialist national culture."[103]

The play also reached the public as a radio and a stage play. The first version, the radio play *The Trial of Lucullus,* was broadcast on 12 May 1940 by the Swiss radio station Beromünster. The same version was also broadcast by the BBC in England in October 1958, with music composed by Humphrey Searle. The BBC had also broadcast *The Condemnation of Lucullus,* conducted by Scherchen, on 20 March 1953.

On 18 April 1947, H. R. Hay's translation of *The Trial of Lucullus* was staged at the University of California at Berkeley, with Henry Schnitzler directing and D. Trevor as Lucullus. The music for this performance was by the American composer Roger Sessions. The play was also performed at Princeton on 29 April 1955.

Brecht's *Lucullus* remains one of his lesser-known works. In the communist states, where it was received coolly, even after Brecht's revisions, it did not fit into the confined mold of socialist realism. In the West, it has not emerged from the shadows of Brecht's so-called great works, such as *Mother Courage* and *Galileo. Lucullus* does, however, deserve wider recognition as an example of Brecht's great crafts-

manship in achieving a successful marriage between
didacticism and artistic beauty.

One-Act Plays: *Dansen* and
What Is the Price of Iron? (1939)

In 1939, while in exile in Sweden, Brecht
wrote two one-act plays, *Dansen* and *What Is the
Price of Iron?*, in which he treated current political
events in parabolic form. The two plays are closely
related; both examine, in a very critical light, the
Scandinavian attitude toward the rise of Hitler. In
Brecht's view, the Scandinavian countries, although
they protested Hitler's violence, did not back up their
words with action. In fact, they actually supported
Hitler indirectly by carrying on trade with Nazi Germany.

It was a rather risky move on Brecht's part to criticize openly his host countries' behavior toward Hitler.
Constantly under threat of invasion by the Nazis,
these countries were very careful not to provoke Hitler. Open propaganda against Hitler by exiled Germans living there was specifically prohibited. Thus
Brecht did not release *Dansen* at that time, and for
the performance of *What Is the Price of Iron?*, he
used the pseudonym John Kent.

The setting for *Dansen* consists of three store-fronts:
a tobacco store belonging to Mr. Austrian; a shoe store
belonging to Mrs. Czech; and Mr. Dansen's food store,
which advertises "Fresh Ham." Next to this last store
is a large gate with a sign saying "Svensson's Iron

German titles: *Dansen* and *Was kostet das Eisen?*

Warehouse." Mr. Dansen is sitting next to the gate, self-righteously praising his independence, his reputation, and his wealth. Suddenly he sees a stranger breaking into the tobacco store and killing its proprietor. Then the man repeats the action in the shoe store. But Dansen's only reaction is to protest this outrage to his friend Svensson over the telephone. He does not want to hear anything about taking up arms to defend himself against intruders; he thinks nothing will happen to him if he remains inconspicuous. But he is soon forced to sign a "friendship treaty" with the murderous stranger, and even to give him the key to Svensson's warehouse. It is only in his dreams that he sees himself courageously resisting all pressures.

What Is the Price of Iron? is introduced by a prologue in which we are told that the following little parable was written by an Englishman (John Kent) after a discussion with two Swedish students in a pub near the Old Vic theater in London.

The setting is Mr. Svensson's iron store; a huge calendar shows the year to be 1938. Mr. Austrian, a traveling tobacco salesman, comes in to sell Austrillo cigars to Mr. Svensson. Mr. Austrian tells Mr. Svensson that his trip was marred by an encounter with a strange man who claimed to be his relative. After Mr. Austrian leaves, this very same stranger enters Mr. Svensson's store to buy iron. He pays for his purchase with blood-stained money, and he also claims to be related to Svensson.

In scene 2, the calendar shows early 1939. A shoe dealer, Mrs. Czech, offers Svensson a pair of yellow shoes. At the same time she tells him that Mr. Austrian has been robbed and murdered, and she is afraid. Svensson, however, wants only to be left alone to sell his iron "peacefully." The stranger returns to buy more iron, offering Svensson some Austrillo cigars he "inherited from a relative" who has just died.

In scene 3, the date is February 1939. Svensson, smoking an Austrillo, has two visitors: Mrs. Gall and Mr. Britt. They inform him that Mrs. Czech has been robbed and murdered—and they suggest an alliance against the marauding stranger. But Svensson wants to remain neutral and sell his iron to anyone who can pay for it. He is confirmed in his attitude by the stranger, who returns to buy more iron, bringing Svensson a present—a pair of yellow shoes.

In scene 4, the calendar shows the year 19?? (indicating some time in the near future). Svensson, wearing his yellow shoes and smoking an Austrillo, suddenly hears the boom of cannon and sees the glare of fire outside his window. In panic, he tries to call his friend Dansen, the food merchant of *Dansen,* but there is no answer. The stranger comes in for more iron. But this time, instead of paying, he points a machine gun and asks menacingly, "What is the price of iron?"[104]

The two plays obviously record events leading up to World War II. In 1938, Hitler (the murderous stranger) occupied Austria; in March 1939, he marched into Czechoslovakia. To build up his war machinery, Hitler needed Swedish (Svensson's) iron ore, which was shipped to Germany via the port of Narvik, Norway. Hitler also imported food products from Denmark (Dansen). The British (Mr. Britt) and the French (Mrs. Gall) had strategic interests in Norway and Sweden. In order to cut off Hitler's supply lines, they landed troops in Norway. The Nazis, however, won the battle; they occupied Denmark and Norway in 1940. Sweden was never occupied, and it continued to supply iron ore to Germany throughout the war.

In a brief note to the play, Brecht suggested that *What Is the Price of Iron?* be played in knockabout style, in the manner of Charlie Chaplin or the Bavarian comedian Karl Valentin. The iron-ore dealer could have a wig with hair that stood up on end; the shoes and the cigar could be very large. He also recommended that projections or prints of actual quotations from Scandinavian statesmen be used for the set.

In addition to the two plays, there are several (now published) fragmentary scenes dealing with the same theme. In one of them Brecht portrays a meeting of Mr. Dansen, Mr. Svensson, and Mr. Norsen (Norway). The plays were quickly written; they are highly topical. Though clearly minor, they are of historic interest. They reveal Brecht's feelings at the time and demonstrate some of his creative methods.

Dansen has never been performed. *What Is the Price of Iron?* was staged in 1939 in Stockholm by a group of young working-class actors under the direction of Ruth Berlau.

The Good Woman of Setzuan
(1938–41)

The Good Woman of Setzuan was written between 1938 and 1941, while Brecht was in Scandinavian exile; his collaborators were Ruth Berlau and Margarete Steffin; Paul Dessau composed the music for the play. The idea for the play goes back to 1930, when Brecht had started a play called *The Commodity Love*. (Unfortunately, the ambiguity of the German title *Die Ware Liebe* gets lost in translation: *Ware* = commodity, *wahre* = true.)

The play is about a prostitute named Shen Te and the difficulties she encounters on account of her natu-

German title: *Der gute Mensch von Sezuan.*

ral goodness. It is set in prewar China, in the capital of the Chinese province of Setzuan, "a half-Europeanized city." The play is divided into a prologue, an epilogue, ten scenes, and seven interludes.

In the prologue, three gods arrive in the capital of Setzuan with the hope of finding at least one good person, for they fear that goodness may have become extinct. They are met by the water seller Wang, who tries to find a place for them to stay. The thought that Wang might be the person they are looking for is dismissed when they discover that he is cheating his buyers—his water jug has a double bottom. After some difficulty, Wang finally finds quarters for the gods in the humble home of Shen Te, a prostitute. Since Shen Te has given them lodging for the night in spite of her poverty, the gods gratefully acknowledge that they have found one good person. When they depart, they admonish her to remain a good person. But she complains: "How can I be good when everything is so expensive?"[105] The gods reply that they cannot meddle in economic affairs. They do give her a substantial sum of money for the night—despite their apprehension that this could be misinterpreted by the people of Setzuan as a generous fee for a night of pleasure.

In the first scene, we see Shen Te setting up a small tobacco shop she has purchased with the thousand silver dollars the gods gave her. Now she hopes to be able to do good. But even before the shop opens, an exploitative family of eight people (her former landlord's family) takes up residence in the store. The landlady, Mi Tzu, appears with the lease and to ask for references. Next, the carpenter bursts in and demands money for the shelves he built, although Shen Te had been told by the previous owner that he had already paid the carpenter. Shen Te realizes that she is being cheated and exploited. She can think of no way out but to invent a cousin, Shui Ta, who will be ruthless and take care of all these problems. Whenever he is needed, Shen Te will impersonate Shui Ta. This means, of course, that wherever Shui Ta appears Shen Te cannot be. The scene ends with Shen Te stepping out of her role and addressing the audience: "The small boat of salvation/ Is immediately pulled under./ Too many sinking people/ Eagerly grab for it."[106]

In the first interlude, we see Wang sleeping under a bridge. In a dream, the gods appear to him and ask him to go back to see how Shen Te is getting along and to report back to them.

In scene 2, Shui Ta "comes to visit" his cousin Shen Te. He bargains with the carpenter and forces him down from one hundred to twenty silver dollars. Then, with the help of a policeman, he evicts the invading family from Shen Te's store. The next problem, however, is more difficult to handle: "Toughness and cunning help only against the lower classes."[107] The houseowner Mi Tzu wants two hundred silver dollars in advance because Shen Te is not a respectable person. Shui Ta is at his wit's end. But the policeman has an idea. He is impressed by Shui Ta's firmness and wants to help: "Don't think that the authorities have no feelings for a hard-fighting businessman."[108] He suggests to Shui Ta that Shen Te should marry a man with some capital. He helps to draw up an advertisement for a suitable marriage partner to put in the newspaper.

Scene 3 takes place on a rainy night in the city park. Yang Sun, a young, jobless pilot pulls a rope out of his pocket and looks for a suitable tree—he plans to hang himself. But Shen Te appears and talks him out of hanging himself. He soon realizes that she has a good heart and genuine compassion for him. What ensues is a beautiful love scene of unsentimental tenderness—in the rain under a tree. But lest the audience forget the harsh realities, Shen Te again steps out of her role and addresses the audience:

"There should not be such dull evenings in our country nor high bridges over rivers. Even the hours between night and morning and the whole winter season are dangerous. For in the face of all the misery around us, even a trifle is sufficient to cause people to throw away their intolerable lives."[109]

Then Wang appears and sings a song about the plight of a water seller in the rain. Nobody buys water —except Shen Te.

In the following interlude, the gods return to Wang in a dream while he is asleep in his "home"—a sewer pipe. They are tired and irritated because they are encountering difficulties in finding suitable accommodations on their trip: "The rich recommended that we stay with the poor, but the poor haven't room."[110] They inquire about Shen Te. Wang reports all of Shen Te's good deeds; she has become the "angel of the slums."[111] But when the gods hear that she has not paid the carpenter for his work, they become indignant: "First the letter of the law must be obeyed, then its spirit."[112]

Scene 4 takes place in a little square in front of Shen Te's tobacco shop. Several poor people are waiting there hoping to be fed by Shen Te. While they wait, they complain about her behavior—"staying away from home for nights."[113] Suddenly Wang stumbles out of the barber shop across the street. He is followed by the fat barber Shu Fu, who hits him on his hand with curling tongs for selling water in his shop. Wang's hand is badly hurt. When Shen Te arrives, she is in high spirits because she has fallen in love with Yang Sun. But when she notices Wang's mangled hand and the apathetic attitude of the people around her, she is disgusted: "What kind of a city is this?! What kind of people are you? When there is injustice in the city there should be an uproar." To this one of the women lamely replies, "Well, we can't change the world."[114]

When Yang Sun's mother comes to tell Shen Te that her son can get a position as a pilot provided he can come up with five hundred silver dollars, Shen Te immediately gives her the two hundred dollars the owner of the carpet store had just lent her: "At least one of us should rise above all this misery."[115] But now, with the money gone that was to pay the rent, Shui Ta must once again come to help.

In the following interlude, Shen Te steps in front of the curtain with her Shui Ta mask and suit in her hands. She presents the "Song of the Defenselessness of the Gods and the Good." ("Why don't the gods have tanks and cannon, battleships and bombers and knives, to cut down the bad and spare the good? . . . The laws of the gods do not help against want. . . . Just to get a meal, it now takes the toughness with which once whole nations were formed."[116]) As she sings, she slowly dresses as Shui Ta, her voice changing to masculine as she changes her clothes.

In scene 5, Shui Ta is behind the counter in Shen Te's store. The cleaning woman, Mrs. Shin, tells Shui Ta of the excellent qualities of the barber Shu Fu, who owns twelve houses. He is already interested in Shen Te. He has inquired about her financial affairs, "a sure proof of true love,"[117] Mrs. Shin says. She thinks that the rich Shu Fu would be a much better match for Shen Te than the dubious Yang Sun.

Yang Sun comes to the store to look for Shen Te. Shui Ta decides to test his love for Shen Te, and soon finds out that Yang Sun is only interested in her money. Shui Ta/Shen Te is deeply hurt. But when she returns again as Shen Te, she still professes her love for Yang Sun: "I will go with the man I love. I will not think about how much it costs."[118]

In an interlude in front of the curtain, Shen Te, in a wedding gown, is on her way to the wedding with Yang Sun. She tries to justify her continuing love for Sun in spite of his callousness to the audience and to herself: "Sun is not bad and he does love me. . . . Will I be strong enough to bring out the good part of him?"[119]

Scene 6 takes place in a cheap restaurant. The ceremony cannot begin until the most important guest arrives. Sun hopes that Shui Ta will serve as his best man and also supply the three hundred dollars he still needs to secure a position as a pilot. Only Shen Te knows that Shui Ta can never appear. Finally she tells Yang Sun: "Where I am, he cannot be."[120] The one jug of wine, which was all they could afford, is empty, the priest and the guests leave, the waiter wants his money. Shen Te, Yang Sun, and his mother are the only people left. The wedding is canceled. Yang Sun sings the "Song of St. Nevercome's Day," referring to the day when goodness will finally pay off —which will be the day when the grass looks down upon the sky, that is to say, never.

In the next interlude, the gods again appear to Wang in a dream. Wang tells them about all of Shen Te's woes ("maybe she is indeed too good for this world"[121]). He asks them to intervene. "Quite impossible," they reply, "we only observe. Suffering purifies."[122]

Scene 7 is in the yard behind Shen Te's store. Her situation is desperate. Her engagement is broken; her money is gone, she is in danger of losing her store, and she is pregnant. Shu Fu sees an opportunity to play the role of the generous savior: he hands Shen Te a large sum and offers his warehouses as refuge for Shen Te and other homeless people. At first, Shen Te is reluctant to accept the money. She still thinks that Yang Sun's meanness is only caused by his poverty. And in a tender pantomime she introduces her still unborn son to the audience and her little world.

Her mood changes drastically when she sees one of the carpenter's abandoned sons rummaging for food in a garbage can. Her son's future must be different. Ruthlessness seems to be the only way, so she changes once more into Shui Ta. Using the substantial check Shu Fu had given her, she pays Mi Tzu the rent for the store, and converts Shu Fu's warehouses into a tobacco factory where all the people Shen Te used to feed are given a job. Reluctantly, the people follow Shui Ta's orders, but secretly they preferred not to work and to receive Shen Te's handouts.

In the interlude, the gods, tired from their long journey in search of good people, again visit Wang in a dream. Wang asks the gods to ease their strict requirements for good people in these bad times. It is very difficult to be good when times are bad. But the gods refuse to relent.

Scene 8 takes place in Shui Ta's tobacco factory. Mrs. Yang, Sun's mother, serves as narrator for this scene. She tells the story of her son's "conversion." Sun wasted Shen Te's money after it became clear that he could not get a position as pilot, and was forced to seek employment in Shui Ta's flourishing tobacco factory. Now, he has even managed to become foreman, but he has turned into a real slave driver and is hated by the other workers. His mother is proud of him—he is a success.

In the next scene, we find Shen Te's tobacco store converted into a comfortable office. Shui Ta is facing serious problems. He/she is getting bigger with child and has dizzy spells. Wang has been spreading rumors that Shui Ta is keeping Shen Te prisoner, and Yang Sun has threatened that he will have the police look into Shen Te's "disappearance." Shui Ta, Shu Fu, and Mi Tzu are in the midst of negotiations about an expansion of business when Yang Sun enters with a policeman. They find a bundle of Shen Te's clothes and arrest Shui Ta on a charge of murder.

In an interlude, the gods again appear to Wang. Their faith in their moral laws and the goodness of the world is badly shaken when they learn that Shen Te has disappeared. They decide to look for Shen Te, their last hope.

Scene 10 is in court, where Shui Ta is on trial for the murder of Shen Te. At first the trial goes quite well for Shui Ta, even though the judge—who had been bribed to decide in Shui Ta's favor—is replaced at the last minute by the three gods. Shu Fu, Mi Tzu, and the policeman testify in Shui Ta's behalf ("a man of principle"[123]).

Finally, Shui Ta collapses; he/she can bear this masquerade no longer. When the courtroom is cleared of spectators, Shui Ta reveals himself to be Shen Te, and tells the gods, "Your order to be good and live at the same time has torn me apart into two halves like lightning.... He who helps those who are lost is lost himself.... But when I was unjust, I was powerful and ate well! Something is wrong in your world."[124] The gods, however, will not listen. Now that they have found Shen Te, their good person, again, they slowly ascend on their private cloud into their realm. When Shen Te implores them to tell her how to continue her life, especially now that she will soon have a child to support, the only advice they can give is, "Be good and everything will be fine."[125] They disappear in a rosy light singing "The Trio of the Gods Disappearing on a Cloud," leaving Shen Te to fend for herself.

In the epilogue, one of the actors steps out in front of the curtain to address the audience: "We know full well that this is not an ending. . . . What could the solution be? . . . You must find the solution yourselves. There must be a good one, must, must, must!"[126]

Thus the play concludes with a Brechtian open ending, and an appeal to the audience to find an ending for themselves. But the ending only appears to be open. The answer, of course, is implied: the structure of society must be changed so that a good person like Shen Te can make a living and still be good, without having to turn into a ruthless person like Shui Ta in order to survive.

Brecht believed in the natural goodness of man, and that it was more difficult to be evil than to be good. In his opinion, only in a socialist society would man have a chance to develop this natural goodness.

The role of the three gods can be taken as a satire on religion; they present a list of commandments to be observed in order to be a good person. But they give no practical advice as to how to follow these commandments and still make a living. But, to a greater extent, the gods are a symbol for the "philanthropists." For the betterment of mankind, they give money, but they are unwilling to bring about the actual effective changes necessary to wipe out social ills.

The gods are also meant to be a contrast to Yang Sun, the flier. For Brecht, the airplane pilot was a symbol of hope for mankind—of progress and positive change. (This is also to be seen in his didactic play *The Flight Across the Ocean.*) To be sure, Yang Sun is not an exemplary character. But the potential is there; the society in which he lives does not allow it to develop. And the hope for the next generation of "fliers" is revealed in Shen Te's "introduction" of her unborn son, who will be a flier: "Welcome a new conqueror of unknown mountain ranges and unreachable territories!"[127]

With the figures of the gods and the image of the flier, Brecht wanted to confront deep-rooted traditional beliefs in gods and religion (which accomplish nothing for mankind) with advanced scientific discoveries (which could accomplish much for mankind). Thus he alluded to the gap between technological and social progress. Many people who readily accept modern technological progress possess an underdeveloped sense of social responsibility.

The Chinese setting, masks, music, and costumes lend a very special poetic and theatrical effect to the play. And, despite the frequent use of the estrangement technique, the play is pervaded with controlled emotion. Yet Brecht never lets his audience forget that they are witnessing a theatrical production.

The first performance of *The Good Woman of Setzuan* took place in the Schauspielhaus Zürich on 4 February 1943, two days after the decisive battle of World War II ended in a defeat for Hitler's troops at Stalingrad (director: Leonard Steckel; sets: Teo Otto; Shen Te/Shui Ta: Maria Becker; Mi Tzu: Therese Giehse).

The reviewer of the *Neue Zürcher Zeitung* called the premiere "an exceptional theatrical delight"—so much better than the "cut-and-dried pattern of epic theater." He thought that the actors performed exceptionally well, especially Maria Becker in her double role. And he thought it was the conception of the double role Shen Te/Shui Ta that helped Brecht avoid the dramaturgic weakness of some of his other plays: the lack of an antagonist. He did find the play somewhat lengthy in parts, but he nevertheless called *The Good Woman of Setzuan* "the most mature and, poetically, the most valuable play of this German playwright."[128]

The Good Woman of Setzuan, Schauspielhaus Zürich, world premiere, 4 February 1943. Director: Leonard Steckel; sets: Teo Otto. Yang Sun: Karl Paryla (left); Shen Te/Shui Ta: Maria Becker.
THEATER-MUSEUM MÜNCHEN

The first American performance was a college production. The Hamline Players of Hamline University, St. Paul, Minnesota, presented Eric and Maja Bentley's adaptation on 16 March 1948. Two days later, the *Minneapolis Star* printed a review by John K. Sherman, who interpreted the plot in an existential light ("a satirical and rather elaborate parable on the difficulties of being good in a savage and self-seeking world"). He found its development rather dull ("the story goes into prolonged and rather tedious complications"). Sherman judged the direction by James R. Carlson "able," and found the staging interesting ("There is artful and fluent use of such devices as asides to the audience, songs with words cast on a screen, and an airy mixture of archaic and modern attitudes and speech"[129]).

The Good Woman of Setzuan has been performed on many campuses around the country—more often than any other play by Brecht. But, as the following review illustrates, it was frequently misunderstood. After the performance on 29 March 1950 at the University of Illinois (directed by Charles H. Shattuck), the reviewer for the student newspaper *The Daily Illini* wrote: "The Illini Theater Guild did an excellent job . . . but the end result was more confusing than amusing. [The play] posed the question, 'Is it worthwhile to be charitable?' but did not attempt to answer it." He may well have been expressing the response of the student audience in his comments on the play's "unusual" form: *"The Good Woman seems to have no real beginning or ending . . .* the continuity is interrupted somewhat by thematic poems and songs, as well as by the basic episodic sequence of action."[130]

The first West German performance of the play took place on 16 November 1952 in Frankfurt on the Main (director: Harry Buckwitz; sets: Teo Otto; Shen Te: Solveig Thomas). The play itself and the production received a very good review in the *Frankfurter Allgemeine Zeitung*. The reviewer saw the play as a powerful and angry indictment against injustice and poverty on earth presented with biblical force and outstanding poetic moments. It was a solid ensemble performance without egoistic "showing off" by individuals; Solveig Thomas' Shen Te was "absolutely superb."[131]

On 31 October 1956, *The Good Woman of Set-zuan* opened at the Royal Court Theater in London (director: George Devine; Shen Te: Peggy Ashcroft). Kenneth Tynan praised the play highly; he found in it "high moments of art," scenes "of the most biting subtlety," and violent emotions curbed only by "that celebrated dam, the alienation-effect." To the critics who asked why Brecht needed "three hours, fourteen scenes, and thirty actors to prove that poor people are often a grasping lot," Tynan countered that, first of all, this synopsis was an oversimplification, and, secondly, that many popular plays—musicals in particular—used at least as much time and apparatus "to say precisely nothing."

But Tynan did have some criticism of the production. As he saw it, George Devine, in trying to direct "his cast along cool, detached Brechtian lines," had lost sight of the fact "that the Brechtian method works only with team-actors of great technical maturity." This criticism could well be leveled against many—if not most—Brecht productions. He thought the play also suffered from the Bentleys' "clumsy" translation. Peggy Ashcroft, as Shen Te, was "only halfway fine." He thought her Shui Ta was "superb," but her Shen Te would not do. Still, Tynan recommended that the production "not be missed by anyone interested in hearing the fundamental problems of human (as opposed to Western European) existence discussed in the theater." He also considered the plot relevant to modern times: "In the context of our present prosperity, these problems may appear irrelevant. They are still cruelly relevant to more than half of the inhabited world."[132]

On 18 December 1956, *The Good Woman of Setzuan*, in the Bentleys' translation, opened in the Phoenix Theater in New York City and ran for twenty-four performances (director: Eric Bentley; sets: Wolf-

gang Roth; music: Paul Dessau; Shen Te/Shui Ta:
Uta Hagen; Yang Sun: Albert Salmi; Shu Fu: Zero
Mostel; Wang: Gerald Hiken). The critical reaction
was mixed. Wolcott Gibbs's review in *The New Yorker*
was outright negative. In his opinion, the performance
attempted to discover "how far a production can go
in the direction of sheer, staggering dullness without
quite emptying the theater at the end of the first act."
He himself left shortly thereafter, and complained that
there was nothing on the stage that was "likely to give
anyone the illusion of looking at life."[133]

The review in *Theater Arts* (February 1957) was
somewhat more positive: "Brecht's parable was given
a very ingenious and lively staging in his own anti-
naturalistic style." The reviewer praised "the wonderfully sardonic quality of Paul Dessau's music." But
he felt that, in the Bentleys' English adaptation, the
message was delivered with "singular lack of thrust."
And he interpreted the message of the play to be "that
men of good will must gain strength and practicality
to cope with the impositions thrust upon them, though
without resorting to tyranny."[134]

Brooks Atkinson of *The New York Times* found the
form of the play particularly interesting, and the play
in general "nonsentimental in theme and stimulating
from several points of view." The style of *The Good
Woman of Setzuan* reminded him of the medieval
morality play and of the classical Peking opera: "It is
pure art—story-telling, songs, orchestra music, moral
homilies, movement. Dispensing with the familiar
principle of trying to create an illusion of actual life,
it uses all the arts of the theater like instruments in
an orchestra." He took "ironic notice of two of the
theater's oldest pieces of hokum"—the prostitute with
a golden heart, and an unborn child who will undoubtedly turn out to be a boy.

As for the performance itself, Atkinson thought that

the setting by Wolfgang Roth was "first rate," and that the principal parts were "extraordinarily well played." But he was critical of the Bentleys' translation and Dessau's "dismal" music.[135]

Walter Kerr's review in the *New York Herald Trib- une* was totally negative. He observed, with regard to this production, that "the possibilities of reducing genuine talent [of the actors] to zero are not yet fully explored." In his opinion, the production lacked mus- cle and vitality; he looked in vain for "the kindling spark." But he attributed the theatrical failings to Bentley's staging and translation.[136]

The premiere of this play by the Berliner Ensemble on 5 October 1957 took place shortly after Brecht's death (director: Benno Besson; sets: Karl von Appen; Shen Te: Käthe Reichel). The question in everyone's mind was how the Ensemble would fare without Brecht. To Fritz Erpenbeck, whose review appeared in the December issue of *Theater der Zeit,* the play itself was beyond criticism. He thought the love scene between Shen Te and Yang Sun "one of the most poetic and beautiful love scenes in our literature." This scene in particular proved to him that Brecht was by no means against emotions. He thought von Ap- pen's sets "beautifully suggestive," and that Besson was "wise enough not to give any room to Chinese folklore or Chinese milieu." But, for his taste, "there were too many gaps, too many estrangement effects, too many underlined passages." However, the produc- tion showed him that the Berliner Ensemble was "alive and well," and that it possessed a cadre of young and talented directors and actors.[137]

In December of 1960, Jean Vilar staged a produc- tion of *The Good Woman of Setzuan* at the Théâtre Récamier in Paris, with excellent performances by Michele Nadal as Shen Te and Gilles Leger as Wang. According to Jean-Pierre Lenoir, in a review for *The*

New York Times, the singing was weak. In general, the French press reviews were mixed.[138]

On 5 November 1970, the Repertory Theater of Lincoln Center opened its sixth season with *The Good Woman of Setzuan* in the Vivian Beaumont Theater (English adaptation: Ralph Manheim; music: Herbert Pilhofer; director: Robert Symonds; Shen Te: Colleen Dewhurst; Yang Sun: David Birney).

The critic of *Variety* observed: "This new treatment ... has more animation than the former edition ... but it's still a heavy, repetitious, attenuated and progressively tiresome show." He found the plot "silly" and "the theme of an individual's conflicting noble and evil impulses ... a soporific cliche." The staging and the acting earned his mild approval, but he did not like Herbert Pilhofer's music.[139]

Clive Barnes of *The New York Times* thought that since Bertolt Brecht was "notoriously difficult to present in English," the production was "bold, and also sensible and necessary, for if New York is to have plays of this quality, properly produced, it is hard to see where they can find a home if not at Lincoln Center." He had some criticisms:

> The play was never quite stylized enough. ...
> There was also a certain ponderousness in Ralph
> Manheim's translation ... where the collaboration
> fell seriously apart here was in the music by
> Herbert Pilhofer. ... The acting was good in its
> realistic passages, less assured in its fantasy.

On the whole, the performance was, in Barnes' opinion, to the Lincoln Center company's credit: "This is a rewarding play for audiences to grapple with and a tough nut for any company to produce. The Lincoln Center company emerges with honor and a certain amount of distinction," although "more delicacy" would have been preferable. Barnes himself seems to have had some misconceptions about the play's message, which he interpreted as being: "While absolute goodness may be impossible, a little goodness is better than no goodness at all."[140]

Walter Kerr's review of the play was scathing. He found a total of about fifteen minutes' worth of "little heart-lifters" in the Vivian Beaumont production, which he regretted, since it made it more difficult for him to bear stoically the other two and a half hours. Otherwise, one would have been able to "settle down to the dull, unhighlighted pace of the production at the Vivian Beaumont and to the coy and placid plaiting of platitudes that constitute so much of Bertolt Brecht's text." In his opinion, Robert Symonds' direction made the text's inescapable flatness even flatter.[141]

In 1973, the Synthaxis Theater Company of Los Angeles presented a rather unorthodox production of *The Good Woman of Setzuan*. The director, Cindy Turtledove, discarded much of the "conventional" Brechtian theater and used modern dance, pantomime, rock music, and the slapstick comedy of early American films. Asked why she chose this new approach, Ms. Turtledove replied: "I think it's about time that Brecht should be a little bit of fun—you know, a little life, a little energy, instead of falling asleep in it." According to the review in the *Brecht Yearbook* of 1974 the production was quite a success.[142]

In February of 1975, director Andrei Serban offered a "work-in-progress" (experimental) production of *The Good Woman of Setzuan* in New York's La Mama Experimental Theater Club. According to Clive Barnes, it was a very successful production, with Priscilla Smith "most appealing" as Shen Te. The music by Elizabeth Swados was "most attractive" with "an unmistakable and apt touch of Kurt Weill to it."[143]

The Good Woman of Setzuan was of particular importance for Brecht. He worked at it for more than ten years. After he had completed the play he wrote in his notebook, "This play cost me more effort than any before."[144] Compared with *Galileo,* the play is a much better example of Brecht's epic, or dialectic, theater. Brecht noted: "When writing for the drawer one does not have to make concessions."[145] At the time Brecht could not foresee that it would ever be produced.

It is a beautifully constructed play of high artistic quality. In the form of a parable, Brecht wanted to show that, in order to survive in a class-oriented society, a person must be a split character. Although this theme of split characters occurs frequently in Brecht's plays, nowhere is it so dominant as in this play.

Herr Puntila and His Servant Matti (1940)

In August 1940, while Brecht and his family were temporary guests on her estate near Helsinki, the Finnish writer Hella Wuolijoki showed Brecht several of her stories and a comedy dealing with a rich landowner and his chauffeur. Immediately interested in the material, Brecht made a play out of it within a month.

The play, consisting of twelve scenes and a prologue, is set in prewar Finland. The main characters are the rich landowner Puntila, his daughter Eve, and his chauffeur and valet Matti.

Prologue. When the theater lights are lowered, the actress who plays the servant who tends the cows appears before the curtain, and informs the audience of the content of the play: "Tonight we are going to

---

German title: *Herr Puntila und sein Knecht Matti.*

show you/ A certain pre-historic animal/ Called estatium possessor or, in English, landowner."[146]

SCENE 1. Puntila is drinking in a hotel in Tavasthus. After two days of drinking, the last of his companions, the judge, has fallen from his chair in a drunken stupor. In a mellow mood, Puntila invites his chauffeur Matti, who has been waiting outside in the car for the two days, to have a drink with him. He then proceeds to tell Matti about a "terrible sickness" that overcomes him every now and then: he has times when he is dead sober—although he tries to fight against it like a man. And, when sober, he degenerates to the level of an animal and is capable of any mean deed.

SCENE 2. Three days later, Puntila, the judge, and Matti arrive (with a lot of noise and a suitcase full of liquor) at Puntila's Kurgela estate. There they are to celebrate the engagement of Eve, Puntila's daughter, to a degenerate diplomat. In his present state of amiable drunkenness, Puntila suggests she marry Matti instead. Eve scolds him and denies him another drop of liquor. Puntila goes to find a drink elsewhere; Eve and Matti are left alone. Eve tries to be very dignified and defends her engagement to her diplomat. Matti, under a cloak of servility, makes witty and ironic comments about Puntila and the diplomat.

SCENE 3. Puntila runs his Studebaker into a telegraph pole in the middle of the village square and curses the pole ("must be a communist"). But since he is drunk, he remains in a good mood. He refuses the illegal alcohol offered to him by Smuggler Emma— a local celebrity—because he is for law and order, but he takes it when he obtains a prescription from a veterinarian. Then he gets engaged to four poor women in succession whom he happens to meet in the town, and he invites them to come to his estate in eight days to celebrate the engagement.

Scene 4. Puntila and Matti are at the servant market. Puntila is looking for servants. He comes close to having one of his fits of sobriety, and accuses Matti of exploiting him when he is drunk. But a few quick drinks in a café remedy the situation. In the meantime, Matti has picked out a servant. But when the now drunk and affable Puntila offers the man a "home" rather than a work contract, the man takes off—the fact that Puntila is friendly to him makes him extremely suspicious.

Puntila and Matti return home with a small, weak worker and another servant, Surkkala, called "the red one." Surkkala had previously been employed by Puntila, but Puntila had dismissed him in one of his sober rages because of his "communist views." Now that Puntila is drunk again, he calls Surkkala "the only intelligent servant I've ever had."[147]

Scene 5. Back on Puntila's estate, Puntila is in the bathhouse, drinking coffee. As soon as he is sober, he becomes ill-tempered. He chases away the servants. Then he scolds Matti for insubordination and stealing. (Puntila had given Matti his wallet, which he now finds in Matti's jacket.)

Eve, in the meantime, is in a desperate situation: she has had a change of heart and does not want to marry the diplomat. Matti offers his help by suggesting that he and she could go to the bathhouse and make it appear as if they were making love. For him, this is a service, like washing the car or any other duty. In a delightfully comic scene, we see Eve and Matti in the bathhouse. They arrange to be seen leaving the bathhouse together when Puntila and the diplomat pass. Puntila is enraged, but not the diplomat (who desperately needs Eve's money and wants to marry her no matter what). "His debts must be even greater than we assumed,"[148] Matti comments drily.

Scene 6. At the end of a long day, Matti is reading

the newspaper in the kitchen. Eve comes in with a seductive swagger and a long cigarette holder. She wants Matti to row her to an island to "find some crabfish." But Matti has worked hard and is tired. Eve leaves, but returns a few minutes later with the request that he take her to the train station. This time she is quite blunt; she tells Matti that she wants to marry him. But Matti knows that he does not belong in Eve's vacuous world.

SCENE 7. Puntila (and the audience) have almost forgotten them by now, but suddenly Puntila's four fiancées from town show up. They overhear the sober Puntila trying to force Eve into a status-raising marriage with the diplomat. Puntila even offers to sell one of his forests in order to have even more money to spend on Eve's wedding. Intercepting the fiancées, Matti informs them they have come at a bad time. He gives them a lesson in upper-class social manners. When Puntila appears, Matti informs him that his four waiting fiancées have formed "a league of Puntila's fiancées." But the sober Puntila is in no mood for jokes. He sarcastically suggests, "Why not a trade union?" He orders the women—whom he does not even recognize —to leave his estate. ("You have come to blackmail me."[149])

SCENE 8. The four fiancées are on their way home again. They tell each other stories about how they or people of their class have been used by people above them.

SCENE 9. Puntila's estate is ready for the engagement ceremonies. Even the minister is there to witness the event. The guests stand around in groups and talk. In these conversations, Eve's fiancé reveals in one episode after another his empty-headedness. Puntila is sitting in a corner, getting drunk—and sensible. Finally, he can no longer bear the diplomat's stupidity and orders him to leave his estate. ("I won't allow the

stück were often crude and earthy, possessing little artistic or aesthetic value. Brecht increased the artistic and poetic qualities in his folk play but he retained some of the crudities and elements of southern German dialect. He also drew upon the revue and the musical comedy. In particular, in his notes he referred to the literary revues of W. H. Auden and Christopher Isherwood, as well as those of Marc Blitzstein. Here he found the loose structure of a series of relatively independent sketches so characteristic of his own epic theater. And, of course, Brecht was influenced by film: his rich landowner Puntila bears many resemblances to Charlie Chaplin's millionaire in *City Lights*.

According to Brecht, a stage production of *Puntila/ Matti* should contain elements of the *commedia dell' arte*[155] and the realistic comedy of manners developed by the French and English in the seventeenth century. Brecht himself was very fond of Molière and Farquhar; he adapted Molière's *Don Juan* and Farquhar's *The Recruiting Officer*.[156] And while working on *Puntila/Matti*, which he found very relaxing after the strenuous work of *The Good Woman of Setzuan*, he enjoyed reading English literature, such as the controversy between Matthew Arnold and Cardinal John Henry Newman about translating Homer. Time and again, he expressed his admiration for English literature: "Those English really have literature!"[157]

Puntila/Matti also contains strong echoes of Hašek's *Schweyk* novel,[158] which Brecht was later to dramatize. (Schweyk is an example of the common man who tries to survive by cunning. Matti has many traits in common with Schweyk.)

With Puntila's near human behavior when drunk and his ruthlessness when sober, Brecht does not want merely to create a humorous effect or characterize an individual. Rather, it is his intention to illustrate a pattern of behavior forced upon an individual in a capitalistic society (just as in *The Good Woman of Setzuan*). Man, as Brecht sees him, is basically good— even Puntila—but the constraints of a class society force him to act otherwise. It is only when Puntila is drunk, thus going against the rules of society, that he is himself, that is to say, good.

Although he used material from Wuolijoki, Brecht's *Puntila/Matti* is a counterplay to one of the most popular German folk plays of the 1920s: Carl Zuck-mayer's *The Merry Vineyard* (1925). In Zuckmayer's play, too, a rich landowner (Gunderloch, the owner of a vineyard) wants to marry his daughter (Klärchen) to an arrogant and empty-headed man (Knuzius) from the upper class. Like Eve in Brecht's play, Klär-chen prefers an honest man from the common people (Jochen Most, a Rhine skipper). *The Merry Vineyard,* however, ends happily; with three engagements, all conflicts are solved. In sharp contrast, the ending of Brecht's play points out the irreconcilable difference between the classes in a class-structured society.[159]

Brecht's play was also directed against the fake "folksiness" with which the Nazis, in order to cover up class differences and their real intentions, tried to embrace the German people. One of the Nazis' main propagators of this kind of obfuscation technique was Hermann Göring, himself basically a Puntila-like figure. He could be as jovial or as brutal as Puntila, but be-cause he was a much more powerful figure, the effects of his brutality were much greater.

It has been said that Brecht made the character of Puntila too attractive. There are indeed fewer scenes showing him in his sober state of ruthlessness and meanness than in his drunk and lovable state, such as the opening scene (Puntila, the lone survivor of a gigantic drinking bout, walking "on a sea of aquavit") and that on the "Hatelma mountain" in Puntila's library (in which Puntila is drunk both with alcohol and patriotism). Brecht realized that the danger is in fact there, and he therefore gave detailed instructions on how he wanted the part of Puntila played. Brecht stressed that the drunken Puntila must not be played in a way that would make him either repulsive or just comic. According to Brecht, the main problem for the actor who plays Puntila is to show that Puntila actually becomes a better person when drunk. When drunk he does not have the blurred language and clumsy, broken gestures of the stage drunk, but rather his language takes on a musical quality and his movements become relaxed and dancelike. At the same time, the actor must not arouse in the theatergoer too much sympathy for Puntila. They must still be able to see him critically.

Puntila's is a fascinating and unusual part to play, but he will not steal the show if Brecht's intentions are realized in the production. In his notes to the Zurich production of *Puntila/Matti,* Brecht wrote: "It is of decisive importance to stress the class antagonism between Puntila and Matti. The role of Matti must be played in such a way that there is a genuine balance, that is to say that he is superior intellectually."[160] For it is clearly Matti, who, with his Schweykian wisdom, is the superior character. Quick-witted and diplomatic, he knows how to get what he wants from his "betters." And most of the time it is Matti's dry comments that expose Puntila's nature and cause us to laugh.

As in many other Brechtian plays, the action is interrupted by songs, and the titles of the individual scenes are projected on a canvas. Between scenes, the cook Laina steps in front of the curtain, accompanied by an accordion player and a guitar player, to sing an appropriate verse of "The Puntila Song," which summarizes and interprets the action we have just seen on stage. Paul Dessau, the composer of the original music for the play, used a melody reminiscent of Slavic folk music for this song.

The first performance in German of *Herr Puntila and His Servant Matti* took place in Switzerland on 5 June 1948, in the Schauspielhaus Zürich (director: Kurt Hirschfeld; Puntila: Leonard Steckel; Matti: Gustav Knuth; sets: Teo Otto). Brecht was in Switzerland at that time, and he actually did most of the directing himself. (It was the second time that he could see and direct one of his plays in a German-speaking theater since his days in Berlin before Hitler came to power. On 15 February 1948 he had directed his adaptation of Sophocles' *Antigone* in Chur, Switzerland.) He was quite happy with the production, considering the time pressure at rehearsals and the inadequate lighting system.

This production of *Herr Puntila and His Servant Matti* was the third premiere of a Brecht play in the Schauspielhaus Zürich. (They had done *Mother Courage and Her Children* in 1941, and *The Good Woman of Setzuan* in 1943.)

The critic of the *Neue Zürcher Zeitung* found it to be "one of the weaker Brechtian dramas." In his opinion, Brecht used some shop worn comedy clichés, and his punch lines were not so witty as in some of his other plays, and the sober Puntila was not convincing—"his maliciousness seems purely the result of a hangover curable with aspirin." But he felt that the Schauspielhaus production and the ensemble made the performance a success. He was particularly impressed with Leonard Steckel's Puntila. Steckel's ascent of the Hatelma mountain in the library was for him the high point of the performance. Despite Steckel's powerful Puntila, he thought that Gustav Knuth held his own as Matti.[161]

On 12 November 1949, *Puntila/Matti* opened in the Deutsches Theater in East Berlin. It was the first play to be performed by the now famous Berliner Ensemble. Brecht himself chose this as their first play (directors: Bertolt Brecht and Erich Engel; sets: Caspar Neher; music: Paul Dessau; Puntila: Leonard Steckel; Matti: Erwin Geschonneck; Eve: Angelika Hurwicz; other roles were played by such illustrious actors and actresses as Regine Lutz, Therese Giehse, Annemarie Hase, and Friedrich Gnass).

The performance was a great success, and the critics even accepted the new "epic" presentation. Brecht noted, however, that it contained only as many epic elements as he felt the audience would accept at that time. He added in his *Work Journal* (13 November 1949): "When will we have a genuine radical epic theater?"[162]

For this production, however, Leonard Steckel wore an unattractive mask throughout the play, because Brecht felt that the character of Puntila had been too attractive in the Zurich production.

Brecht justified the performance of a play about class struggle in "the classless society" of East Germany by adding a prologue. He stressed the historical aspect of the play: "Why is *Herr Puntila and His Servant Matti* still meaningful to us? Because one does not learn only from the [class] struggle, but also from the history of [class] struggles."[163]

Friedrich Luft, the leading theater critic in West Berlin, returned from his excursion to East Berlin with an excellent review: "There were salvos of laughter, plenty of applause. This performance, masterly in detail, bold in concept, was a [theatrical] highlight." Luft thought the high points of comedy that were achieved by the quick and witty repartee proved that Brecht was "the writer of the most poignant dialogue and the craftiest manipulator of language in our time."

Puntila and His Servant Matti, Schauspielhaus Zürich, world premiere, 5 June 1948. Director: Kurt Hirschfeld; sets: Teo Otto. Puntila: Leonard Steckel (left); Matti: Gustav Knuth.

Puntila and His Servant Matti, Berliner Ensemble, 1949. Puntila: Leonard Steckel (left); Matti: Erwin Geschonneck.

He pointed to the scene on Hatelma mountain as a particularly good example. In his opinion, the acting was superb throughout.[164]

On 14 May 1959, *Puntila/Matti,* in an English adaptation by Gerhard Nellhaus and Richard Grenier, entitled simply *Puntila,* had its world premiere. Alex Horn directed the production by Repertory Boston in the Wilbur Theater (sets: Robert Skinner and Lorna Kreuger; music: Caldwell Titcomb; Puntila: Ray Reinhardt; Matti: John Lasell).

Brooks Atkinson of *The New York Times* encouraged the fledgling theater company with a good review: "The management is entitled to take pride. For *Puntila* is a sophisticated, original and amusing theatrical escapade, shrewdly directed by Alex Horn and played in the leading parts with comic gusto." In the play, Atkinson found "some class-conscious didacticism dropped into the conclusions." But—so far as he could tell from the English adaptation—Brecht was "primarily interested in inventing a humorous form to tell a commedia dell'arte story of an epochal conflict among three strong-minded characters [Puntila, Matti, Eve]."[165]

In November 1964, *Puntila/Matti* had its French premiere at the Théâtre National Populaire, directed by Georges Wilson. According to the critic for *The New York Times,* the play, produced "in the Epic Theater manner," was met by a protest of Le Mouvement Lettriste, an "eccentric literary group," which tossed a shower of leaflets from the balcony protesting the play as Stalinist propaganda.

In October 1974, the Montreal International Theater, in their small theater La Poudrière (which was formerly the powder magazine of an old fort on an island in the St. Lawrence River), gave a delightful performance of *Puntila/Matti* in German. Erwin Potitt adapted and directed the play; he also played the part of Matti. Max Fleck was quite successful in arousing both laughter and disgust as the rich landowner Puntila. Potitt played Matti with wit, successfully imbuing him with the aura of superiority. The play was considerably shortened and the cast reduced to only seven characters (Puntila's four fiancées were cut altogether). But the production showed that *Puntila/Matti* can be very effectively staged by a small theater with a small cast and a limited budget.

In March 1977 the Yale Repertory Theatre produced its version of *Puntila/Matti* (director: Ron Daniels; sets: David Lloyd Gropman; translation: Gerhard Nellhaus; music: William Bolcom, with lyrics adapted by Michael Feingold; Puntila: Thomas Hill; Matti: Ron Faber; Eve: Shaine Marinson). Daniels chose a carnival setting for the play, complete with a sideshow barker (who replaced Brecht's dairymaid as commentator) and fair-type happenings before the play and during the intermission. In an attempt to Americanize the play, Daniels used elements of a TV quiz show when Matti examined Eve on whether she would make a good wife for a chauffeur.

Mel Gussow of *The New York Times* found the play "timely," and he asked: "With low wages, high unemployment, and a plethora of Puntilas—could this also be Middle America?" Despite occasional "slow moments" and "too much stage business" he judged the production "convivial ... a worthy addition to Yale's repertory of uncommon Brecht."[165a]

In a rather lengthy review in *Newsweek* Jack Kroll praised both the play and the production: "The texture of this enormously appealing play is well served by Daniels, who gets funny and touching performances from Yale's quite Brechtian mixture of professionals and advanced students."[165b]

In December 1966, the Deutsche Staatsoper in East

Berlin staged Paul Dessau's opera *Puntila,* based on Brecht's play, adapted for opera by Peter Palitzsch and Manfred Wekwerth, both of whom had been as-asistant directors under Brecht at the Berliner Ensemble. The producer was Ruth Berghaus, who had been one of Brecht's friends and collaborators. (From 1971 to 1977 she was the director of the Berliner Ensemble.) Dessau's score was very modern and ambitious, but Joachim Kaiser, in a review in *Theater heute,* felt that the opera as a whole was less effective than the play.[166]

In 1955, the Austrian film company Wien Film Rosenhügel made a color film of Brecht's play, with Alberto Cavalcanti as director and Curt Bois as Puntila, and with music by Hanns Eisler.

Many critics have interpreted *Puntila/Matti* as a rather harmless folk comedy and a welcome reprieve from Brecht's political plays. They justify this view by Brecht's own subtitle, "folk play." But Brecht quite deliberately chose this term in order to upgrade the genre. As he pointed out in 1940: "For a long time the folk play has been a much despised genre, given to dilettantism and routine. The time has come to use it for those noble purposes to which the name of this genre obligates us in the first place."[167] Thus he set out, as a Marxist, to write a Marxist folk play—a play for the people. The result of his work, *Herr Puntila and His Servant Matti,* is one of Brecht's wittiest plays. Translated into Finnish by Hella Wuolijoki, it was even called a "classic Finnish national comedy."[168]

The Resistible Rise of Arturo Ui
(1941)

Brecht's last play in Scandinavian exile before he emigrated to the United States was *The Resistible Rise of Arturo Ui*. On 10 March 1941, Brecht noted in his *Work Journal*: "Thinking of the American theater, I remembered an idea I once had when I was in New York [he was there in 1935]—namely to write a gangster play about certain events [the rise of Hitler] we all know." Thus in March and April of 1941, he wrote *Arturo Ui*, a gangster play depicting Hitler's rise to power. The Nazi leaders are presented as Mafia-type gangsters; the setting is Chicago at the beginning of the 1930s. Brecht noted that this play was "an attempt to explain the rise of Hitler to the capitalist world by placing the action in a well-known milieu."[169] Just as organized crime was believed to have taken over Chicago and the suburb of Cicero, Hitler and his gang took over Germany and Austria.

Brecht changed the names of the historical Nazis and other historical figures, but in most cases their real identity can easily be recognized:

Dogsborough = Paul von Hindenburg (dog = *Hund*, borough = *Burg*; president of Germany before Hitler);

Arturo Ui, gangster boss = Adolf Hitler;

Ernesto Roma, Arturo's lieutenant = Ernst Röhm (head of the Nazi storm troopers);

Emanuele Giri and Giuseppe Givola, flower dealers = Hermann Göring (head of the Nazi airforce) and Josef Goebbels (propaganda minister);

German title: *Der aufhaltsame Aufstieg des Arturo Ui.*

Dullfeet = Dollfuss (chancellor of Austria, 1932–34);

Clark = von Papen (landowner and industrialist who became German chancellor in 1932 and helped to pave the way for Hitler);

Cauliflower Trust = Prussian landowners (Junkers);

Chicago = Germany; Cicero = Austria.

Brecht intended that in the play these characters should also resemble their historical models by the use of masks, gestures, figures of speech, and tones of voice.

The play begins with a prologue. An announcer steps in front of the curtain, and, in the fashion of the ringmaster at the circus, gives a preview of the action to follow: "Ladies and gentlemen, today we will bring you . . . a great historical gangster show." Then he introduces the main characters in the "show," each of whom steps forward as he is introduced. Shrill circus music can be heard in the background. On the curtain, newspaper headlines are projected: "News from the dock scandal! Sensation in warehouse fire trial! Gangster Ernesto Roma assassinated by his friends! Dullfeet blackmailed! Cicero conquered by gangsters!"[170] These captions not only create the atmosphere of gangsterland, but also point out the actual historical events depicted in the play. (To keep the historical parellels clearly in the theatergoer's mind, similar projections are used throughout the play for each scene. Some scenes, however, lack direct historical parallels.)

SCENE 1. In the city of Chicago, five bosses of the Cauliflower Trust discuss their difficulties: business is bad. Gangster boss Arturo Ui has offered them his services and promised to double their business. But they turned him down. They feel that they, as good taxpayers, are entitled to a loan from the city government. Officially they claim that the money will be used to improve the docks to facilitate imports and help the city. Their true motives, however, are of a more dubious nature; they want the money for personal gains. They hope to gain bar owner Dogsborough's assistance. ("He is an honest man—or at least has the reputation of being honest, which is even better."[171]) He is known to have great influence with the city government.

Historical background: In 1929–31 the economic crisis hits especially hard in Germany. Prussian landowners (Junkers) try to get a loan from the government.

SCENE 2. Flake and Butcher of the Cauliflower Trust go to Dogsborough's bar to ask him to help. Dogsborough refuses to intercede with the city government on behalf of their loan ("Your request sounds fishy").[172] They resort to a ploy: in recognition of Dogsborough's services to the city, they offer him a special deal. For only $20,000 they will sell him the majority of the stocks in a shipping company worth much more. (They had previously extracted the stocks from the company's owner, Sheet, who was in serious financial difficulties.) Dogsborough hesitates, but finally accepts this "gift."

Historical background: In order to win his support, the Junkers honor President Hindenburg with a present of an estate. They receive their loan.

SCENE 3. In a shabby gambling office on 122nd Street, Arturo Ui, Roma, and their gang are listening to race track reports. They, too, have fallen on hard times (lack of cash, lack of morale). Roma develops a plan: they will harass small businessmen and then bully them into paying protection money. But first, Ui wants to be sure of some protection for himself from government quarters.

Giri appears with a shady character named Bowl, and things take a turn for the better for Ui's gang. Bowl knows about Dogsborough's deal with the Cauliflower Trust. Ui rejoices, "By God, Dogsborough has spots on his vest!"[173] He sees the opportunity to blackmail him.

Historical background: In the fall of 1932, the Nazis faced serious problems—loss of financial support and voters.

SCENE 4. At Dogsborough's estate, he is having second thoughts about taking the gift from the Cauliflower Trust. When "a certain Mr. Ui" appears, he orders him to leave. But Ui, with the help of his hoods, is persistent in his request that Dogsborough intervene on his behalf with the police so that he can provide "effective" protection for the small businessmen. ("The small businessman is industrious, but stupid; often honest, but seldom far-sighted. He needs strong leadership."[174]) When his appeal to Dogsborough's "humanity" fails, Ui resorts to shouts, screams and tears, and threatens to expose Dogsborough's part in the shady Cauliflower Trust loan arrangements. Still to no avail. Ui departs threatening to expose Dogsborough to city officials. Shortly after he leaves, two city councilmen appear to inform Dogsborough that the council intends to probe into his dealings with the Cauliflower Trust.

Historical background: President Hindenburg denies Hitler the chancellorship. But he fears an inquiry into the government loan to the landowners. He also fears exposure about his handling of state funds because he has used part of them for his own private ends.

SCENE 5. In city hall, the hearing before the city council is hampered by the sudden and mysterious death of Sheet, who was a most important witness for the investigation. And when the investigator gets close to exposing Dogsborough's deal, Ui comes to Dogsborough's aid by putting all the blame on the dead Sheet and by having another witness assassinated on the steps of the city hall. He now has Dogsborough in his hands, and he has also impressed the members of the Cauliflower Trust as a man of action.

Historical background: Hitler gains importance in the eyes of the Junkers and industrialists.

SCENE 6. Ui's suite in the Mammoth Hotel. In a highly comic theatrical scene, Ui hires a down-and-out second-rate actor to teach him how to walk, stand, sit, and speak with great style. He wants to learn how to impress the man in the street. Antonio's great speech from Shakespeare's *Julius Caesar* ("Friends, Romans, countrymen") serves as a model for a demagogic speech.

Historical background: Rumor has it that Hitler took acting lessons.

SCENE 7. In the office of the Cauliflower Trust, Ui is speaking to a gathering of produce merchants, with "honest" and popular Dogsborough at his side. In the face of increasing violence (actually perpetrated by his gang, of course), Ui calls for "law and order," which only he can provide. He has Dogsborough's backing ("Providence has joined us"[175]) and the backing of the trust, who fear uprisings of the workers. Ui is quick to point out that the "individual worker" has his full sympathy. But workers who "band together and dare to meddle in affairs they know nothing about"[176] must be opposed.

The following question-and-answer session shows that the produce dealers do not feel sufficiently threatened to want protection. But suddenly a produce warehouse nearby bursts into flames. (It has deliberately been set on fire by Ui's men.) Ui hopes that now everyone "sees the light." Those people who happened to see Giri and his men walk by with gasoline cans just minutes before the fire are threatened at gun point to keep them quiet. The scene ends with the usual trappings of a political meeting—there is a sentimental patriotic song and Ui pats children on the head.

Historical background: Big business, afraid of worker unrest, supports Hitler. On 30 January 1933, Hitler becomes chancellor with Hindenburg's approval. The investigation into the loan scandal is stopped.

SCENE 8. The warehouse fire trial. This travesty of a trial is presented in seven small episodes, separated by short periods of darkness and underscored by the music of Chopin's funeral march—played as a lively dance.

An unemployed working man named Fish, who has just arrived in Chicago, has been accused by Giri of having deliberately started the fire. To the derisive laughter of Giri and his people, the defense tries to prove that Giri himself was at the scene of the fire. The produce merchant Hook testifies that he saw Giri carrying gasoline, and Fish denies that he had anything to do with the fire. But by using force and threats, Giri and his gang manage it so that—against all evidence—Fish is sentenced to fifteen years in prison.

Historical background: In February 1933, the Reichstag, the seat of the legislature in Berlin, burned down. Accusing the communists of this act, the Nazis took this opportunity to move against the "enemies of the people." A jobless Dutchman, van der Lubbe, was sentenced to death by the highest court (Reichsgericht). It is alleged that the Nazis themselves started the fire.

SCENE 9. This scene is divided into two short episodes. In Cicero, a woman, covered with blood, stumbles from a truck and shouts: "My husband . . . murderers . . . Ui, you monster, you scum. Is there no one to stop him?"[177] A machine-gun blast silences her.

Switch to Dogsborough's estate. Dogsborough is writing his will. In a monologue, he relieves his conscience and confesses that he has known all along about Ui's shameful deeds. Fear and greed made him an acquiescent conspirator.

Historical background: The first part is an illustration of Nazi brutality. There is no proven historical evidence for the second part, but Brecht is obviously hinting that Hindenburg, out of personal greed, helped to pave the way for Hitler.

SCENE 10. Ui's suite in the Mammoth Hotel. Hostilities that have long been brewing among Giri, Givola, and Roma erupt. Ui barely manages to prevent bloodshed by delivering one of his emotional speeches: "He who does not trust me blindly can go his own way. My motto is 'Do your duty to the utmost' . . . How do you think I was able to accomplish all this? Because I had the faith, the solid faith that I was destined to be a leader!"[178] Giri and Givola leave.

Ui tells Roma about his new plans: once he has conquered Chicago, he wants to extend his business to Cicero and beyond. His method will be the same: "With threats and pleas, with wooing and cursing, with gentle force and iron-clad embraces."[179] Cicero's business leader Dullfeet can be "dealt with." Roma warns Ui that Clark and other leaders of the Cauliflower Trust are using him for their own ends. After the dirty work is done they plan to abandon him in order to preserve their respectability. According to Roma, they are supported by Giri and Givola. He proposes to take care of this matter. Ui promises to give a little pep talk to Roma's men before they move.

Roma has just left when Clark, Mrs. Betty Dullfeet (representing her husband) and Giri appear to assure Ui that there is nothing standing in the way of the planned business expansion into Cicero—except Roma: "Friendship and business are two different things."[180]

Historical background: Soon after Hitler came to power, serious differences among the Nazi leaders became apparent. Hitler's friend Röhm insisted that his storm troopers have the greatest influence. Göring was on the side of Hindenburg and the generals, who wanted the army (*Reichswehr*) to remain the controlling faction. Hitler prepared the way for the takeover of Austria. (Mrs. Dullfeet is symbolic of the Austrian people, whom Hitler "courted.")

SCENE 11. On a rainy night, Roma and his men are waiting in a garage for Ui, who is late. Suddenly Ui appears with Givola. Ui reaches out and shakes Roma's hand—to prevent him from drawing his own gun. Givola cuts down Roma and his men with a machine gun.

Historical background: During the night of 30 June 1934, Hitler had his friend Röhm and many of Röhm's companions assassinated.

SCENE 12. In Givola's flowershop, Dullfeet and Ui discuss Ui's business expansion into Cicero. Dullfeet does not like Ui's methods. Ui wants Dullfeet's press to stop the "slander" against him. With gentle pressure, Ui cajoles Dullfeet into an agreement. Then, in a marvelous parody on the famous garden scene in Goethe's *Faust* (in which Faust is courting Gretchen), Ui and Mrs. Dullfeet, Givola and Dullfeet, stroll around an arrangement of flowers in the shop, and talk in beautiful iambic pentameter.

But Ui does not trust Dullfeet; he arranges to have him killed.

Historical background: Giving in to Hitler's threats, the Austrian chancellor Engelbert Dollfuss agrees to forbid anti-Nazi reports in the Austrian press.

SCENE 13. Dullfeet has conveniently died. He is being given a ceremonious funeral. Ui, Giri and Givola arrive, carrying large wreaths to show their "grief." Clark and the Cauliflower Trust people now see that they may not be able to control Ui.

In a parody of Shakespeare's *Richard III*, Ui woos

Betty Dullfeet in the cemetery, offering her and Cicero his protection: "The last and only protection you have is me." But Mrs. Dullfeet resists: "And that you say to the widow of the man you murdered? Monster!"[181]

Historical background: Hitler had Dollfuss assassinated in July 1934 and continued to woo Austria. All the while he was preparing for an invasion.

SCENE 14. Ui's bedroom in the Mammoth Hotel. Just as the ghost of the murdered Banquo appeared before Macbeth in Shakespeare's play, Roma now appears to Ui in a nightmare. He warns: "The day will come when everyone you killed and everyone you will yet kill will rise against you, Ui."[182] Ui orders his bodyguards to shoot at the apparition.

SCENE 15. A gathering of the produce merchants of Chicago and Cicero. Those present curse Ui and pretend they had nothing to do with his rise to power. They hope someone will stop him. Fanfares sound. Ui, flanked by his bodyguards, enters with Betty Dullfeet, Clark, Giri, and Givola. Clark announces that Betty Dullfeet's produce business (she had taken over from her husband) is now part of the Cauliflower Trust. It means that it, too, is under Ui's protection. Then Ui speaks. He tells them that Dullfeet had asked him, before he died, to extend his protection to Cicero. But he claims that he wants to be "freely chosen by the people." When one man believes the talk of "free elections" and prefers to leave the room rather than vote for Ui, he is followed by one of Ui's men and shot. Now the vote for Ui is unanimous.

The scene ends with Ui's address to the people: "After fifteen years, peace in Chicago's produce business is no longer a dream but a hard reality." But he has ordered new and more sophisticated weapons, "because other cities besides Chicago and Cicero are crying for protection: Washington and Milwaukee! Detroit! Toledo! Pittsburgh! Cincinnati!"[183]

Historical background: On 11 March 1938, Hitler marched into Austria. This was the first of his incursions into other countries. He then invaded Czechoslovakia, Poland, Denmark, Norway, The Netherlands, Belgium, Luxemburg, France, Yugoslavia, Greece, the Soviet Union, and others.

In an epilogue Brecht added after World War II, the audience is admonished to prevent those events from ever happening again: "But you must learn how to see instead of to stare, and to act instead of talk, talk, talk. Someone like this once almost ruled the world! The people overcame him, but lest someone rejoice too soon, the womb from which this creature crawled is fertile still."[184]

In *Arturo Ui* Brecht hoped "to destroy the widespread and common respect great murderers seem to command."[185] To accomplish this, he postulated that "great political criminals must be ... exposed to ridicule."[186] The effect is achieved by what is referred to as a double estrangement effect: the Nazi leaders are presented as Chicago gangsters, who, however, speak mostly in blank verse—the verse of Shakespeare. Portions of the play are pure comedy. (There are many similarities to Charlie Chaplin's film *The Great Dictator*, Chaplin's brilliant satire on Hitler, made in 1940.) But Brecht also warned against playing it as travesty; the comedy must not overshadow the barbaric truth.

In 1961, Martin Esslin wrote in his book on Brecht that "the parallels between Hitler's dealings with the German capitalists and the connection between Chicago gangsters and businessmen are labored and unconvincing. Brecht knew Hitler; he knew very little about Chicago."[187] Actually, however, it has been established that Brecht knew a good bit about Chicago and the world of organized crime. Throughout his life, and especially shortly before he came to America, he read many books and articles on this country. Among them was F. D. Pasley's biography of Al Capone. Many details that appear in the play are found in that biography. (Among them are Capone's move into Cicero on 1 April 1924; Capone's headquarters in Chicago's Metropole Hotel—in the play the Mammoth Hotel; the St. Valentine's Day massacre of 1929, in which Capone assassinated seven members of Bugs Moran's gang in a garage; the trick of killing someone by locking him in a handshake while someone else shoots him; the florist shops Capone used as cover; and the fact that he took huge wreaths to the funerals of his adversaries.) Details about the protection racket came from Louis Adamic's book *Dynamite,* which describes the control organized crime had over trade unions, businessmen, and politicians.[188]

In writing *Arturo Ui,* Brecht had an American audience in mind. For a time he thought of doing a kind of music hall production on Broadway. On an American audience, however, the situation would be reversed: instead of seeing something they were familiar with take place in a strange environment, theatergoers would see something they were *not* familiar with take place in a familiar environment.[189]

Brecht himself was not sure how effective the play would be, and did not release it for many years. A few months before his death, Brecht decided that the time had come for a performance of *Arturo Ui.* (He felt that fascism was on the rise again in West Germany.) But his death prevented him from realizing this project.

To the criticism that the Nazi crimes were too cruel and inhuman to become the object of satire, Brecht answered that the satiric parable was an apt medium for exposing big political criminals because it could destroy the awe and even respect they inspire in many people. The satire depicts them as the little, ridiculous creatures they actually were.

Arturo Ui was first performed in Stuttgart, West Germany, on 19 November 1958. Peter Palitzsch, from the Berliner Ensemble, directed the actors of the Württembergisches Staatstheater, (Arturo Ui: Wolfgang Kieling; sets: Gerd Richter; music: Hans-Dieter Hosalla).

A Brecht expert, André Müller, of the East German theater magazine *Theater der Zeit*, had ample praise for the direction, the acting, and the sets. But he did criticize the fact that the play does not show who could (and should) have resisted Ui's rise—namely the people—and how they could have done it. He also thought that Kieling overemphasized Ui's pathological side. But he stressed that the production was a venture into new territory and deserved attention.[190]

A West German critic, Johannes Jacobi, in *Die Zeit*, was less generous. He called the play outdated; it was suitable only for discussion in a literary seminar.[191]

On 23 March 1959, *Arturo Ui* opened in the famous Theater am Schiffbauerdamm of the Berliner Ensemble (directors: Peter Palitzsch and Manfred Wekwerth; sets: Karl von Appen; Arturo Ui: Ekkehard Schall).

The East German critic Heinz Hofmann, in *Theater der Zeit*, saw room for improvement in the play. He would have liked the play to show the force which finally did stop Ui (which was, according to him, the Soviet Union). But he deemed the play necessary as a warning against neofascist tendencies in the West. Artistically, he found the performance a delight, especially Schall's Ui, "who comes close to Chaplin in artistic perfection."[192]

West Berlin's most famous critic, Friedrich Luft,

The Resistible Rise of Arturo Ui, Berliner Ensemble, 1959. Directors: Peter Palitzsch and Manfred Wekwerth; sets: Karl von Appen; Arturo Ui: Ekkehard Schall.

emphasized that Schall's impersonation of Hitler was as good as Chaplin's in *The Great Dictator.* Although he thought it was not Brecht at his best, Luft was impressed with the Ensemble's "masterly" presentation of Brecht's "crude comedy full of wit and gags." He strongly disliked the program notes that claimed to find parallels between West Germany of 1959 and the Third Reich; between Adenauer (West German chancellor at the time) and Hitler.[193]

In 1965 the Berliner Ensemble performed *Arturo Ui* in German in London. The drama critic of *The*

Times who reviewed the play did not know any German. It is therefore difficult to see how he could have judged anything but the acting. Presumably he had read a translation beforehand. Nevertheless, he doubly welcomed the performance, "partly to justify the legend of the 1956 season [the Ensemble's successful first visit to London] and partly to reestablish Brecht's basic claim to attention," because "we have rarely found the knack of playing Brecht in English." This critic did not find *Arturo Ui* a "consistently satisfactory play" because Brecht, "in his determination to explain the rise of Hitler in Marxist terms, has misrepresented history and failed to convey the evil of the subject." But despite these shortcomings, he felt that "there is no doubt at all that [the Ensemble production] works splendidly in the theatre, whether or not one knows German." He singled out Ekkehard Schall's Ui as "a great piece of comic acting."[194]

As of July 1968, the Ensemble had given 404 performances of the play, including those they presented on tour in other East and West German cities, in Warsaw (1960), Prague (1965), Budapest (1965), London (1965), Venice (1966), Moscow (1968), and Leningrad (1968). In 1960, the Ensemble received first prize in an international theater festival in Paris with a group of Brecht plays that included *Arturo Ui*. At the same festival, this play was awarded the prize of an organization of theater and music critics as the best theater production offered at the festival.

In November 1960, Jean Vilar directed the Théâtre National Populaire in a production of *Arturo Ui* at the Palais de Chaillot. Vilar also played the title role. The play and the production were well received ("a chronicle play comparable to those of Shakespeare"). According to Jean-Pierre Lenoir (in a *New York Times* review), Vilar used a huge budget, a cast of thirty-eight, and almost innumerable set changes, and

the presentation was "synchronized to the second."
Vilar's Ui was "an extraordinary tour de force, even
for such an accomplished actor."[195]

Somewhat belatedly, *Arturo Ui* reached Broadway
on 11 November 1963 for eight performances in the
Lunt-Fontanne Theater, with Christopher Plummer
in the title role (English adaptation: George Tabori;
director: Tony Richardson; sets: Rouben Ter-Arutu-
nian; music: Jule Styne). Howard Taubman of *The
New York Times* was not at all impressed with the
production. Although he realized that the play "is not
first-rate Brecht," he had seen *Ui* productions elsewhere (in Berlin and Warsaw) and knew that this
Broadway production would not do: "The trouble is
everywhere—in George Tabori's adaptation, in the
vacillating styles that make a confusion of the scenes,
in the wild mixture of individual acting styles and in
the hopped-up scenic effects. Despite a few redeeming moments, particularly near the end, one cannot
speak the comforting words." He found the most encouraging aspect was "that Broadway at last acknowl-
edges the significance of Brecht. Now it must master
the art of presenting him with the coherence and
eloquence that are his right."[196]

Walter Kerr's review in the *New York Herald Tribune* was less lucid and less informed, but equally
negative, the difference being that he was not sure
whether it was the play, the production, or both, that
failed. Kerr recognized some good moments, but said
that the three elements in the play—the rise of Hitler,
gangland Chicago, and the circus—remained uncon-
nected. He found the gestures of bufoonery "almost
uniformly obvious, heavy, half-hearted." In short, he
found the performance lacked coherence and vitality:
"The issue is not enlarged; it is not even lightened;
it is only made remote, and insufficient."[197]

The reviewer for *Variety* wondered whether the

parallel of Hitler to Capone might not actually be "a bit puzzling to a generation that doesn't remember the two notorious criminals." The scenes of gang warfare appealed to him more than the play's "slow and rather heavy scenes stressing the big business-big crime relationship underlying the rise of both the monstrous political adventurer and the pathologically vicious racketeer." His overall impression of the play: "As usual with the late German playwright's works, it's questionable boxoffice material, but depends primarily on gimmicky production uproar." That, however, was the last thing Brecht had in mind; nothing could have been further from his intention than the "garish, blatant and exaggeratedly stylized caricature," which the *Variety* reviewer found in this production.[198]

On 7 August 1968, *Arturo Ui* (in George Tabori's translation) opened in Minneapolis at the Tyrone Guthrie Theater (director: Edward Payson Call; Ui: Robin Gammell; sets: Richard L. Hay; music: Herbert Pilhofer). Dan Sullivan of *The New York Times* called it "a splendid production" despite some "yawns and inadvertent giggles." But for him the relevance of the play was "more theatrical than political"—notwithstanding the epilogue. It gave the Minnesota Theater Company an opportunity "to show off its considerable dramatic and technical resources." He gave particular credit to Robin Gammell as Ui.[199]

In December 1968, the Tyrone Guthrie Theater took their successful production of *Arturo Ui* to the Billy Rose Theater in New York City. It was equally well received. Dan Sullivan "loved it." In his opinion, Robin Gammell's Ui was even better than in Minneapolis. Sullivan credited Call with being one of the few directors who "knows how to make Brecht live on a stage."[200]

In August 1968, *Arturo Ui* was staged at the Edinburgh Festival by the Glasgow Citizens' Theater. According to a *New York Times* review by Irving Wardle, the production emerged "as one of the few satisfactory stagings of Brecht;" Leonard Rossiter's performance as Ui stood comparison with "Berlin's Ekkehard Schall; and one cannot pay a bigger compliment than that." As to the play itself, Wardle had some reservations—he found no reference to the "final solution" for the Jews "and other nightmare elements of the regime."[201]

When the Nottingham Playhouse Company staged their production of *Arturo Ui* in London's Saville Theater in August 1969, Clive Barnes of *The New*

The Resistible Rise of Arturo Ui, Minnesota Theater Company (Tyrone Guthrie Theater), 1968. *Above,* Giri: Charles Keating; Givola: Richard Ramos; Roma: Lee Richardson; Arturo Ui: Robin Gammell. *Left,* Robin Gammell and Richard Ramos.

York Times found it much better than the Tyrone Guthrie production he had seen in New York City ("good as that was"). He had high praise for Michael Blakemore's staging ("uncommon skill"), and especially for Leonard Rossiter, who played Ui. ("Mr. Rossiter is perfect—a trampled paranoid, comically mean-minded.... Even at his funniest, Mr. Rossiter never lets us forget the gas chambers, the bombs, the slaughter."[202])

From 28 March to 4 May 1975, the Goodman Theater Center in Chicago presented a highly successful staging of *Arturo Ui* (director: William Woodman; Arturo Ui: Kenneth Welsh; music: Hans-Dieter Hosalla; sets: Joseph Nieminsky). The production made careful, yet effective, use of local color: the scenes took place in well-known Chicago locations, photographs of which were projected on two large sliding screens.

The production was well received by Chicago newspaper critics. Roger Dettmer of the *Chicago Tribune* found the production "both stylish and spellbinding," and the play "remarkable ... ahead of its time.... Seen in historical perspective on a Chicago stage, with projection of actual places on two large sliding screens, the shoe may pinch, but dammit it fits."[203]

Sidney J. Harris of the *Chicago Daily News* called the play "uneven ... yet one that is immensely worthwhile, as much today as when [Brecht] wrote it more than thirty years ago.... *The Resistible Rise of Arturo Ui* is flawed Brecht ... but even flawed Brecht is superior to the pink of perfection of most other playwrights."[204]

That *Arturo Ui* can also be a success at the box office was demonstrated by a production of the Williamstown Theater in Williamstown, Virginia, presented in July 1972. The final performance "produced

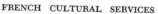

The Resistible Rise of Arturo Ui, Théâtre National Populaire, Paris, 1969. Director: Georges Wilson. *Above*, Hindsborough (Dogsborough): Georges Wilson (left); Arturo Ui: Robert Hirsch. *Right*, Robert Hirsch.
A.D.N.P./E. LAMY, UNIVERSAL PHOTO
FRENCH CULTURAL SERVICES

the largest gross of a single performance of a straight play in the [Williamstown] theater's history."[205]

Artistically, *Arturo Ui* does not measure up to *Mother Courage* or the *Caucasian Chalk Circle;* it lacks the depth and subtlety of those plays. But then it is also quite different in nature and intent. In addition, it must be remembered that it was written in a very short time and never revised. It is safe to assume that Brecht, had he been able to stage the play himself, would have made changes. Nevertheless, it is a most interesting play and can be a powerful theatrical experience if produced by an imaginative director.

The early 1970s saw a resurgence of interest in Nazi Germany and Hitler, not only in West Germany but also in England and the United States. This interest manifested itself in numerous works about Nazi Germany, like the Hitler biographies by Werner Mauser and Joachim Fest, the memoirs of the former Nazi Albert Speer, and purely commercial products like the British film *Hitler: The Last Ten Days,* with Alec Guinness.

Brecht's *Arturo Ui* shows the Nazis for what they were: criminals. The play is needed as an antidote against morbid fascination with and blissful ignorance about that gruesome period of modern history. It is an important contribution to the process of coming to terms with the past. At the same time it serves as a warning to future generations.

With the passage of time the objections raised against the play, that the inhuman Nazi period is not a proper subject for satire, have lost their strength. For new generations, satire is one of the most effective means of preventing respect—let alone admiration—from arising for the types portrayed in the play.

The Visions of Simone Machard
(1942–43)

World War II began on 1 September 1939, when Hitler's armies invaded Poland, which was defeated in a few weeks. After occupying Denmark and Norway in April 1940, the German troops began the war on the western front in the early morning hours of 10 May 1940. By 20 May, German tanks had reached the French Atlantic coast, trapping the main force of the French and British armies near Dunkirk in northwestern France. (This could have been a decisive battle in World War II. But since the German forces did not attack, over 300,000 French and British troops could be evacuated to Britain.) On 22 June 1940, the French government, under Marshal Pétain, concluded an armistice with the Germans. In 1945, when the war was over, Pétain and his Vichy government were severely criticized for collaborating with the German occupation forces; Pétain himself was sentenced to death. Later his sentence was commuted to life imprisonment; he died in 1951, at ninety-five. (In Brecht's play, the French Captain Fétain was clearly conceived after Pétain.)

This is the historical background for *The Visions of Simone Machard*, which Brecht finished in exile in California in 1943. For the second time (the first was *Saint Joan of the Stockyards*, 1929–31) Brecht used the well-known Joan of Arc theme for a play.

Only seventeen years old, driven by inner voices, the historic Jeanne d'Arc (1412–31) led the French armies of Charles VII to victory against the English and freed the city of Orleans in 1429. Through treason

German title: *Die Gesichte der Simone Machard.*

she fell into the hands of the English. She was tried by the Inquisition (that claimed her voices came from the devil) and burned at the stake. (In 1920 she was canonized by the Roman Catholic Church.)

In Brecht's play a simple young servant girl named Simone becomes a French resistance fighter against the invading Nazi armies. The play is set in the yard of a hostelry and trucking business, Au Relais, in 1940. There is a large garage in the background, and, as seen by the audience, the back entrance of the hostelry is to the right. To the left are a storage room and the truck drivers' quarters. The action takes place in eight days—from the evening of 14 June to the morning of 22 June—in the small French town of Saint-Martin in central France, on the main highway from Paris to the south.

Four employees of the hostelry are discussing the rapidly deteriorating military situation in France. German planes control the skies, and German tanks are advancing quickly. The roads are clogged with French refugees fleeing from the German armies, which hampers French military efforts: "The civilian population has turned out to be a great nuisance in wartime. . . . Either you abolish the people or the war, you can't have both."[206]

According to Henri Soupeau, the wealthy owner of the hostelry, only another Saint Joan can help France in her present predicament. But Soupeau is only trying to cover up the establishment's abdication of responsibility. They are all more concerned with saving their own skins and their possessions than their country. The refugees and soldiers go hungry, but Soupeau treats a French colonel—who has simply abandoned his men at the front—to a lavish meal. Soupeau's truckers are told to take Captain Fétain's wines, rather than the refugees, to safety. In the meantime, Soupeau tries to imbue Simone, a young and naive servant girl in his hostelry, with a feeling for France's great past by giving her a book on Joan of Arc.

During the night, Simone sees herself as Joan in a dream. An angel, closely resembling Simone's brother who is a soldier, hands her a drum and bids her to save France. In her vision, the employees of the hostelry arm themselves and follow her. She forms an alliance with the mayor of Saint-Martin, who, in her dream, appears as Charles VII, against the enemies of France.

Early the next morning, Monsieur Soupeau prepares to leave because the German tanks have come dangerously close to Saint-Martin. He orders his employees to load the trucks with his possessions, as well as the hostelry's food and wine supplies. But they refuse to carry out his orders: "He wants to protect his supplies from the French, not from the Germans."[207] Simone, emboldened by her dream, has called in the mayor to stop Soupeau from leaving without taking the refugees. Soupeau is enraged ("this is anarchy"). But the situation becomes outright dangerous when the desperate refugees threaten to storm the hostelry.

At this crucial moment, however, Madame Soupeau, Monsieur Soupeau's mother, emerges from the building and defuses the tension by ordering Simone to provide the people with as many supplies as they wish. She also promises to feed those who will remain. Her son watches in silent rage, but by giving in only a little, Madame Soupeau has cleverly saved most of their possessions. The refugees disperse, the employees load the trucks, and Soupeau's secret gasoline reserves seem to be saved. By her natural inclination to help people in need Simone has become a threat to the Soupeaus. She is dismissed.

In another dream during the following night, Simone is knighted for her good deeds by King Charles (the mayor). But when she urges him to fight on, there is no answer. The king, his court, and the people, withdraw into the darkness. Again the angel appears to admonish her not to give up her struggle: "When the conqueror comes to your city, it shall be as if he has conquered nothing. . . . Go and destroy."[208]

The next day, the German tanks arrive. Madame Soupeau, who stayed behind when her son left, is afraid for herself and her property. But she has nothing to fear. The German captain, the French Captain Fétain, and Madame Soupeau quickly discover they hold common views and interests, and they breakfast together. One of the hostelry employees dryly comments, upon seeing the comfortable relationship between the rich Germans and the rich Frenchmen: "Rich and rich stick together."[209] (Brecht has used this line once before, as the subtitle for *The Roundheads and the Pointed Heads*.) The refugees, who had remained in Saint-Martin upon Madame Soupeau's promise that they would be fed by the hostelry, are now told to keep away. The promise turns out to have been a clever ruse.

The mayor, too, has had a change of heart. Earlier he seemed to be concerned about the fate of France and the refugees. Now he refuses to listen when Simone suggests that the secret gasoline reserves be destroyed to keep the Germans from getting them. Instead he joins Madame Soupeau and the German and French captains inside the hostelry to talk about the terms of collaboration.

In a vision Simone sees all of them as figures in the Joan of Arc legend: the mayor as King Charles, the French captain as the Duke of Burgundy, the German captain as an English general, and Madame Soupeau as queen mother Isabeau. While they are inside "playing with the fate of France,"[210] a German private comes to the hostelry cursing the war and his superiors. The employees immediately understand him. This underscores the bond between the common people of both countries.

When Madame Soupeau and her guests emerge from the hostelry, they have reached an agreement. One point is that the gasoline reserves are to be handed over to the Germans. But a red glow in the sky indicates that the brickyard, where the fuel was stored, is ablaze.

During the night Monsieur Soupeau returns to his hostelry. Simone confides to him that she has set the brickyard on fire for the sake of France. But instead of praising her for her patriotic deed, he is upset about the loss of his property, and he fears reprisals from the Germans. When two of his employees support Simone's action, he angrily dismisses them: "Arsonists, all of you! Criminals! . . . You are worse than the Germans."[211]

In a fourth dream during the night of 21/22 June, Simone sees the medieval court assembled in the hostelry's yard. The German captain, wearing a suit of armor, and Simone as Joan, are surrounded by soldiers in suits of black mail with red swastikas on them. The French judges, the colonel, the captain, Monsieur Soupeau, and the mayor, all clad in the ceremonial robes of the church, announce that Simone has been sentenced to death. And the "angels' voices" she heard are averred to have been the voices of the "rabble," especially that of her brother André—a mere private in the French army.

The next morning, 22 June, the French flag is flying at half mast. France has surrendered. The hostelry employees feel guilty because they did not resist: "The child was the only person in the hostelry who did her duty."[212] But Monsieur Soupeau will have none of this. Life for him could now have returned to normal if it had not been for Simone's patriotic deed: "We were just about to make a nice gesture by handing the gasoline over to the Germans, gasoline that we kept away from the French army, when the rabble with their patriotism interfered!"[213] Addressing the employees, Madame Soupeau feels, of course, that she and her kind are the true patriots: "We are quite capable of telling you when war is necessary and when it is better to make peace. Do you want to do something for France? Well, *we* are France, understand?"[214]

Simone, who had disappeared from the hostelry, is brought back by two German soldiers. She was apprehended while taking food from the hostelry to the refugees who have found shelter in the local gymnasium. To prevent her from doing any more "damage," she is committed to an insane asylum.

The play ends with the angel appearing to Simone in her dreams and giving her courage: "Be not afraid, daughter of France. None will survive who fights against you."[215]

The lesson to be learned from the play, according to Brecht, is that the rich Frenchmen collaborated with the rich Germans while the common people in both countries had to bear the main burden of the war: "The Pétains used the defeat and the foreign occupation as an excuse to crush their social enemies."[216] Brecht saw the real issues of the war as being rich versus poor rather than Frenchmen versus Germans. Simone received a patriotic education. She believed that it was every Frenchman's duty whether rich or poor to resist the German invaders. But her patriotism only caused her difficulties; she did not recognize that economic interests outweighed patriotism. Nor did she realize that patriotism was only used as a means to keep her and her class subservient.

With Simone's case Brecht wants to show that patriotism can be used to deceive people about real issues such as wars being conducted to further certain economic and political interests. When patriotism subsequently proves to be an obstacle, as was the case with Simone's patriotism, it is effectively muzzled.

Brecht's plans for this play go back to 1940. Shortly after France's defeat in 1940, Brecht—at that time still in Scandinavia—made his first notes for a Saint Joan play in a contemporary setting:

> A young French girl, operating a gas station in her brother's absence, dreams day and night that she is Joan of Arc suffering her fate. The Germans advance to Orleans. The voices Joan hears are the voices of the people, those of the black-smith and the farmer. She obeys those voices, thus saving France from the enemy from without. But she is defeated by the enemy from within.[217]

In December 1941, in California, Brecht returned to this play, which he at that time called *The Voices*. The ideological outline was clear: "The voice of God is the voice of the people.... In wars between two countries, the ruled classes of both countries are bound by common interests, and the ruling classes are also bound by common interests."[218] But Brecht was still having difficulties writing the individual scenes.

While in California, Brecht was reunited with Lion Feuchtwanger, with whom he had already collaborated in the 1920s. In October 1942, Brecht discussed with Feuchtwanger his plans for the play (which he then called *Saint Joan of Vitry*), and a fruitful collaboration ensued. First they worked on a detailed outline of the structure. Then Brecht wrote individual scenes at home. The two writers then discussed these in regular morning sessions in Feuchtwanger's house on Sunset Boulevard in Santa Monica. In the afternoons, Brecht occasionally stopped by the United Artists film studio to observe Fritz Lang shooting the film *Hangmen Also Die*, for which Brecht had written the scenario. The work on the play, now entitled *The Visions of Simone Machard,* was a relief for Brecht after what he felt was degrading and frustrating work on the film. But the $10,000 he earned for the film-writing stint enabled Brecht to move into a new house in Santa Monica and concentrate on his new play.

At times, Feuchtwanger and Brecht differed in their opinions about certain aspects of the play. Feuchtwanger preferred that Simone be psychologically motivated and that the play be written in a more naturalistic style. Brecht, on the other hand, insisted on a more epic presentation and a social motivation for the characters. This Feuchtwanger tolerated only as an aspect of Brecht's personal style. But Brecht accepted Feuchtwanger's suggestions concerning the French milieu, which Feuchtwanger knew much better than Brecht. (In 1940, he had been interned in a French camp near Aix-en-Provence, from which he escaped to Spain and then to the United States.) And it was largely upon Feuchtwanger's advice that Brecht made Simone a child of not more than thirteen. Originally, Brecht had conceived his heroine as a mentally disturbed person.

Despite some differences in opinion, the collaboration between the two writers was pleasant and productive. Brecht noted in his *Work Journal:* "He [Feuchtwanger] has a good sense for structure, appreciates linguistic subtleties, has poetic and dramaturgical ideas, knows a lot about literature, respects arguments, and is a very pleasant human being, a good friend."[219]

Feuchtwanger, fourteen years Brecht's senior, was equally satisfied with Brecht: "He eagerly listened to suggestions and objections, and whenever they seemed reasonable to him, he made revisions, even if it meant

starting again from the beginning. . . . He was domi-
neering and proud, and he demanded patient cooperation from his friends. But he was without haughtiness;
he did not brag and gave [of himself] generously and
without envy."[220] Feuchtwanger also benefited from
this collaboration. His novel *Simone* (published in
1944) includes many ideas which emerged in the
discussions with Brecht.

Simone Machard contains epic elements and estrangement effects. But taken as a whole it is written
in a more traditional vein; it carefully observes the
unities of time, place, and action demanded by the
tradition of the so-called Aristotelian drama. It is also
less doctrinal than other Brechtian plays. In fact it is
so much less so that Hanns Eisler, who composed the
music for the play, criticized Brecht for having failed
to stress that Simone is a victim of nationalistic education.

When working on *Simone Machard,* Brecht and
Feuchtwanger apparently also had a film version in
mind. This probably accounts for the fact that the
play is more conventionally structured than most of
his other plays. Brecht wrote in his *Work Journal* that
Feuchtwanger did indeed succeed in getting a film
contract for it, but the film was never made.

For the staging of the dreams in which Simone
relives the legend of Saint Joan, Brecht suggested that
projections could be used—illustrations (preferably
woodcuts) from a book about Joan of Arc.

The play was first performed on 8 March 1957 in
Frankfurt, West Germany (director: Harry Buckwitz;
sets: Teo Otto; music: Hanns Eisler; Simone: Dorothea
Jecht). Brecht had repeatedly stressed that Simone
should be played by a child, not just a young actress.
This advice was followed in the very successful premiere, for which Buckwitz had especially trained a
young girl, not quite eleven years old.

Hans Schwab-Felisch, the reviewer of the *Frankfurter Allgemeine Zeitung*, felt that "the play is not among Brecht's best, but it contains some very beautiful passages." In his view Simone is one of Brecht's "good people in a world of corruption." But he objected that at times she tended to radiate too much emotional patriotism. (This feature of the play and the production was also criticized by Hanns Eisler, who found Simone "too heroic.") The reviewer was also skeptical of Brecht's rather "simplistic" view of the nature of war. Nevertheless, according to Schwab-Felisch the production was successful with the audience, and Dorothea Jecht, as Simone, fulfilled Brecht's prescribed wishes "ideally."[221]

With its blend of dream and reality and the interaction of different time levels (historic legend and current events), the play can be much more effective on stage than Brecht's *Saint Joan of the Stockyards*. But it has seldom been performed. Primarily this is because it is to some extent bound to a definite historical situation.

Brecht did, of course, have a specific historical situation in mind when he wrote the play. But beyond that, Brecht would argue that all capitalist societies act in a similar fashion.

Schweyk in the Second World War (1943)

Between 1920 and 1923, a serialized novel appeared in Prague, Czechoslovakia, which was to become a major work of world literature: Jaroslav

---

German title: *Schweyk im zweiten Weltkrieg.*

Hašek's *The Adventures of Good Soldier Schweyk During the World War*. Soon afterward, in 1926 and 1927, a German translation by Grete Reiner appeared. In his novel, Hašek gives a very witty and satirical description of the experiences of a common man, named Schweyk, with the bureaucracy, the police, and the military during World War I. This novel was immediately dramatized by Max Brod (Kafka's friend and editor of his posthumous novels) and Hans Reimann, a German humorist.

Erwin Piscator, one of the foremost German theater directors and producers of the 1920s, selected this play for production in his own Theater am Nollendorfplatz in Berlin. With Bertolt Brecht, Felix Gasbarra and Leo Lania, Piscator reshaped Brod and Reimann's play to suit his purposes. The Brecht/Piscator version, first performed on 23 January 1928, was an unusual but highly successful performance, with Max Pallenberg playing Schweyk.

Piscator used many innovative techniques. Film strips provided a live backdrop and grotesque marionettes designed by George Grosz[222] moved across the stage on conveyor belts. Brecht's contribution to this production was considerable, and he also learned a great deal from this experience. It helped him shape his own play about Schweyk, which he wrote in 1943 while in exile in California.

Brecht's Schweyk has survived World War I. He is now trying to do the same in World War II, although this turns out to be a much more difficult task. Brecht's play is set in Prague and on the Russian front during World War II.

The play opens with a prelude "in higher regions." Hitler, Göring (Air Force), Goebbels (Propaganda), and Himmler (SS, a Nazi elite troop) are standing around a globe planning new conquests. Martial music is playing. All figures are caricatures, and all are larger than life except Goebbels, who is smaller than life size—the real Goebbels was a tiny, thin man. (Technically this can be accomplished with projections and masks.) Hitler is wondering aloud what the common man thinks of him, in Europe as well as Germany. Himmler assures him: the common man is enthusiastic.

SCENE 1. In Anna Kopecka's bar, The Goblet, in Prague. The dog trader Schweyk hears from an SS man that an assassination attempt on Adolf Hitler almost succeeded. Schweyk pretends he only knows two Adolfs, one a druggist's assistant and the other a collector of dog droppings. Both of them are now in concentration camps.

Schweyk's friend Baloun, who is fond of good food, is thinking of joining the German army because the rations are said to be much better than those available to Czechs: "I can no longer be a good Czech on an empty stomach."[223] As a warning to Baloun, Mrs. Kopecka, a young widow, sings "The Song of the Nazi Soldier's Wife." This is about a young wife who has been receiving gifts from her husband from all over Europe. From Russia she receives only a widow's veil. Baloun is impressed by this warning, and promises not to join the German army if she will give him one good meal. In order to give Baloun a good meal, Anna Kopecka induces young Prochazka, a butcher's son and one of her lovers, to go and try to get some meat. This is dangerous because of strictly controlled food rationing.

When Brettschneider, who works for the Gestapo, stops in for a drink, Schweyk talks with him about politics, despite Mrs. Kopecka's plea that politics be avoided. ("I have no opinions, I have a bar.")[224] Schweyk's remarks are deliberately naive—but he is arrested for making anti-Nazi remarks.

SCENE 2. Schweyk's interrogation in the Gestapo headquarters. Schweyk pretends to be very stupid.

SS Officer Bullinger orders Schweyk jailed. On his way out, Schweyk turns around, raises his right arm, and salutes: "Long live our leader Adolf Hitler; we will win this war!" Bullinger is baffled: "Are you stupid?" Schweyk: "Yes, sir."[225] He produces an official document from the army confirming that he is stupid. (This passage is a good example of Brecht's own Schweykian method of presentation—someone who could make such a statement about Hitler and the war was indeed stupid!) At this point, Bullinger is furious at Brettschneider for having brought in what seems to be the village idiot. He orders that Schweyk be sent to a concentration camp. But when he hears that Schweyk is in the dog business, he changes his mind and orders Schweyk to get a certain type of spitz dog for him.

INTERLUDE IN THE LOWER REGIONS. Schweyk and an SS man on their way back to The Goblet. We again detect the satirical overtones in Schweyk's apparent praise of Hitler's simple life style: "And all the things he did, he did while he was sober; not everyone could do that."[226]

SCENE 3. In The Goblet. Baloun is selling picture postcards. One of them has a photograph of the bombed-out city of Bremen, with the caption: "Hitler is one of the greatest architects of all times."[227] The cards quickly disappear when Schweyk and the SS man enter. Schweyk has Mrs. Kopecka read the SS man's future. She predicts for him a hero's death, and he leaves—badly shaken, at the thought of imminent death.

In the meantime, Prochazka has returned—but without the meat. Schweyk's arrest had frightened him out of attempting to get meat. Someone suggests that a more active resistance against the Nazis should be considered. To this Schweyk replies, "Don't demand too much of yourself. These days it means a lot if one is still alive. The fight to survive takes so much time and energy that nothing is left for anything more."[228]

INTERLUDE IN THE HIGHER REGIONS. Hitler and Göring are standing in front of a model of a tank. Martial music. Hitler wants more weapons: "Is the common man in Europe willing to work for me?" Göring: "Most certainly, that's why we have the forced labor camps."[229]

SCENE 4. A park near the Moldau River in Prague. Baloun and Schweyk scheme to kidnap a dog for Bullinger. Two servant girls appear, walking a dog that belongs to a high Czech official who collaborates with the Germans. Schweyk and Baloun befriend the girls. After a while, Schweyk pretends that he must leave. Then, without being seen, he entices the dog away with a twelve-inch sausage. He hides the dog in Kopecka's bar. The girls leave. A grim-looking official arrests Schweyk and Baloun for loitering. Schweyk's argument that his profession (dog vendor) and that of Baloun ("he photographs soldiers so that their families have at least a picture left"[230]) are vital for the success of the war, does not convince him.

SCENE 5. Noon break at Prague's freight yard. Baloun and Schweyk, now in Hitler's labor force, are guarded by a heavily armed German soldier. The soldier is trying to remember the number of a freight car that is supposed to be sent to Munich. Schweyk pretends to help him remember. But he gets him so confused that the wrong car goes to Munich. Schweyk philosophizes: "Perhaps a car with machine guns is now going to Bavaria. But by the time the trains arrive, they might need harvesting equipment in Stalingrad and machine guns in Munich. Who knows?"[231]

SCENE 6. Saturday evening in The Goblet. The guests are dancing the *beseda*, a Czech folk dance.

By this they hope to drive away the SS men and to create so much noise that Mrs. Kopecka can secretly hear radio Moscow. Schweyk appears with a package of meat—dog meat. He had to kill the spitz intended for Bullinger in order to get some meat to keep Baloun from joining the German army. Suddenly Bullinger appears, accuses Mrs. Kopecka of running a black market, strikes her, arrests Schweyk, and confiscates the package of meat. The situation seems hopeless.

But at this point Mrs. Kopecka sings "The Song of the Moldau River," a key song of the play that indicates that times will change. In this faith lies the hope of the people: "At the bottom of the Moldau the rocks are moving,/ Three emperors are buried in Prague./ That which is big does not remain big, and that/ Which is small does not remain small./ The night has twelve hours, and then comes the day."[232]

INTERLUDE IN THE HIGHER REGIONS. Hitler and Nazi General von Bock are standing in front of a map of the Soviet Union. Martial music. Von Bock warns that the war is getting too expensive. But Hitler wants Stalingrad at all costs and is confident that the common man will support him.

SCENE 7. A military prison full of Czechs, including Schweyk. They are waiting for their induction into the German army. They all pretend to have terrible diseases. Schweyk sarcastically wonders why his countrymen are not anxious to go into a war that is being conducted "to defend civilization against bolshevism."[233] A band outside the prison plays the official Nazi anthem ("The flag is raised. The ranks are closed./ SA [storm troopers] are marching with calm and solid steps"). Schweyk parodies it by singing the "Cattle March" to the same tune (refrain: "The butcher calls. With eyes firmly closed/ The cattle march with calm and solid steps"[234]). All join in the refrain. The result is that the doctor declares them all fit to fight without further examination.

SCENE 8. Several weeks later. In search of his regiment that is stationed near Stalingrad, Schweyk is wandering through the vast snow covered prairies of Russia. Theatrically, this is a most impressive scene. Schweyk meets two German deserters whom he advises on how to successfully surrender to the Russians. He marches on, and in a mirage he sees The Goblet.

In the mirage he sees Baloun who has sworn not to join the Nazi army. He will marry Anna, the servant girl. He and Mrs. Kopecka have given up hope that Prochazka will find some meat. But at this moment Prochazka appears with meat, and is reinstated in Mrs. Kopecka's favors. The vision disappears.

Schweyk encounters a drunken priest, SS man Bullinger's brother, who asks Schweyk "Are you a German Christian?" To this Schweyk retorts, "No, a normal one."[235] They proceed in different directions. Schweyk marches on and reads the same sign he has seen before: "Stalingrad 50 kilometers." He has been walking in circles.

Again he has a vision of The Goblet. Baloun is eating and talking about the fabulous meals he had in the past, while Mrs. Kopecka sings the "Song of the Goblet." The vision disappears.

Schweyk encounters an armored car carrying German soldiers. The soldiers sing the "German Miserere" ("One day our superiors ordered us to conquer the small city of Danzig ..."[236]). They now find themselves lost on the Russian plains in icy winter.

Schweyk marches on, and is joined by a dog. He admonishes him: "If you want to survive the war, stick to the others and do nothing unusual. Lie low until the time comes to bite."[237]

Postlude. Wild music. A huge figure emerges—

Hitler. A "historic meeting" takes place between Schweyk and Hitler. Schweyk asks him the way to Stalingrad. But Hitler does not know: "This winter is a bolshevik plot!" They try north—too much snow; south—too many dead; east—the Soviet army; and west—"My German people! I can't go there!"[238] There is no way out, they are trapped.

To end the play, all players take off their masks and address the audience with the last verse of the "Song of the Moldau River:" "Times will change. The great plans/ Of the mighty finally come to naught./ Even if they strut about like fighting cocks/ Times will change, no force can oppose it."[239]

Schweyk in the Second World War[240] is the tale of a common man who is forced to go to war. He tries to survive, not by revolutionary confrontation, but through wit and opportunism. In his *Work Journal,* Brecht emphasized that:

> Schweyk must absolutely not become a cunning and insidious saboteur. He is only taking advantage of the limited opportunities still available to him. Although it may destroy him, he even approves of the existing order as much as he can—even of its nationalist elements. His wisdom is amazing. His indestructibility makes him an object of abuse, but at the same time it is also his source of liberation.[241]

The machinery of government makes no sense to him. In order to keep his sanity, he decides to play the role of an "ingenious fool." He is not strong enough to directly oppose the system, but he manages to take advantage of it and to point out some of its absurdities to the audience.

In his Schweyk play Brecht also drew upon the folk-play tradition. Most of his characters, notably Schweyk and the Czech people, speak dialect (a southern Germany variety), whereas the Nazi officials usually speak the proper high German. Hanns Eisler's music incorporates the melodies of many German and Czech folk tunes and other well-known Czech music. The first six notes of the "Song of the Moldau River," for example, are taken from the Czech composer Smetana's symphonic piece *The Moldau*. A key instrument in the *Schweyk* music is a pianola—a player piano.

Brecht also gave some hints as to the staging:

> The center of the scenery is the bar The Goblet in Prague, with darkish paneling and brass edging on the bar.... The interludes should be presented in the style of horror stories. The whole Nazi hierarchy can appear in each of them.... Their lackeys can accentuate the verses by shouting "Heil!"[242]

Originally Brecht had hoped to produce *Schweyk* in New York City, and he had in mind that Kurt Weill would compose the music. He had found a translator (Alfred Kreymborg) and a famous actor to play the lead (Peter Lorre). But these plans never materialized because Weill, who had gained fame on Broadway, envisioned this project as a kind of musical in which Brecht functioned only as librettist. As a matter of fact, Weill had already written songs for a Schweyk play on Broadway: It was Paul Green's comedy *Johnny Johnson*, "a jeering antiwar play," which was based on Hašek's *The Good Soldier Schweyk*. It ran for sixty-eight performances.[243]

Thus Brecht shelved all plans for an American production of *Schweyk*. His untimely death in 1956 also prevented him from staging the play with the Berliner Ensemble.

The world premiere of *Schweyk in the Second World War* was given on 17 January 1957 by the

Teatr Dramatyczny in Warsaw. (Translator: Andrej Wirth; director: Ludwik René; sets: Jan Kosinski; Schweyk: Aleksander Dzwankowski; Mrs. Kopecka: Wanda Luczycka.) Although this theater was well qualified to produce Brecht in Poland, the play was not well received. After all of their suffering during World War II, the Polish people were not ready to view Nazi officials as comic characters.

The first West German performance of *Schweyk* was given on 22 May 1959 in Frankfurt on the Main (director: Harry Buckwitz; sets: Teo Otto; Schweyk: Hanns Ernst Jäger; Mrs. Kopecka: Lola Müthel). *The New York Times* reported that it was "greeted with thunderous applause."[244] The critic of *Die Zeit*, Johannes Jacobi, felt that the play was dated. Though he credited it with some great poetic moments, it was not to be ranked as one of Brecht's masterpieces, such as *Galileo* and *Mother Courage*.[245]

Kenneth Tynan, on the other hand, who saw the Frankfurt production, enjoyed the performance very much, particularly the mixture of lyric lines ("some of the loveliest lyrics Brecht ever wrote") and acid comments ("the text is rough, acid, and brutally contemptuous of Nazi sympathizers"). According to him, the Frankfurt audience liked the play: "The night I was there, the Frankfurt audience cheered it."[246] Hans Schwab-Felisch, critic for the *Frankfurter Allgemeine Zeitung*, concurred with Tynan and confirmed the tremendous success of the Frankfurt performance: "Applause before curtain falls, an ovation at the end . . . a great and unforgettable evening."[247] But, according to Schwab-Felisch, the play itself was not without faults. Particularly weak was the encounter between Hitler and Schweyk that occurs at the end of the play. Brecht was himself aware of this, but he died before he could revise it.

How great an impact the Frankfurt premiere had

was demonstrated by a panel discussion of the play held in Frankfurt the night after the first performance. Brecht's closest associates, Helene Weigel, Elisabeth Hauptmann, Hanns Eisler, Erich Engel, and Manfred Wekwerth, had even come from East Berlin to discuss the play with West German critics, the director Harry Buckwitz, and actors of the Frankfurt cast.

The public's interest was overwhelming. Two thousand people, most of them young, had gathered; hundreds more had to be turned away. Contributions from the audience clearly showed that Brecht had succeeded in demythologizing the Nazis. Especially for the young people, his play had provided shocking insights into the Nazi era.

In 1961, Giorgio Strehler staged *Schweyk in the Second World War* in his Piccolo Teatro in Milan, with Tino Buazzelli in the title role. According to Antonio Monti, who reviewed the play for *Theater der Zeit,* the production was a great success with critics and audiences. After fifty performances—each one completely sold out—the production was withdrawn. But to satisfy the great demand, *Schweyk* was again produced in the following season.

Since Brecht never produced the play himself, or made any of the changes he would probably have made, Strehler himself proceeded to make the necessary changes. In Monti's opinion, he did it in a masterly fashion. Strehler had achieved a superb blend of the comic and the tragic elements. And, in Monti's view, Buazzelli, two hundred and fifty pounds of wit and vitality, played Schweyk extremely well.[248]

On 31 December 1962, after a relatively short rehearsal period, the Berliner Ensemble presented *Schweyk in the Second World War* (directors: Erich Engel and Wolfgang Pintzka; sets: Manfred Grund; Schweyk: Martin Flörchinger; Mrs. Kopecka: Gisela

May). Ernst Wendt, in the leading West German theater magazine *Theater heute,* found the production
too low in key and lacking in vitality and freshness.
It was his opinion that Engel had reduced Schweyk
to an ordinary everyday citizen who lacked aggres-
sive obstinacy and the Chaplinesque gestures that this
characterization required. Wendt even detected a
certain insecurity about the production. This led him
to speculate that this resulted from the awareness on
the part of the directors that Schweyk's resourceful-
ness could be construed by the audience to be as
necessary in present day East Germany as it was in
occupied Prague: "Schweyk could have walked directly from the Friedrichstrasse into the theater."[249]

Kenneth Tynan was again among the first-nighters.
He liked the production specifically because of the
subdued tone; to him it was "more genuine and more
comical."[250] Manfred Nössig, in the East German
theater magazine *Theater der Zeit,* called the production "memorable" but "almost Spartan" in its simplicity. He wondered whether a more exaggerated style à
la Chaplin might not have been more effective.[251]
Brecht, after all, had visualized the play as a horror
story. This quality was especially to be conveyed in
the interludes.

On 21 August 1963, *Schweyk* opened in London's
Mermaid Theater (director: Frank Dunlop; Schweyk:
Bernard Miles; Mrs. Kopecka: Joan Heal). In a very
lucid review, the drama critic of *The Times* called
Schweyk "the Falstaff of the modern battlefield." He
pointed out that the play "provides an excellent introduction to the dramatist. Its subject matter is common property, and its light operatic idiom shows
Brechtian stage-craft operating on a modest and easily
accessible scale." He was less enthusiastic about the
production ("not perfect"). But "enough of the work

emerges for one to feel heartily grateful to the Mermaid for bringing it to London."[252]

Schweyk has been widely performed in East and West Germany; it has also played in Milan, Helsinki, Copenhagen, Budapest, The Hague, Tel Aviv, Stockholm, Geneva, and many other cities around the world. But, with the exception of several college productions, it has not been performed in the United States. On the college campuses, it has not always been a success. A case in point is the performance by the Department of Dramatic Art's Professional Resident Theater of the University of California in Davis on 6 March 1968. The production, directed by Theodore Shank, with John Coe as Schweyk and Jean LeBouvier as Mrs. Kopecka, was announced in the *Davis Enterprise* as presenting "the horrors of war through a strange mixture of farce and drama." But the *Davis Enterprise* wrote the next day: "PRT Production Fails to Come Off." It continued: "Almost nothing came across ... the production failed on every score at least once— musical, technical, acting, directing, and most of all, writing."[253]

The American premiere of *Schweyk in the Second World War* was staged by the professional theater company of Brandeis University in Waltham, Massachusetts, in November 1967 (director: Peter Sander, who also did the translation; music: Hanns Eisler; Schweyk: Morris Carnovsky). Julius Novick of *The New York Times* remained unimpressed; to him the production chiefly showed "just how heavy-handed and dull Brecht could be on his off-days." He found Schweyk's "interminable anecdotes" boring. The jokes were unfunny: "The play seems to have been composed on the assumption that every line containing a reference to excrement becomes *ipso facto* hilarious." As to the production itself, Novick found it "competent on the whole, but also almost entirely lacking

Schweyk in the Second World War, Berliner Ensemble, 1962. Director: Erich Engel and Wolfgang Pintzka; sets: Manfred Grund; Mrs. Kopecka: Gisela May (left); Schweyk: Martin Flörchinger (center, with pipe).

PERCY PAUKSCHTA; BERLINER ENSEMBLE

Schweyk in the Second World War, Théâtre des Champs Élysées, Paris, 1964. Director: Roger Planchon; sets and costumes: René Allio; Schweyk: Jean Bouise (center).

AGENCE DE PRESSE BERNAND, PARIS;
FRENCH CULTURAL SERVICES

in the kind of imaginative theater magic that alone
might have made this play worth watching."[254]

Hašek's novel continued to inspire Brecht. He re-
read it on 26 May 1943 during a train ride from New
York to Los Angeles: "I am again overwhelmed by
Hašek's vast panoramic view."[255] Hašek's *Schweyk*
was of such great importance to Brecht that its influence can also be seen in many of his other works, such
as *Mother Courage, Puntila,* and *Refugee Dialogues.*
Brecht called his *Schweyk* a counterplay to *Mother
Courage.* Schweyk recognizes the evils of war from
the beginning; he is a helpless victim. Mother Courage, on the other hand, makes her living from the war
and has only momentary and fleeting insights into its
cruelties.

Some elements in Brecht's *Schweyk in the Second
World War* may appear dated today. But as the critic
of *The Times* pointed out in his review of the 1963
Mermaid Theater production in London, the play can
still be good theater. And certainly the main character,
Schweyk, will survive the test of time. In Schweyk,
Hašek—and after him, Brecht—created a character
who transcends a particular time and a particular
locale. He is the representative of a certain type of behavior. As Hanns Eisler wrote, there are Schweyks
everywhere, millions of them. (Schweyk's example
was effective enough to lead the U.S. Army to forbid
the reading of Hašek's novel in World War II.) Brecht
himself always recommended Hašek's novel—even as
standard reading for East Germany's People's Army
(*Volksarmee*).

The Caucasian Chalk Circle
(1944–45)

The Caucasian Chalk Circle is the last of Brecht's major plays, and it is one of his most often performed works. He wrote the play between 1943 and 1945, while he was still in California. By this time it was apparent that fascism in Germany would soon be defeated. Brecht began to think about a reorganization of society after the war and the principles upon which it should be based. He expressed some of these ideas in *The Caucasian Chalk Circle*.

Sources for Brecht's play are the original Chinese play about the Chalk Circle, a German adaptation of it by Klabund (pen name of Alfred Henschke) in 1925, and the familiar story of King Solomon's judgment in the Bible: I Kings, 3:16–28. In each instance the story is centered around a child who is claimed by two women. The decision is made by a trial by means of which the natural mother is discovered, who then receives the child.

In the period of his Scandinavian exile, Brecht had already used the plot of the chalk circle for a short story, which, like *Mother Courage,* is set in the time of the Thirty Years' War in central Europe (1618–48). In both the short story and the play, however, Brecht changed the plot: it is not the natural mother who is awarded the child, but the woman who loved it and cared for it. Thus Brecht wanted to show that social ties and humane feelings supersede blood relationship.

In the play, the setting is a village in the Caucasus in the southern part of the Soviet Union. The time is toward the end of World War II. The village is in

German title: *Der kaukasische Kreidekreis.*

ruins. The invading Nazi forces have been defeated.
Two Soviet collectives claim the land of a fertile
valley. One is comprised of the people of the collective
Galinsk, who formerly inhabited the valley and were
goat breeders. The other is the collective Rosa Luxemburg, which now wants to cultivate fruit trees in this
valley. The goat breeders want to return to their home,
and, according to the law, the valley is theirs. But
both collectives agree that "the old laws have to be
reviewed to see whether they still apply."[256] The standard of measurement in the new Soviet society is the
principle of what is most useful for the whole Soviet
society. In the discussion between the two groups,
which is carried out amicably, both sides bring forth
good arguments. The collective Galinsk finally con-
cedes the valley to the collective Rosa Luxemburg
because it is decided that they can use the land
more productively. To celebrate the result of the debate, the people of the collective Rosa Luxemburg
perform an adaptation of the old Chinese saga of the
chalk circle, which "has something to do with our
problem."[257]

The play actually consists of two stories, which the
singer of the collective Rosa Luxemburg tells with the
help of musicians and the actors from the collective.
The first story is the story of Grusha, the servant girl;
the second story is the story of Azdak, the judge. Both
stories, however, take place at the same time and are
connected in the last scene.

When the people of the collective Galinsk have
settled down to watch, Arkadi Tscheidse, the singer,
sits on the ground in front of his musicians, opens a
well-thumbed book, and introduces the first story. He
takes his audience back in time to "bygone and
bloody" days in the province of Grusinia (today the
Soviet Republic of Georgia in the southern part of the
Soviet Union):

"In olden times, in bloody times, a governor named Georgi Abashvili ruled in this city, called the city of the damned. He was as rich as Croesus. He had a beautiful wife. He had a healthy child. . . . On one Easter Sunday morning, the governor and his family went to church. . . ."[258]

And at this point the story is continued by the actors, who begin to act.

Soldiers clear the way for the governor and his family, lashing out with whips at the multitudes of beggars and petitioners who are eager to present their requests and wish to get a glimpse of Abashvili's heir, his newly born son Michael. When the baby coughs ever so slightly, Natella, the governor's wife, angrily turns to his two doctors, who in turn accuse each other of miscalculating the temperature of the baby's bath water. The governor seems to be at the pinnacle of his power. But there is trouble ahead. A messenger on horseback brings bad news about a war the governor is conducting. But the governor refuses to hear any bad news on this day. This costs him dearly, for before the day is over, the fat duke Kazbeki has staged a coup. His brother, the grand duke, is overthrown, and his governor, Abashvili, is beheaded. But the war goes on.

The singer, who serves as commentator throughout the play, interrupts the action with the words: "O change of times! You are the hope of the people!"[259]

In the disorder following the coup, Natella hastily prepares to flee. Only a few hours ago she had seemed concerned about Michael's slightest cough. Now she thinks only about saving her expensive dresses. She abandons Michael because, as the executed governor's son and heir, he has become a liability to her, rather than an instrument for obtaining power.

The baby is passed from one servant to another and finally to Grusha, a simple scullery maid. She is the only one who sees the baby for what he is—a helpless human being. Grusha realizes the danger in helping the child. The singer comments: "Terrible is the seduction to goodness!"[260] But her humane feelings win, and she takes the baby. The inner turmoil in Grusha is not expressed in a heart-rending monologue but in a pantomime in which Grusha acts out what the singer —in beautiful poetic language—describes.

In the middle of all the disorders, love develops between Grusha and Simon, a soldier of Abashvili's palace guard. But there is no time for romance; Simon is ordered to leave with the governor's widow as her bodyguard. But before he leaves, he and Grusha exchange promises of marriage.

Grusha's fate is now tied to that of the high-born child for whom the new rulers are searching all over Grusinia, and on whose head a high reward has been placed. Pursued by soldiers, she flees into the northern mountains with Michael. In several episodes, we see the dangers and hardships of her journey.

A farmer asks an outrageous price for his milk, but Michael needs it, so she pays.

In front of a caravansery, Grusha discovers a wagon full of rich refugees. She joins them, pretending to be one of their class. The ladies decide to spend the night at the caravansery despite the exorbitant prices. The servant tells them they will have to straighten out their own rooms. All others are aghast at this indignity. But Grusha immediately sets to work, thereby giving herself away as a person of low birth. The servant comments: "Believe me, nothing is more difficult than imitating a lazy and useless person."[261]

Again she has to move on, barely keeping ahead of the pursuing soldiers, or Ironshirts, as they are called in the play. But soon Michael becomes too much of a burden for her, and she decides she must find someone else to take care of him. She leaves him in front of a farmer's house. When she sees that the farmer's wife takes him in, she moves on. But she quickly runs into the Ironshirts, who demand to know where the baby is. She pretends that she has no knowledge of the child. But she is overcome with anxiety about the baby, and turns around and runs back to the farmhouse to warn the farmer's wife. At first the soldiers think Grusha has run away because she is afraid they will rape her. But the submissive and fearful farmer's wife directs the soldiers' attention to the child. Grusha pretends that the child is hers, but the baby's fine clothing reveals that she is lying. In desperation, Grusha takes a piece of wood, hits the soldiers' leader over the head, grabs the child, and runs.

Again she is close to being captured when she comes to a ravine and the only bridge across the ravine is in almost impassable condition. But when the Ironshirts close in on her, she dares to cross the footbridge and reaches the other side safely. The abyss is two thousand feet deep, but she says "These people are worse."[262]

Finally she reaches her destination, her brother's home. But he indicates that she and little Michael cannot stay there long because Grusha, who pretends that the baby is hers, cannot name his father. This makes her pious sister-in-law suspicious that Grusha is not married; it offends her "sense of decency." And Grusha's brother, Lavrenti, is completely under his wife's influence because she owns the property. Grusha, however, is in no condition to move on. Despite her sister-in-law's resentment, she is reluctantly allowed to stay.

After a half year has passed, a husband must be found for Grusha, because people are beginning to talk about the "child out of wedlock." After some time, Lavrenti informs Grusha that he has found the right man for her: "The son of the farm woman with whom I made a deal is just about to die. Isn't that marvelous?"[263] Thus legitimacy is bought for Michael for six hundred piasters. The wedding ceremony is conducted at the dying man's bedside by an alcoholic monk, and the celebration is attended by scores of gluttonous neighbors who are anxious to share the wedding feast. In the midst of the festivities, the news arrives that the war is over. This has a remarkable effect upon Jussup, now Grusha's legal husband, who immediately recovers from his terminal disease, drives all the wedding guests away, and begins to tyrannize her.

Years pass and Michael grows. One day while Grusha is washing clothes in a brook, her old fiancé, Simon, appears. When he hears that she is married and has a child, he walks away, deeply disappointed. At the same moment, two Ironshirts appear and take Michael away, because his real mother is demanding his return. Grusha follows them to town, where the case comes to court. The presiding judge is Azdak.

At this point, the Grusha story is interrupted, and the singer proceeds to tell us the story of Azdak: "And now you will hear the story of the judge: how he became judge, how he passed judgment, and what kind of a judge he is."[264]

Azdak's story begins on that same Easter Sunday— the revolt breaks out, the grand duke is overthrown, the governor Abashvili is killed. Azdak, a clerk in the village—a derelict rogue, always drunk, ragged, and crude—on this morning hides a fugitive in his shack. But he soon recognizes by the fine hands—and gross eating habits—that the stranger is a person of high birth. Later, he learns that this stranger is the former grand duke. He turns himself in, accusing himself of a terrible crime and demanding that he be sentenced in a public trial, for he believes that "a new time" has come—a time "in which everything will be examined, everything will be brought to light."[265] But there has just been an uprising of discontented carpet weavers, who have hanged the judge. Before Azdak can be tried, a new judge has to be found.

The fat duke Kazbeki is in power, but he is not firmly established, so long as the former grand duke and the former governor's son are still alive. The Ironshirts, that is to say, the military, hold a key position. At Kazbeki's request they kill the weavers for two piasters per head. The fat duke then comes to them to present his nephew as candidate for the judge-ship. The Ironshirts jokingly ask the prisoner Azdak what he thinks of the prospective judge. Azdak suggests a mock trial to test the nephew, in which he himself plays the part of grand duke. He plays this part so amusingly well—particularly when he makes a case for the people of Grusinia against the exploitative dukes—that the Ironshirts decide to make him the new judge: "Always the judge has been a rascal; now a rascal shall be the judge."[266]

For two years, Azdak decides the law in the province of Grusinia, and his judgments are unusual indeed. Of course, he takes bribes. But he also contributes toward the equal distribution of income by taking from the rich and giving to the poor. He uses the book of law only to sit on. Thus some of his sentences "are often just." He is called "a good bad judge."

One of the several cases he decides is that of three rich farmers versus an old woman. The farmers are suing the old woman for stealing a cow, a big ham, and a piece of land. She claims that Saint Banditus interfered on her behalf. But the farmers identify the alleged "saint" as the much dreaded bandit Irakli, who robbed and threatened the farmers in order to help the old woman. Azdak's sympathies lie with the old woman. In her he sees the oppressed people of

Grusinia, and he calls her "Mother Grusinia, full of grief," with obvious reference to Mary, the mother of Christ. The phrase also echoes the Catholic hymn *Stabat Mater Dolorosa*. He sentences the farmers to a fine of five hundred piasters each for impiety, since they do not believe in Saint Banditus.

The times change again. The grand duke is restored to power, and the fat duke is beheaded. The short period of chaos during which Azdak brought some justice to the common people has come to an end. Azdak comes close to being hanged. But through an order from the grand duke (whom Azdak had hidden that Easter Sunday) he is released and reinstated as judge. But he realizes that, with the kind of justice he metes out, his days are numbered. Yet before he leaves, he has to decide one last case. Two women appear before him, Grusha and Natella, both of whom claim the same child. Azdak must decide which is the real mother.

As usual, Azdak is drinking heavily. He sits down on the law book, takes the bribes offered him, and opens the trial. The lawyers for Natella Abashvili base their argument on the blood relationship: "Blood is thicker than water. . . . The bonds of blood are the strongest of all bonds."[267] Grusha, with no legal aid, can only claim that she has raised the child at great sacrifice, even to the point of jeopardizing her own life: "I have brought him up to the best of my ability; I have always found something for him to eat."[268]

Then the real reason for Natella Abashvili's renewed interest in the child becomes apparent: without the child she cannot inherit her late husband's estate. Grusha thinks that the judge will surely be partial to Natella because her lawyers can bribe well and talk fluently. She does not restrain her indignation, and freely tells Azdak what she thinks of him and his justice: "I have no respect for you. No more than for a thief and a robber with a knife who does what he wants."[269] But instead of being angry, Azdak is delighted with her.

After he has heard both sides, he announces that he will decide the child's fate by the test of the chalk circle. He has his clerk draw a chalk circle on the ground and orders the two women to stand on opposite sides of the circle and try to pull the child out. Whoever succeeds will be the real mother and will be granted custody of the child. Twice Grusha tries, but she cannot bring herself to hurt the child. In desperation she turns to the judge: "I have raised him. Shall I now tear him apart? I cannot do it."[270] Thereupon Azdak rises and declares Grusha the real mother. Then he proceeds to sign the divorce papers for Grusha so that she and Simon can get married. (Simon had watched the trial and now understands why Grusha had to marry Jussup.) Soon afterward, Azdak disappears.

The play ends with a dance by all those who are still present after Natella and her entourage have left. The singer sums up the story and turns to the audience: "But you, the listeners to the story of the chalk circle, take notice of the wisdom of the ancients: that which exists shall belong to those who can make it flourish, that is to say, the children to those who are motherly, so that they may thrive, the wagons to those who drive well, and the valley to those who irrigate it, so that it will bring forth plenty of fruit."[271]

There has been some debate as to whether the prologue is necessary to the play. The message is clear without the prologue. But there are several reasons for the prologue.

The first version of the play (June 1944) does include an epilogue in which the action returns to the two collectives. In this version, the decision about the ownership of the valley is made after the performance of the play. And in this early version, the time of the prologue is 1934.

The second version was written in 1945. It does not return to the two collectives; the decision about the valley is made before the performance of the play. The impact of the second version is much stronger because the audience is directly addressed with the last lines of the singer. The setting for the prologue in the second version is the year 1945 (the year of Hitler's defeat). Thus it stresses much more clearly the need and the opportunity for a new beginning after the crushing defeat of fascism. Brecht felt that a new beginning was an absolute necessity for Germany.

In his annotations to the play Brecht explained that the story of the chalk circle is meaningful only in relation to a concrete situation, which proves the practicability of the play's lesson in a definite historic context. This context in the play is the dispute about the valley. It illustrates the practical application of the singer's last words. Consequently, the prologue is essential for Brecht's intentions in this play. It is also important for his philosophy behind play-writing in general, since "practicability" and Karl Marx's dictum "The truth is concrete" were his guiding principles.

To underline the close relationship between prologue and play, Brecht, in 1956, replaced the title "prologue" with "the quarrel about the valley." He also added two new sentences ("According to the law, the valley is ours," and "The old laws must be reviewed to see if they still apply") in order to make the play's message more widely applicable.

The prologue also serves a dramaturgic function: it strengthens the epic structure of the play. The singer is introduced to relate a story and uses actors as demonstrators. He creates distance between the audience and the material presented. And the play within a play also brings home to the audience the fact that they are watching a play, not reality.

The prologue was omitted from all American productions of the play until 1965. During the time of the cold war, the arguments against it may well have been motivated more by ideological than by artistic reasons. The prologue might have been a bit of a shock to American audiences because they would have been confronted with two Soviet collectives and people who call each other "comrade."[272]

But the play is by no means a one-dimensional propaganda piece. The audience is not only treated to good theater but is also moved to think about the basic principles of society. In Grusha, the play celebrates the victory of true humanity over inhumanity, and in Azdak's verdict, the victory of reason and progress for all over unreason and preservation of the status quo for a privileged few.

In the play within a play, we get a glimpse of a golden age of justice through such a dubious character as Azdak—and in a time of chaos. But we are challenged to think how much better it would be if the exception—true justice—became the rule.

The play is full of contradictions, the main function of which is to point out the contradictions inherent in the society portrayed. By caring for Michael's life, Grusha endangers her own life. In finding a father for the child, she loses the man she loves (Simon). Azdak is corrupt, degenerate, and contemptuous of the laws of the land, but during his term as judge, more real justice is dispensed than the country ever knew before.

The main characters of the play are not painted in black and white. In order to counter the impression that Grusha is too attractive a heroine, Brecht stated that she should show all the backwardness of her class. And he advised actresses who play Grusha to study the peasant scenes in Bruegel's paintings, particularly his picture *Dulle Griet* (*Dull Greta*).[273] Brecht also described Grusha as a "sucker." Although Grusha is basically a good person, endowed with a natural mother instinct, she has human weaknesses. At the beginning, she is not at all sure that she should take the baby. Later, during her flight, she makes an attempt to abandon him.

Azdak is surely far from being an exemplary judge. Yet he is somewhat like the Shakespearean fool, who is the smartest of the lot.

The first performance of *The Caucasian Chalk Circle* took place on the campus of Carleton College, Northfield, Minnesota, on 4 May 1948 (directed by Henry Goodman). The reviewer for *The Northfield Independent* of 6 May 1948 praised the production highly. He recognized the unconventional nature of the play and the performance and confessed to being somewhat baffled by its meaning:

> Come prepared to see and hear the work of a playwright who does not "pull his punches" when expressing himself, which at times may "rough you up" a bit. . . . You will also see a play that is different from the conventional and novel in its presentation. Just what is meant by the maze of scenes and often surprising lines is not always clear, but the impression remains that government, justice in particular, administered under popular selected authority, even under corrupt circumstances, is preferred to that administered by inherited or despotic authority, and good acts win over evil.[274]

Brecht's own theater group, the Berliner Ensemble, staged the play on 7 October 1954 (Azdak: Ernst Busch, who also played the singer; Natella Abashvili: Helene Weigel; Grusha: Angelika Hurwicz; director: Bertolt Brecht). The music for this production was

composed by Paul Dessau, who invented a special
instrument for the ballads of the "good bad judge"
Azdak. This instrument consisted of eight differently
tuned gongs. Played with a flute, a violin, and drums,
a special rhythmical effect was achieved.

The reviewer of the West German paper *Die Zeit*
found the production too long (it lasted more than
four hours), and recommended some cuts. But she had
high praise for the "brilliantly executed details" and
for the performances by Busch, Weigel, and Hurwicz.[275]

The first West German performance of the *Chalk
Circle* was on 28 April 1955 in Frankfurt on the Main
(director: Harry Buckwitz; Grusha: Käthe Reichel;
Azdak: Hanns Ernst Jäger). Unfortunately, this was
offered during the cold war. The political feeling
clearly affected the judgment of most western critics.
Party members of Adenauer's Christian Democrats,
then in power, objected vociferously to the presentation of a play by Brecht, because only a short time
before (on 17 June 1953) Brecht had openly supported the regime of East Germany during an uprising of rebellious workers.

Possibly because of the adverse political climate
Buckwitz omitted the prologue. This was generally
approved of by the West German theater critics because most of them regarded the prologue only as naive
communist propaganda and a concession to the East
German Communist party. This was also the opinion
of the reviewer for the *Frankfurter Allgemeine Zeitung* of 30 April 1955. (She had obviously read
the prologue because she did give some considera-
tion to its artistic merits.) She found the play too
long-winded, particularly the "long passages of tedious
and tiring social criticism." Her only forthright praise
went to the scenes that revolved around Judge Azdak
—mainly because of the actor Hanns Ernst Jäger. An-

other reviewer in the same paper strongly disliked Dessau's music. Yet, the play was enthusiastically received by the audience.[276]

Because of the political climate the organizers of the annual Recklinghausen-Ruhr Festival, at which a guest performance of the Frankfurt production was given, took the precautionary measures of informing the Bonn government and of securing police protection against possible disturbances. This proved to be unnecessary because the performance turned out to be a resounding success. The review in the *Frankfurter Allgemeine Zeitung* of 18 June 1955 was ambivalent. Hailing the poetic qualities of the play, the reviewer called it "a doctrinaire fairy tale." He expressed his amazement at the fact that "such a piece of poetry (although brought into party line by a prologue that we were fortunately spared) [could] originate in the Eastern zone." He somewhat condescendingly recommended that the "free western world" also take notice of its message.[277]

On 30 October 1961 the Arena Stage Theater Company officially opened its new theater in Washington, D.C., with a production of *The Caucasian Chalk Circle,* in the English adaptation by John Holmstrom (director: Alan Schneider; sets: Peter Wingate; music: Teiji Ito; Grusha: Melinda Dillon; Azdak: David Hurst). Howard Taubman of *The New York Times* traveled from New York to see this production of "an outstanding contemporary work," and he found it "well worth a trip." Taubman was impressed with the play itself: "It is a measure of Brecht's special gift that out of Grusha's inability to resist the terrible temptation [of goodness] he can construct a work with so much moral fervor couched in such entertaining and moving terms." He found that Alan Schneider, although clearly influenced by the style of the Berliner Ensemble, had "caught in his own way the rare amalgam of theatrical flair, tenderness, and passion that distinguishes Brecht and the interpreters he trained before his death." Taubman called Holmstrom's new English text "effective" but wished the Ironshirts had not talked like "tough guys on television."[278]

A highly successful performance of *The Caucasian Chalk Circle* in the English-speaking world (in John Holmstrom's translation) was given by the Royal Shakespeare Company on 29 March 1962 in the Aldwich Theater in London (director: William Gaskill; Grusha: Patsy Byrne; Azdak: Hugh Griffith). According to the British critic Kenneth Tynan, there were a few minor flaws. "But on the whole the production need not shrink from comparison with that of the Berliner Ensemble. Under-rehearsed though it is by continental standards, it towers over everything else in London."

Some quarters chided Tynan for judging plays more by their ideology than their artistic merits. His answer to this charge was that the two cannot be separated from each other: "No message can confer greatness on a play unless a man of genius delivers it. The touchstone, in other words, is not what Brecht says, but the fact that it is Brecht who says it."[279]

On 13 December 1963, the Actors' Workshop in San Francisco opened a production of the play, in Eric Bentley's translation, at the Marines' theater (director: Carl M. Weber; producer/directors: Jules Irving and Herbert Blau; sets: James H. Stearns; music: Morton Subotnick; Grusha: Elizabeth Huddle; Azdak: Ray Fry). The review in the *San Francisco Chronicle* is a good example of how Brecht can be misunderstood. The reviewer, Paine Knickerbocker, called it "a production of many excellences ... a richly mounted, triumphant visual presentation" by the Workshop's "theatrical magicians," the producer/directors Jules

Irving and Herbert Blau. But he wrote: "What faults there are belong to Brecht." These "faults" were, according to Knickerbocker, the sudden switch of the story line to Azdak, which jolts the audience out of its engrossment with the plight of Grusha, "Brecht's insistence on occasional scatological dialogue," and the songs ("without trained voices...they simply clutter up a most distinguished production"[280]).

On 24 March 1966 the play, in Eric Bentley's translation, opened in the Vivian Beaumont Theater of New York City's Lincoln Center, presented by the Repertory Theater of the Lincoln Center (directors: Jules Irving and Herbert Blau; singer: Brock Peters; Grusha: Elizabeth Huddle; Natella Abashvili: Beatrice Manley; Azdak: Robert Symonds; music: Morton Subotnick).

Director Irving divided the play into three acts, as compared with six scenes in Brecht's own version (the first scene, "The Dispute over the Valley" functions as prologue).

The expectations were high, as Walter Kerr wrote in his review, "and nearly every last man of us was waiting to see Brecht whole. Brecht has for many years been advertised as one of the truly influential movers and shakers of the contemporary theatrical consciousness—advertised, but not effectively represented in New York." But disillusionment was soon to follow: "No such luck," Kerr continued, "the very worst, far and away the most frustrating, aspect of the Blau-Irving *Caucasian Chalk Circle* was its ineptitude in projecting what is unconventional about the play." His disappointment, then, was mostly due to the staging rather than to the play itself.

According to Kerr, the whole production was characterizd by an extraordinary stylistic insecurity. He illustrates his criticism with a rather detailed description of the inadequate beginning of the play, which seemed to him to be symptomatic of the whole performance. Several peasants along with the storyteller appeared before the curtain and stared intensely at the audience. This immediately arrested everyone's attention and created an expectant tension. But that was destroyed, when the storyteller suddenly left the stage to roam freely through the aisles of the theater and sternly confront some embarrassed latecomers struggling to find their seats. What was probably conceived as a provocative confrontation ended in absurdity.

To Kerr, it seemed that Mr. Irving was desperately trying to do "something else," something unusual. And, Kerr comments dryly: "Else was all over the place." Eric Bentley's translation also received its share of the criticism. Kerr found it too scholarly and dry. "We come to the end of a speech feeling we have navigated a tunnel in which there were no variations of shape or course . . . Mr. Bentley's ear would not seem to be attuned to the auditorium."

Kerr questions whether part of the weakness is not to be attributed to the "venerable playwright" himself, since (a) the play is "considered close to foolproof" and (b) the principals involved in the production did have some credentials to their credit. Otherwise the only conclusion would be that "Messrs. Blau and Irving were themselves without any powerful or very practical theatrical sensibilities." Yet, despite Kerr's criticism, the play survived the entire season.[281]

Stanley Kauffmann of *The New York Times* saw *The Caucasian Chalk Circle* of the Repertory Theater twice during the season, and enjoyed it both times. He found it "a good production by any standards" and the play ("a circus-like show") "a diversion from [Brecht's] activist political plays into the arena of theatrical high jinks, with plentiful opportunities for pageantry, music, horseplay, and sheer heart-tugging."

But Kauffmann was not without criticism of Brecht's play:

> The play was written by a man whose theater theories have proved weak; it derives from a political philosophy with which I disagree; and it teaches a moral point which is simple—possibly too simple. . . . Central to Brecht's view of the theater is the Alienation Effect, which is probably the most over-exploded idea in modern drama.

Nevertheless, Kauffmann thought it was a fine play. And apart from the play's high dramatic qualities, he gave two further reasons why the play was (and still is) of interest for the noncommunist. First he felt that Marxism had indeed "altered our view of society. The materialist view of history and behavior cannot now be ignored any more than it need be solely venerated. Brecht is far and away the best dramatist of this view who has so far written." And Kauffmann's second reason: "In general artistic terms, it seems increasingly possible that we are moving to the end of a long age of subjective art—art that reproduces the individual and whose chief purpose is 'identification'." This is a view Kauffmann found well expressed in Sartre's essay "Beyond Bourgeois Theater."

According to Kauffmann, "Brecht, from his own sources and impulses, anticipated this. Whatever his theoretical formulations, his artistic instincts and insights were those of a genius who had outdistanced his time."[282]

The Caucasian Chalk Circle is perhaps the best illustration of Brecht's epic theater. The two plots are not interwoven as they are in conventional plays, but are presented one after the other. By introducing the singer as narrator, Brecht combines a device of the novel with the devices of a drama. The narrator functions as an omniscient storyteller who illustrates

The Causasian Chalk Circle, The Guthrie Theater, 1965.
Director: Edward Payson Call; sets: Lewis Brown;
Governor's wife: Helen Harrelson; Young Michael: Matt
Talberg; Grusha: Zoe Caldwell; Azdak: Ed Flanders.
The Caucasian Chalk Circle, Repertory Theater of Lincoln
Center, New York, 1966. Translator: Eric Bentley; direc-
tors: Jules Irving and Herbert Blau; sets and costumes:
James Hart Stearns; music and songs: Morton Subotnick.
Grusha Vachnadze: Elizabeth Huddle (left); Peasant
Woman (Grusha's mother-in-law): Shirley Jac Wagner.

his narrative with pantomime and dramatic action. He is the only link between the episodic scenes, which span long periods of time. Through him, we learn Grusha's thoughts, and it is he who describes for us her inner turmoil at the end of the second scene when she looks at the abandoned child. But the singer is not always a detached observer. He also serves as commentator and interpreter, similar to the chorus in the classical Greek drama. In highly poetic language, he comments upon the palace revolt in the first scene: "O blindness of the great! They walk like eternal gods/ On bent backs, assured/ Of hired fists, trusting/ In their power which has lasted a long time./ But long is not forever./ O change of the times! Hope of the people!"[283] This hope for change and assurance of change is an essential message in this and many of Brecht's plays. It is a positive and optimistic view of the future.

EAST BERLIN (1948–1956)

The Days of the Commune
(1948–49)

In *The Days of the Commune* Brecht dramatized one of the most important events in the history of socialism: the rise and fall of the Paris Commune in the spring of 1871. Today the Paris Commune is recognized as the prototype of a leftist revolution. Marx, Engels, and Lenin have described it as the first genuine revolution of the proletariat. In the socialist world, the Paris Commune is regarded as the predecessor of all workers' and peasants' states. In preparation for the successful 1917 revolution in Russia, for example, Lenin most thoroughly studied the history of the Paris Commune. He was determined not to repeat its mistakes (the Commune failed immediately and firmly to smash all opposition).

The formation of the Commune in Paris came in the wake of the French defeat in the war with Germany in 1871. On 2 September 1870, the Germans won the decisive Battle of Sedan, in which more than one hundred thousand French soldiers, along with Emperor Napoleon III, were taken prisoner. Two days later, on 4 September 1870, a republican government,

German title: *Die Tage der Commune.*

a government of national defense, was formed with
General Trochu as president and Jules Favre as secretary of foreign affairs.

On 18 September 1870, German troops began their
beleaguerment of Paris, which lasted more than four
months. The greatest humiliation for France during
this period was the bombardment of Paris and the
crowning of the King of Prussia as Emperor Wilhelm
I at Versailles on 18 January 1871.

Tensions in the city of Paris increased. The poor
people of Paris had suffered severely under the hardships of war. With the blockade of the city, their lot
grew worse. They felt that they were being exploited
and that the government was not resisting the Germans forcefully enough. Tensions came to a boiling
point on 22 January 1871, when government troops
opened fire on a demonstration by the National
Guardsmen outside the Hôtel de Ville (City Hall),
the seat of the republican government. (The Paris
National Guard, a sort of militia, originally formed
from the bourgeoisie under Napoleon III, was enlarged during the war against Prussia. It now also
comprised many men from lower socioeconomic
classes, some of whom were radical leftists.) 22 January 1871 marked a turning point; the Parisians were
divided into two irreconcilable camps.

On 28 January 1871, Paris and the rest of France
capitulated to the Germans after Thiers and Favre had
negotiated the terms of surrender with Bismarck. A
small contingent of German troops (thirty thousand)
occupied Paris for two days.

The war was over, but the social tensions between
upper and lower classes in Paris continued. The government became increasingly afraid of a rebellion in
the city. When the French government, since 17 February 1871 under Aldolphe Thiers, ordered the army

to take away the cannons of the National Guard (during the night of 17–18 March), the troops refused orders, shot two of their generals (Thomas and Lecomte), and sided with the National Guard. The Thiers government fled to Versailles and the Central Committee of the National Guard's left wing took over the government of Paris.

In the elections to the municipal council of Paris on 26 March, the candidates of the Central Committee of the National Guard won a large majority. The "Reds" assumed the name of "Commune de Paris" and took official residence in the Hôtel de Ville. On 28 March the Commune of Paris was officially proclaimed.

For a brief period life in Paris returned more or less to normal. The city was calm, theaters, cafés, restaurants were open, and for the poor at least the future looked much brighter. But there were signs of trouble ahead. Various factions of the Commune lost vital time arguing about which course to follow. There were plans for an immediate march to Versailles to crush Thiers. It could have been accomplished, because the National Guard outnumbered Thiers' demoralized army, had they marched in time. But the plans were shelved for fear of violence and German intervention.

Another setback for the Commune was that Beslay, one of their delegates, failed to take over the national Bank of France. Instead, Beslay left Marquis de Ploeuc in office, who lost no time in providing Thiers with badly needed funds.

The internal dissent and lack of firmness on the part of the Commune, and the receipt of de Ploeuc's money gave Thiers the time and opportunity to assemble an army against the insurgents in Paris. The victorious Bismarck, who had limited the size of Thiers' army, permitted an enlargement of Thiers' forces for this purpose. The sooner the red Commune of Paris was crushed, the sooner Bismarck could cope with his own German socialists at home.

On 2 April 1871, Thiers began to wage a civil war that ended in a total and extremely bloody defeat for the Commune on Sunday, 28 May 1871.[1]

These are the historic events that Brecht followed rather closely in his play. Some of his characters are historical figures, as in the cases of Thiers, Favre, Bismarck, and the delegates of the Paris Commune, Beslay, Delescluze (perhaps the outstanding Communard), Ranvier, Rigault, and Varlin. Other characters he created, such as the members of the Cabet family and the National Guardsmen Papa, Coco, François.

SCENE 1. The action in Brecht's play begins on that crucial day of 22 January 1871, with the shooting of demonstrating National Guardsmen. Brecht, however, does not recreate the highly dramatic events outside the Hôtel de Ville. Instead the setting for the first scene of his play is a small café in Montmartre. A fat bourgeois customer is complaining about the impudence of the masses, when three members of the National Guard—Papa, Coco, and François (with a captured German in their midst)—enter the café and drive him away by their "unpatriotic talk." They are tired of fighting against the Germans so that the rich Frenchmen can prosper. The guardsmen feel exploited and betrayed by the establishment and are preparing an insurrection.

SCENE 2. 25 January 1871. Over breakfast in Thiers' home in Bordeaux, Thiers and Favre are discussing the terms of the French capitulation. They are more afraid of the people of Paris than of the Germans. In order to protect "our civilization, which is based on private property,"[2] Thiers wants to end the war as quickly as possible and to reach a favorable agreement with the Germans. His key word is "pacification," even if it means a blood bath for the Parisians.

SCENE 3. It is the night of 17–18 March in the Rue Pigalle. Guardsmen Jean Cabet and François Faure are guarding a cannon. Thiers has bread distributed to calm down the people in the workers' quarters and to prevent an uprising. But the talk of some lower-class women who are standing in front of the baker's shop indicates that the mood of the people is ugly. ("Thiers is getting five million francs from the Germans! . . . They capitulate, although there are more than three hundred thousand National Guardsmen in Paris alone! Maybe *because* there are three hundred thousand of them in Paris!"[3]) When army soldiers appear outside the bakery—among them Philippe, the baker—to take away the National Guard's cannon, they are confronted by National Guardsmen. After some tense moments, the army soldiers are persuaded by the women (Madame Cabet, Jean's mother, is the most persuasive of them) to give up and align themselves with the National Guardsmen.

SCENE 4. 19 March 1871, the day after the revolutionaries take over the government of Paris. Delegates of the Central Committee of the National Guard are assembled in city hall to discuss the future development of the people's movement. There is disagreement among them as to which course to take. Papa and Madame Cabet listen to the debates at the open door. Papa is of the opinion that they must march directly to Versailles against Thiers. But delegate Pierre Langevin, who has joined them, wants to prevent bloodshed and civil war. He argues for a democratic election process. In the meantime, no one thinks of preventing Thiers from taking supplies, troops, and artillery to Versailles.

SCENE 5. The same day, at the Gare du Nord in

Paris. Posters on the station walls urge the people of Paris to vote for the leftist candidates for the Commune in the upcoming municipal elections on March 26, but all the bourgeois papers call on Parisians not to vote at all. Bourgeois families and Thiers government officials scramble on trains to leave Paris for Versailles. An aristocratic lady is worrying about her hat collection, and army soldiers load the treasury coffers of Paris onto the train. Jean Cabet attempts to stop them, but is beaten up. He is rescued by National Guardsmen. He is bitterly disappointed that they allow the money to be taken to Versailles.

SCENE 6. 26 March 1871. The leftists have won the elections. At the café in Montmartre, the owner has left and the waiter now runs it. The Cabet family, Papa, Langevin and others gather at the café to celebrate the beginning of a new time of a classless society and international brotherhood. This also includes the captured German who has joined the commune. The bourgeois papers, which are still allowed to publish, spread lies about the "terror" of the left. Most communards are in a festive mood; only Pierre Langevin wonders whether they did not make a mistake when they decided not to march on Versailles.

SCENE 7. 29 March 1871. The Commune is now officially governing the city of Paris. The inside of city hall is decorated with red flags and posters such as "Freedom of the Individual," "Freedom of Speech." At the opening session of the Commune in the city hall, sweeping reforms are announced.

But immediately the practical difficulties become apparent. The scene switches to the new Ministry of the Interior, where, for the eighth day, not a single employee has come to work (either out of resistance to the Commune or a misunderstood sense of "freedom"). The Commune has to rebuild from the beginning; each person must share in the responsibility.

SCENE 8. Beslay, a representative of the Commune, pays a visit to the governor of the National Bank of France, Marquis de Ploeuc, to obtain money, mainly to pay the men in the National Guard. The Marquis de Ploeuc is most polite but refuses. (A few minutes earlier, he promised a representative of the archbishop of Paris that the money would be shipped to Versailles.)

SCENE 9. On his return to city hall, Beslay faces protesting fellow communards who want to take over the bank and take the money by force. Others, Beslay included, prefer to find a peaceful and "legal" solution. Trusting in the peaceful progress of socialism and fearful of starting a civil war, the majority of the communards vote down delegate Rigault's proposal to march on Versailles and liberate the countryside.

But a drastic change in the political situation gives their deliberations a new direction: The Thiers forces in Versailles have begun an offensive to recapture Paris; Thiers has, in effect, started the civil war. The troops of the National Guard—so far successful in defending the Commune—are dedicated to the cause but not well equipped and well disciplined. Because of a distorted image of a people's democracy, people insisted prematurely on too much freedom and too many rights for the individual. What was needed was strict discipline in the interest of the whole Commune.

The scene ends with the reading of the German Socialist August Bebel's declaration of support for the Paris Commune, which Bebel had delivered in the German Reichstag the day before.

SCENE 10. Frankfurt, Germany. German Chancellor Bismarck and the French foreign secretary Jules Favre meet during a performance of Bellini's opera *Norma*. (Favre is in Frankfurt to sign the peace agreement.) Bismarck agrees to free French prisoners-of-war to strengthen Thiers' force in suppressing the Commune, and to defer reparation payments until after the Commune has been defeated. He does this not for his love of the French, who were then regarded as the "hereditary enemies" of the Germans, but out of fear that the example of a proletarian revolution might spread to Germany.

SCENE 11. It is late at night, and Pierre Langevin is still hard at work in city hall. Difficulties for the Commune have multiplied. As he recognizes, they are due to the Commune's own mistakes. Worst of all was their failure to march against Versailles ("of course we should have marched on Versailles"[4]), and their lack of discipline ("we were not ready . . . to forego personal freedom until freedom for all was achieved"[5]).

In the face of civil war delegates to the Commune, assembled in city hall, are debating whether to resort to restrictions of individual freedom and repressive measures against the bourgeois class. Delegates Varlin and Rigault argue that the Commune must use the same means of terror as the enemy or face certain destruction ("terror against terror, oppress or be oppressed, destroy or be destroyed"[6]). But the majority of delegates are opposed to violent tactics. With naive idealism they believe that truth does not need to take up the sword. ("In a few weeks the Commune has done more for human dignity than all other governments for eight centuries."[7]) They vote to proceed with organizational matters at hand.

SCENE 12. Place Pigalle: Easter Sunday 1871. With the thunder of cannons in the distance, the people of Paris are erecting barricades. Among them are Jean, his fiancée Babette, François, and Geneviève, a young teacher. Philippe, the baker, who had joined the Commune, has left it again because he wants to be on the winning side. When Geneviève's fiancé arrives, disguised as a nun and serving as informer for Thiers,

Geneviève recognizes him. He is delivered to Papa and Coco, who intend to execute him as a traitor. But Madame Cabet persuades them to spare him.

SCENE 13. Barricade on the Place Pigalle. As though it were a symbol of hope, an apple tree is in full bloom. François, Jean, Geneviève, and the German soldier fight until they are killed by Thiers' forces.

SCENE 14. From the bastions of Versailles the bourgeoisie watch the defeat of the Commune through opera glasses: "What a sublime spectacle! The fires, the mathematical movement of the troops!" An aristocratic lady congratulates Thiers: "You have returned Paris to her true mistress, to France." The play closes with Thiers' reply: "And France, that is—you, Mesdames et Messieurs."[8]

In preparation for this play Brecht consulted various historical works. One of his major sources was Olivier Lissagaray's *Histoire de la Commune* (1876; first German edition 1878; first English edition 1886, translated by Eleanor Marx-Aveling, Karl Marx' daughter). Lissagaray himself was a member of the Paris Commune.

Brecht also used Nordahl Grieg's *The Defeat,* another play about the Paris Commune, as an inspiration for his own play: "The play *The Days of the Commune* was written in Zürich in 1948–49 after I read Nordahl Grieg's *The Defeat.* I adopted some features and characters from *The Defeat,* but seen as a whole, *The Days of the Commune* is a kind of counterversion."[9]

Thus reads Brecht's introduction to the printed version of the play when it was published in the fifteenth and last volume of his *Versuche* (a title meaning attempts or experiments) in 1957. Brecht never regarded this version as finished but rather as a preliminary sketch of what he considered one of the most complicated events in modern history. His death in 1956 prevented him from completing the extensive revisions he had already planned.

Nordahl Grieg, a Norwegian socialist playwright, born in 1902, and shot down as a member of a Canadian bomber crew in an air raid on Berlin in December of 1943, attempted to dramatize important historical events of his time. Brecht appreciated Grieg's attempts, but for him Grieg's play *The Defeat* remained too personal and failed to lead the theatergoer to see the wider historical significance. Grieg's tone, which ranges from naturalism to the romantic and lyrical (the play concludes with Beethoven's Ninth Symphony), appealed little to Brecht.

Brecht's play, which closely follows Lenin's views of the Paris Commune, is an "optimistic tragedy," a description of the first step—though it failed—toward the rule of the proletariat. It is a monument to the Commune of Paris and a warning for the working classes everywhere not to repeat the mistakes the Commune made. "The Paris Commune may fall, but the Social Revolution it has initiated will triumph. Its harbingers are everywhere," Karl Marx himself wrote in his second outline of *The Civil War in France*.[10]

When Brecht wrote the play in 1948 and 1949 at the beginning of the cold war, he undoubtedly had in mind the Western propaganda against the formation of a separate East German state under communist rule. As the program notes from the Berliner Ensemble production in 1962 point out: "With the production of this play, Brecht intended to leave nothing unclear about the dictatorship of the proletariat in our state [the German Democratic Republic]."

The play was first performed on 17 November 1956 at the municipal theater in Karl Marx Stadt, East Germany (director: Benno Besson; sets: Caspar Neher; music: Hanns Eisler; Jean Cabet: W. D. Voigt; Papa:

H. Hoff). According to A.D.N., the official news agency of East Germany, the play "had an extremely deep effect on the audience."[11]

Brecht's own theater, the Berliner Ensemble, first produced the play on 7 October 1962 (directors: Manfred Wekwerth and Joachim Tenschert; sets: Karl von Appen; music: Hanns Eisler; Madame Cabet: Gisela May; Jean Cabet: Hilmar Thate; Papa: Hermann Hiesgen). The producers carefully researched Brecht's texts and notes, as well as numerous historical sources in addition to the ones Brecht himself used. It was their intention to show the greatness of the experiment and the tragedy of its failure, particularly since history has attributed the downfall of the Commune to the Commune's own mistakes.

In August 1965 the Berliner Ensemble presented this play in German in London. It was well received by *The Times*'s drama critic:

> This is the most thoroughgoing ensemble production in the company's London repertoire (Schall and Weigel both taking tiny parts): it may not be to everyone's taste, but its final image of men behind a wall holding up a banner inscribed "We are just like you" invites something more generous than an iron-curtain response. . . . Brecht manages to charge the ensemble street scenes with a gaiety and human warmth that is worlds removed from the stuffy propriety of Communist virtue.[12]

The Days of the Commune is unknown in the English-speaking world. The only reference to a production I could find is in Claude Hill's book *Bertolt Brecht*,[13] where he mentions that a student production of the play was done at Harvard University in a translation by Leonard J. Lehrman.

Brecht did not present the events in Paris in the spring of 1871 on a grand scale but as they affected the Cabet family. In the play the fate of the Cabets

Scenes from *The Days of the Commune*, Berliner Ensemble, 1963. Directors: Manfred Wekwerth and Joachim Tenschert. *Above*, Madame Cabet: Gisela May; Jean Cabet: Hilmar Thate; Papa: Wolf Kaiser; François: Manfred Karge.

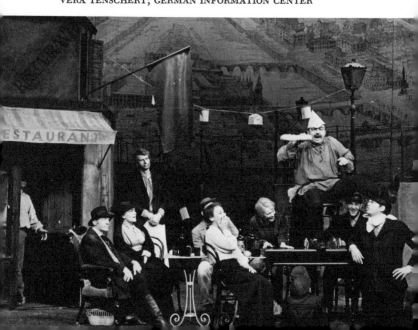

and the historic events are not always perfectly blended. At times the Cabets seem to recede too far into the background. Nevertheless Brecht succeeds in showing us the human side of the Commune as opposed to its "reign of terror," as the rule of the Commune has been labeled by conservatives.

Brecht's play is one of the best dramatizations of these important historical events. It is not one of the best examples of his epic or dialectic theater. There is little use of estrangement effects and other features of epic theater. Yet it is decidedly Brechtian in its restraint and in its concerns for a just and humane society.

Turandot, or The Congress of Whitewashers (1953–54)

The Venetian dramatist Carlo Gozzi (1720–1806) took several tales from *The Thousand and One Nights* for the purpose of dramatization. One of them was the tale of the beautiful but cruel Chinese Princess Turandot and the handsome Prince Calaf. Turandot declared that she would marry the man who could solve three riddles; but those who tried, and failed, would be killed. Many tried and failed. Finally, Calaf, Prince of Astrakhan, arrived at the court of the Chinese emperor, Turandot's father, solved all the riddles, won Turandot, and lived happily ever after.

Gozzi's work influenced several German writers, particularly the German romantic poets. Before Brecht's version, Gozzi's *Turandot* was produced in several adaptations, the most prominent of them being

---

German title: *Turandot, oder Der Kongress der Weisswäscher.*

those by Friedrich Schiller and Karl Vollmoeller. Schiller's *Turandot,* written in 1799, was staged in Weimar in 1804. Karl Vollmoeller's *Turandot,* written in 1911, was produced by Max Reinhardt on 27 October 1911 in the Deutsches Theater Berlin:

> Turandot was to enjoy a renaissance on the stage which was to surpass anything that even Gozzi might have fondly dreamed for her; she was to be reborn in the twentieth century as a rococo figure of daintiness incarnate; Max Reinhardt was to wave his magic wand over her, and a new Turandot was to arise in undreamed-of splendor.[14]

(On 18 January 1913, Vollmoeller's *Turandot,* in an English translation by Jethro Bithel, was successfully staged at the St. James Theater, London. It should also be noted that two famous composers chose the Turandot theme for their opera libretti: Ferruccio Busoni for his *Turandot,* composed in 1917, and Giacomo Puccini for his *Turandot,* composed in 1926.)

Brecht was familiar with the ancient fairy tale of Turandot and the dramas by Gozzi and Schiller. (It is likely he also knew Vollmoeller's version.) He set out to use the Turandot theme for a play of his own. The play was written in 1953 and 1954, but its beginnings go back to 1930, when Brecht planned to write the play as a vehicle for the actress Carola Neher.

However, Brecht changed the story substantially. The setting is still in China, there are still riddles to solve and a maiden to be won, the men who fail are still decapitated—until Gogher Gogh, Brecht's version of Calaf, arrives. But Brecht changed the play from a fanciful fairy tale to a satiric parable about capitalist economics and unprincipled intellectuals.

The action of the play takes place in a mythical China. The characters are the emperor of China; his daughter, Princess Turandot; his brother, Jau Jel; a farmer, A Sha Sen; a street robber, Gogher Gogh; Gogh's bodyguards; Ma Gogh, his mother; policemen; soldiers; robbers; and various Tuis. The Tuis in the play are the court officials, lawyers, teachers, writers, and other intellectuals of the country. The country is in deep trouble, and they are supposed "to find the reason for the confusion" and "the source of all evil."[15]

SCENE 1. The emperor's palace in Peking. The emperor laments he is broke. He wants to resign. China is suffering from a terrible disaster—the cotton harvest was too good and therefore the prices are too low. Even the best educated Tuis cannot explain this misfortune.

SCENE 2. In the Tuis' teahouse, there are various signs, advertising Tui skills: "We recycle opinions; afterward like new" and "Do what you like, but formulate it properly."[16] Tui Ka Mü sells only personalized opinions, for he dislikes mass production. Another Tui laments that soon poor people will no longer be able to afford opinions, due to rising prices. As the imperial court Tui explains to the visiting Turandot, this teahouse is visited mostly by lower-class Tuis, not by those who make the laws, write books, or educate the young. Turandot, nevertheless, likes to sample their opinions because the posing of problems and the articulation of beautifully phrased sentences arouse her sexually. She is particularly attracted by Gogher Gogh, a street robber, who has twice taken and failed the examination to become a Tui. But he has not given up. He supports himself in these bad times by collecting fees for protecting suburban laundries—from attacks by his own gang.

SCENE 3. The imperial palace. The emperor's situation and his mood have improved. The emperor has secretly stashed away quantities of cotton, thereby creating an artificial scarcity. The supply-and-demand principle operates to drive up the price of cotton. This situation brings about an alliance of the union of clothesmakers and the union of the clothesless. Representatives of both unions demand to know where the cotton is. In addition, a certain Kai Ho ("an undisciplined agitator"),[17] has taken advantage of the situation to stir up social unrest. And the people have begun to read the writings of Ka Me, an activity that has intensified social unrest. In order to calm down the people the emperor promises to call a Tui congress, which will search for the missing cotton. (The emperor himself, of course, knows full well where the cotton is. The congress is used purely as a diversionary measure.) And he proceeds to pacify the people with a patriotic gesture, by paying homage to a national symbol—a cotton coat that is revered in the country because the first Manchu emperor, one of his ancestors, used to wear it. And he promises his daughter's hand in marriage to whichever Tui reestablishes the people's trust in him. (He has no intention of keeping his promise.)

SCENE 4. In the Tui school they are still debating the problem raised by the German philosopher Kant: Do things exist in themselves outside of any sensory perception? The last Tui congress, which was convened to answer this question, was swept away by the flooding Yellow River—the existence of which they doubted.

The farmer A Sha Sen has come to study at the school because "thinking is such a pleasure . . . it is so useful."[18] But he leaves in disappointment after seeing what goes on there—particularly the examination of the Tui candidates Shi Meh and Gogher Gogh. Shi Meh has to answer the question: "Why is Kai Ho wrong?"[19] Whenever his answers please the examining Tui, a bread basket is lowered; whenever the answers displease him, the basket is raised out of Shi Meh's reach. (Thus Brecht illustrates with an effective the-

atrical device that survival depends on one's possession of the "correct" opinions.)

Gogher Gogh fails the examination for a third time,
because he cannot answer the question, "How much
is three times five?"[20] He declares that the examiners
are inefficient because they cannot find the right questions for his answers. He departs in disgust.

SCENE 5. From all corners of the country, learned
Tuis assemble in the Palace of the Tui Association to
find an answer to the question about the missing cotton that will whitewash the emperor's image. The
task seems monumental. It is like proving that two
times two is five. Ki Leh, the chancellor of the imperial university, argues that it was a bad harvest
and there is no cotton. Because he does not lie cleverly, he is beheaded. The learned Hi Wei maintains
that the shortage is the result of overbuying. He recommends paper clothes. He, too, is beheaded. Munka
Du, the next speaker, must first pass an examination
that tests for un-Chinese thought. (Here, Brecht obviously paraphrased his own experiences with the
House Committee on *Un-American Activities*.) Munka
Du appeals to the Chinese qualities of patience and
self-denial. When he inadvertently reveals that the
cotton is in the imperial warehouses, he, too, is beheaded.

SCENE 6. Turandot is walking along the city wall,
which is now adorned with Tui heads. She encounters
Gogher Gogh, who had tried unsuccessfully to enter
the Tui convention. His solution to the crucial question is simple: forbid the question. To Turandot's
probing personal questions, he declares that the Chinese woman is faithful, industrious, and obedient, and
that he likes literature provided it is not decadent.

SCENE 7. In the imperial palace, the emperor is having difficulties. The vital question remains unan-
swered, and a large crowd moves menacingly toward

the palace. Turandot introduces Gogher Gogh to her father. The fact that he is not a Tui and his views ("the people are dangerous; they attack the state . . . their questions about cotton must be forbidden")[21] impress the emperor. Gogher is granted authority to command. He begins to imprison the Tuis. He declares that from now on he will pay only for opinions that suit him. "Anyway, this continuous thinking is abhorrent to me."[22] In addition, he orders half the cotton burned—it helps keep the prices up and demonstrates to the people that they need strong protection against the unknown "arsonists." Turandot is fascinated and adores Gogh.

SCENE 8. The farmer Sen is shopping at a small Tui market, which offers books on medicine, love, and economics. Suddenly flames blaze in the background. Gogher Gogh, now chancellor, appears with armed bandits, who have now been made policemen. He blames the Tuis, the clothesmakers, and the clothesless, for setting fires as a signal for the revolutionary Kai Ho, who has already reached the province of Setzuan. He orders that the "intellectual firebugs be eliminated."[23] Sen, who has seen and heard all of this, now decides to secretly buy Kai Ho's famous book.

SCENE 9. In front of the Almond Blossom laundry. The possession of works of art has been prohibited by the new government. The Tuis are trying to hide the forbidden objects in an armorer's house across the street from the laundry. Ma Gogh has renounced her son Gogher. Sen has made his decision to embrace the teachings of Kai Ho: "There is injustice in the country and the Tui schools teach that it has to be that way. . . . But there is Kai Ho; here I have his booklet. . . . Where he once walked and thought, there are now large rice and cotton fields, and apparently the people are happy."[24]

SCENE 10. In a small Manchu temple, Gogher Gogh

and Turandot are to be married. Gogh is to be presented with the revered cotton coat of the first Manchu emperor as symbol of his new powers. But complications arise: the emperor plots against Gogh; Gogh plots against the emperor; Turandot changes her mind; the Manchu coat is stolen. Kai Ho's forces end the rule of the Tuis, the emperor, and Gogh. The corrupt rulers are swept away by the power of the people, as the last line of the play, spoken by one of Kai Ho's soldiers, indicates: "This is what you were, and now away with you!"[25]

According to Brecht's preface, "The play *Turandot, or The Congress of Whitewashers,* is part of a larger body of my literary works, which as of now consist mostly of plans and drafts. It incorporates a novel, *The Fall of the Tuis,* a volume of stories, *Tui-Stories,* a sequence of playlets called *Tui-Pranks,* and a small volume of treatises, *The Art of Adulation, and Other Tricks.* All of these works, which have engaged the author's attention for several decades, deal with the misuse of the intellect."[26] While in exile, he wrote the fragmentary Tui novel (from 1939 to 1943), but of the treatises he mentioned, only two have been found. None of the Tui-pranks have come to light.

The term Tui is derived from the first letters of "*t*ellect-*u*al-*in*," Brecht's inversion of intellectual. It is his name for intellectuals whose intellectual capacities can be hired by people in power. The Tuis serve as "whitewashers," "hired heads," "lessors of intellect," "formulators," and "evaders."[27]

The play is in many ways a counterversion to Brecht's *Galileo.* In *Galileo,* Brecht, in his own words, had "described the dawn of the age of reason." In *Turandot,* he intended to portray "the dusk of reason, namely that kind of reason, which, toward the end of the sixteenth century, had opened the age of capitalism."[28]

In notes for the Tui novel in 1934, Brecht made clear what he meant to say with the parable of *Turandot:* "The golden age of the Tuis is the liberal republic [the Weimar Republic], but Tuism reached its peak in the Third Reich." Under Hitler, who in the play is called Gogher Gogh, the people had fallen into the hands of "the most corrupt and lowest Tuis."[29] Brecht blamed many of the German intellectuals for paving the road to fascism.

The main opponents of Gogher Gogh and his regime in Brecht's play are the armies of Kai Ho and the writings of Ka Me—thinly veiled allusions to Mao Tse-tung and Karl Marx.

The play can also be interpreted from a strictly Marxist point of view as Brecht pointed out in an entry in his *Work Journal.* In Brecht's view, *Turandot* was a comedy similar to Molière's *The Miser.* Each play, as Brecht saw it, exposes and ridicules one weakness in a capitalistically organized society: avarice (*The Miser*) and unproductive thought (*Turandot*). "In *Turandot,* mere formulative, unproductive thought is caught at a point in time when the capitalist system does not allow a further development of the productive forces; therefore, it appears impractical, ridiculous."[30] In this context, the Tuis serve as whitewashers for capitalism.

Since Brecht never saw the play staged, we do not know what changes he would have made after a production had tested the text. But in his notes to the play, Brecht gave us some hints as to how he wanted it performed:

> It must be possible to change the stage quickly; the street scenes and the imperial palace can be played before the small curtain. The scenery must be light with poetic and realistic allusions. The Whitewashers' Congress is best played on a revolving stage without a curtain. The Tuis are

characterized by little hats after the fashion of Tibetan and European priests. The hats differ according to rank—more or less opulent—and are different in color. The costumes can be mixtures, based on Chinese costumes. The play must be acted with tempo.[31]

This work is probably one of Brecht's least-known plays. It was not available in print until 1967, and as yet there is no generally available English translation.

The play was first performed on 5 February 1969 in the Schauspielhaus Zürich (director: Benno Besson, sets: Horst Sagert; Turandot: Erla Prollius; Gogher Gogh: Peter Ehrlich).

The reviewer of the *Neue Zürcher Zeitung* claimed that, measured against other plays by Brecht, this play "occupies a rather modest place" in the hierarchy of Brecht's works. But the production on the whole was a success, particularly the acting and the sets: "The audience applauded enthusiastically." This critic also tried to fathom why the play had its world premiere in Zurich rather than in Brecht's own theater in East Berlin. He drew a parallel between the play's Tuis and the political functionaries in the east who have the task of justifying the questionable actions of their governments to the people.[32] (An example of such an episode is the invasion of Czechoslovakia by Russian and East German troops in 1968, in order to squelch a move toward a more liberal form of communism.) When Brecht, the Marxist playwright, wrote the play, he presumably had the capitalist world in mind. The financial speculation and manipulation described in the play is indeed possible only under capitalism. But history has shown that the communist countries are certainly not without their Tuis, a fact Brecht must have been aware of when he wrote the play in 1953, the year of Stalin's death.

In 1969 the San Francisco Mime Troupe staged an

English-language premiere of *Turandot* in an outdoor performance in a County Park in the San Francisco Bay Area (first performance: 12 March 1969; translation: Juris Swendson; director: R. G. Davis; Gogher Gogh: R. G. Davis). Davis used the highly formal and presentational form of the Peking Opera, mixed with the company's own commedia-style. Eleven actors were cast in fifty-five, later forty-five roles. Reviews, though mixed, tended to be unfavorable. The play apparently seemed beyond the artistic abilities of the Mime Troupe and not a suitable vehicle for their intentions.[33]

Early in 1973, *Turandot* was staged by the Berliner Ensemble in East Berlin (directors: Peter Kupke and Wolfgang Pintzka; sets: Karl von Appen; A Sha Sen: Martin Flörchinger; emperor: Curt Bois; Turandot: Olga Strub; Gogher Gogh: Franz Viehmann).

The East German critic Manfred Nössig pointed out that the play was directed against the misuse of intellectual skills. In addition it was a parable for a corrupt capitalist society.[34] The events were seen from the point of view of the peasant A Sha Sen. He showed "caution and wisdom, craftiness and courage, an unalterable will to know, and, most of all, development" (Nössig). The artistic highlight of the evening was the whitewashers' congress, with outstanding performances by Ekkehard Schall, Stefan Lisewski and Dieter Knaup as Hi Wei, Ki Leh, and Munka Du, the three leaders of the academic Tuis. Karl von Appen's sets were praised for being simple but effective.

Turandot is not among Brecht's great plays. The unrevised text is not always clear, and the ending is unsatisfactory. As a parable portraying the rise of Adolf Hitler, Brecht's *The Resistible Rise of Arturo Ui* is a much better play. But Brecht never considered *Turandot* ready for the stage. However with a good cast, an imaginative director, and appropriate adjustments the play can be staged successfully, as the Zurich premiere proved.

Although Brecht had particularly in mind the German intellectuals, who, at best, did nothing to prevent Hitler from coming to power, the play has not lost its point. The misuse of intellectual abilities is still with us, as are Tuis and whitewashers.

Brecht's Adaptations

Adaptation is an important feature of Brecht's work as a playwright and a producer-director. Many of his plays can be considered as adaptations, for example *The Threepenny Opera* (of Gay's *Beggar's Opera*), *The Mother* (of Gorky's novel *The Mother*), and his *Lehrstücke He Who Says Yes* and its counterpart *He Who Says No* (of the Japanese No play *Taniko*). Brecht's play *The Round Heads and the Pointed Heads* started out as an adaptation of Shakespeare's *Measure for Measure*.

It is often difficult to determine when a play ceases to be an adaptation in the strict sense and becomes the playwright's own creation. In a broad sense, all of Brecht's plays are adaptations. Shaping a given topic or a familiar theme in his own ways was an intrinsic part of Brecht's dramatic concept. A large number of his plays are counterversions to or re-interpretations of well known plays or themes. This concept of counterversion is the literary expression of Brecht, the anti-bourgeois, and Brecht, the Marxist. In his earlier works, his attitude was mainly anti-bourgeois. As a Marxist playwright he supported the

Marxist effort to reinterpret history and reshape society according to Marxist-Leninist principles.

Brecht's adaptations in the stricter sense are those plays which he, in cooperation with others, adapted for specific productions, mostly for the Berliner Ensemble. Brecht himself considered them adaptations, and he planned to publish them separately.

Six of his adaptations are now published as volume six of the twenty-volume Suhrkamp edition of Brecht's work of 1967 (English translations in volume nine of the Manheim-Willett edition of Brecht's works). They are: Sophocles, *Antigone* (1947); Jacob Michael Reinhold Lenz (a German playwright of the so-called "Storm and Stress" period who lived from 1751 to 1792), *The Tutor* (1949–50); Shakespeare, *Coriolanus* (1951–53); Anna Seghers (a German prose writer, born in 1900), *The Trial of Joan of Arc at Rouen 1431* (1952); Molière, *Don Juan* (1952–53); and George Farquhar, *The Recruiting Officer* (1945–55; Brecht's new title is *Trumpets and Drums*).

These are not Brecht's only adaptations. Among his other adaptations are: Christoper Marlowe, *Edward II* (together with Feuchtwanger, in Munich, 1923–24); John Webster, *The Duchess of Malfi* (together with H. R. Hays and W. H. Auden, in Santa Monica and New York, 1943–45, first performed in Boston in September of 1946); and Gerhart Hauptmann (a German playwright, 1862–1946), *The Beaver Coat* and *The Red Cock* (*Biberpelz* and *Roter Hahn*, 1950–51).

In his adaptations, Brecht pursued two objectives, one artistic and one sociopolitical. He wanted to show the beauty of the dramatic literature of past ages on a modern stage: "The old works have value, . . . beauty and truth of their own. It is up to us to discover them."[35] In addition, he wanted to bring out the sociopolitical significance of the plays he selected. In Lenz's play *The Tutor*, for example, he wanted to expose the servility and docility of the Germans which was instilled by the feudal class and perpetuated by generations of German philosophers and schoolmasters. In *Coriolanus* Brecht intended to destroy the belief that great men are irreplaceable. His adaptation of *Don Juan* was meant to demonstrate the antisocial and parasitic nature of the hero.

Brecht combined the qualities and abilities of a playwright with those of a producer-director and practical theater man. In his adaptations we see more of Brecht, the producer-director.

BRECHT AND AMERICA

After World War I, many German writers, including Brecht, looked to America for new ideas. To them, Europe no longer offered any inspiration. On 18 June 1920 Brecht noted in his diary: "How boring this Germany is for me! It is a good country with beautiful pale colors and plains, but what inhabitants! Degenerated peasants whose coarseness does not even give birth to fabulous monsters, only slow bestialization; a middle class grown fat, and fading intellectuals! The alternative: America!"[1]

In their enthusiasm, many of the young writers in the early 1920s embraced everything American—jazz, sports (particularly boxing), and also the language. They even changed their names. Brecht's friend Hellmut Herzfelde changed his name to John Heartfield, and young Brecht himself changed his first name from Bertold to Bertolt and Bert. America was considered to be the land of technological progress, rapid change, and individual freedom, a land in which every hard-working individual could succeed, unhampered by the burden of a sterile tradition.

No modern German writer occupied himself more with America than did Brecht. Numerous works, fragments, and notes bear evidence of this. But from his school years in Augsburg to his death in East Berlin, Brecht's view of America underwent several changes.

For the young Brecht, America was an exotic country of impenetrable jungles, wide open prairies, and towering cities. The earliest manifestation of his fascination with America was his Walt Whitman-style poem, "Song of the Railroad Gang of Fort Donald," written in 1916.

In 1920, Brecht read two novels set in Chicago: *The Jungle* by Upton Sinclair and *The Wheel* by the Danish novelist Johannes V. Jensen. Both novels had a lasting influence upon the fledgling playwright. "The cold Chicago," as Brecht called the city, is the setting for several of his plays: *In the Jungle of Cities, Saint Joan of the Stockyards,* and *The Resistible Rise of Arturo Ui.*

In the 1920s especially, Brecht preferred to use the American scene for his works. Thus in 1924 he planned to write an opera entitled "Man from Manhattan." In 1925 he wrote scenes for a play he called "Dan Drew." It is based on Daniel Drew, railroad king Vanderbilt's arch rival. (About three-quarters of it was written when Brecht put it aside.)

An eager reader of newspapers (the Brecht Archives contain numerous clippings he saved), he also showed a particular interest in the natural catastrophes that sometimes afflicted the United States, such as tornados and hurricanes. They inspired such projects as *The Destruction of Miami, the Paradise City,* and *The Flood.* These plays were never completed, but some of the same motifs are found in the opera *The Rise and Fall of the City of Mahagonny.* This opera contains, in the original German text, such "American" songs as "The Alabama Song"—"Oh moon of Alabama, we now must say goodbye"—and, in the earlier version, "The Telephone Song." The city of Mahagonny, which Brecht placed on the West coast of the United States, is threatened by a hurricane moving west from Pensacola, Florida.

In *Joe Fleischhacker* (also known as *Wheat,* 1927), Brecht planned to show the disintegration of the Mitchell family, which moved from the great plains to the city of Chicago. They are destroyed when the speculator Joe Fleischhacker corners the wheat market. This project, too, remained a fragment, but it was an important step on the way to *Saint Joan of the Stockyards.*

Critics have noted that Brecht's details about Chicago and other places in the United States are often vague or simply wrong. This is true, and some of it is certainly due to ignorance of the actual geography of the place. But we must also bear in mind that it was never his intention to write naturalistic plays. Brecht knew, of course, that ships do not sail directly from Chicago to Tahiti (as they do in *In the Jungle of Cities,* forty years before the St. Lawrence Seaway was built). But all of this was part of his mythological America and served his dramatic technique of epic theater. "Chicago," for example, was a much wider concept than just the real city itself.

In the early 1920s Brecht saw himself as the poet of the big city. As he wrote in his famous poem "Of Poor B.B.," written in 1920, he felt at home in the asphalt cities. In this early anarchic-nihilistic phase even the cold, man-made city jungle of Chicago had a positive value for him.

During the mid-1920s, however, Brecht's attitude toward America underwent a gradual, but radical, change. By the time he wrote *Saint Joan,* he had converted to Marxism. Consequently he saw America as a stronghold of capitalism and, thus, as a country of exploitation and social injustice.

The *Mahagonny* opera still betrays some of Brecht's earlier fascination with America. But the ballet *The Seven Deadly Sins* is a biting satire on the capitalistic society. And especially his *Saint Joan* play, set in Chicago's stockyards, is a virulent attack on the capitalist system.

In his last play with an American setting, *The Resistible Rise of Arturo Ui,* Brecht employed the gangster world of Chicago in the 1920s as a means of explaining the rise of Hitler to the capitalist world, particularly America. For Brecht, the methods of gangster bosses like Al Capone were not much different from those of prominent capitalists like Morgan and those of the politicians, the capitalists' puppets. And, as the epilogue to *Arturo Ui* indicates, the danger of fascism did not pass with Hitler's defeat. According to Lenin, fascism is an inevitable offshoot of capitalism, and the potential for fascism exists so long as capitalism exists.

Brecht's attitude did not change when he came to live in the United States. He felt isolated and out of touch in his exile in Santa Monica. The blatant commercialism that permeated every aspect of life, including the arts, was abhorrent to him. He tried to write film scripts, since he did have to earn a living, but the only script that was accepted by a producer, *Hangmen Also Die,* was so mutilated in the actual filming that he never repeated the attempt. By the time he was called before the House Committee on Un-American Activities to testify in its inquiries into communist activities in the film industry in 1947, he was ready to leave the United States.

But upon his return to East Berlin, he did not turn his back on "the new world." If anything, his interest in the United States increased, but his opinions of the American political system grew more and more negative. He deplored the steadily widening gap between

America's revolutionary origins and its present day policies and directions. America had betrayed its revolution and turned reactionary. In his view, the country that had just defeated fascism in Germany was rapidly turning into a fascist country itself. America was in the throes of the McCarthy era from 1951 to 1954. Senator Joseph McCarthy (Republican, Wisconsin, 1909–57), as chairman of the Senate committee investigating subversive influences in the United States government, was bullying and terrorizing all those who had ever had affiliations or sympathy with the left. In 1954, he was finally censured by his senatorial colleagues. Brecht saw parallels between the McCarthy era and the end of the Weimar Republic, when Hitler came to power, and everything "un-German" began to be ruthlessly persecuted.

In his eyes, America had become the major threat to world peace. He found it particularly shocking that it was America that encouraged the rearmament of West Germany and the development of the hydrogen bomb. He carefully studied the Rosenberg and the Oppenheimer cases. (Ethel and Julius Rosenberg were executed in 1953 for allegedly passing atomic secrets to the Soviet Union. Dr. J. Robert Oppenheimer had supervised the making of the first atomic bomb. But when he opposed the development of the hydrogen bomb, he was suspended as chairman of the advisory committee to the Atomic Energy Commission and declared a security risk. It was alleged that he had harbored communist leanings in the 1930s. He was cleared in 1963. He died in 1967.) Brecht deplored Albert Einstein's naiveté in making his services available to the American power elite. His early death prevented him from writing a play on Einstein's life (for which he had already gathered a good deal of material). It was no coincidence that he planned to stage *Galileo* at that time, a play about the social responsibilities of a scientist. (He died while the production was in preparation.)

With clear reference to the West German rearmament, he wrote an adaptation of George Farquhar's *The Recruiting Officer* (Brecht's title was *Trumpets and Drums,* written in 1954 and 1955). The point he wanted to make in the play was that the Americans only pursued selfish—and mostly financial—interests in their creation of the new West German army (so they could sell more arms).

But for all his criticism of the American system, he always admired the American people and claimed that they were manipulated by those in power: "One hundred and fifty million industrious people, alert, sober-minded, and trained in many trades and practical matters, find themselves under a regime that is insulting their intelligence and love of justice."[2]

America, in turn, did not accept Brecht and his works with open arms. Before and during the Nazi period, Brecht was hardly known on this side of the Atlantic. In 1933, his *Threepenny Opera* was brushed off as a poor imitation of Gay's *Beggar's Opera.* When the didactic play *He Who Says Yes* was performed in New York in the same year, the critics did not even mention Brecht's name (only the composer, Weill). A critic who saw the 1935 production of *The Mother* wrote: "Whether Brecht is the playwright's first or last name, the program saith not."[3]

The Nazis quickly squelched the violently antifascist writer just as his star began to rise in Germany. In exile he was deprived of the opportunity to gain recognition through productions of his plays. He expressed his frustration in an entry into his *Work Journal* on 30 June 1940: "It is impossible to finish a play without a stage, *the proof of the pudding. . . .*"[4] (The italicized words are in English in the German text.) And Hitler's war certainly did not help the production of German drama abroad. After the war, especially during the McCarthy era and the cold war, Brecht's Marxist philosophy alienated him from American producers. And, as the Brecht scholar Ulrich Weisstein pointed out, the production and exaggerated acclaim of *The Private Life of the Master Race,* staged in 1945 in Berkeley and New York, proved more an obstacle than a help so far as productions of Brecht's great plays were concerned.[5] The exaggerated acclaim of this play's artistic significance by some critics (among them Eric Bentley) overshadowed Brecht's major achievements in his other plays.

It was only in the late 1950s that Brecht began to gain wider recognition in America. By the late 1960s Brecht's work was known wherever there was interest in serious theater. His acceptance, even popularity, on college campuses goes back to the early 1950s, when he was regarded primarily as a great innovator of the theater. Many of his plays were performed in college theaters between 1948 and 1953. In those years not one Brecht play was produced on Broadway. In the second half of the 1950s it was *The Threepenny Opera* in Marc Blitzstein's adaptation that enthralled millions for eight glorious seasons. (This popularity may perhaps be attributed largely to Kurt Weill's catchy music.) The only other Brecht play Broadway offered in the 1950s was *The Good Woman of Setzuan,* which ran for twenty-four performances in the 1956–57 season. Brecht had become by then one of the great names in European theater admired by Americans. The 1956 edition of *Theater World* described him in his obituary as "one of Germany's leading playwrights" but he was seldom performed in commercial theaters.

Although Brecht was a fervent supporter of the socialist cause after his conversion to Marxism, his plays were not readily accepted by the socialist theater in America. To a large extent, this was due to the unpleasant encounter between Brecht and the most famous of all American Socialist theaters, the Theater Union in New York City, in 1935, elicited by their production of his play *The Mother*. In his detailed analysis of this production Lee Baxandall states, "The effects of the Theater Union fiasco on the American stage were . . . lasting, for doors slammed shut to Epic Theater."[6]

In the world of the commercial theater, success on Broadway (and to some extent, off Broadway) is still the leading indicator of success with the public in general. That Brecht's plays have never, with the exception of *The Threepenny Opera*, found appreciation on Broadway is not really surprising. As Brooks Atkinson writes in his excellent book *Broadway:* "Broadway . . . is a holiday promenade not equipped to cope with intellectual problems. . . . It does not want its mind improved. It wants to be bewitched and entertained."[7] It is obvious that this audience would not be interested in plays that were written to appeal to the intellect. But there were other factors, too. Many critics objected to Brecht on ideological grounds. Moreover, when a theater must operate at a profit, Brecht is too great a financial risk. (German theaters, and many other European theaters, on the other hand, are substantially subsidized by local and state governments.)

Then, there was—and to some extent there still is— the general and often astounding ignorance of many producers and critics about Brecht's theater and his intentions. Many of the producers and directors who studied Brecht's theories in detail, approached the plays from such a theoretical angle that the result was sterile, stereotyped epic theater.

They overemphasized the outward trappings of epic theater at the expense of vitality on stage. In their intent to imitate the famous Berliner Ensemble as

closely as possible, they often overlooked the fact that
the working conditions in New York City are quite
different from those of the Berliner Ensemble in East
Berlin.

This is also true of many college productions, although Brecht, in general, fared much better on college campuses than in the commercial theater. Martin
Esslin noted in 1961: "During the author's lifetime . . .
Brecht seems to have been performed more in the great
country of capitalism than anywhere else except West
(not East) Germany."[8] Brecht himself preferred to be
performed in noncommercial theaters. He wrote in a
letter to Eric Bentley on 12 November 1949: "I prefer
the university productions to the commercial ones."[9]

It may seem ironic that Brecht, who wanted his
political theater to reach the widest possible audience, would be satisfied with a campus community.
But Brecht's tactical remark of 1949 must be regarded
in context. A campus production was and still is better than no production at all. And, as recent developments have shown, after years of fruition, important
impulses have spread from college campus productions into surrounding communities. Many of them
have gone unnoticed. One interesting example came
to light at the Fourth Congress of the International
Brecht Society held in November 1976 in Austin,
Texas. Ian McLachlan, Professor of English and Comparative Literature at Trent University in Peterborough, Ontario, discussed his 1976 production of *The
Measures Taken* in Peterborough, staged jointly by
actors, students, and workers of local factories. In
order to establish a link from the past to the present,
the play was paired with a staged reenactment of
Brecht's hearing before the House Committee on Un-
American Activities in 1947, at which chief investigator Stripling himself quoted extensively from Brecht's
The Measures Taken. The production was performed

on campus and in local factories, and, according to Mr. McLachlan, it worked "exceedingly well."

Brecht is still widely produced on college campuses, but the number of interesting and effective productions in other than campus theaters has also increased. To name only a few: *The Good Woman of Setzuan* by the Synthaxis Theater Company in Los Angeles in 1973; *The Resistible Rise of Arturo Ui* in Minneapolis' Guthrie Theater in 1968, and in Chicago's Goodman Theater in 1975; even the most doctrinal of all Brecht's plays, *The Measures Taken,* in Los Angeles in 1973, staged by the Center Theater Group (together with *The Little Mahagonny*), and in New York City's Public Theater in 1974.

Brecht has also inspired such theater groups in America as the San Francisco Mime Troupe and El Teatro Campesino. When the latter group, which developed out of the Chicano-dominated grape pickers' strike in California in 1965, gave guest performances in the Westside Theater of New York's Chelsea Center in October of 1974, their play *La Carpa de los Rasquachis* (*The Tent of the Underdogs*) seemed to Clive Barnes of *The New York Times* to be "a mixture of morality play, street theater, and Bertolt Brecht. Brecht would certainly have approved a key line in the play—'There are only two kinds of people in this world, those who take us and those who are taken.'" It was pure political theater, and for Barnes "a salutary experience."[10]

And Lee Baxandall concluded: "As a result of the emergence of a thoroughly critical outlook among a considerable and growing number of Americans, Brecht has gained a positive Americanization to an extent not to be thought possible a few years ago. . . . His life work has passed the barrier of its national and political culture."[11]

IN CONCLUSION

On the international scene, Bertolt Brecht has emerged as one of the most influential playwrights of the twentieth century—in both east and west. His plays are performed all over the world. Modern theater cannot be grasped without a knowledge of Brecht, as the famous producer Peter Brook points out in his book *The Empty Space*. He calls Brecht "the strongest, most influential, and the most radical theater man of our time." He goes on to say: "No one seriously concerned with the theater can bypass Brecht. Brecht is the key figure of our time, and all theater work today at some point starts or returns to his statements and achievements."[1]

The sources for Brecht's plays are as varied as his plays themselves. Through his sources Brecht is connected with the large body of German and international literature and culture. To name only a few writers and genres, Brecht is indebted to: the Japanese No play; the Chinese theater, notably the actor Mei Lan-fang and the playwright Li Hsing-tao; the Bible; the *commedia dell'arte;* Jesuit drama; Aristophanes; Homer; Pindar; Sophocles; Goethe; Hölderlin; Schiller; Wagner; Molière; Rimbaud; Verlaine; Villon, Gay;

Kipling; Marlowe; Shakespeare; Shaw; Sinclair; R. L. Stevenson; Synge; Gorky; Grieg; Hašek; Stanislavski.

Like Shakespeare or Bernard Shaw before him, Brecht borrowed freely from other writers. He was indifferent to their ideological persuasion so long as their creations in some way served his dramatic purpose. Brecht's originality lies not in the invention of new materials but in the careful adaptation of the heritage of world literature for his own purposes. His dramatic work is characterized by a very original and successful integration of economics, politics, and world literature.

It is true that some of Brecht's plays deal only with particular situations at particular times in Germany. Such plays as *Fear and Misery of the Third Reich* may be of more historic interest than contemporary relevance today. But the parabolic form of most of his plays allows for a much wider and much more general frame of reference.

Brecht's plays are neither pure form nor pure politics, but a highly artistic blend of both. Brecht himself stressed that a play's effectiveness is directly proportional to its artistic qualities. In order to make Brecht's plays meaningful for another environment, Brecht's own principles should be applied to his own plays: adapt them to different times and different circumstances. A fixed canon of untouchable masterpieces would mean that Brecht had ceased to be the provocative playwright he always wanted to be.

NOTES

Introduction: Life, Times, and Work

1. Bertolt Brecht, *Tagebücher 1920–1922: Autobiographische Aufzeichnungen 1920–1954* (Diaries 1920–1922. Autobiographical Notes 1920–1954) (Frankfurt on the Main: Suhrkamp, 1975), p. 42. Cited as *Diary*.

2. *Diary*, p. 61.

3. Klaus Völker, *Bertolt Brecht: Eine Biographie* (München, Wien: Hanser Verlag, 1976), p. 13.

4. Bertolt Brecht, *Gesammelte Werke* (Collected Works), vol. 14 (Frankfurt on the Main: Suhrkamp, 1967), p. 1404. In the following, this edition is cited as GW.

5. GW 14, 1402.

6. See GW 14, 1403–04.

7. GW 15, 26.

8. *Diary*, p. 109 (19 April 1921).

9. *Diary*, p. 122.

10. *Diary*, p. 186.

11. *Diary*, p. 125.

12. *Diary*, p. 109 (18 April 1921).

13. *Diary*, p. 168 (25 October 1921).

14. *Diary*, p. 108 (18 April 1921).

15. *Diary*, p. 138 (17 June 1921).

16. *Diary*, p. 98 (24 March 1921).

17. *Diary*, p. 98 (23 March 1921).

18. *Diary*, p. 136 (4 June 1921).

19. *Diary*, p. 195 (2 May 1920).

20. Reinhold Grimm, *Bertolt Brecht* (Stuttgart: Metzler, 1971), p. 10.

21. Bernard Reich, "München 1923," Bertolt Brecht, *Leben Eduards des Zweiten von England. Vorlage, Texte und Materi-*

alien, ed. Reinhold Grimm (Frankfurt on the Main: Suhrkamp, 1968), pp. 242–63.

22. Arnolt Bronnen, *Tage mit Bertolt Brecht* (Munich: Desch, 1960), p. 98.

23. John B. Watson, *Psychology from the Standpoint of the Behaviorist,* Philadelphia, 1924, p. xii.

24. GW 20, 46.

25. Reinhold Grimm, *Brecht und die Weltliteratur* (Nürnberg: Hans Carl, 1961), p. 35.

26. GW 16, 714.

27. GW 15, 202.

28. GW 9, 725.

29. Bertolt Brecht, *Arbeitsjournal* (Work Journal), vol. 1 (Frankfurt on the Main: Suhrkamp, 1973), p. 68 (7 November 1939). Cited as *Work Journal.*

30. *Work Journal,* vol. 1, p. 171.

31. *Work Journal,* vol. 1, p. 285.

32. For more details, see John Fuegi, "The Soviet Union and Brecht: The Exile's Choice," *Brecht Heute—Brecht Today,* vol. 2 (Frankfurt on the Main: Athenäum, 1972), pp. 209–21.

33. GW 10, 848.

34. Reinhard Heydrich (1904–42), high-ranking SS officer and deputy governor of the protectorate of Bohemia and Moravia, which the Nazis created after their destruction of the state of Czechoslovakia. In 1942, Heydrich was assassinated by Czech nationalists and resistance fighters. The SS (*Schutzstaffel*) developed from a private army to protect the Nazi Party in the 1920s to the most loyal terror organization of the Third Reich.

35. *Work Journal,* vol. 1, p. 291 and 293 (8 and 9 August 1941).

36. See Chapter II for a discussion of Brecht's dramatic theory.

37. *Work Journal,* vol. 2, p. 848.

38. *Work Journal,* vol. 2, p. 889.

39. Wolfgang Bernard Fleischmann, ed., *Encyclopedia of World Literature in the Twentieth Century* (New York: Ungar, 1971), p. 299.

40. For details on this debate, consult Eugene Lunn, "Marxism and Art in the Era of Stalin and Hitler: The Brecht-Lukacs Debate," *New German Critique,* no. 3 (Fall 1974): 12–44.

41. GW 10, 1009.

42. GW 10, 1008.

BRECHT'S THEORY OF THEATER

1. Brecht explained his theory of theater in numerous articles, essays, annotations to plays, reviews, diary notes, and dis-

cussions. Some of his more important theoretical works are the theater reviews from his years as a critic for the Augsburg paper *Volkswillen* (1919 to 1921); annotations to *The Rise and Fall of the City of Mahagonny* (1930), *The Threepenny Opera* (1931), and *The Mother* (1932 and 1935–36); the essays "Dialectic Theater" (1939–40); and two larger works, *The Purchase of Brass* and *The Short Organum for the Theater*.

2. GW 15, 241.

3. GW 15, 301.

4. GW 15, 302.

5. GW 15, 302.

6. A thorough and detailed study of the function of estrangement effects in Brecht's works is to be found in Reinhold Grimm's *Bertolt Brecht: Die Struktur seines Werkes* (Nürnberg: Hans Carl, 1968).

7. GW 5, 2128.

8. GW 5, 2025.

9. *The Purchase of Brass*, "inspired by Galileo's Dialogues," as Brecht noted, was written between 1937 and 1951, but it was never finished. Brecht intended this work to be a staged discussion of his epic theater. A philosopher, an actor, an actress, and a *Dramaturg* discuss the principles of epic theater. Their discussions are interspersed with practical examples, for which Brecht wrote several "Practice Pieces for Actors," such as *Murder in the Porter's Lodge* (based on Shakespeare's *Macbeth*, Act II) and "The Quarrel of the Fishwives" (based on Schiller's *Mary Stuart*, Act III). *The Purchase of Brass* was never performed during Brecht's lifetime. But after his death, the Berliner Ensemble prepared a production that had its premiere on 12 October 1963; Ekkehard Schall acted the role of the philosopher.

10. GW 16, 546.

11. *The Short Organum* (which was, according to Brecht, "a summary of *The Purchase of Brass*") was written in 1948. Its seventy-seven paragraphs, together with several additions from 1954, are a concise outline of the kind of theater Brecht envisioned: "It describes the theater in the age of science." The title is derived from Francis Bacon's *Novum Organum*, which, in turn, refers to Aristotle's *Organon*. Aristotle's philosophical writings on logic are known as "Organon," a "tool" to acquire knowledge. Bacon's *Novum Organum* summarized his theory of logic. Bacon, 1561–1626, stressed the importance of inductive, empirical thought, whereas Aristotle's logic rests upon the deductive process of thought.

12. GW 16, 683.

13. GW 15, 453.

14. GW 15, 454.

15. GW 16, 756.

16. GW 16, 757.

17. GW 16, 759–60.
18. GW 16, 760.
19. GW 15, 428.
20. *Diary,* p. 17–18 (7 July 1920).
21. *Diary,* p. 13 (27 June 1920).
22. *Diary,* p. 15 (1 July 1920).
23. *Diary,* p. 15 (1 July 1920).
24. *Diary,* p. 187.
25. GW 17, 1008–09.
26. GW 17, 1009–10.
27. GW 17, 1011.
28. GW 17, 1010.
29. GW 17, 1036.
30. GW 17, 1144.
31. GW 15, 305.
32. GW 15, 305.
33. The quotation is taken from John Fuegi, *The Essential Brecht* (Los Angeles: Hennessey & Ingalls, Inc., 1972), p. 1.
34. GW 15, 267.
35. Wolfgang Roth, "Working with Bertolt Brecht," *Brecht Heute-Brecht Today,* vol. 2 (1972), p. 132.
36. Giorgio Strehler, "Begegnung mit Brecht," *Theater der Zeit,* no. 11 (1974): 37.

AUGSBURG, MUNICH, BERLIN

1. GW 1, 14.
2. GW 1, 15.
3. GW 1, 23.
4. GW 1, 22.
5. GW 1, 25.
6. GW 1, 29.
7. GW 1, 35.
8. GW 1, 41.
9. GW 1, 41.
10. GW 1, 42.
11. GW 1, 53.
12. GW 1, 56.
13. GW 1, 60.
14. GW 1, 62.
15. GW 1, 63.
16. GW 1, 64.
17. GW 1, 64.
18. GW 1, 66.
19. GW 1, 67.
20. Völker, *Brecht Biographie,* p. 54.
21. Dieter Schmidt, *"Baal" und der junge Brecht* (Stuttgart: Metzler, 1966), p. 62.

22. GW 17, 954.

23. Hans Otto Münsterer, *Brecht, Erinnerungen aus den Jahren 1917–22.* Zürich: Arche, 1963.

24. GW 17, 954.

25. GW 17, 954–55.

26. A detailed discussion can be found in Dieter Schmidt's books: *Baal under der junge Brecht* (Stuttgart: Metzler, 1966); *Baal: Der böse Baal, der asoziale: Texte, Varianten und Materialien* (Frankfurt on the Main: Suhrkamp, 1968).

27. GW 1, 24.

28. GW 1, 18.

29. GW 1, 59.

30. GW 1, 53.

31. GW 1, 17.

32. GW 1, 16.

33. GW 17, 947.

34. GW 17, 948.

35. The reviews of *Baal* in Leipzig and Berlin mentioned here were taken and translated from Günther Rühle's book *Theater für die Republik* (Frankfurt on the Main: Fischer, 1967), pp. 486–93 and 683–90.

36. *Evening Standard,* 8 February 1963.

37. *The Observer Weekend Review,* 10 February 1963.

38. *The New York Times,* 7 May 1965.

39. *New York Herald Tribune,* 7 May 1965.

40. Münsterer, p. 99.

41. The quotations are taken from Lion Feuchtwanger, "Bertolt Brecht Presented to the British," in *Brecht: As They Knew Him,* ed. Hubert Witt, trans. John Peet (New York: International Publishers, 1974), p. 17.

42. GW 1, 77.

43. GW 1, 76–77.

44. GW 1, 79.

45. GW 1, 83.

46. GW 1, 85.

47. GW 1, 87.

48. GW 1, 89.

49. GW 1, 92.

50. GW 1, 97.

51. GW 1, 105.

52. GW 1, 114.

53. GW 1, 114.

54. GW 1, 117–18.

55. GW 1, 118.

56. GW 1, 120.

57. GW 1, 123.

58. GW 17, 965.

59. Martin Esslin, *Brecht: The Man and His Work* (Garden City: Anchor Books, 1961), p. 279.

60. GW 1, 70 and 123.
61. GW 1, 123.
62. GW 17, 945.
63. GW 17, 945.
64. GW 17, 946.
65. GW 17, 967.
66. GW 1, 70.
67. Rühle, p. 402.
68. Rühle, pp. 406–08.
69. Bronnen, p. 104.
70. Rühle, pp. 408–10.
71. *The New York Times,* 18 May 1967.
72. Münsterer, p. 141.
73. GW 7, 2733–34.
74. *The New York Times,* 25 November 1970.
75. GW 7, 2749.
76. Münsterer, p. 141.
77. GW 7, 2773.
78. See Herbert Knust and Leonie Marx, "Brechts Lux in Tenebris," *Monatshefte,* 65, no. 2 (1973): 117–25.
79. Herbert Knust, "Brechts Fischzug," *Brecht Heute-Brecht Today,* vol. 1 (Frankfurt on the Main: Athenäum, 1971), pp. 98–109.
80. GW 1, 126.
81. GW 1, 128.
82. GW 1, 134.
83. Bertolt Brecht, *Im Dickicht der Städte: Erstfassung und Materialien* (In the Jungle of Cities: First Version and Other Materials), edited by Gisela E. Bahr (Frankfurt on the Main: Suhrkamp, 1968), p. 136.
84. GW 1, 186.
85. GW 1, 187.
86. GW 1, 187.
87. GW 1, 190.
88. GW 1, 190.
89. GW 1, 193.
90. GW 17, 948.
91. Bertolt Brecht, *Im Dickicht der Städte: Erstfassung und Materialien.*
92. GW 15, 69.
93. Brecht, *Materials to In the Jungle of Cities,* pp. 140–41.
94. *Ibid.,* p. 134.
95. GW 17, 970.
96. The reviews of the Munich and Berlin performances can be found in Rühle, pp. 446–453 and pp. 564–572.
97. *The New York Times,* 21 December 1960.
98. *New York Herald Tribune,* 21 December 1960.
99. *The New York Times,* 1 March 1970.

100. *Theater der Zeit* (an East German theater journal), no. 2 (1973): 15.

101. *Theater heute,* no. 5 (1971).

102. GW 1, 302.

103. GW 1, 315.

104. GW 1, 330.

105. GW 1, 333.

106. GW 1, 335.

107. GW 1, 336.

108. GW 1, 348.

109. GW 1, 338.

110. GW 1, 338.

111. GW 1, 349.

112. GW 1, 361.

113. GW 1, 362.

114. GW 1, 369.

115. GW 17, 977.

116. GW 17, 978.

117. GW 17, 978.

118. GW 17, 978.

119. GW 17, 987–88.

120. GW 17, 951.

121. Reviews of the Darmstadt and Berlin productions in Rühle, pp. 728–735 and pp. 1068–1076.

122. *The New York Times,* 15 April 1928.

123. Rühle, p. 1076.

124. *New York Herald Tribune,* 19 September 1962.

125. *The New York Times,* 19 September 1962.

126. *The New York Times,* 20 September 1962.

127. *New York Herald Tribune,* 20 September 1962.

128. *New York Herald Tribune,* 19 September 1962.

129. *The New York Times,* 19 September 1962.

130. *Theater der Zeit,* no. 7 (1967).

131. *Theater heute,* no. 4 (1967).

132. *The New York Times,* 13 February 1971.

133. *The New York Times,* 5 March 1971.

134. GW 15, 365.

BERLIN (1926–33)

1. GW 2, 395.

2. GW 2, 422.

3. GW 2, 425.

4. GW 2, 427.

5. GW 2, 428.

6. GW 2, 436.

7. GW 2, 444.

8. GW 2, 457.

9. GW 2, 462.

10. GW 2, 463.

11. GW 2, 465.

12. GW 2, 482.

13. William Eben Schultz, *Gay's "Beggar's Opera": Its Content, History and Influence* (New York: Russell & Russell, 1923, reissued 1967), p. xxi.

14. John Gay, *The Beggar's Opera*, Act III, Scene XVI.

15. Lotte Lenya, Preface to *The Threepenny Opera*, Grove edition; also in *Brecht: As They Knew Him*, ed. Hubert Witt, pp. 54–62.

16. *The New York Times*, 2 December 1928.

17. GW 18, 149.

18. *The New York Times*, 14 April 1933.

19. *New York Herald Tribune*, 14 April 1933.

20. *New York Herald Tribune*, 11 March 1954.

21. *The New York Times*, 11 March 1954.

22. *The New York Times*, 21 September 1955.

23. *New York Herald Tribune*, 21 September 1955.

24. *The New York Times*, 12 March 1965.

25. *The New York Times*, 24 October 1972.

26. *The New Yorker*, 10 May 1976.

27. *Daily News*, 3 May 1976.

28. *Time*, 17 May 1976.

29. Friedrich Luft, *Berliner Theater 1945–1961* (Velber: Friedrich Verlag, 1962), pp. 362–64.

30. *The Times*, 12 August 1965.

31. Quotes taken from *The New York Times*, 12 February 1956.

32. *Theater der Zeit*, no. 4 (1956).

33. *The New York Times*, 27 October 1929.

34. *The New York Times*, 30 April 1972.

35. GW 2, 482.

36. GW 17, 962.

37. GW 2, 502.

38. Esslin, p. 22.

39. GW 2, 502.

40. GW 2, 505.

41. GW 2, 508.

42. GW 2, 514.

43. GW 2, 520.

44. GW 2, 523.

45. GW 2, 524.

46. GW 2, 526.

47. GW 2, 530.

48. GW 2, 530.

49. GW 2, 531.

50. GW 2, 532.

51. GW 2, 532.
52. GW 2, 532.
53. GW 2, 535.
54. GW 2, 546.
55. GW 2, 551.
56. GW 2, 555.
57. GW 2, 561.
58. GW 2, 561–62.
59. GW 17, 1011.
60. Alfred Polgar, *Ja und Nein* (Hamburg: Rowohlt, 1956), pp. 300–01.
61. H. H. Stuckenschmidt, supplement to the Columbia record K3L243, p. 13.
62. *The Times,* 17 January 1963.
63. *The New York Times,* 29 April 1970.
64. *The New York Times,* 10 May 1970.
65. Lee Baxandall, "The Americanization of Bert Brecht," *Brecht Heute-Brecht Today,* vol. 1, pp. 150–67.
66. *The New York Times,* 24 December 1972.
67. Mel Gussow, *The New York Times,* 13 February 1974.
68. Julius Novick, *The New York Times,* 17 February 1974.
69. *The New York Times,* 13 February 1974.
70. *The New York Times,* 17 February 1974.
71. *The Times,* 24 April 1967.
72. *The Times,* 12 July 1968.
73. Review in *Brecht-Jahrbuch 1974,* edited by John Fuegi et al. (Frankfurt on the Main: Suhrkamp, 1975), pp. 129–31.
74. GW 2, 670.
75. GW 2, 671.
76. GW 2, 672.
77. GW 2, 688.
78. GW 2, 689.
79. GW 2, 696.
80. GW 2, 704–05.
81. GW 2, 717.
82. GW 2, 718.
83. GW 2, 734.
84. GW 2, 738.
85. GW 2, 742.
86. GW 2, 748.
87. GW 2, 749.
88. GW 2, 753.
89. GW 2, 771.
90. GW 2, 778.
91. GW 2, 780.
92. GW 2, 783.
93. Peter Wagner, "Bertolt Brechts *Die heilige Johanna der Schlachthöfe,*" *Jahrbuch der Deutschen Schillergesellschaft,* vol. 12 (1968), pp. 493–519.

94. See Bertolt Brecht, *Die heilige Johanna der Schlacht-höfe: Bühnenfassung, Fragmente, Varianten* (Saint Joan of the Stockyards: Stage Version, Fragments, Variants), ed. by Gisela Bahr (Frankfurt on the Main: Suhrkamp 1971), pp. 223–31.

95. *Ibid.*, p. 217–22.

96. *Theater der Zeit,* no. 6 (1959).

97. *Die Zeit,* 8 May 1959.

98. *Theater der Zeit,* no. 6 (1959).

99. *Die Zeit,* 8 May 1959.

100. *The New York Times,* 12 June 1964.

101. Program notes and *Theater der Zeit,* no. 15 (1968).

102. *Theater der Zeit,* no. 15 (1968).

103. *Theater der Zeit,* no. 12 (1970).

104. From *Theater der Zeit,* no. 1 (1974): 69.

105. Bertolt Brecht, *Die heilige Johanna der Schlachthöfe: Bühnenfassung, Fragmente, Varianten.*

106. GW 17, 1022–23.

107. GW 17, 1033.

108. GW 17, 1023.

109. Bertolt Brecht, *Die Massnahme: Kritische Ausgabe* (The Measures Taken: Critical Edition), edited by Reiner Steinweg (Frankfurt on the Main: Suhrkamp, 1972), pp. 249–50.

110. GW 17, 1024.

111. GW 17, 1024 and 1025.

112. GW 17, 1024.

113. GW 2, 585.

114. GW 2, 575.

115. GW 18, 129.

116. Roswell, May Mac, "Bertolt Brecht's Plays in America" (unpublished dissertation, University of Maryland, 1961) p. 87.

117. GW 2, 591 and 593.

118. GW 2, 611.

119. GW 2, 592.

120. Lee Baxandall, "B.B.'s J.B.," in Erika Munk, ed., *Brecht* (New York: Bantam Books, 1972), p. 175.

121. *The New York Times,* 26 May 1969.

122. Judith Malina, Julian Beck, *Paradise Now* (New York: Vintage Books, 1971), p. 5.

123. GW 2, 615.

124. GW 2, 629.

125. Luft, pp. 20–21.

126. *The New York Times,* 26 April 1933.

127. *New York Herald Tribune,* 26 April 1933.

128. GW 17, 1034.

129. GW 2, 633.

130. GW 2, 633.

131. GW 2, 637.

132. GW 2, 638.

133. GW 2, 657.

134. GW 2, 658.

135. GW 2, 661 and 662.

136. GW 2, 663.

137. Esslin, p. 294.

138. See Elisabeth Hauptmann's note in Bertolt Brecht, *Die Massnahme: Kritische Ausgabe,* edited by Reiner Steinweg, p. 271.

139. *Ibid.,* p. 325.

140. Review in *Brecht Jahrbuch 1974,* pp. 131–32.

141. *Newsweek,* 11 November 1974.

142. *The New York Times,* 16 October 1974.

143. *The New York Times,* 27 October 1974.

144. Steinweg, p. 265.

145. GW 2, 793.

146. GW 2, 808.

147. GW 2, 811.

148. GW 2, 821.

149. GW 2, 820.

150. GW 2, 822.

151. *The New York Times,* 21 May 1965.

152. *New York Herald Tribune,* 21 May 1965.

153. Lee Baxandall, "The Americanization of Bert Brecht," p. 160.

154. GW 17, 1075.

155. GW 17, 1080.

156. GW 2, 826.

157. GW 2, 827.

158. GW 2, 829.

159. GW 2, 837.

160. GW 2, 840.

161. GW 2, 852.

162. GW 2, 857.

163. GW 2, 856.

164. GW 2, 860.

165. GW 2, 867.

166. GW 2, 871.

167. GW 2, 872.

168. GW 2, 872.

169. GW 2, 875.

170. GW 2, 879.

171. GW 2, 882 and 884.

172. GW 2, 887.

173. GW 2, 888.

174. GW 2, 895.

175. GW 2, 895.

176. GW 17, 1071.

177. GW 17, 1071.

178. Rühle, pp. 1103–04.

179. Helene Weigel et al, eds., *Theaterarbeit* (Berlin: Henschelverlag, 1967), p. 157.

180. Reviews of 1932 premiere quoted from Rühle, pp. 1102–1108.

181. For more details see Lee Baxandall, "Brecht in America, 1935," in *Brecht,* edited by Erika Munk (New York: Bantam, 1972), pp. 33–60.

182. GW 17, 1058.

183. *The New York Times,* 20 November 1935.

184. GW 17, 1060.

185. GW 17, 1056.

186. Werner Hecht, ed., *Materialien zu Bertolt Brechts "Die Mutter"* (Materials re the Mother) (Frankfurt on the Main: Suhrkamp, 1969), p. 125.

187. *Ibid.,* p. 166.

188. *Ibid.,* pp. 166–71.

189. *The New York Times,* 22 November 1974.

190. Review in *Brecht-Jahrbuch 1974,* pp. 138–41.

191. GW 17, 1036.

EXILE (1933–47)

1. GW 7, 2860.

2. GW 7, 1.

3. Roswell, p. 26.

4. See Reinhold Grimm, *Bertolt Brecht* (Stuttgart: Metzler, 1971), p. 57.

5. GW 3, 1059.

6. GW 3, 910.

7. GW 3, 921.

8. GW 3, 920.

9. GW 17, 1092.

10. GW 3, 1096.

11. *Work Journal,* p. 744 (June–middle of July 1945).

12. *New York Herald Tribune,* 13 June 1945.

13. *The New York Times,* 13 June 1945.

14. Luft, pp. 25–26.

15. *The New York Times,* 31 January 1956.

16. *The New York Times,* 15 November 1961.

17. *Bergische Morgenpost,* 27 September 1973.

18. John Willett, *The Theater of Bertolt Brecht* (New York: New Directions, 1968), p. 45.

19. GW 3, 1221.

20. GW 3, 1213.

21. GW 3, 1228.

22. GW 17, 1100.

23. Esslin, p. 299.

24. *Work Journal,* 25 February 1939.

25. Klaus Völker, *Brecht-Chronik* (Munich: Hanser, 1971), p. 69.

26. GW 17, 1100–02.

27. Luft, pp. 19–20.

28. *The New York Times,* 10 December 1968.

29. *The New York Times,* 28 March 1972.

30. GW 3, 1232.

31. GW 3, 1255.

32. GW 3, 1256.

33. GW 3, 1278.

34. GW 3, 1283.

35. GW 3, 1288.

36. GW 3, 1290.

37. GW 3, 1296.

38. GW 3, 1297.

39. GW 3, 1312.

40. GW 3, 1318.

41. GW 3, 1321.

42. GW 3, 1322–23.

43. GW 3, 1326 and 1300.

44. GW 3, 1328.

45. GW 3, 1329.

46. GW 3, 1337.

47. GW 3, 1340–41.

48. Ernst Schumacher, *Bertolt Brechts "Leben des Galilei"* (Life of Galileo) (Berlin: Henschelverlag, 1965), p. 116.

49. GW 17, 1106.

50. GW 17, 1133.

51. GW 17, 1132.

52. Werner Hecht, ed., *Materialien zu Brechts "Leben des Galilei"* (Materials re Brecht's Galileo) (Frankfurt on the Main: Suhrkamp, 1967), p. 87.

53. GW 17, 1118.

54. GW 17, 1120.

55. Gerhard Szczesny, *The Case Against Bertolt Brecht,* tr. by Alexander Gode. New York: Ungar, 1969. This book deserves to be read because it does present some interesting facts and challenging ideas. But the reader should be forewarned that Szczesny's position is considerably influenced by the cold war and that he uses *Galileo* mostly to support his own somewhat biased theories about Brecht.

56. Guy Stern, "The Plight of the Exile: A Hidden Theme in Brecht's *Galileo Galilei*," *Brecht Heute-Brecht Today,* vol. 1 (1971), pp. 110–16.

57. GW 17, 1126.

58. *The New York Times,* 1 August 1947.

59. Schumacher, *Leben des Galilei,* pp. 202–03.

60. Brooks Atkinson, *Broadway* (New York: Macmillan, 1970), p. 404.

61. *The New York Times,* 8 December 1947.

62. Friedrich Luft, p. 260.

63. Kenneth Tynan, *Curtains* (New York: Atheneum, 1961), p. 468.

64. Kenneth Tynan, *Tynan Right and Left* (New York: Atheneum, 1967), pp. 23–24.

65. *The New York Times,* 5 January 1963.

66. *The New York Times,* 14 April 1967.

67. GW 4, 1349.

68. GW 4, 1351.

69. GW 4, 1360.

70. GW 4, 1373.

71. GW 4, 1374.

72. GW 4, 1379.

73. GW 4, 1398.

74. GW 4, 1409.

75. GW 4, 1410.

76. GW 4, 1437.

77. GW 4, 1404.

78. GW 4, 1438.

79. Tynan, *Curtains,* p. 100.

80. GW 4, 1352.

81. GW 4, 1378.

82. GW 9, 656.

83. GW 17, 1138.

84. GW 4, 1375.

85. *Neue Zürcher Zeitung,* 21 April 1941.

86. *Work Journal,* p. 271 (22 April 1941).

87. GW 4, 1439.

88. *Work Journal,* p. 1004.

89. Tynan, *Curtains,* pp. 100–101.

90. *San Francisco Chronicle,* 17 January 1956.

91. Tynan, *Tynan Right and Left,* p. 137.

92. *The New York Times,* 30 March 1963.

93. *The New York Times,* 17 November 1967.

94. *The New York Times,* 25 February 1975.

95. *The New York Times,* 16 February 1975.

96. GW 4, 1449.

97. GW 4, 1453.

98. GW 4, 1478.

99. *Work Journal,* p. 943 (15 January 1951).

100. *Neues Deutschland,* 22 March 1951.

101. GW 17, 1153.

102. GW 4, 1485.

103. *Theater der Zeit,* no. 11 (1974).

104. GW 7, 2849.

105. GW 4, 1498.
106. GW 4, 1508–09.
107. GW 4, 1519.
108. GW 4, 1520.
109. GW 4, 1524.
110. GW 4, 1530.
111. GW 4, 1529.
112. GW 4, 1530.
113. GW 4, 1531.
114. GW 4, 1536.
115. GW 4, 1538.
116. GW 4, 1539–40.
117. GW 4, 1540.
118. GW 4, 1552.
119. GW 4, 1553–54.
120. GW 4, 1558.
121. GW 4, 1564.
122. GW 4, 1565.
123. GW 4, 1598.
124. GW 4, 1603.
125. GW 4, 1605.
126. GW 4, 1607.
127. GW 4, 1568.
128. *Neue Zürcher Zeitung,* 6 February 1943.
129. *The Minneapolis Star,* 18 March 1948.
130. *The Daily Illini,* 30 March 1950.
131. *Frankfurter Allgemeine Zeitung,* 18 November 1952.
132. Tynan, *Curtains,* pp. 146–48.
133. *The New Yorker,* 29 December 1956.
134. *Theatre Arts,* February 1957.
135. *The New York Times,* 19 December 1956.
136. *New York Herald Tribune,* 19 December 1956.
137. *Theater der Zeit,* no. 12 (1957).
138. *The New York Times,* 25 December 1960.
139. *Variety,* 11 November 1970.
140. *The New York Times,* 6 November 1970.
141. *The New York Times,* 15 November 1970.
142. Henry G. Huettich, "Zwischen Klassik und Kommerz: Brecht in Los Angeles," *Brecht-Jahrbuch 1974,* p. 129.
143. *The New York Times,* 4 February 1975.
144. *Work Journal,* p. 120 (29 June 1940).
145. *Work Journal,* p. 45 (15 March 1939).
146. GW 4, 1611.
147. GW 4, 1639.
148. GW 4, 1656.
149. GW 4, 1671.
150. GW 4, 1681.
151. GW 4, 1684.
152. GW 4, 1687.

153. GW 4, 1705.

154. GW 4, 1708–09.

155. The *commedia dell'arte* originated in Italy in the middle of the sixteenth century. It is a comedy with stereotyped scenario and stock characters; its success depends chiefly on the actors' ability to improvise. Some stock characters, still well-known today, are Pantalone, the simpleton and cheated husband; his clever servant, Harlequin; and Harlequin's sweetheart, Columbina.

156. A remark Farquhar made in reply to criticism that his dialogue was unpolished, undoubtedly endeared him to Brecht, the non-Aristotelian playwright: "The rules of English comedy don't lie in the compass of Aristotle or his followers, but in the Pit, Box, and Galleries." Quoted from George Sampson, *The Concise Cambridge History of English Literature* (Cambridge: University Press, 1961), p. 424.

157. *Work Journal,* p. 169 (14 September 1940).

158. Jaroslav Hašek (1883–1923), whose novel, *The Adventures of the Good Soldier Schweyk During the World War,* written 1920–22, was adapted by Brecht in 1943.

159. See Jost Hermand, *"Herr Puntila und sein Knecht Matti:* Brechts Volksstück," *Brecht Heute-Brecht Today,* vol. 1 (1971), pp. 117–36.

160. GW 17, 1172.

161. *Neue Zürcher Zeitung,* 8 June 1948.

162. *Work Journal,* p. 912 (13 November 1949).

163. GW 17, 1175.

164. Luft, pp. 91–94.

165. *The New York Times,* 15 May 1959.

165a. *The New York Times,* 13 March 1977.

165b. *Newsweek,* 21 March 1977.

166. *Theater heute,* no. 1 (1967).

167. *Theaterarbeit,* p. 16.

168. *Work Journal,* p. 193 (28 October 1940).

169. GW 17, 1176.

170. GW 4, 1721.

171. GW 4, 1728.

172. GW 4, 1734.

173. GW 4, 1746.

174. GW 4, 1752.

175. GW 4, 1777.

176. GW 4, 1776.

177. GW 4, 1790.

178. GW 4, 1797.

179. GW 4, 1799.

180. GW 4, 1805.

181. GW 4, 1825.

182. GW 4, 1827.

183. GW 4, 1834.

184. GW 4, 1835.
185. GW 17, 1179.
186. GW 17, 1177.
187. Esslin, p. 306.
188. Detailed information in Helfried W. Seliger. *Das Amerikabild Bertolt Brechts* (Bonn: Bouvier, 1974).
189. The problem concerns almost all of Brecht's plays set in America. E.W. White therefore suggested changing the setting for American productions so that the quality of the exotic is retained. See Ulrich Weisstein, "Brecht in America: A Preliminary Survey," *Modern Language Notes,* no. 4 (1963): 380.
190. *Theater der Zeit,* no. 1 (1959).
191. *Die Zeit,* 5 December 1958.
192. *Theater der Zeit,* no. 5 (1959).
193. Luft, pp. 318–20.
194. *The Times,* 10 August 1965.
195. *The New York Times,* 22 December 1960.
196. *The New York Times,* 12 November 1963.
197. *New York Herald Tribune,* 12 November 1963.
198. *Variety,* 13 November 1963.
199. *The New York Times,* 8 August 1968.
200. *The New York Times,* 23 December 1968.
201. *The New York Times,* 30 August 1968.
202. *The New York Times,* 18 August 1969.
203. *Chicago Tribune,* 30 March 1975.
204. *Chicago Daily News,* 30 March 1975.
205. *The New York Times,* 28 July 1972.
206. GW 5, 1846.
207. GW 5, 1870.
208. GW 5, 1880–81.
209. GW 5, 1887.
210. GW 5, 1887–88.
211. GW 5, 1892.
212. GW 5, 1903.
213. GW 5, 1903.
214. GW 5, 1909.
215. GW 5, 1910.
216. *Work Journal,* p. 563 (5 January 1943).
217. *Work Journal,* p. 131 (7 July 1940).
218. *Work Journal,* p. 338 (19 December 1940).
219. *Work Journal,* p. 562 (3 January 1943).
220. Lion Feuchtwanger, "Bertolt Brecht" (1957). In Hubert Witt, ed., *Erinnerungen an Brecht* (Remembering Brecht) (Leipzig: Reclam, 1966), p. 358 and p. 360.
221. *Frankfurter Allgemeine Zeitung,* 11 March 1957.
222. George Grosz (1893–1959), best known for his satirical caricatures of the German Kaiserreich and the Weimar Republic.

223. GW 5, 1922.
224. GW 5, 1919.
225. GW 5, 1930.
226. GW 5, 1935.
227. GW 5, 1937.
228. GW 5, 1945.
229. GW 5, 1947.
230. GW 5, 1952.
231. GW 5, 1957.
232. GW 5, 1968.
233. GW 5, 1972.
234. GW 5, 1976.
235. GW 5, 1982.
236. GW 5, 1989.
237. GW 5, 1990.
238. GW 5, 1992–93.
239. GW 5, 1993–94.
240. The spelling of the name Schweyk with a *y* instead of an *i* is of importance in the play because it was the *y* in his name that kept Schweyk from being immediately drafted into the German army, since it made it a Czech name.
241. *Work Journal,* p. 569 (27 May 1943).
242. GW 5, 1995.
243. Brooks Atkinson, *Broadway* (New York: Macmillan, 1970), p. 246.
244. *The New York Times,* 23 May 1959.
245. *Die Zeit,* 12 June 1959.
246. Tynan, *Curtains,* p. 459.
247. *Frankfurter Allgemeine Zeitung,* 25 May 1959.
248. *Theater der Zeit,* no. 6 (1961).
249. *Theater heute,* no. 5 (1963).
250. *Theater heute,* no. 2 (1963).
251. *Theater der Zeit,* no. 3 (1963).
252. *The Times,* 22 August 1963.
253. *Davis Enterprise,* 7 March 1968.
254. *The New York Times,* 12 November 1967.
255. *Work Journal,* p. 569 (27 May 1943).
256. GW 5, 2003.
257. GW 5, 2006.
258. GW 5, 2008.
259. GW 5, 2015.
260. GW 5, 2025.
261. GW 5, 2033.
262. GW 5, 2043.
263. GW 5, 2050.
264. GW 5, 2065.
265. GW 5, 2069.
266. GW 5, 2078.
267. GW 5, 2095.

268. GW 5, 2096.
269. GW 5, 2100.
270. GW 5, 2104.
271. GW 5, 2105.
272. Bentley also gives another reason for the omission of the prologue. In 1965, he added an introduction to his translations of *The Caucasian Chalk Circle* and *The Good Woman of Setzuan* in the volume entitled *Parables for the Theater* (Minneapolis: University of Minnesota Press, 1965). In it Bentley explained that "it was on the advice from him [Brecht] that the appearance of this Prologue was postponed" at that time. ("That time" was 1947, when Bentley first translated Brecht's play.) Thus the play was printed without it until 1959.

273. Pieter Bruegel the Elder (1525–69), Flemish painter, especially of peasant scenes. Bruegel's painting *Dulle Griet* was actually pasted onto the title page of the earliest versions.

274. *The Northfield Independent,* 6 May 1948.

275. *Die Zeit,* 14 October 1954.

276. *Frankfurter Allgemeine,* 30 April 1955.

277. *Frankfurter Allgemeine,* 18 June 1955.

278. *The New York Times,* 1 November 1961.

279. Tynan, *Tynan Right and Left,* pp. 121–23.

280. *San Francisco Chronicle,* 17 December 1963.

281. Walter Kerr, *Thirty Plays Hath November* (New York: Simon and Schuster, 1969), pp. 277–84.

282. *The New York Times,* 25 March 1966 and 10 April 1966.

283. GW 5, 2015.

East Berlin (1948–56)

1. Good introductions to the history of the Paris Commune are: Alistair Horne, *The Terrible Year: The Paris Commune 1871,* New York: The Viking Press, 1971 (illustrated); Alistair Horne, *The Fall of Paris: The Siege and the Commune 1870–71,* Garden City, N.Y.: Anchor Books, 1967; Olivier Lissagaray, *History of the Commune of 1871,* tr. Eleanor Marx Aveling, 1886; reprint ed., New York: Monthly Review Press, 1967; Karl Marx and Friedrich Engels, *Writings on the Paris Commune,* ed., Hal Draper, New York, London: Monthly Review Press, 1971; Edward S. Mason, *The Paris Commune: An Episode in the History of the Socialist Movement.* New York: Macmillan, 1930.

2. GW 5, 2119.
3. GW 5, 2123.
4. GW 5, 2173.
5. GW 5, 2174.
6. GW 5, 2179.

7. GW 5, 2180.

8. GW 5, 2192.

9. GW 5, 2.

10. Karl Marx and Frederick Engels, *On the Paris Commune* (Moscow: Progress Publishers, 1971), p. 210.

11. *The New York Times,* 20 November 1956.

12. *The Times,* 13 August 1965.

13. Claude Hill, *Bertolt Brecht* (New York: Twayne, 1975), p. 187.

14. Hedwig Hoffmann Rusack, *Gozzi in Germany* (New York: Columbia University Press, 1930), p. 111.

15. GW 12, 4.

16. GW 5, 2198.

17. GW 5, 2205.

18. GW 5, 2212.

19. GW 5, 2212.

20. GW 5, 2215.

21. GW 5, 2243.

22. GW 5, 2247.

23. GW 5, 2253.

24. GW 5, 2264.

25. GW 5, 2269.

26. GW 5, 2194.

27. GW 12, 3.

28. GW 5, 3.

29. GW 12, 4.

30. *Work Journal,* p. 1011 (13 September 1953).

31. GW 5, 2270.

32. *Neue Zürcher Zeitung,* 6 February 1969.

33. See Elizabeth B. Edelson, "The San Francisco Mime Troupe as Radical Theater" (Ph.D. dissertation, University of Wisconsin, 1975), pp. 212–17.

34. *Theater der Zeit,* no. 5 (1973).

35. GW 17, 1260.

BRECHT AND AMERICA

1. *Diary,* p. 11.

2. GW 20, 338.

3. Quotation taken from Ulrich Weisstein, "Brecht in America: A Preliminary Survey," p. 383.

4. *Work Journal,* p. 122 (30 June 1940).

5. Weisstein, pp. 384–85.

6. Lee Baxandall, "Brecht in America, 1935," p. 58.

7. Atkinson, *Broadway,* p. 360 and pp. 404–05.

8. Esslin, p. 340.

9. Quoted from Esslin, p. 340.

10. *The New York Times,* 26 October 1974.

11. Lee Baxandall, "The Americanization of Bert Brecht," p. 167.

CONCLUSION

1. Peter Brook, *The Empty Space* (New York: Avon, 1969), p. 65.

BIBLIOGRAPHY

1. WORKS BY BERTOLT BRECHT IN GERMAN

The standard edition of Brecht's works is *Gesammelte Werke* ("Collected Works"). 20 vols., Frankfurt on the Main: Suhrkamp, 1967.

Versuche ("Attempts, Experiments"). Vols. 1–7, Berlin: Kiepenheuer, 1930–33. Vols. 9–15, Frankfurt on the Main: Suhrkamp, 1949–56, and Berlin, Weimar: Aufbau Verlag, 1949–56. Vols. 1–8, Frankfurt: Suhrkamp, 1959, and Berlin, Weimar: Aufbau Verlag, 1963.

Stücke ("Plays"). 14 vols., Frankfurt on the Main: Suhrkamp, 1953–67, and Berlin, Weimar: Aufbau Verlag, 1953–67.

Gedichte ("Poems"). 9 vols., Frankfurt on the Main: Suhrkamp, 1960–69, and Berlin, Weimar: Aufbau Verlag, 1960–69.

Schriften zum Theater ("Writings on Theater"). 7 vols., Frankfurt on the Main: Suhrkamp, 1963–64, and Berlin, Weimar: Aufbau Verlag, 1963–64.

Prosa ("Prose"). 5 vols., Frankfurt on the Main: Suhrkamp, 1965.

Schriften zur Literatur und Kunst ("Writings on Literature and Art"). 3 vols., Frankfurt on the Main: Suhrkamp, 1966–67; 2 vols., Berlin, Weimar: Aufbau Verlag, 1966–67.

Schriften zur Politik und Gesellschaft ("Writings on Politics and Society"). 1 vol., Frankfurt on the Main: Suhrkamp, 1968; 2 vols., Berlin, Weimar: Aufbau Verlag, 1968.

Texte für Filme ("Texts for Films"). 2 vols., Frankfurt on the Main: Suhrkamp, 1969.

Arbeitsjournal ("Work Journal"). 2 vols. and 1 vol. of notes. Frankfurt on the Main: Suhrkamp, 1973.

Tagebücher 1920–1922, Autobiographische Aufzeichnungen 1920–1954 ("Diaries, Autobiographical Notes"). Frankfurt on the Main: Suhrkamp, 1975.

Materialien ("Materials"). Commentaries and materials relating to the origin and variants of the play, available for many plays, all of them published by Suhrkamp.

2. TRANSLATIONS

Collections

Early Plays. Edited and translated by Eric Bentley. New York: Grove Press, 1964. (*Baal, A Man's a Man* and *The Elephant Calf.*)

Collected Plays. Edited by Ralph Manheim and John Willett. New York: Random House, Vintage Books, 1971–. In progress. At this time, volumes 1, 5, 6, 7, and 9 have appeared. This edition, which includes copious notes, is by far the best English-language edition. Translators' names given in parentheses.

Vol. 1: *Baal, Drums in the Night* (both tr. by William E. Smith and Ralph Manheim), *In the Jungle of Cities* (tr. by Gerhard Nellhaus), *The Life of Edward the Second of England* (tr. William E. Smith and Ralph Manheim), *Five One-Act Plays* (tr. Martin and Rose Kastner, Peter Hertz).

Vol. 5: *Life of Galileo* (tr. Wolfgang Sauerlander and Ralph Manheim), *The Trial of Lucullus* (tr. Frank Jones), *Mother Courage and Her Children* (tr. Ralph Manheim).

Vol. 6: *The Good Person of Szechwan, Puntila and Matti, His Hired Man, The Resistible Rise of Arturo Ui* (all tr. by Ralph Manheim), *Dansen, How Much Is Your Iron?, Practice Pieces for Actors* (The Murder in the Porter's Lodge, The Battle of the Fishwives, Ferry Scene, The Servants) (tr. Rose and Martin Kastner).

Vol. 7: *The Visions of Simone Machard* (tr. Ralph Manheim), *Schweyk in the Second World War* (tr. Max Knight and Joseph Fabry), *The Caucasian Chalk Circle* (tr. Ralph Manheim), *The Duchess of Malfi.*

Vol. 9: The adaptations *The Tutor* (tr. Ralph Manheim and Wolfgang Sauerlander), *Coriolanus* (tr. Ralph Manheim), *The Trial of Joan of Arc at Rouen, 1431* (tr. Ralph Manheim and Wolfgang Sauerlander), *Trumpets and Drums* (tr. Rose and Martin Kastner), *Don Juan* (tr. Ralph Manheim).

Collected Plays. Edited by John Willett and Ralph Manheim. London: Methuen, 1970.

Vol. 1: *Baal* (tr. Peter Tegel), *Drums in the Night* (tr. John Willett), *In the Jungle of Cities* (tr. Gerhard Nellhaus), *The Life of Edward II of England* (tr. William E. Smith and Ralph Manheim), *Five One-Act Plays* (tr. Jean Benedetti, Michael Hamburger, Richard Grunberger, Eva Geisel and Ernst Borneman, Eric Bentley).

The Jewish Wife, and Other Short Plays. Tr. by Eric Bentley. New York: Grove Press, 1965. (*The Jewish Wife, In Search of Justice, The Informer, The Elephant Calf, The Measures Taken, The Exception and the Rule, Salzburg Dance of Death*).

Jungle of Cities, and Other Plays. New York: Grove Press, 1966. [*Jungle of Cities* (tr. Anselm Hollo), *Drums in the Night* (tr. Frank Jones), *Roundheads and Peakheads* (tr. N. Goold-Verschoyle).]

Plays. 2 vols., London: Methuen, 1960–62 (and later reprints).

Vol. 1: *The Caucasian Chalk Circle* (tr. James and Tania Stern, with W. H. Auden), *The Threepenny Opera* (tr. Eric Bentley and Desmond I. Vesey), *The Trial of Lucullus* (tr. H. R. Hays), *The Life of Galileo* (tr. Desmond I. Vesey).

Vol. 2: *Mother Courage and Her Children* (tr. Eric Bentley), *St. Joan of the Stockyards* (tr. Frank Jones), *The Good Person of Szechwan* (tr. John Willett).

Plays, in single editions, also by Methuen, in the Methuen Modern Plays series (*The Caucasian Chalk Circle, The Good Person of Szechwan, The Life of Galileo, Mother Courage and Her Children, Saint Joan of the Stockyards, The Threepenny Opera, The Resistible Rise of Arturo Ui*).

Parables for the Theater: The Good Woman of Setzuan and The Caucasian Chalk Circle. Revised English version by Eric Bentley. Minneapolis: University of Minnesota Press, 1965.

Seven Plays. Edited by Eric Bentley. New York: Grove Press, 1961. [*In the Swamp, A Man's a Man* (both tr. by Eric Bentley), *Saint Joan of the Stockyards* (tr. Frank Jones), *Mother Courage* (tr. Eric Bentley), *Galileo* (tr. Charles Laughton), *The Good Woman of Setzuan* (tr. Eric Bentley), *The Caucasian Chalk Circle* (tr. Eric Bentley and Maja Apelman).]

Works of Bertolt Brecht. In single editions. General editor Eric Bentley. New York: Grove Press, since 1964: *The Threepenny Opera* (tr. Desmond I. Vesey and Eric Bentley), *The Mother* (tr. Lee Baxandall), *Galileo* (tr.

Charles Laughton), *Mother Courage* (tr. Eric Bentley), *The Good Woman of Setzuan* (tr. Eric Bentley), *The Visions of Simone Machard* (tr. Carl Richard Mueller), *The Caucasian Chalk Circle* (tr. Eric Bentley), *Edward II* (tr. Eric Bentley).

Theoretical Writings

A *Little Organum for the Theater* (tr. Beatrice Gottlieb). *Accent* 11 (Winter 1951): 13–40.

The Messingkauf Dialogues (tr. John Willett). London: Methuen, 1965.

"On Chinese Acting" (tr. Eric Bentley). *The* [*Tulane*] *Drama Review* 6 (September 1961): 130–36.

"On the Experimental Theater" (tr. Carl Richard Mueller). *The* [*Tulane*] *Drama Review* 6 (September 1961): 3–17.

"Theater for Learning" (tr. Edith Anderson). *The* [*Tulane*] *Drama Review* 6 (September 1961): 18–25.

Brecht on Theater: The Development of an Aesthetic. Edited and translated by John Willett. New York: Hill and Wang, 1964.

Individual Editions of Plays

The Rise and Fall of the City of Mahagonny (tr. W. H. Auden and Chester Kallmann). Boston: David R. Godine, 1976

St. Joan of the Stockyards (tr. Frank Jones). Bloomington: Indiana University Press, 1969.

The Flight Across the Ocean (tr. George Antheil). Vienna: Universal Edition, 1930 (with score).

The Didactic Play of Baden: On Consent. Two translations: a.) by Lee Baxandall. *The* [*Tulane*] *Drama Review* 4 (May 1960): 118–33. Reprinted in Erika Munk, ed. *Brecht* (New York: Bantam, 1972), pp. 177–97; b.) by Gerhard Nellhaus. *Harvard Advocate* 134 (February 1951).

He Who Says Yes/ He Who Says No (tr. Gerhard Nellhaus). *Accent* 7 (Autumn 1946): 14–24.

The Seven Deadly Sins. Tr. by W. H. Auden and Chester Kallmann as *The Seven Deadly Sins of the Lower Middle Class. The* [*Tulane*] *Drama Review* 6 (September 1961): 123–29.

The Horatians and the Curiatians (tr. H. R. Hays). *Accent* 8 (Autumn 1947): 3–22.

The Private Life of the Master Race. Tr. by Eric Russel Bentley. New York: New Directions, 1944.

Señora Carrar's Rifles. Two translations: a.) by Keene Wallis. *Theatre Workshop* 2 (April–June 1938): 30–50; b.) by George Tabori as *The Guns of Carrar.* New York: S. French, 1971.
The Days of the Commune (tr. Leonard J. Lehrman). *Dunster Drama Review* 10 (1971).

3. WORKS ON BRECHT

Alter, Maria P. "Bertolt Brecht and the *Noh* Drama." *Modern Drama* 11 (1968): 122–31.

Bathrick, David. *The Dialectic and the Early Brecht. An Interpretive Study of Trommeln in der Nacht.* Stuttgart: Akademischer Verlag Hans-Dieter Heinz, 1975.

Bauland, Peter. *The Hooded Eagle: Modern German Drama on the New York Stage.* Syracuse: Syracuse University Press, 1968.

Baxandall, Lee. "The Americanization of Bert Brecht." *Brecht Yearbook 1971,* pp. 150–67. (See *Brecht Heute.*)

Beckley, Richard. "Adaptation as a Feature of Brecht's Dramatic Technique." *German Life and Letters* 25 (1962): 274–84.

Bentley, Eric. "Ibsen, Shaw, Brecht: Three Stages," in *The Rarer Action: Essays in Honor of Francis Fergusson,* eds. Cheuse, Alan, and Koffler, Richard. (New Brunswick, N.J.: Rutgers University Press, 1970), pp. 3–23.

Bentley, Eric. *The Playwright as Thinker: A Study of Drama in Modern Times.* New York: Harcourt, Brace and World, 1967.

Borchardt, Frank K. "Marx, Engels and Brecht's Galileo." *Brecht Yearbook 1972,* pp. 149–63. (See *Brecht Heute.*)

Brecht Heute-Brecht Today. Yearbook of the International Brecht Society, ed. by John Fuegi, Reinhold Grimm, Jost Hermand et al., vols. 1–3, Frankfurt on the Main: Athenäum, 1971–1973. Beginning with vol. 4 (1974) as *Brecht Jahrbuch* in Frankfurt on the Main: Suhrkamp, 1974. (The yearbook contains articles and reviews in English, French, and German.)

Brook, Peter. *The Empty Space.* New York: Atheneum, 1968.

Brown, Thomas K. "*Verfremdung* in Action at the Berliner Ensemble." *German Quarterly* 46 (1973): 525–39.

Brustein, Robert. *The Theater of Revolt: An Approach to the Modern Drama.* Boston, Toronto: Little, Brown and Co., 1962.

Brustein, Robert. *The Third Theater.* New York: Knopf, 1969.

Demetz, Peter, ed. *Brecht: A Collection of Critical Essays.* Englewood Cliffs, N.J.: Prentice-Hall, 1962.

Esslin, Martin. *Bertolt Brecht.* New York, London: Columbia University Press, 1969.

Esslin, Martin. "Brecht, and the Dangers of Being a Classic." *Encounter,* 31, iii (1968): 63–65.

Esslin, Martin. *Brecht: The Man and His Work.* Garden City, New York: Doubleday & Co. (Anchor Books), 1961.

Ewen, Frederic. *Bertolt Brecht.* New York: Citadel, 1967.

Fergusson, Francis. *The Human Image in Dramatic Literature: Essays.* Garden City: Doubleday, 1957.

Fuegi, John. *The Essential Brecht.* Los Angeles: Hennessey & Ingalls, 1972.

Fuegi, John. "*The Caucasian Chalk Circle* in Performance." *Brecht Yearbook 1971,* pp. 137–49.

Fuegi, John. "The Soviet Union and Brecht: The Exile's Choice." *Brecht Yearbook 1972,* pp. 209–21.

Gassner, John. *The Theater in Our Times: A Survey of the Men, Materials and Movements in the Modern Theater.* New York: Crown Publishers, 1954.

Glade, Henry. "Brecht and the Soviet Theater: A 1971 Overview." *Brecht Yearbook 1972,* pp. 164–73.

Gorelik, Mordecai. "Rational Theater." *Brecht Yearbook 1971,* pp. 48–67.

Gorelik, Mordecai. *New Theaters for Old.* New York: Dutton, 1962.

Gray, Ronald. *Brecht.* Edinburgh, London: Oliver and Boyd, 1961.

Gray, Ronald. *Brecht the Dramatist.* Cambridge, London, New York, Melbourne: Cambridge University Press, 1976.

Grimm, Reinhold. *Bertolt Brecht.* Stuttgart: Metzler, 1971. (An excellent bio-bibliographical study in German, which, unfortunately, is not available in English.)

Hill, Claude. *Bertolt Brecht.* Boston: Twayne Publishers, 1975.

Kenney, William. *The Plays of Bertolt Brecht.* New York: Monarch Press, 1965.

Knust, Herbert, and Mews, Siegfried, eds. *Essays on Brecht: Theater and Politics.* Chapel Hill: University of North Carolina Press, 1974.

Ley, Ralph. "Brecht as Bolshevist: The Commune in Memoriam." *University of Dayton Review,* 8, ii (1971): 49–70.

Lyon, James K. "Bertolt Brecht's Hollywood Years: The Dramatist as Film Writer." *Oxford German Studies* 6 (1971): 145–74.

Lyon, James K. "Bertolt Brecht's American Cicerone." *Brecht Yearbook 1972*, pp. 187–208.

Lyon, James K. *Bertolt Brecht and Rudyard Kipling: A Marxist's Imperialist Mentor*. The Hague, Paris: Mouton, 1975.

Lyons, Charles R. *Bertolt Brecht: The Despair and the Polemic*. Carbondale: Southern Illinois University Press, 1968.

McLean, Sammy K. *The "Bänkelsang" and the Work of Bertolt Brecht*. The Hague: Mouton, 1972.

Munk, Erika, ed. *Brecht: A Selection of Critical Pieces from The Drama Review*. New York: Bantam Books, 1972.

Nelson, G. E. "The Birth of Tragedy out of Pedagogy: Brecht's 'Learning Play' *Die Massnahme*." *German Quarterly*, 46 (1973): 566–80.

Roth, Wolfgang. "Working with Bertolt Brecht." *Brecht Yearbook 1972*, 131–35.

Shaw, Leroy. *The Playwright and Historical Change: Dramatic Strategies in Brecht, Hauptmann, Kaiser, Wedekind*. Madison: University of Wisconsin Press, 1970.

Sokel, Walter H. "Brecht's Concept of Character." *Comparative Drama*, 5 (1971): 177–92.

Spalter, Max. *Brecht's Tradition*. Baltimore: Johns Hopkins Press, 1967.

Stern, Guy. "The Plight of the Exile: A Hidden Theme in Brecht's *Galileo Galilei*." *Brecht Yearbook 1971*, pp. 110–16.

Szczesny, Gerhard. *The Case Against Bertolt Brecht*. Translated by Alexander Gode. New York: Frederick Ungar, 1969.

Theaterarbeit. Sechs Aufführungen des Berliner Ensembles (Working with theater. Six performances of the Berliner Ensemble). Edited by the Berliner Ensemble under Helene Weigel. Berlin: Henschelverlag, 1961, 1967.

Weideli, Walter. *The Art of Bertolt Brecht*. New York: New York University Press, 1963. (Translated from French).

Weisstein, Ulrich. "Brecht in America: A Preliminary Survey." *Modern Language Notes*, 4 (1963): 373–96.

Weisstein, Ulrich. "From the Dramatic Novel to the Epic Theater: A Study of the Contemporary Background of Brecht's Theory and Practice." *Germanic Review*, 38 (1963): 257–71.

Willett, John. "The Poet Beneath the Skin." *Brecht Yearbook 1972*, pp. 88–104.

Willett, John. *The Theater of Bertolt Brecht*. 3rd rev. ed. New York: New Directions, 1968.

Williams, Raymond. *Modern Tragedy.* Stanford: Stanford University Press, 1967.

Williams, Raymond. *Drama from Ibsen to Brecht.* New York: Oxford University Press, 1969.

Witt, Hubert, ed. *Brecht: As They Knew Him.* Translated by John Peet. New York: International Publishers, 1974.

INDEX